I0446014

Trip Advisor

Trip Advisor

Notes from over 25 Years
of Psychedelic Voyages

Ryan McGinness

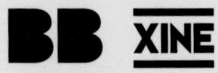

Published by
BLURRING BOOKS + XINE
New York

Dedicated to My Best Friend & Trip Sitter,
TRISH GOODWIN

Trip Advisor
Notes from over 25 Years
of Psychedelic Voyages
Ryan McGinness

Published in 2025 by
BLURRING BOOKS, New York.
XINE, New York.

Texts, Design, and Artwork
© Ryan McGinness / Artists
Rights Society (ARS), New York.

International Standard Book Numbers
978-1-963814-22-4

Library of Congress Control Number:
2025932348

All rights reserved.
No part of this publication may be
reproduced, stored in a retrieval
system, or transmitted in any form
or by any means, electronic,
mechanical, photocopying, recording,
or otherwise, without written prior
consent of the author and publisher.

RyanMcGinness.com
@McGinnessWorks

Note to the Reader:
This book is intended for informational and educational purposes only.
All recounted actions undertaken
by the author were done so at his
own risk and with the benefit of years
of experience. None of the author's
ventures should be blindly copied
by others. Neither the author nor the
publisher assumes any responsibility
for physical, psychological, or social
consequences resulting from the
ingestion of psilocybin.

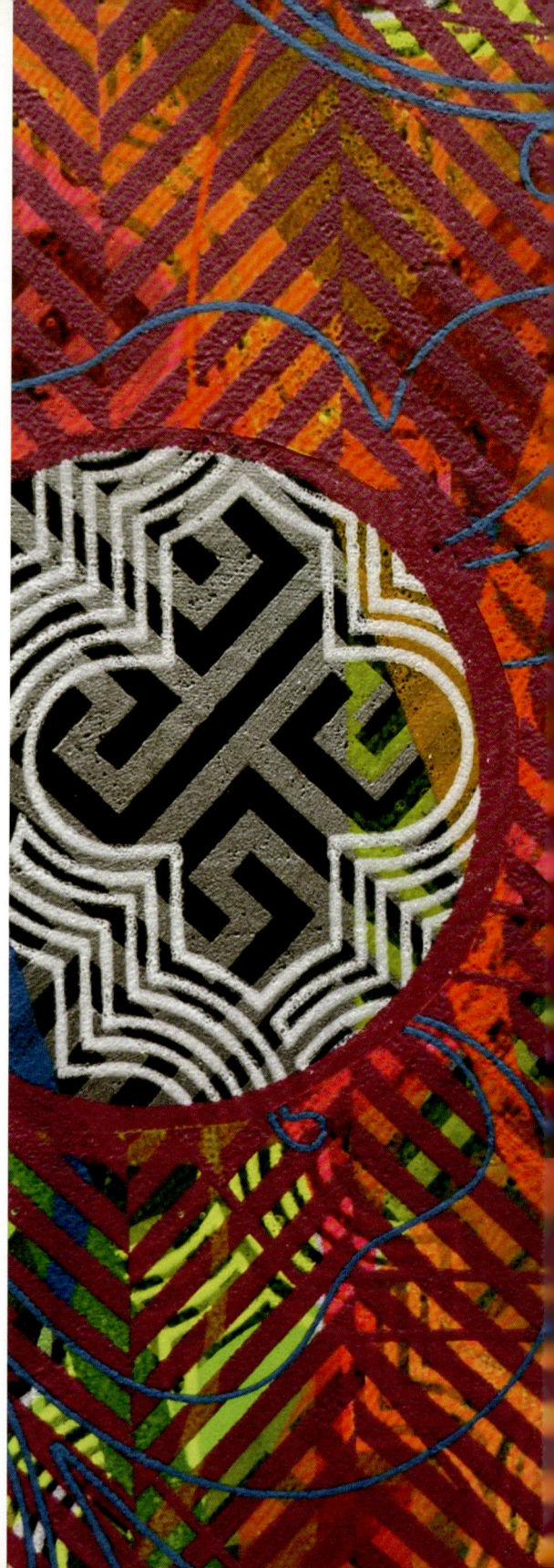

CONTENTS

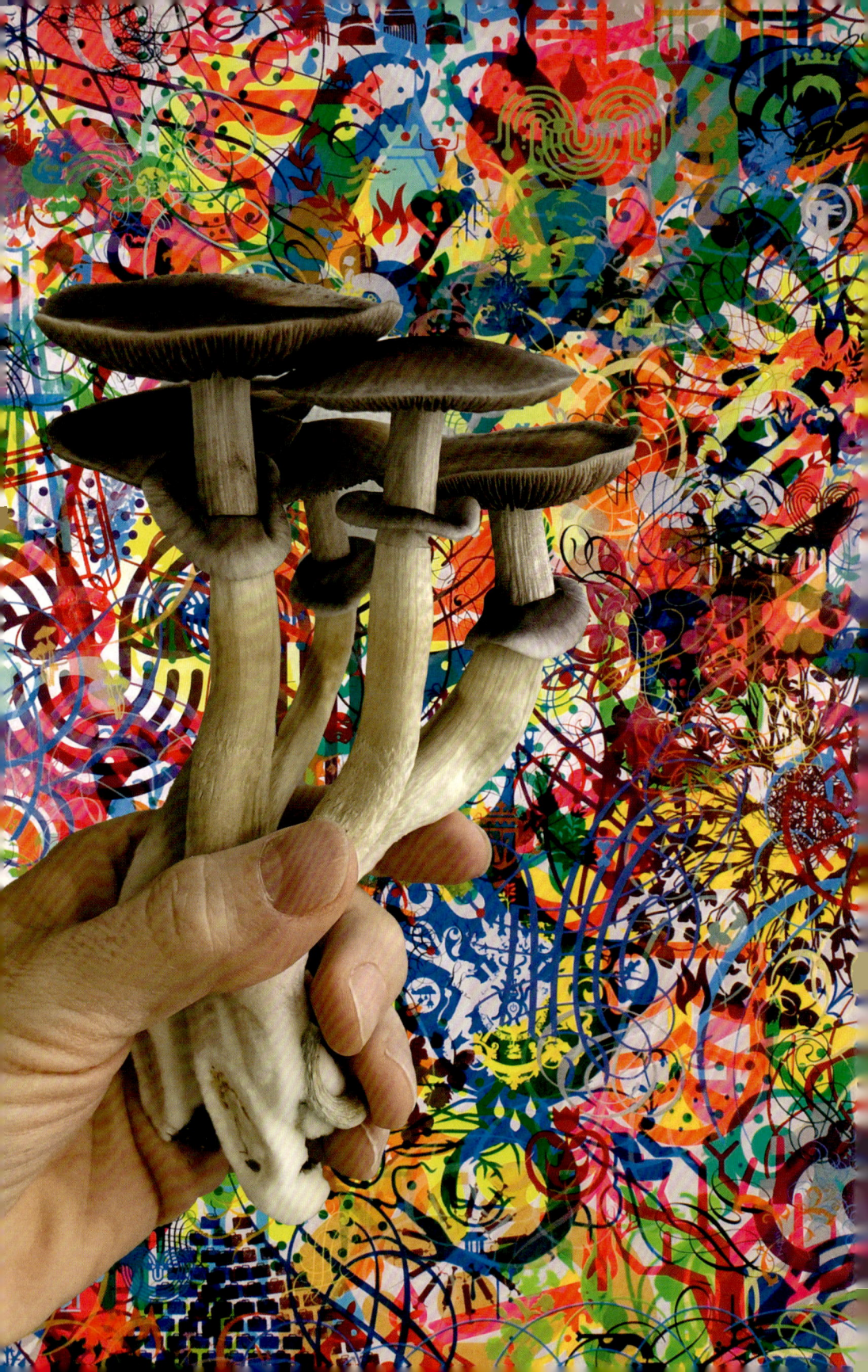

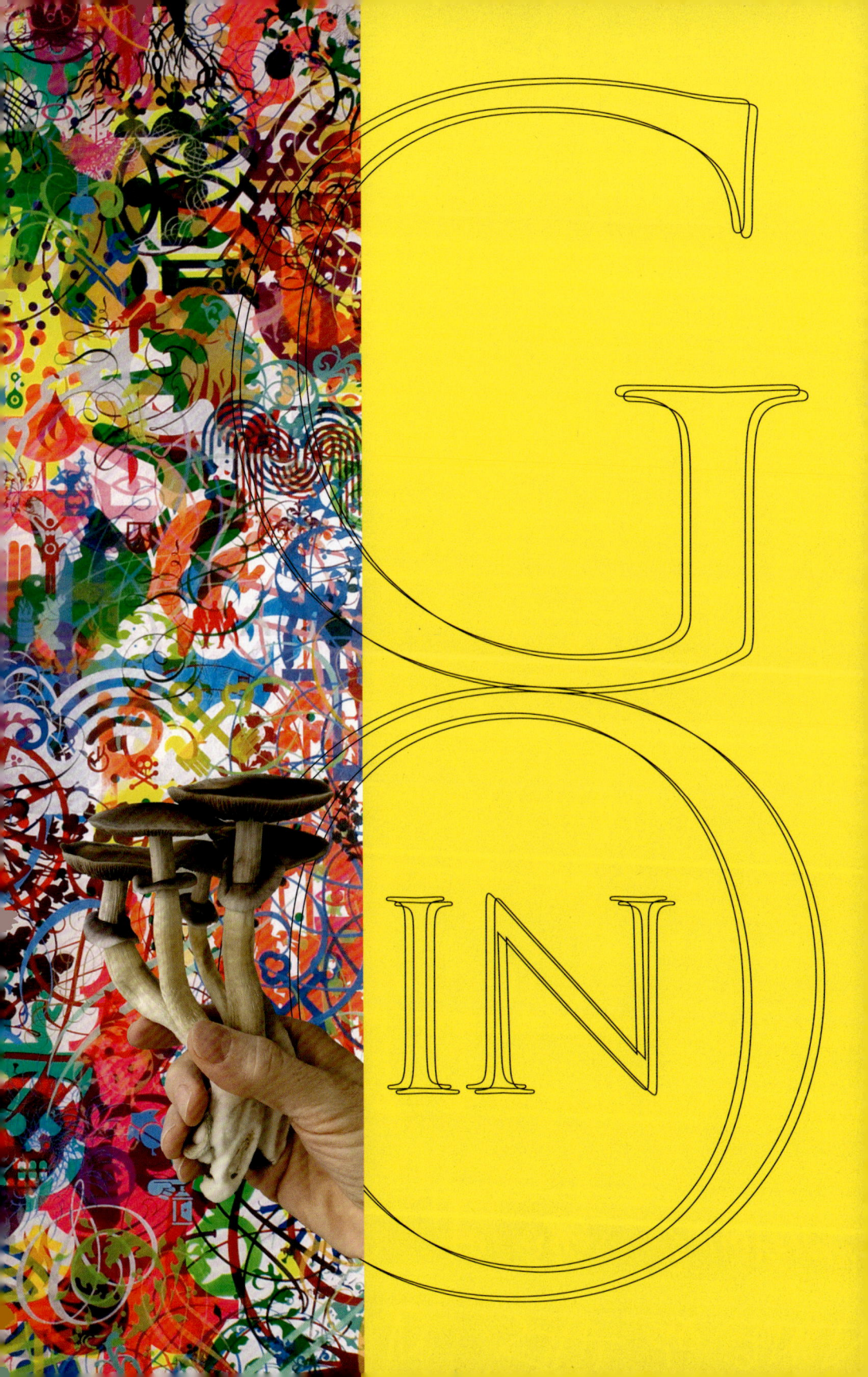

At w/ ~~HEAD DOWN~~. clown head they

could jump into quickly.

trish talking on phone. keepin

me here. i'm SEARCHING for

SOMETHING to ~~TAKE~~ BACK.

ENJOY LIFE.

it doesn't matter. so insignificant

reality is scary.

5. 52 : HAVE to start

writing

5:55 just threw up. guided

by or dictated by.

overwhelming sense of otherness.

NONE OF THIS MATTERS

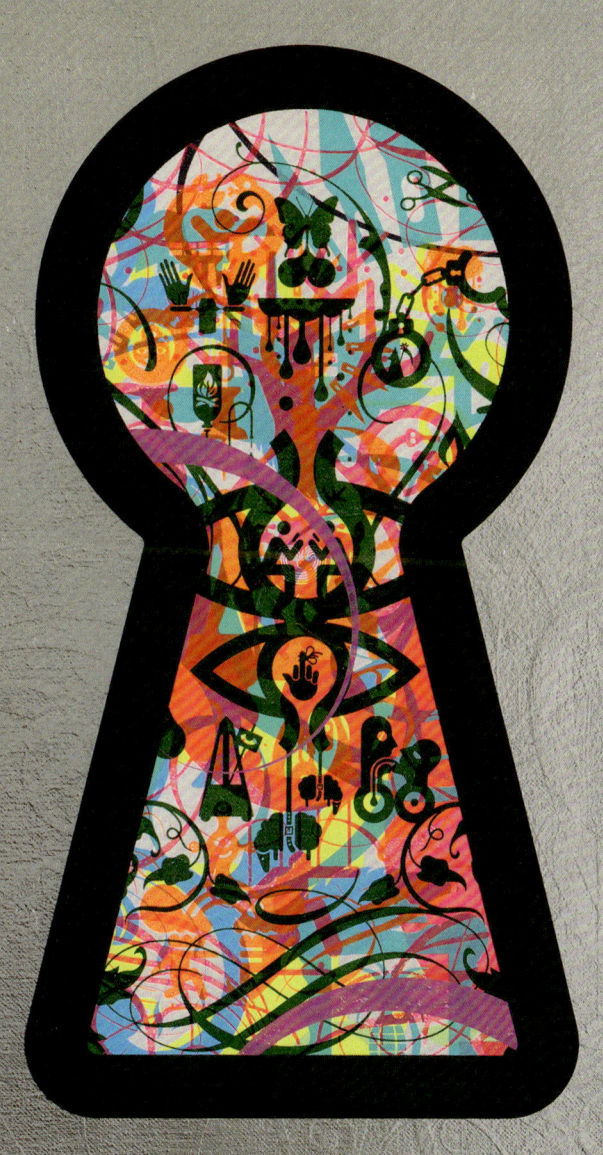

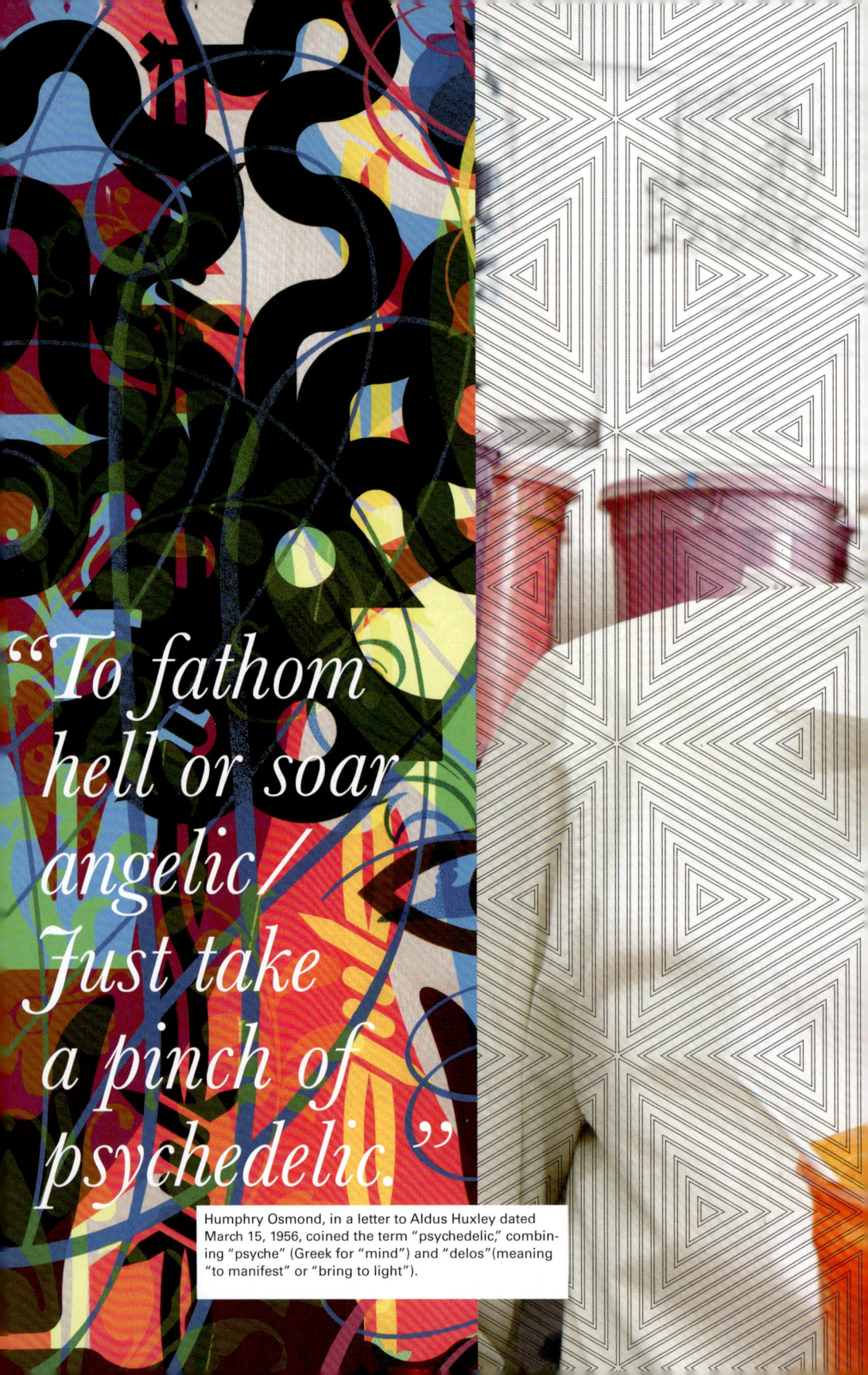

> "To fathom
> hell or soar
> angelic/
> Just take
> a pinch of
> psychedelic."

Humphry Osmond, in a letter to Aldus Huxley dated March 15, 1956, coined the term "psychedelic," combining "psyche" (Greek for "mind") and "delos" (meaning "to manifest" or "bring to light").

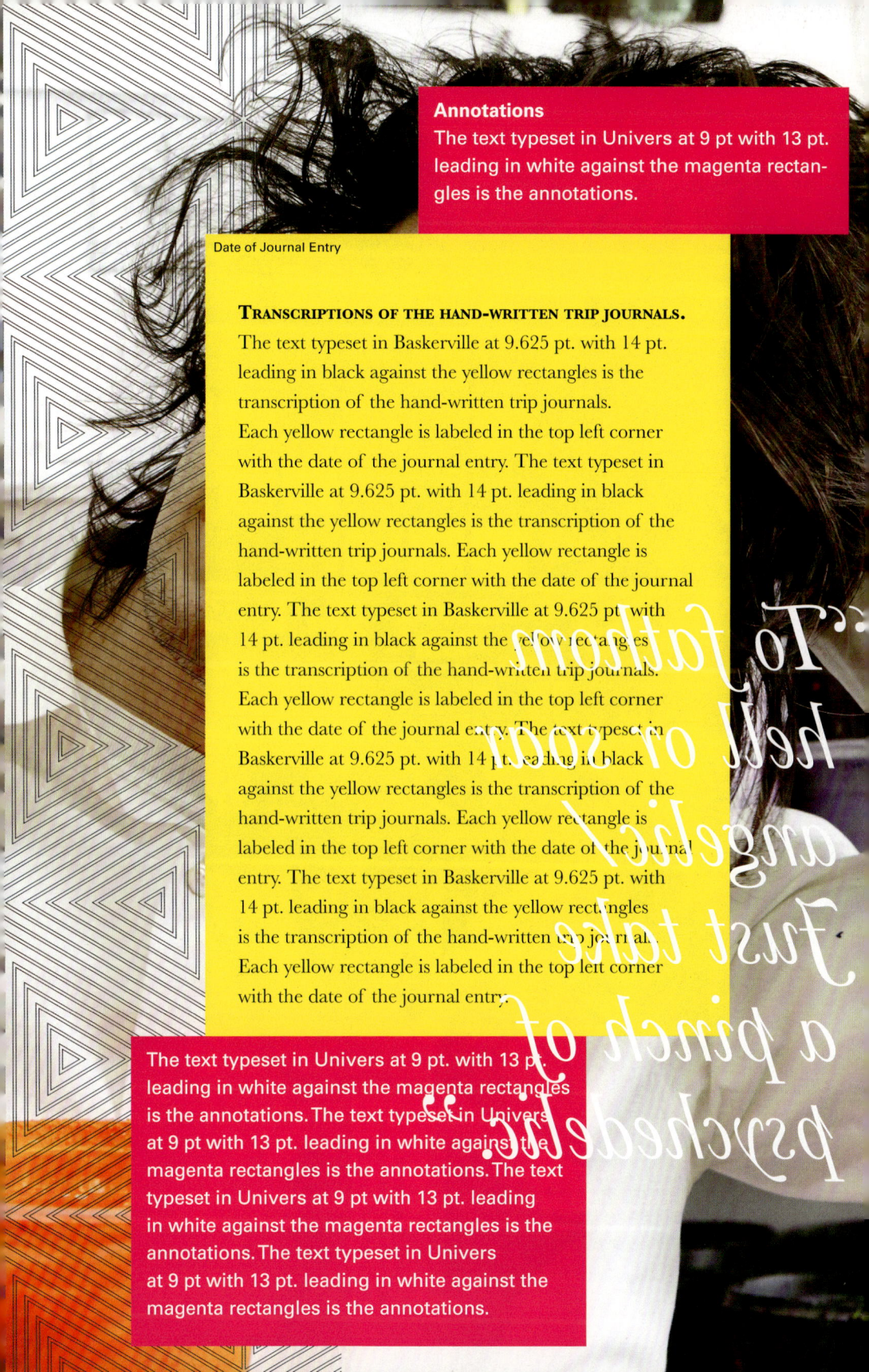

Annotations
The text typeset in Univers at 9 pt with 13 pt. leading in white against the magenta rectangles is the annotations.

Date of Journal Entry

TRANSCRIPTIONS OF THE HAND-WRITTEN TRIP JOURNALS.
The text typeset in Baskerville at 9.625 pt. with 14 pt. leading in black against the yellow rectangles is the transcription of the hand-written trip journals. Each yellow rectangle is labeled in the top left corner with the date of the journal entry. The text typeset in Baskerville at 9.625 pt. with 14 pt. leading in black against the yellow rectangles is the transcription of the hand-written trip journals. Each yellow rectangle is labeled in the top left corner with the date of the journal entry. The text typeset in Baskerville at 9.625 pt. with 14 pt. leading in black against the yellow rectangles is the transcription of the hand-written trip journals. Each yellow rectangle is labeled in the top left corner with the date of the journal entry. The text typeset in Baskerville at 9.625 pt. with 14 pt. leading in black against the yellow rectangles is the transcription of the hand-written trip journals. Each yellow rectangle is labeled in the top left corner with the date of the journal entry. The text typeset in Baskerville at 9.625 pt. with 14 pt. leading in black against the yellow rectangles is the transcription of the hand-written trip journals. Each yellow rectangle is labeled in the top left corner with the date of the journal entry.

"…To fathom hell or soar angelic, just take a pinch of psychedelic."

The text typeset in Univers at 9 pt. with 13 pt. leading in white against the magenta rectangles is the annotations. The text typeset in Univers at 9 pt with 13 pt. leading in white against the magenta rectangles is the annotations. The text typeset in Univers at 9 pt with 13 pt. leading in white against the magenta rectangles is the annotations. The text typeset in Univers at 9 pt with 13 pt. leading in white against the magenta rectangles is the annotations.

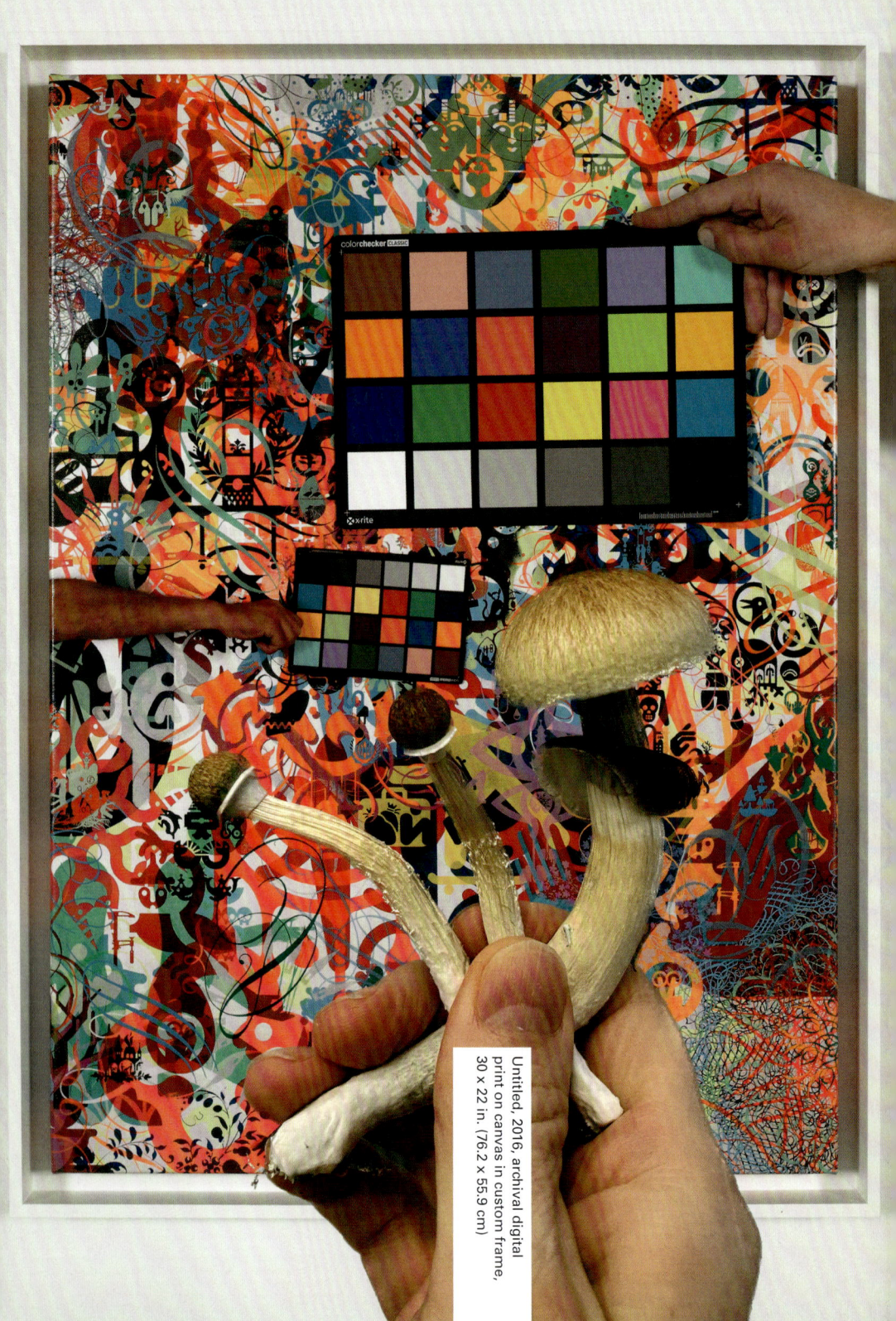

Untitled, 2016, archival digital print on canvas in custom frame, 30 x 22 in. (76.2 x 55.9 cm)

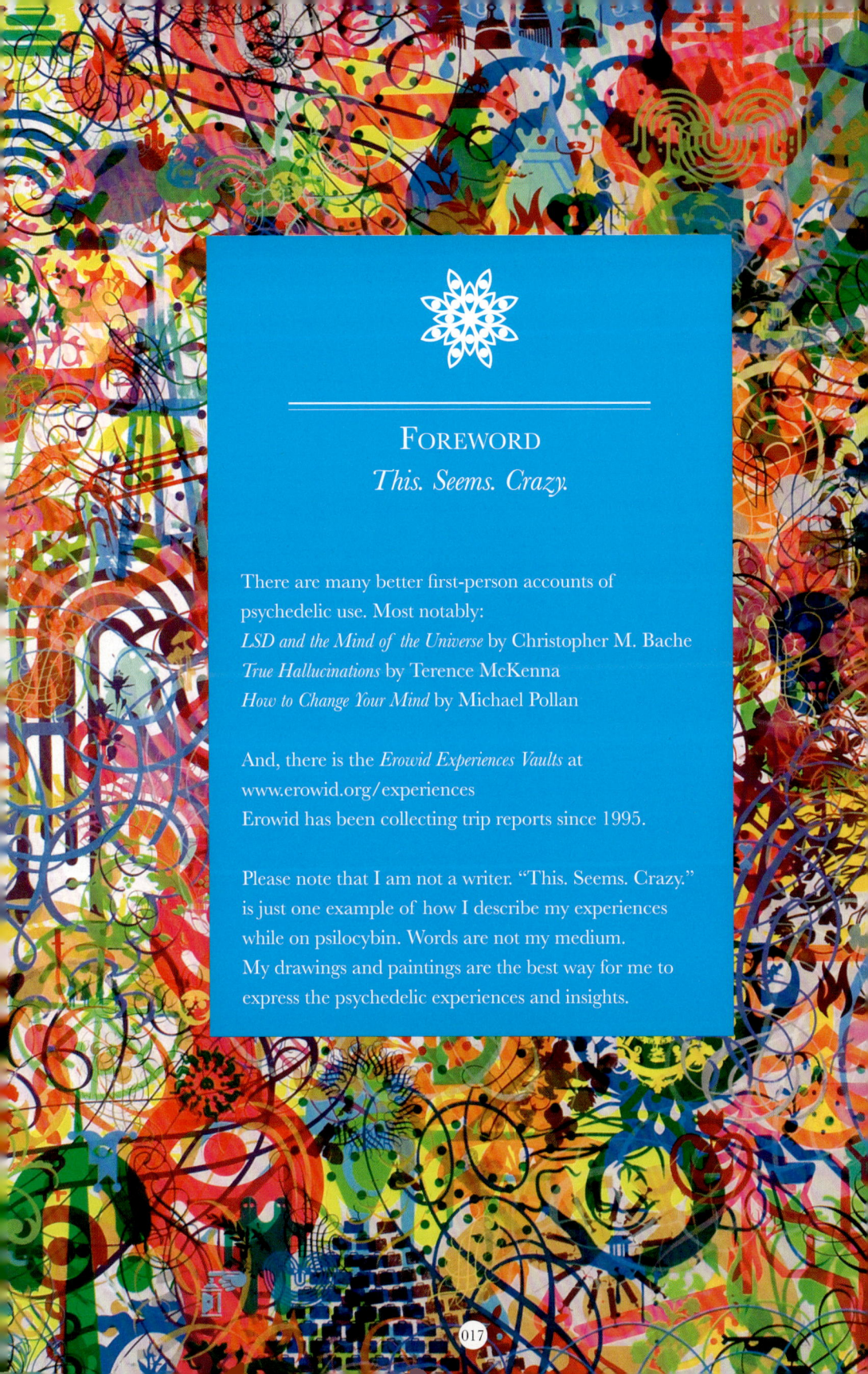

FOREWORD
This. Seems. Crazy.

There are many better first-person accounts of
psychedelic use. Most notably:
LSD and the Mind of the Universe by Christopher M. Bache
True Hallucinations by Terence McKenna
How to Change Your Mind by Michael Pollan

And, there is the *Erowid Experiences Vaults* at
www.erowid.org/experiences
Erowid has been collecting trip reports since 1995.

Please note that I am not a writer. "This. Seems. Crazy."
is just one example of how I describe my experiences
while on psilocybin. Words are not my medium.
My drawings and paintings are the best way for me to
express the psychedelic experiences and insights.

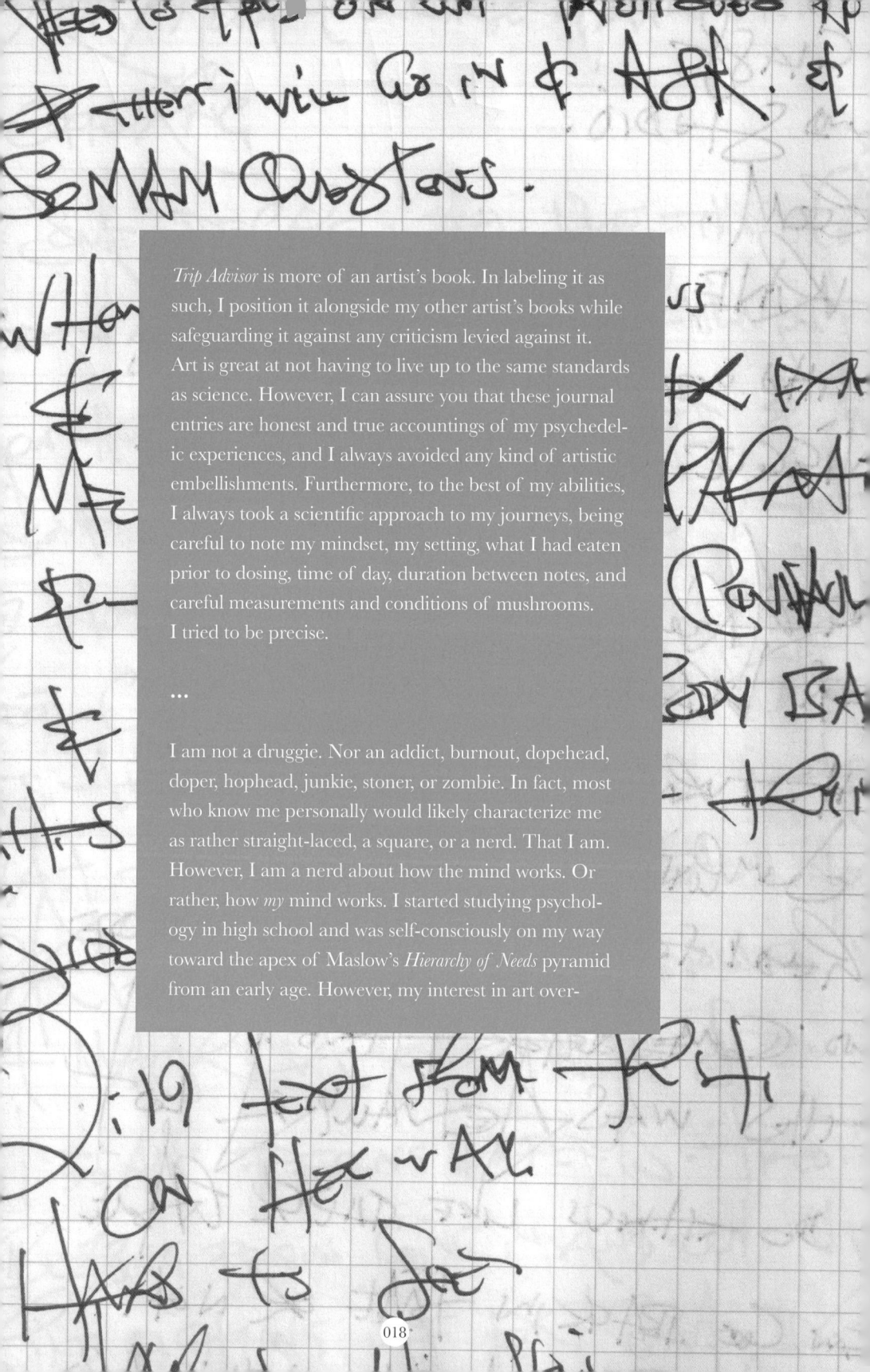

Trip Advisor is more of an artist's book. In labeling it as such, I position it alongside my other artist's books while safeguarding it against any criticism levied against it. Art is great at not having to live up to the same standards as science. However, I can assure you that these journal entries are honest and true accountings of my psychedelic experiences, and I always avoided any kind of artistic embellishments. Furthermore, to the best of my abilities, I always took a scientific approach to my journeys, being careful to note my mindset, my setting, what I had eaten prior to dosing, time of day, duration between notes, and careful measurements and conditions of mushrooms. I tried to be precise.

...

I am not a druggie. Nor an addict, burnout, dopehead, doper, hophead, junkie, stoner, or zombie. In fact, most who know me personally would likely characterize me as rather straight-laced, a square, or a nerd. That I am. However, I am a nerd about how the mind works. Or rather, how *my* mind works. I started studying psychology in high school and was self-consciously on my way toward the apex of Maslow's *Hierarchy of Needs* pyramid from an early age. However, my interest in art overshadowed all other interests as I found art to be a more valuable tool for exploring philosophical curiosities about how we symbolize the world around us—in our minds. I found my life's purpose and meaning through art-making. To supplement that exploration, I turned to psychedelics for the first time when I was 27 years old. Before then, coffee and alcohol were the strongest substances I had ever ingested.

My intentions have always been purposeful and considered—from learning how to grow the mushrooms myself to always ensuring the *set and setting* were conducive to my research. I have always had a sober sitter in my supportive best friend and partner, Trish. She has always served as my tether to this world and allowed me to "go in" and completely abandon this reality. "Going in" is how I have always described the experience of completely letting go of…everything. It's a wild experience.

Virtually all of my trip sessions were under very controlled settings: alone with Trish in a quiet and calm place (usually my studio) on a day on which nothing was scheduled and we had no place to be. I would usually write a bit, take my prepared dose all at once, and write down what I was feeling until I could not write letters

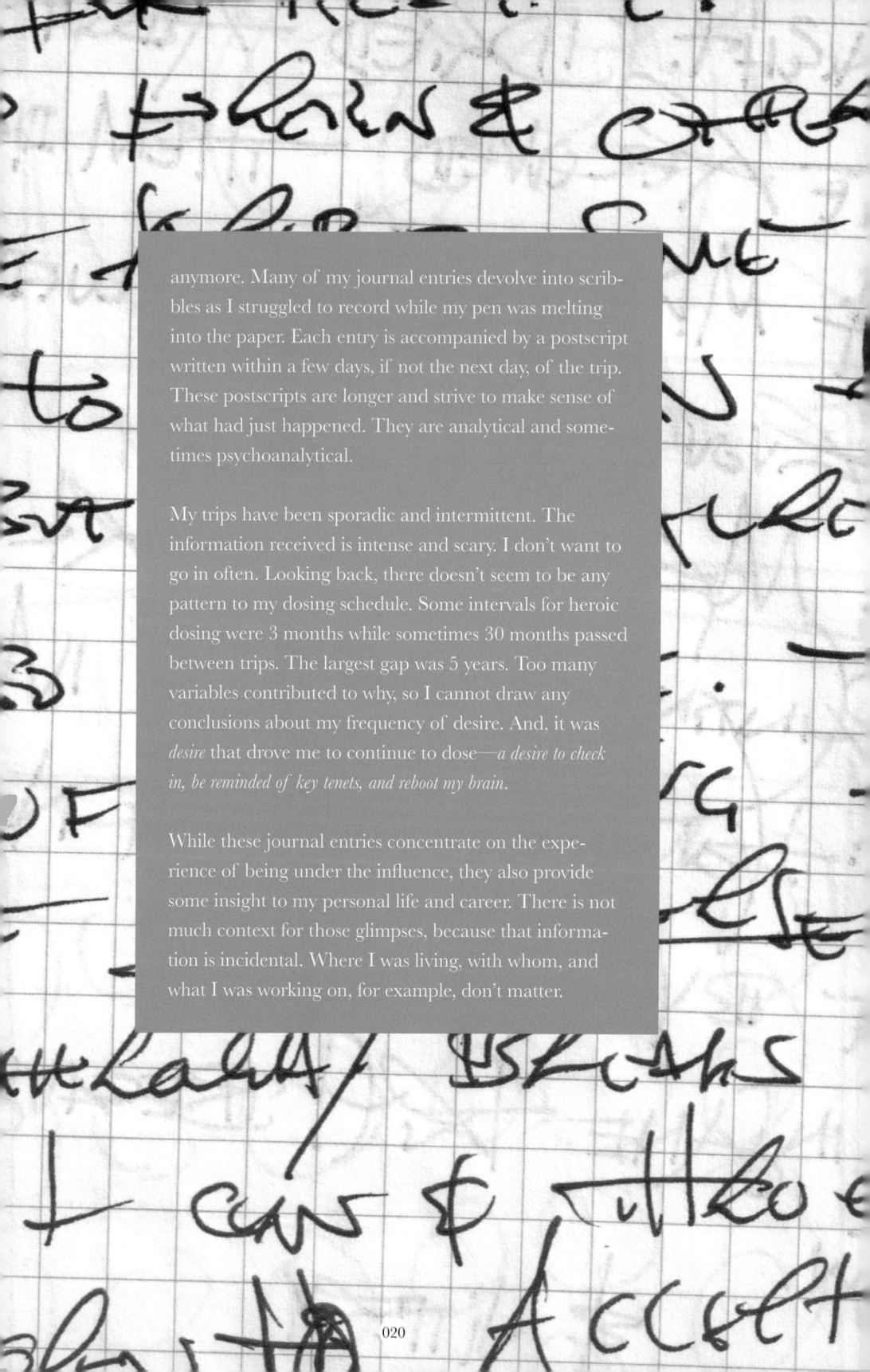

anymore. Many of my journal entries devolve into scribbles as I struggled to record while my pen was melting into the paper. Each entry is accompanied by a postscript written within a few days, if not the next day, of the trip. These postscripts are longer and strive to make sense of what had just happened. They are analytical and sometimes psychoanalytical.

My trips have been sporadic and intermittent. The information received is intense and scary. I don't want to go in often. Looking back, there doesn't seem to be any pattern to my dosing schedule. Some intervals for heroic dosing were 3 months while sometimes 30 months passed between trips. The largest gap was 5 years. Too many variables contributed to why, so I cannot draw any conclusions about my frequency of desire. And, it was *desire* that drove me to continue to dose—*a desire to check in, be reminded of key tenets, and reboot my brain.*

While these journal entries concentrate on the experience of being under the influence, they also provide some insight to my personal life and career. There is not much context for those glimpses, because that information is incidental. Where I was living, with whom, and what I was working on, for example, don't matter.

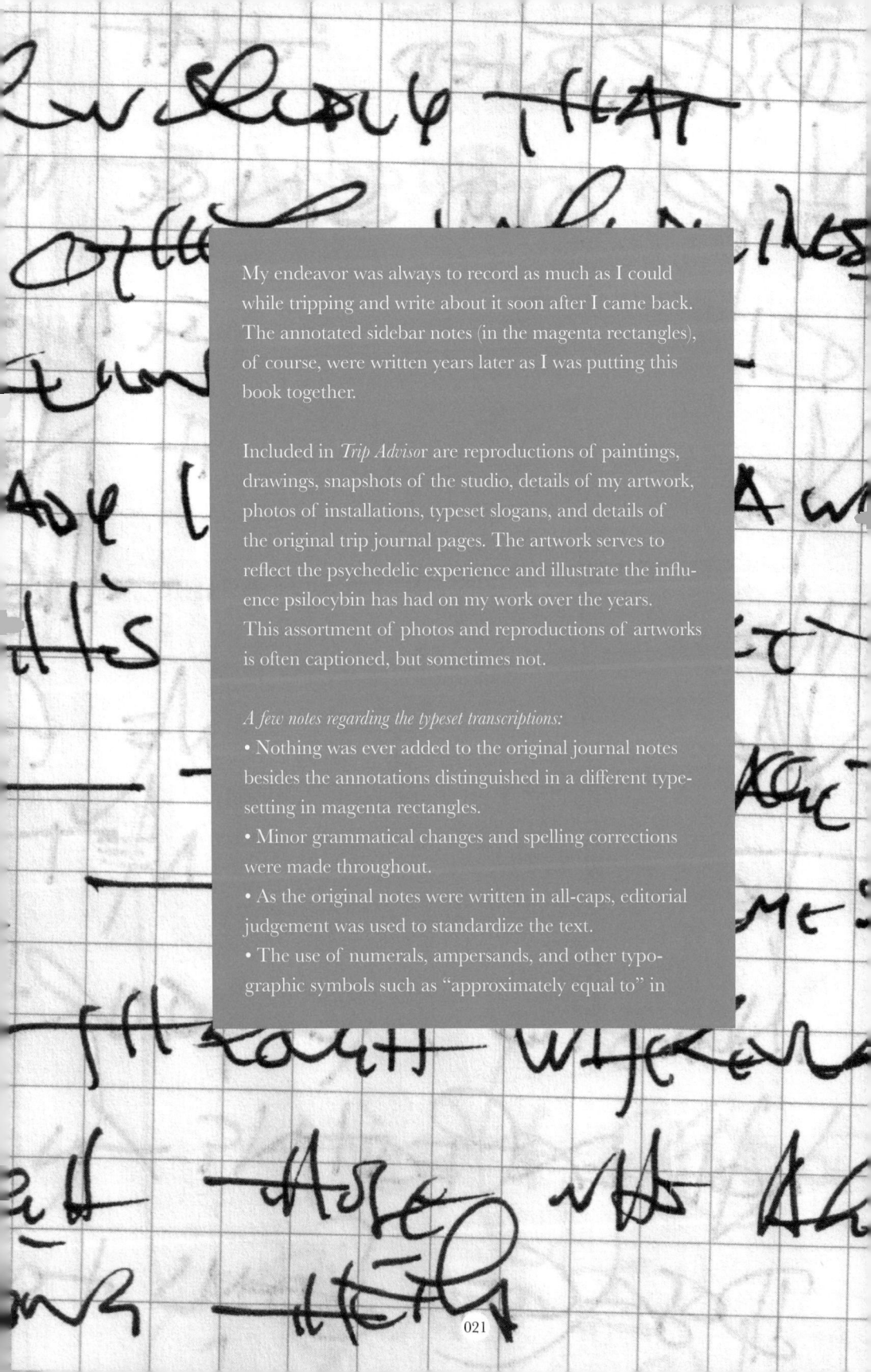

My endeavor was always to record as much as I could while tripping and write about it soon after I came back. The annotated sidebar notes (in the magenta rectangles), of course, were written years later as I was putting this book together.

Included in *Trip Advisor* are reproductions of paintings, drawings, snapshots of the studio, details of my artwork, photos of installations, typeset slogans, and details of the original trip journal pages. The artwork serves to reflect the psychedelic experience and illustrate the influence psilocybin has had on my work over the years. This assortment of photos and reproductions of artworks is often captioned, but sometimes not.

A few notes regarding the typeset transcriptions:
• Nothing was ever added to the original journal notes besides the annotations distinguished in a different type-setting in magenta rectangles.
• Minor grammatical changes and spelling corrections were made throughout.
• As the original notes were written in all-caps, editorial judgement was used to standardize the text.
• The use of numerals, ampersands, and other typo-graphic symbols such as "approximately equal to" in

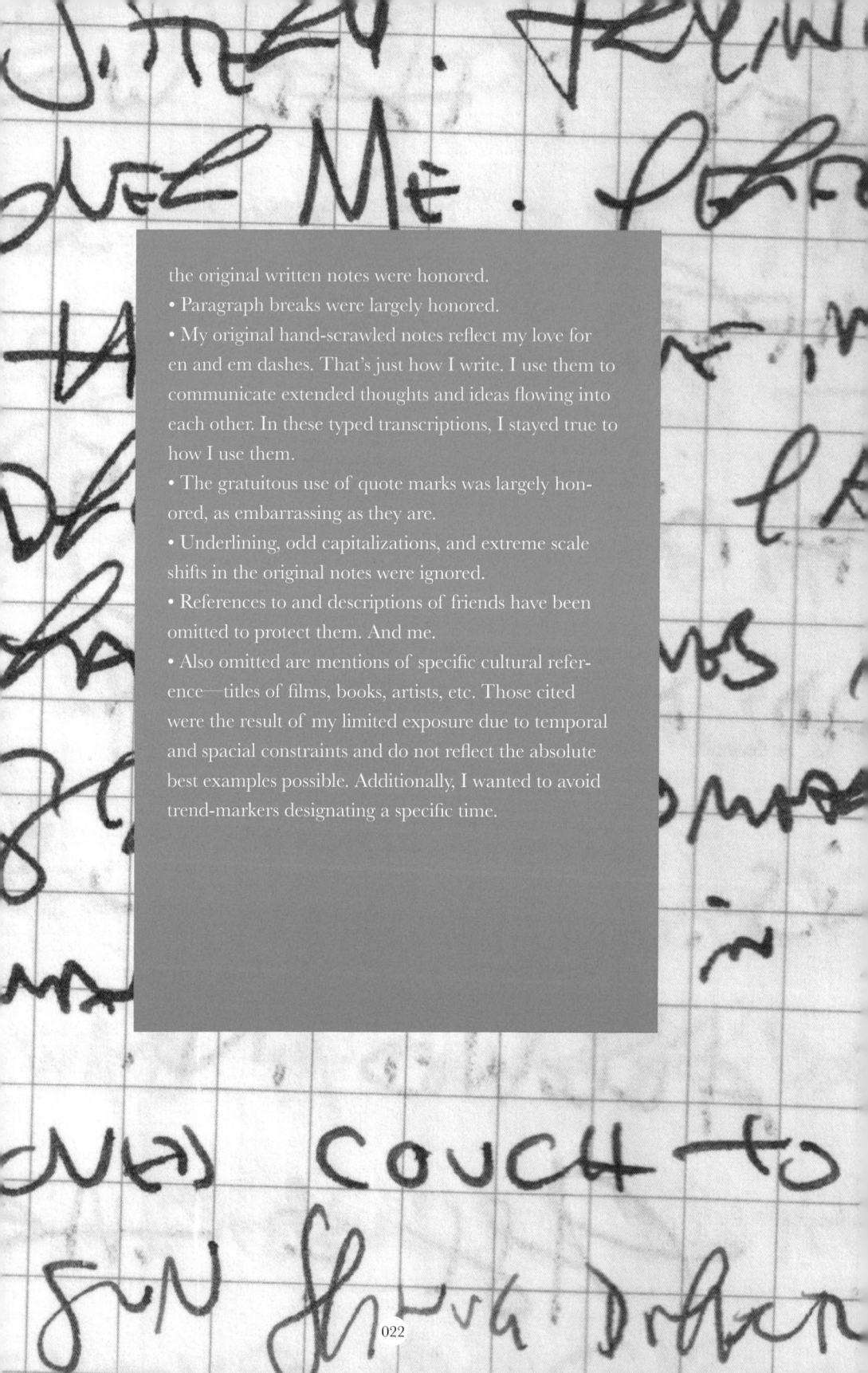

the original written notes were honored.

• Paragraph breaks were largely honored.

• My original hand-scrawled notes reflect my love for en and em dashes. That's just how I write. I use them to communicate extended thoughts and ideas flowing into each other. In these typed transcriptions, I stayed true to how I use them.

• The gratuitous use of quote marks was largely honored, as embarrassing as they are.

• Underlining, odd capitalizations, and extreme scale shifts in the original notes were ignored.

• References to and descriptions of friends have been omitted to protect them. And me.

• Also omitted are mentions of specific cultural reference—titles of films, books, artists, etc. Those cited were the result of my limited exposure due to temporal and spacial constraints and do not reflect the absolute best examples possible. Additionally, I wanted to avoid trend-markers designating a specific time.

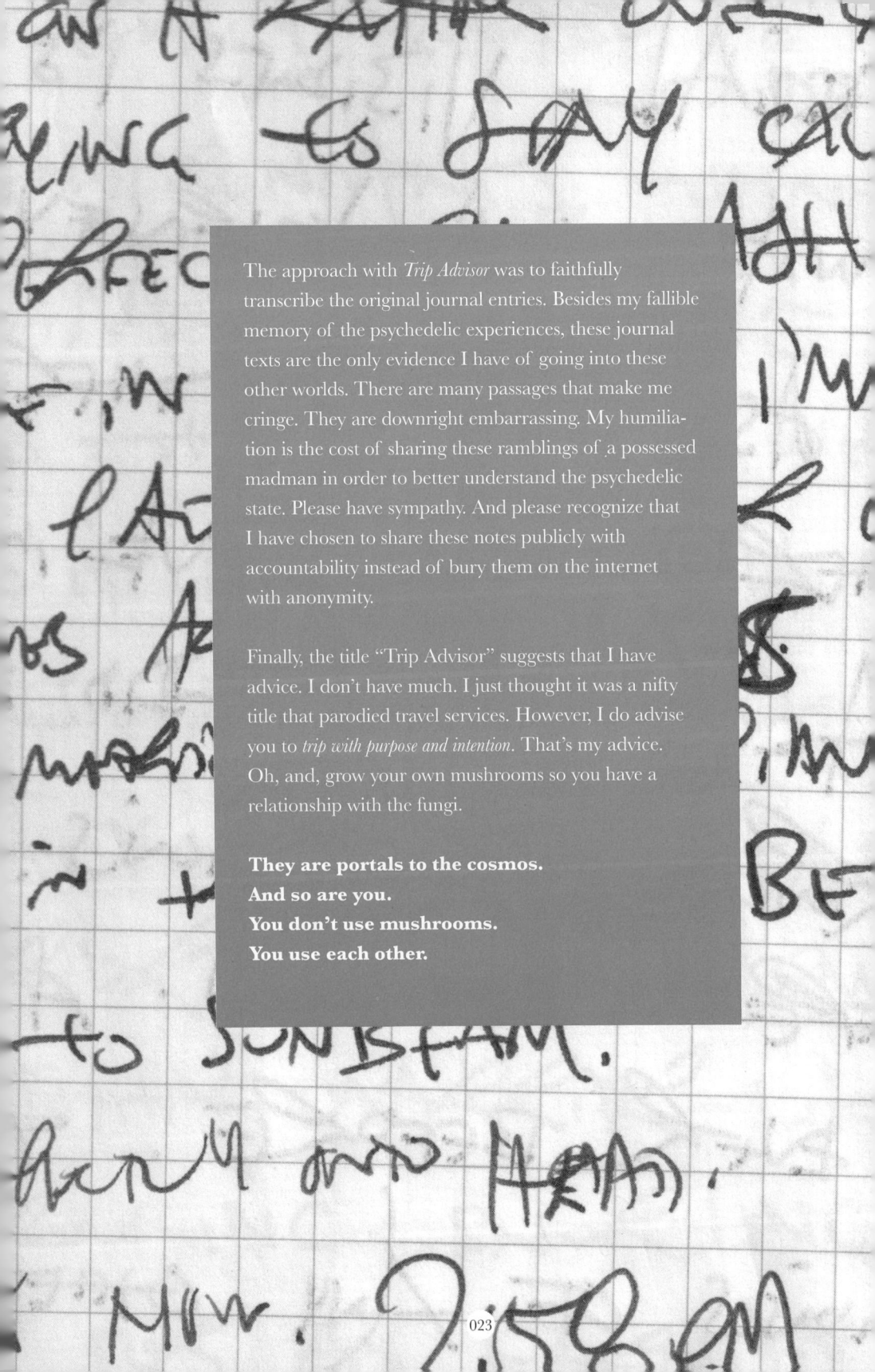

The approach with *Trip Advisor* was to faithfully transcribe the original journal entries. Besides my fallible memory of the psychedelic experiences, these journal texts are the only evidence I have of going into these other worlds. There are many passages that make me cringe. They are downright embarrassing. My humiliation is the cost of sharing these ramblings of a possessed madman in order to better understand the psychedelic state. Please have sympathy. And please recognize that I have chosen to share these notes publicly with accountability instead of bury them on the internet with anonymity.

Finally, the title "Trip Advisor" suggests that I have advice. I don't have much. I just thought it was a nifty title that parodied travel services. However, I do advise you to *trip with purpose and intention*. That's my advice. Oh, and, grow your own mushrooms so you have a relationship with the fungi.

They are portals to the cosmos.
And so are you.
You don't use mushrooms.
You use each other.

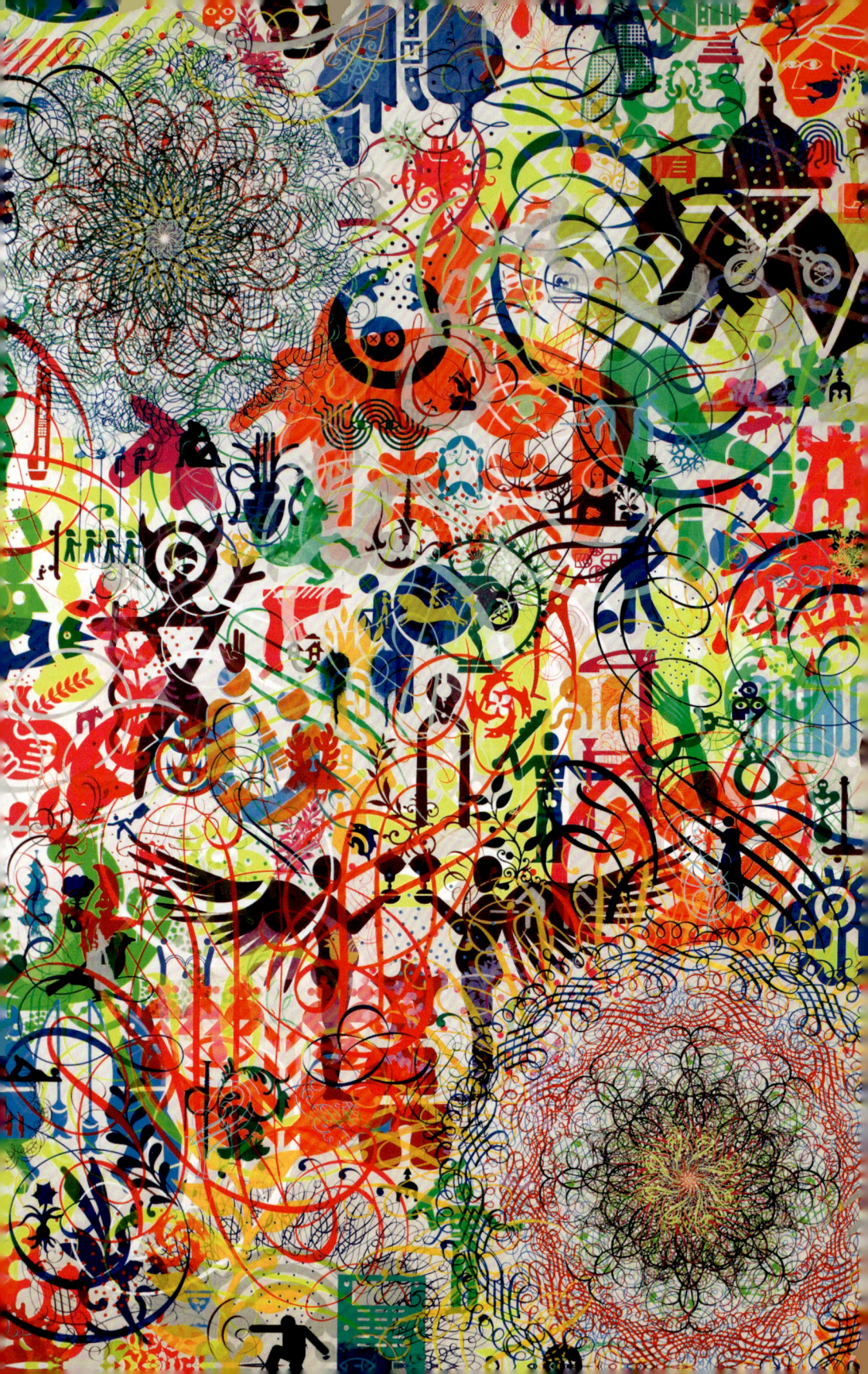

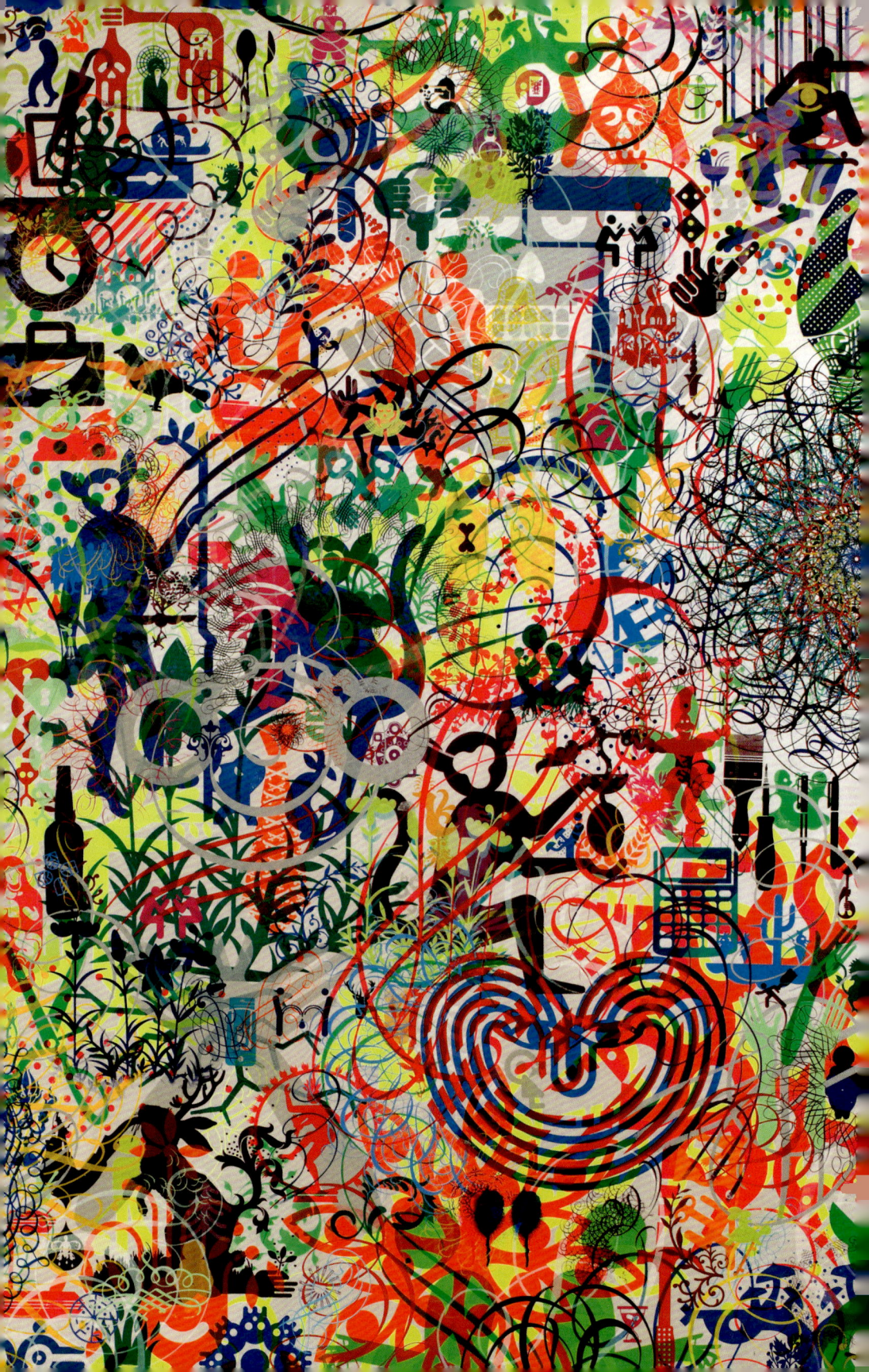

SATURDAY, NOVEMBER 6, 1999

2:30 ATE LARGE CHICKEN ROLL & 1 GLASS ORANGE JUI
FINISHED EATING ABOUT 2:50

FINISHED CLEANING LOFT & TOOK SHOWER.
ATE 4 MUSHROOMS. STALKS ≈ 3-4 INCHES
WITH 1 LARGE GLASS OF FRESH ORANGE JUICE
WILL READ SOME OF MY RESEARCH MATERIAL
UNTIL EFFECTS KICK IN.
MOSTLY WORRIED ABOUT STOMACH / GETTING SICK.
TRISH STANDING BY & WILL BE BY IN CASE
OF ANY EMERGENCY.
A LITTLE SCARED. NERVOUS. ANXIOUS.
WISH I HAD A CONTROL DOUBLE FOR THIS EXPERIMENT
I IMAGINE IT WILL BE HARD TO TELL WHAT
THOUGHTS / SENSATIONS / EXPERIENCES ARE DUE TO
THE PSILOCYBIN.
4:15 : NOTHING REALLY.
THERE'S NO GOING BACK. LIKE GETTING ON A
ROLLERCOASTER. YOU WANT TO HAVE ALREADY
GONE. THEN IT GETS GONE.
4:30 EXCITEMENT. DIZZINESS. WALKING / RACING A

MUSH
SEMI
DRIE
ANY
PICK
THIS

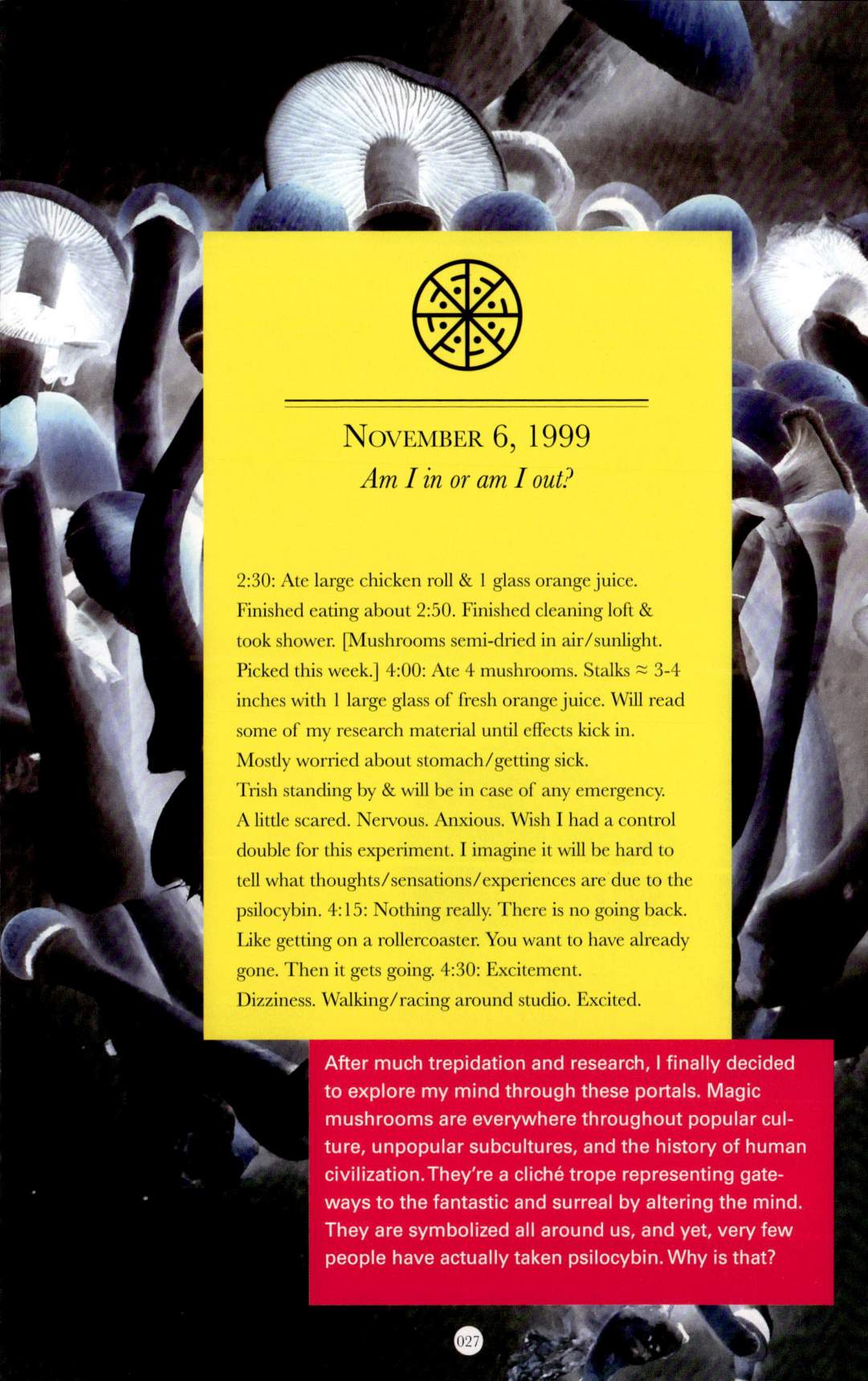

November 6, 1999

Am I in or am I out?

2:30: Ate large chicken roll & 1 glass orange juice.
Finished eating about 2:50. Finished cleaning loft &
took shower. [Mushrooms semi-dried in air/sunlight.
Picked this week.] 4:00: Ate 4 mushrooms. Stalks ≈ 3-4
inches with 1 large glass of fresh orange juice. Will read
some of my research material until effects kick in.
Mostly worried about stomach/getting sick.
Trish standing by & will be in case of any emergency.
A little scared. Nervous. Anxious. Wish I had a control
double for this experiment. I imagine it will be hard to
tell what thoughts/sensations/experiences are due to the
psilocybin. 4:15: Nothing really. There is no going back.
Like getting on a rollercoaster. You want to have already
gone. Then it gets going. 4:30: Excitement.
Dizziness. Walking/racing around studio. Excited.

After much trepidation and research, I finally decided
to explore my mind through these portals. Magic
mushrooms are everywhere throughout popular culture, unpopular subcultures, and the history of human
civilization. They're a cliché trope representing gate-
ways to the fantastic and surreal by altering the mind.
They are symbolized all around us, and yet, very few
people have actually taken psilocybin. Why is that?

My "soul" transcended my body several times to the point where I was manipulating my environment—making some things disappear & appear.

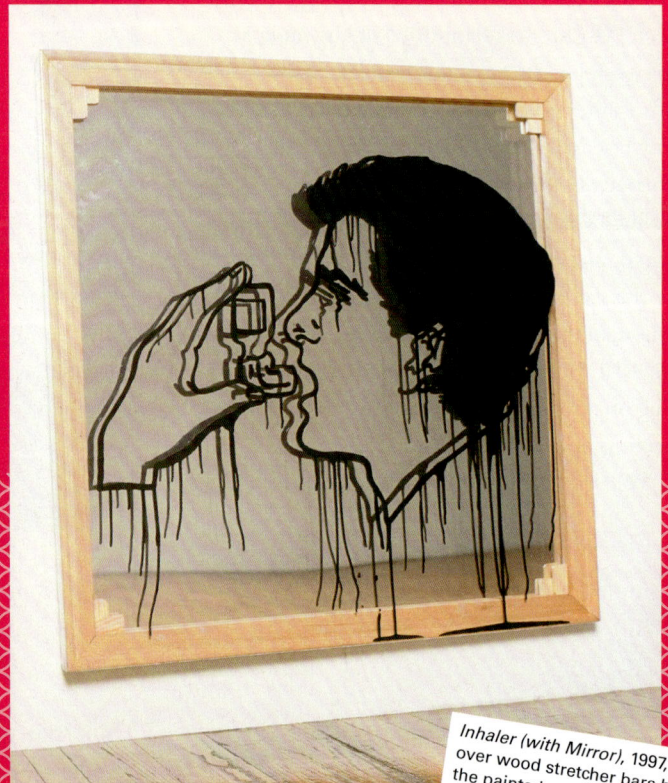

Inhaler (with Mirror), 1997, oil on verso of clear plastic stretched over wood stretcher bars backed with mirrored acrylic reflecting the painted surface, 36 x 36 in. (91.4 x 91.4 cm)

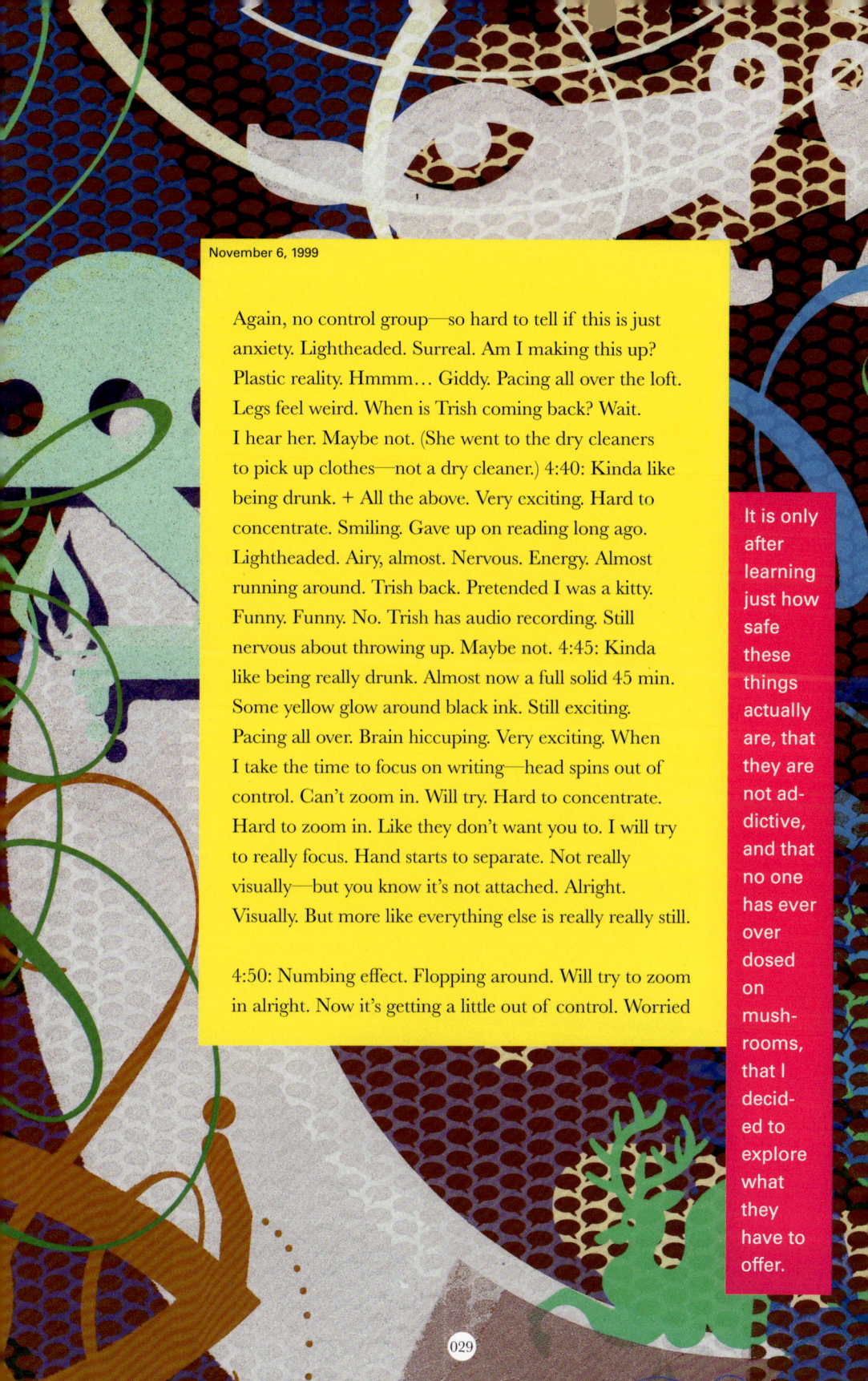

November 6, 1999

Again, no control group—so hard to tell if this is just anxiety. Lightheaded. Surreal. Am I making this up? Plastic reality. Hmmm… Giddy. Pacing all over the loft. Legs feel weird. When is Trish coming back? Wait. I hear her. Maybe not. (She went to the dry cleaners to pick up clothes—not a dry cleaner.) 4:40: Kinda like being drunk. + All the above. Very exciting. Hard to concentrate. Smiling. Gave up on reading long ago. Lightheaded. Airy, almost. Nervous. Energy. Almost running around. Trish back. Pretended I was a kitty. Funny. Funny. No. Trish has audio recording. Still nervous about throwing up. Maybe not. 4:45: Kinda like being really drunk. Almost now a full solid 45 min. Some yellow glow around black ink. Still exciting. Pacing all over. Brain hiccuping. Very exciting. When I take the time to focus on writing—head spins out of control. Can't zoom in. Will try. Hard to concentrate. Hard to zoom in. Like they don't want you to. I will try to really focus. Hand starts to separate. Not really visually—but you know it's not attached. Alright. Visually. But more like everything else is really really still.

4:50: Numbing effect. Flopping around. Will try to zoom in alright. Now it's getting a little out of control. Worried

It is only after learning just how safe these things actually are, that they are not ad-dictive, and that no one has ever over dosed on mush-rooms, that I decid-ed to explore what they have to offer.

about not being allowed to focus. Head buzzing.
Yellowing around dark ink. Almost 5:PM: 5:00 Now now.
Like really really drunk. Can't rely on analogy. Analogies
anymore. Still a little after 5. Now visuals. 5:05: 3-D is
hyperreal. 3D. 3D on top of 3D. Been talking to Trish.
5:08: Trish takes over.

1:15AM Now. I was completely out of control. I felt as
though I had or could completely transcend this body,
this world, this dimension. I kept going back & forth.
In and out. I believed that you were either chosen &
could go in, or you weren't & remained out. I could go
in, or I could go out. I went in a repeated # of times.
The world disappeared & dissolved into good & evil.
Light & dark. White & black. I felt like I was a chosen
one who could go in. I wanted Trish to come with me,
but because she was not chosen, she kept me tied. Out.
Down. Black. I felt like I had achieved a complete & total
understanding of the larger picture. The total plan.
We make up such a tiny tiny tiny part of it. My "soul"
transcended my body several times to the point where
I was manipulating my environment—making some
things disappear & appear. Disappear & appear audibly.
Aurally. I could touch things like the plant above

I learned how to grow mushrooms. As this was before off-the-shelf solutions were available on the internet, there was a bit of a learning curve, but I liked the idea of having a relationship with these fungi—organisms that are not plants and are not animals. They are somewhere in-between. They literally breathe like humans and share more of their DNA with us than with plants.

Double Happiness, 1998, oil on canvas, 48 x 48 in. (121.9 x 121.9 cm)

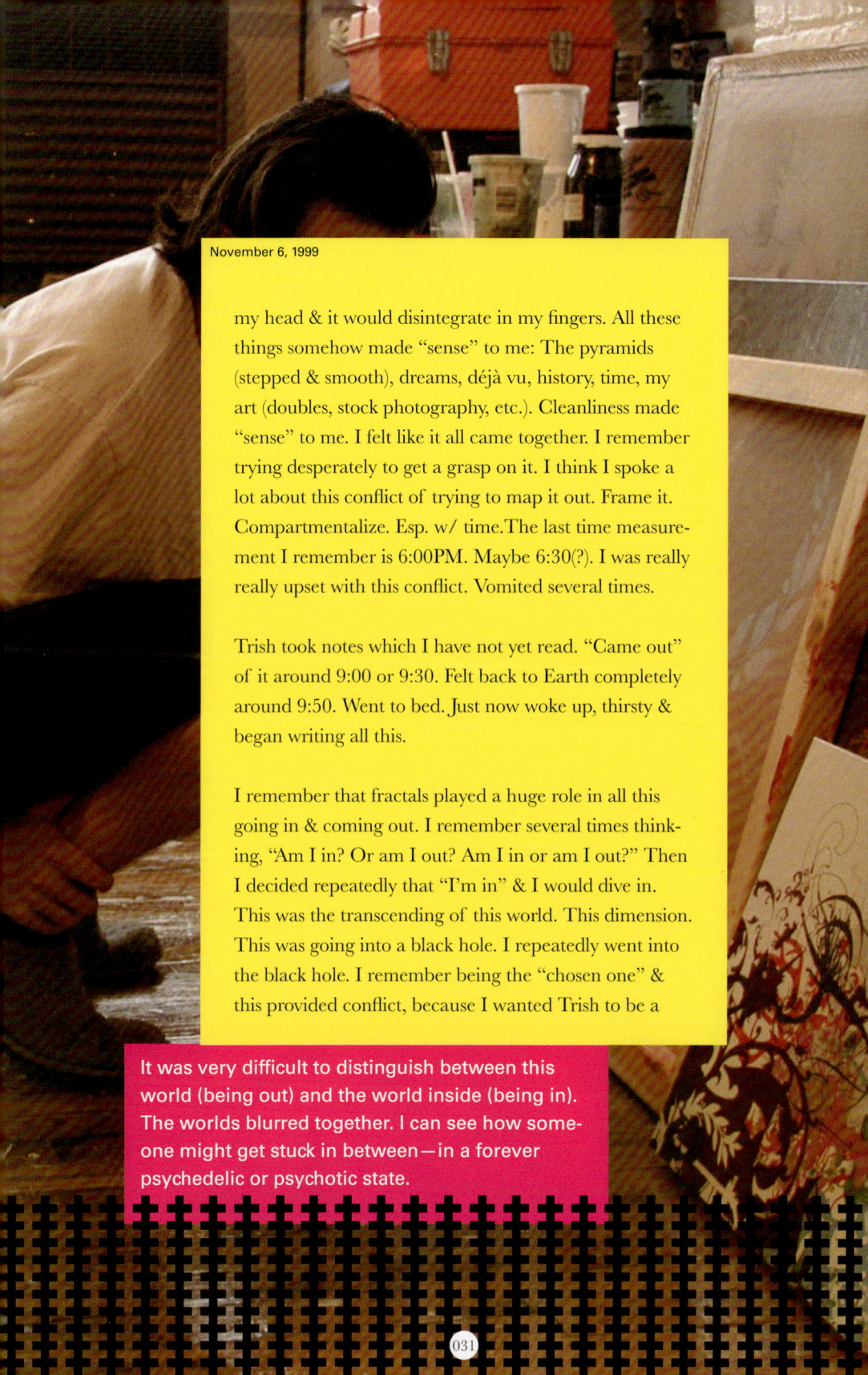

November 6, 1999

my head & it would disintegrate in my fingers. All these things somehow made "sense" to me: The pyramids (stepped & smooth), dreams, déjà vu, history, time, my art (doubles, stock photography, etc.). Cleanliness made "sense" to me. I felt like it all came together. I remember trying desperately to get a grasp on it. I think I spoke a lot about this conflict of trying to map it out. Frame it. Compartmentalize. Esp. w/ time. The last time measurement I remember is 6:00PM. Maybe 6:30(?). I was really really upset with this conflict. Vomited several times.

Trish took notes which I have not yet read. "Came out" of it around 9:00 or 9:30. Felt back to Earth completely around 9:50. Went to bed. Just now woke up, thirsty & began writing all this.

I remember that fractals played a huge role in all this going in & coming out. I remember several times thinking, "Am I in? Or am I out? Am I in or am I out?" Then I decided repeatedly that "I'm in" & I would dive in. This was the transcending of this world. This dimension. This was going into a black hole. I repeatedly went into the black hole. I remember being the "chosen one" & this provided conflict, because I wanted Trish to be a

It was very difficult to distinguish between this world (being out) and the world inside (being in). The worlds blurred together. I can see how someone might get stuck in between—in a forever psychedelic or psychotic state.

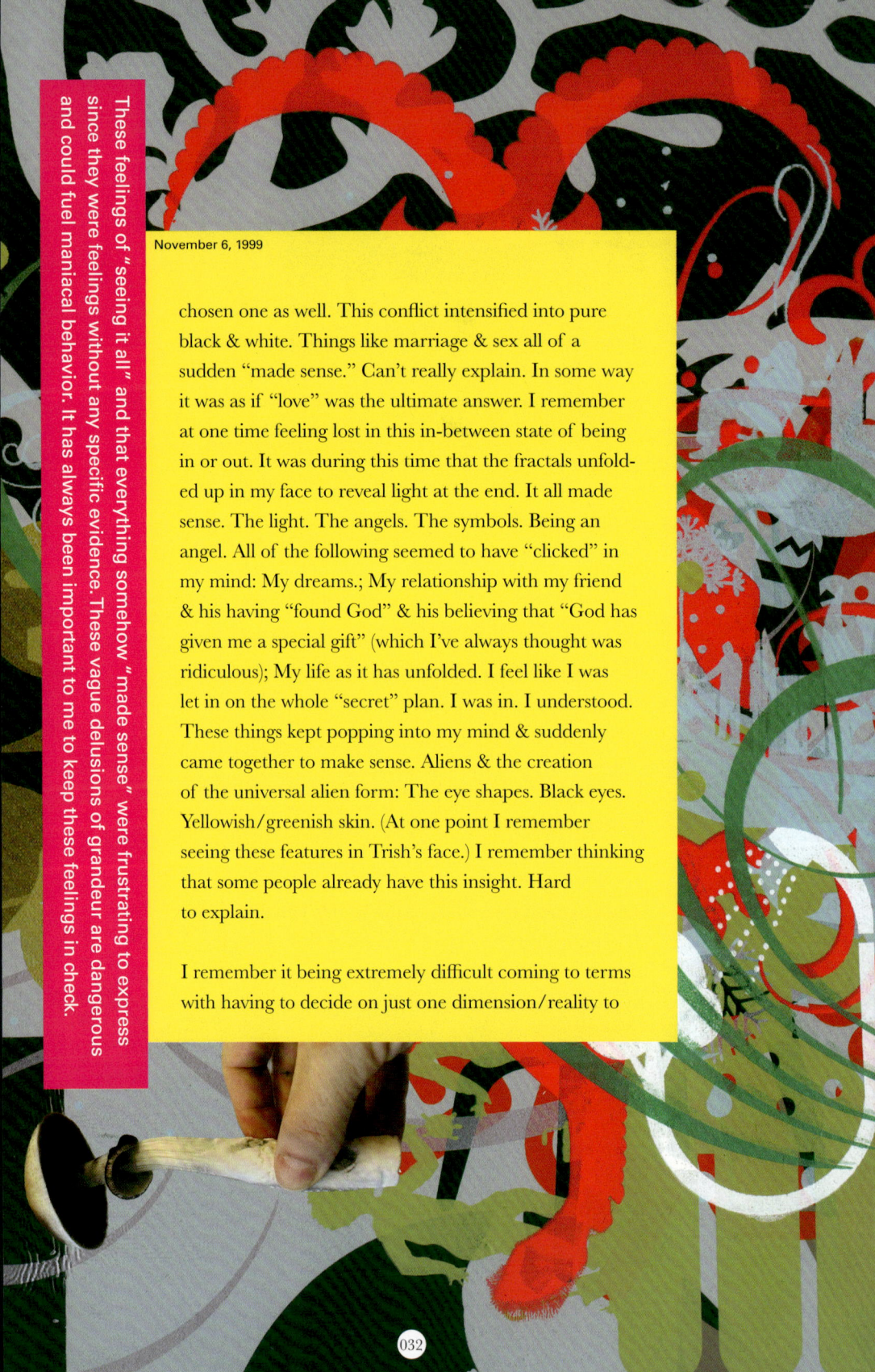

These feelings of "seeing it all" and that everything somehow "made sense" were frustrating to express since they were feelings without any specific evidence. These vague delusions of grandeur are dangerous and could fuel maniacal behavior. It has always been important to me to keep these feelings in check.

chosen one as well. This conflict intensified into pure black & white. Things like marriage & sex all of a sudden "made sense." Can't really explain. In some way it was as if "love" was the ultimate answer. I remember at one time feeling lost in this in-between state of being in or out. It was during this time that the fractals unfold-ed up in my face to reveal light at the end. It all made sense. The light. The angels. The symbols. Being an angel. All of the following seemed to have "clicked" in my mind: My dreams.; My relationship with my friend & his having "found God" & his believing that "God has given me a special gift" (which I've always thought was ridiculous); My life as it has unfolded. I feel like I was let in on the whole "secret" plan. I was in. I understood. These things kept popping into my mind & suddenly came together to make sense. Aliens & the creation of the universal alien form: The eye shapes. Black eyes. Yellowish/greenish skin. (At one point I remember seeing these features in Trish's face.) I remember thinking that some people already have this insight. Hard to explain.

I remember it being extremely difficult coming to terms with having to decide on just one dimension/reality to

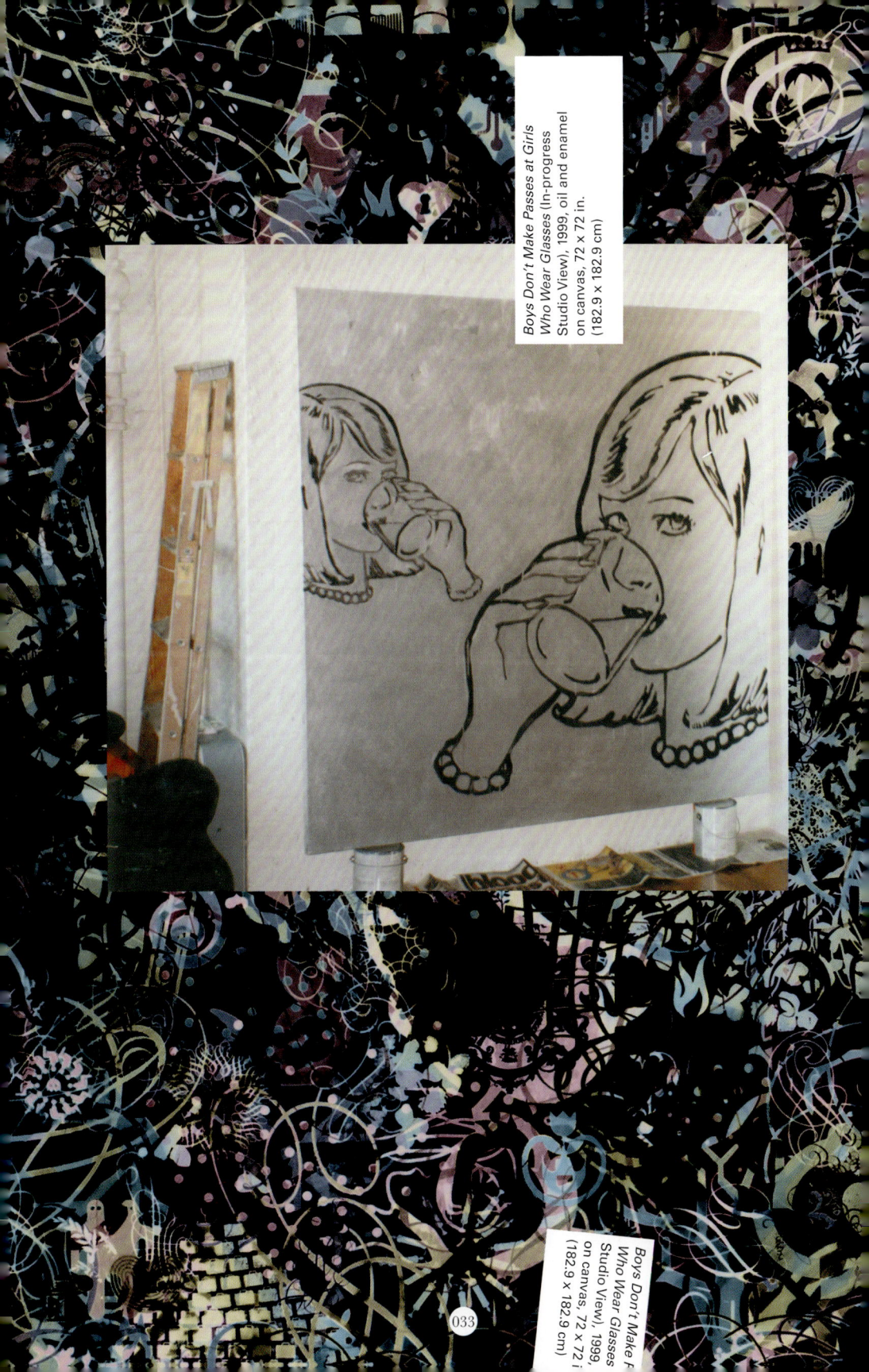

Boys Don't Make Passes at Girls
Who Wear Glasses (In-progress
Studio View), 1999, oil and enamel
on canvas, 72 x 72 in.
(182.9 x 182.9 cm)

Boys Don't Make P
Who Wear Glasses
Studio View), 1999,
on canvas, 72 x 72 i
(182.9 x 182.9 cm)

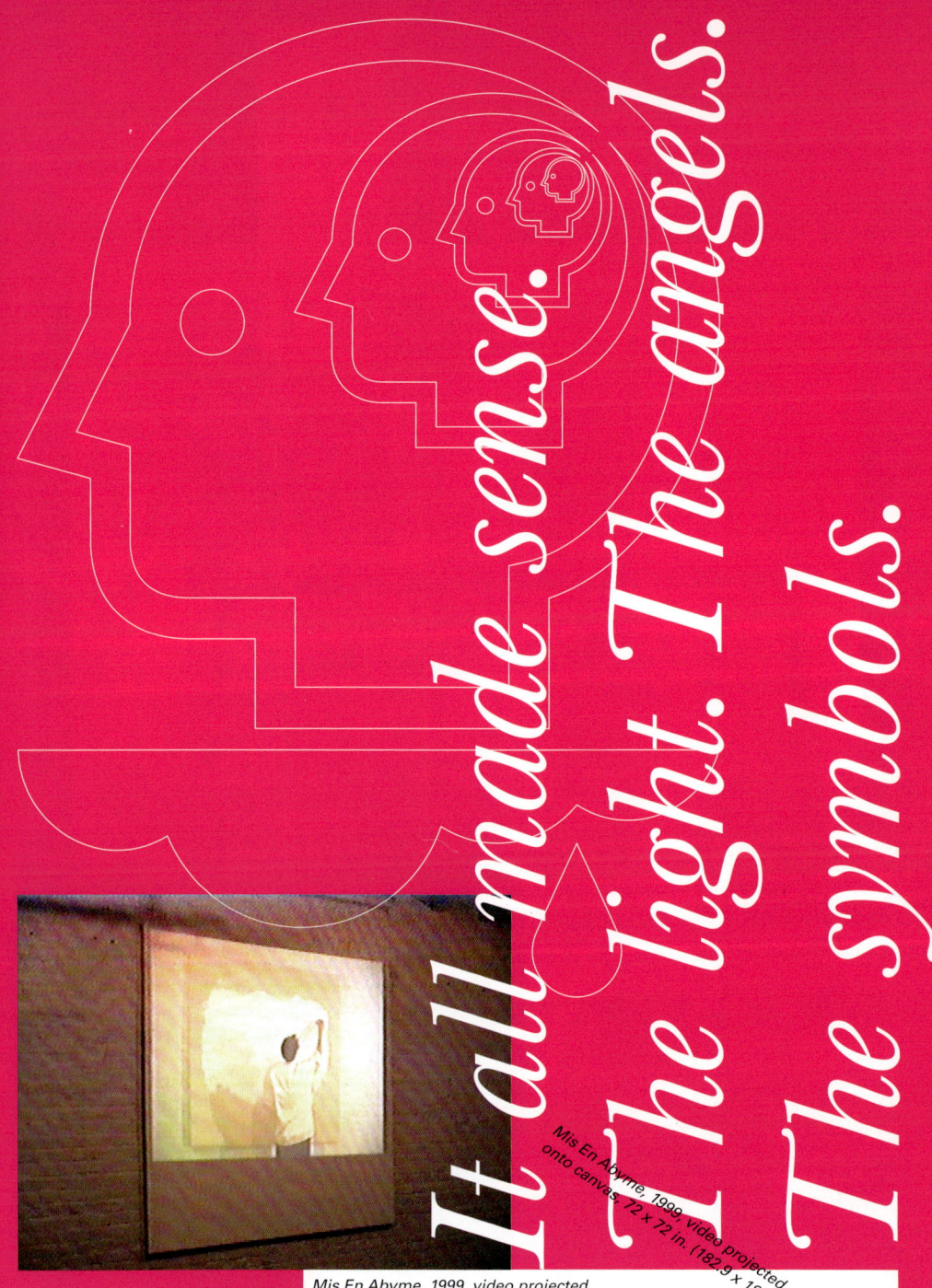

It all made sense. The light. The angels. The symbols.

Mis En Abyme, 1999, video projected onto canvas, 72 x 72 in. (182.9 x 182.9 cm)

Mis En Abyme, 1999, video projected
onto canvas, 72 x 72 in. (182.9 x 182.9 cm)

Mis En Abyme, 1999, video projected
onto canvas, 72 x 72 in. (182.9 x 182.9 cm)

Mis En Abyme, 1999, video projected
onto canvas, 72 x 72 in. (182.9 x 182.9 cm)

Mis En Abyme, 1999, video projected
onto canvas, 72 x 72 in. (182.9 x 182.9 cm)

Mis En Abyme, 1999, video projected

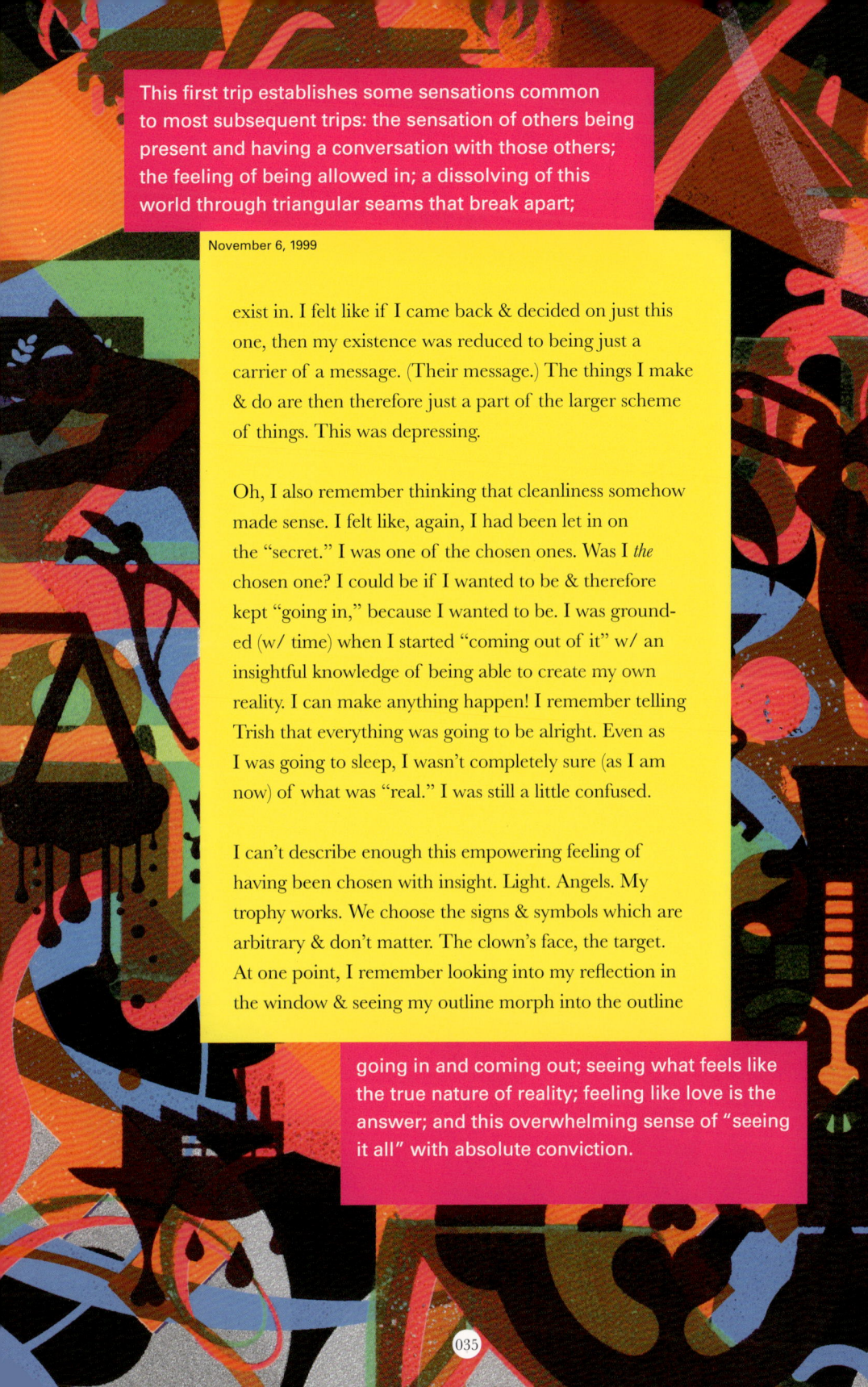

November 6, 1999

exist in. I felt like if I came back & decided on just this one, then my existence was reduced to being just a carrier of a message. (Their message.) The things I make & do are then therefore just a part of the larger scheme of things. This was depressing.

Oh, I also remember thinking that cleanliness somehow made sense. I felt like, again, I had been let in on the "secret." I was one of the chosen ones. Was I *the* chosen one? I could be if I wanted to be & therefore kept "going in," because I wanted to be. I was grounded (w/ time) when I started "coming out of it" w/ an insightful knowledge of being able to create my own reality. I can make anything happen! I remember telling Trish that everything was going to be alright. Even as I was going to sleep, I wasn't completely sure (as I am now) of what was "real." I was still a little confused.

I can't describe enough this empowering feeling of having been chosen with insight. Light. Angels. My trophy works. We choose the signs & symbols which are arbitrary & don't matter. The clown's face, the target. At one point, I remember looking into my reflection in the window & seeing my outline morph into the outline

going in and coming out; seeing what feels like the true nature of reality; feeling like love is the answer; and this overwhelming sense of "seeing it all" with absolute conviction.

035

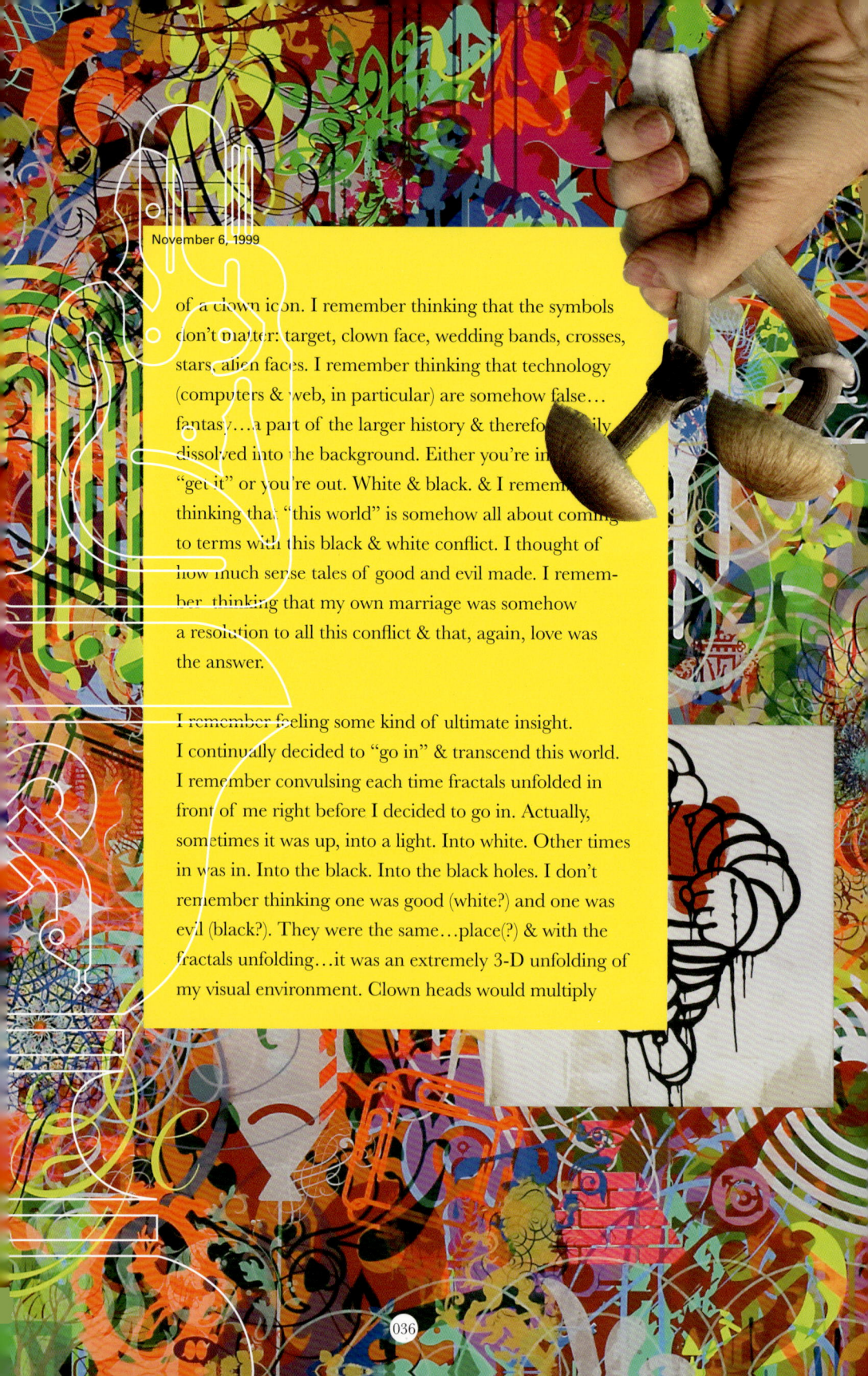

of a clown icon. I remember thinking that the symbols don't matter: target, clown face, wedding bands, crosses, stars, alien faces. I remember thinking that technology (computers & web, in particular) are somehow false… fantasy….a part of the larger history & therefore easily dissolved into the background. Either you're in & "get it" or you're out. White & black. & I remember thinking that "this world" is somehow all about coming to terms with this black & white conflict. I thought of how much sense tales of good and evil made. I remember thinking that my own marriage was somehow a resolution to all this conflict & that, again, love was the answer.

I remember feeling some kind of ultimate insight. I continually decided to "go in" & transcend this world. I remember convulsing each time fractals unfolded in front of me right before I decided to go in. Actually, sometimes it was up, into a light. Into white. Other times in was in. Into the black. Into the black holes. I don't remember thinking one was good (white?) and one was evil (black?). They were the same…place(?) & with the fractals unfolding…it was an extremely 3-D unfolding of my visual environment. Clown heads would multiply

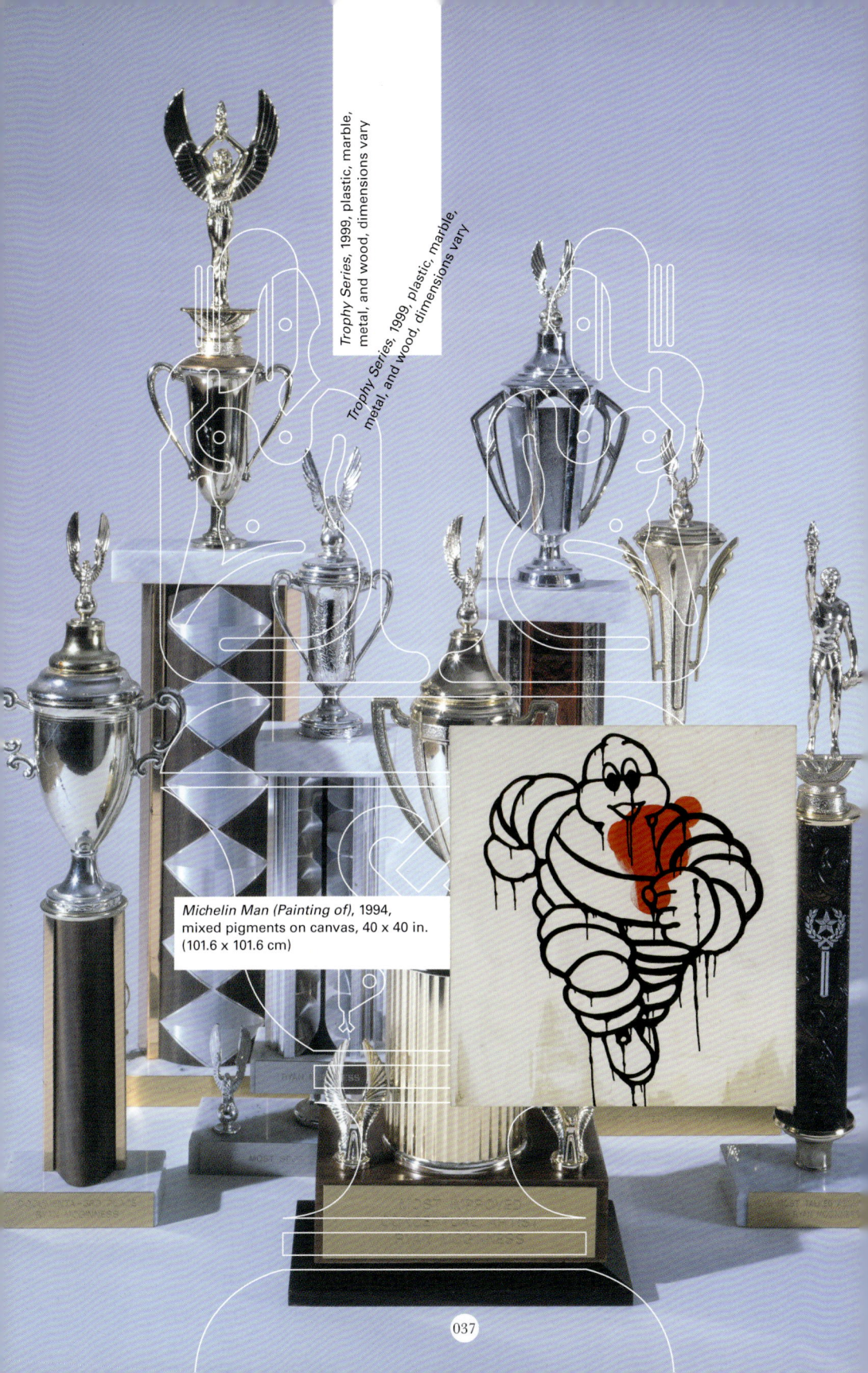

Trophy Series, 1999, plastic, marble, metal, and wood, dimensions vary

Trophy Series, 1999, plastic, marble, metal, and wood, dimensions vary

Michelin Man (Painting of), 1994, mixed pigments on canvas, 40 x 40 in. (101.6 x 101.6 cm)

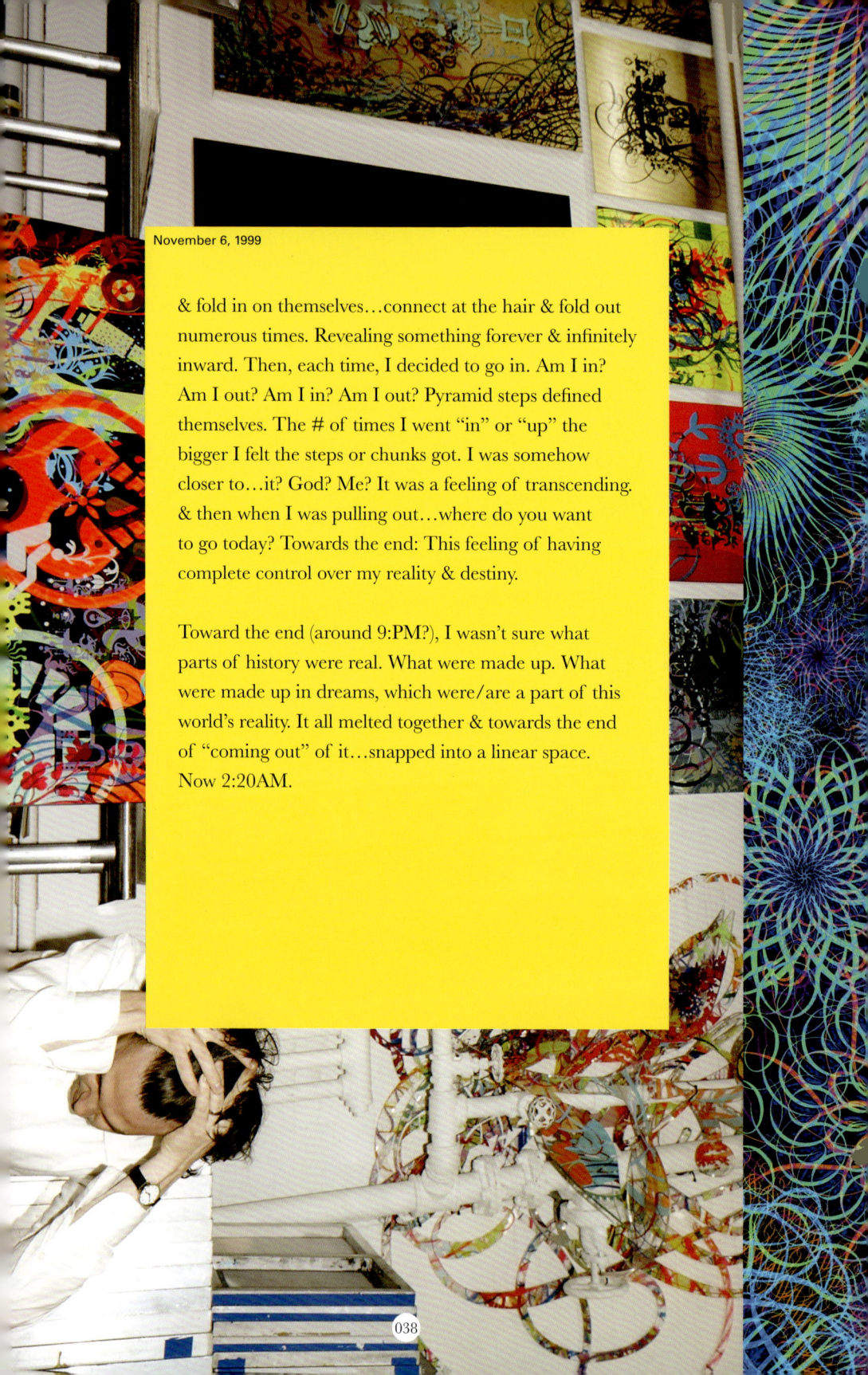

November 6, 1999

& fold in on themselves…connect at the hair & fold out numerous times. Revealing something forever & infinitely inward. Then, each time, I decided to go in. Am I in? Am I out? Am I in? Am I out? Pyramid steps defined themselves. The # of times I went "in" or "up" the bigger I felt the steps or chunks got. I was somehow closer to…it? God? Me? It was a feeling of transcending. & then when I was pulling out…where do you want to go today? Towards the end: This feeling of having complete control over my reality & destiny.

Toward the end (around 9:PM?), I wasn't sure what parts of history were real. What were made up. What were made up in dreams, which were/are a part of this world's reality. It all melted together & towards the end of "coming out" of it…snapped into a linear space. Now 2:20AM.

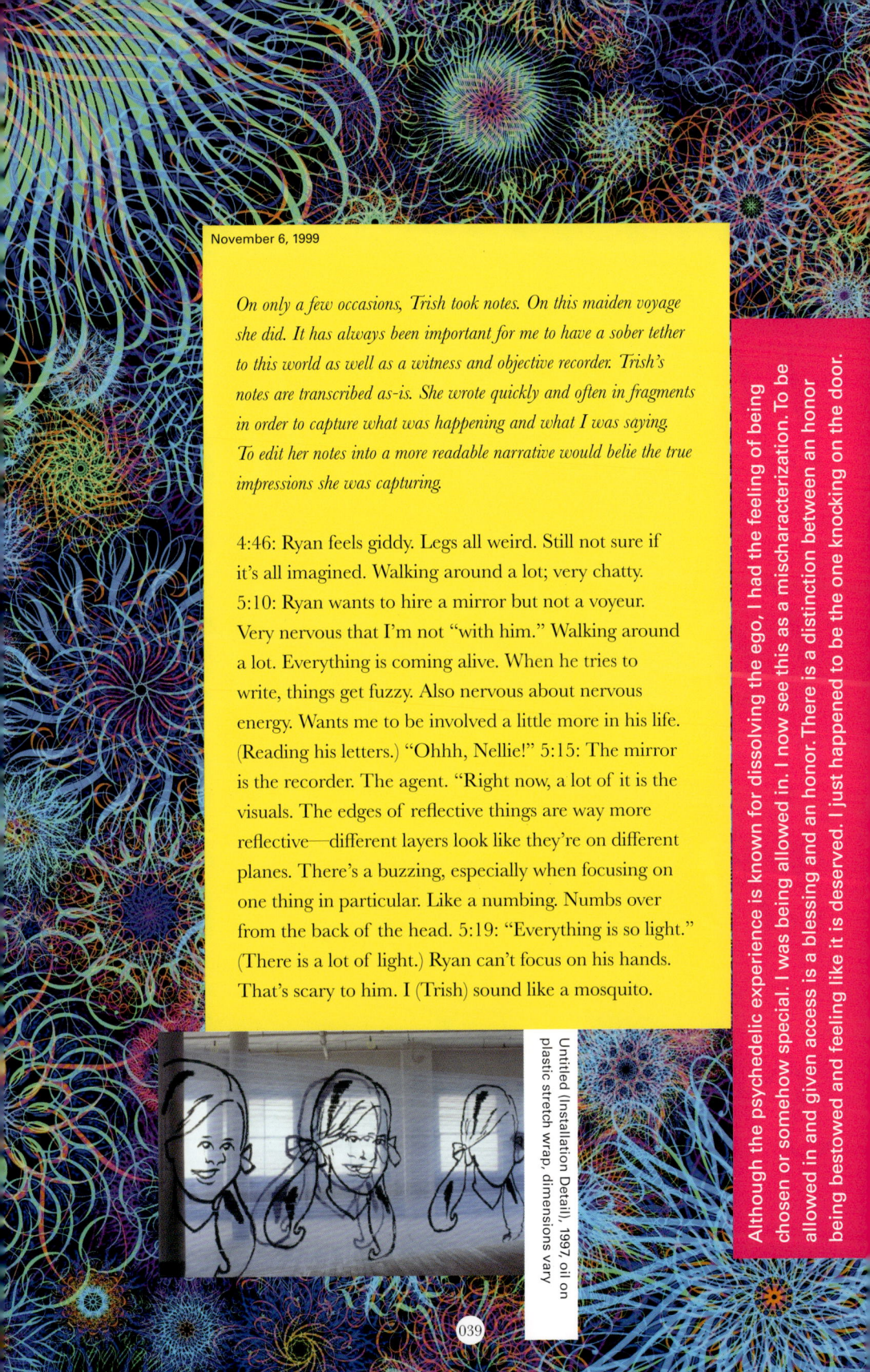

November 6, 1999

On only a few occasions, Trish took notes. On this maiden voyage she did. It has always been important for me to have a sober tether to this world as well as a witness and objective recorder. Trish's notes are transcribed as-is. She wrote quickly and often in fragments in order to capture what was happening and what I was saying. To edit her notes into a more readable narrative would belie the true impressions she was capturing.

4:46: Ryan feels giddy. Legs all weird. Still not sure if it's all imagined. Walking around a lot; very chatty. 5:10: Ryan wants to hire a mirror but not a voyeur. Very nervous that I'm not "with him." Walking around a lot. Everything is coming alive. When he tries to write, things get fuzzy. Also nervous about nervous energy. Wants me to be involved a little more in his life. (Reading his letters.) "Ohhh, Nellie!" 5:15: The mirror is the recorder. The agent. "Right now, a lot of it is the visuals. The edges of reflective things are way more reflective—different layers look like they're on different planes. There's a buzzing, especially when focusing on one thing in particular. Like a numbing. Numbs over from the back of the head. 5:19: "Everything is so light." (There is a lot of light.) Ryan can't focus on his hands. That's scary to him. I (Trish) sound like a mosquito.

Although the psychedelic experience is known for dissolving the ego, I had the feeling of being chosen or somehow special. I was being allowed in. I now see this as a mischaracterization. To be allowed in and given access is a blessing and an honor. There is a distinction between an honor being bestowed and feeling like it is deserved. I just happened to be the one knocking on the door.

Untitled (Installation Detail), 1997, oil on plastic stretch wrap, dimensions vary

I remember
that technol
(computers
in particula
somehow fa

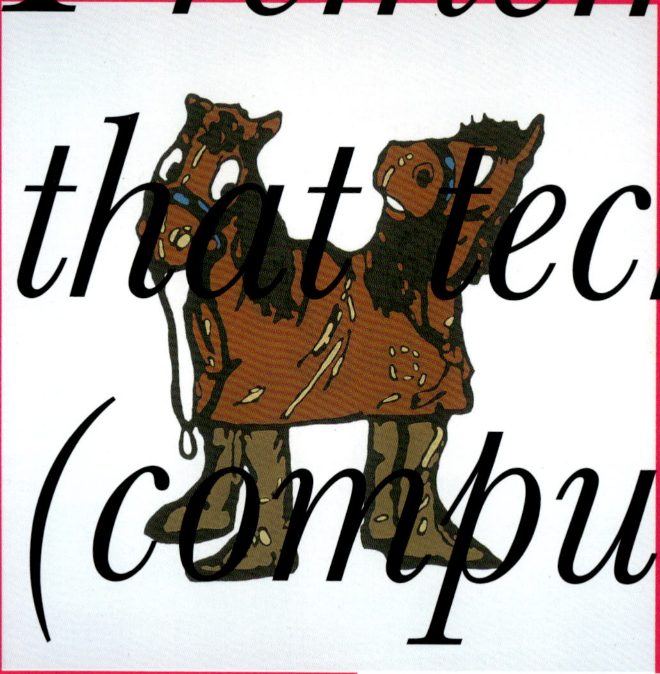

I'm Rubber You're Glue, 1999,
mixed pigments on canvas,
72 x 72 in. (182.9 x 182.9 cm

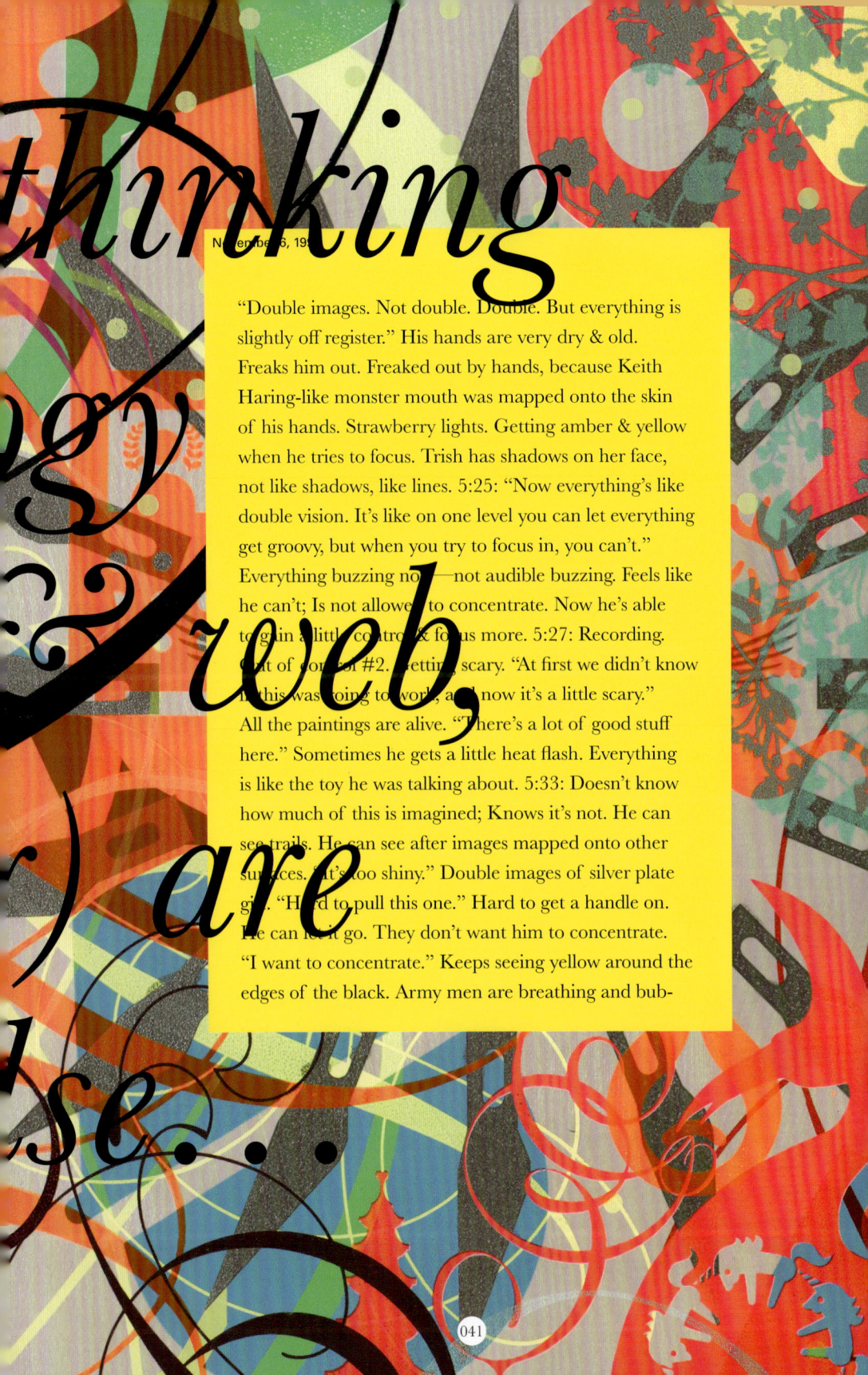

November 6, 199

"Double images. Not double. Double. But everything is slightly off register." His hands are very dry & old. Freaks him out. Freaked out by hands, because Keith Haring-like monster mouth was mapped onto the skin of his hands. Strawberry lights. Getting amber & yellow when he tries to focus. Trish has shadows on her face, not like shadows, like lines. 5:25: "Now everything's like double vision. It's like on one level you can let everything get groovy, but when you try to focus in, you can't." Everything buzzing no —not audible buzzing. Feels like he can't; Is not allowed to concentrate. Now he's able to gain a little control & focus more. 5:27: Recording. Out of control #2. Getting scary. "At first we didn't know if this was going to work, and now it's a little scary." All the paintings are alive. "There's a lot of good stuff here." Sometimes he gets a little heat flash. Everything is like the toy he was talking about. 5:33: Doesn't know how much of this is imagined; Knows it's not. He can see trails. He can see after images mapped onto other surfaces. It's too shiny." Double images of silver plate girl. "Hard to pull this one." Hard to get a handle on. He can let it go. They don't want him to concentrate. "I want to concentrate." Keeps seeing yellow around the edges of the black. Army men are breathing and bub-

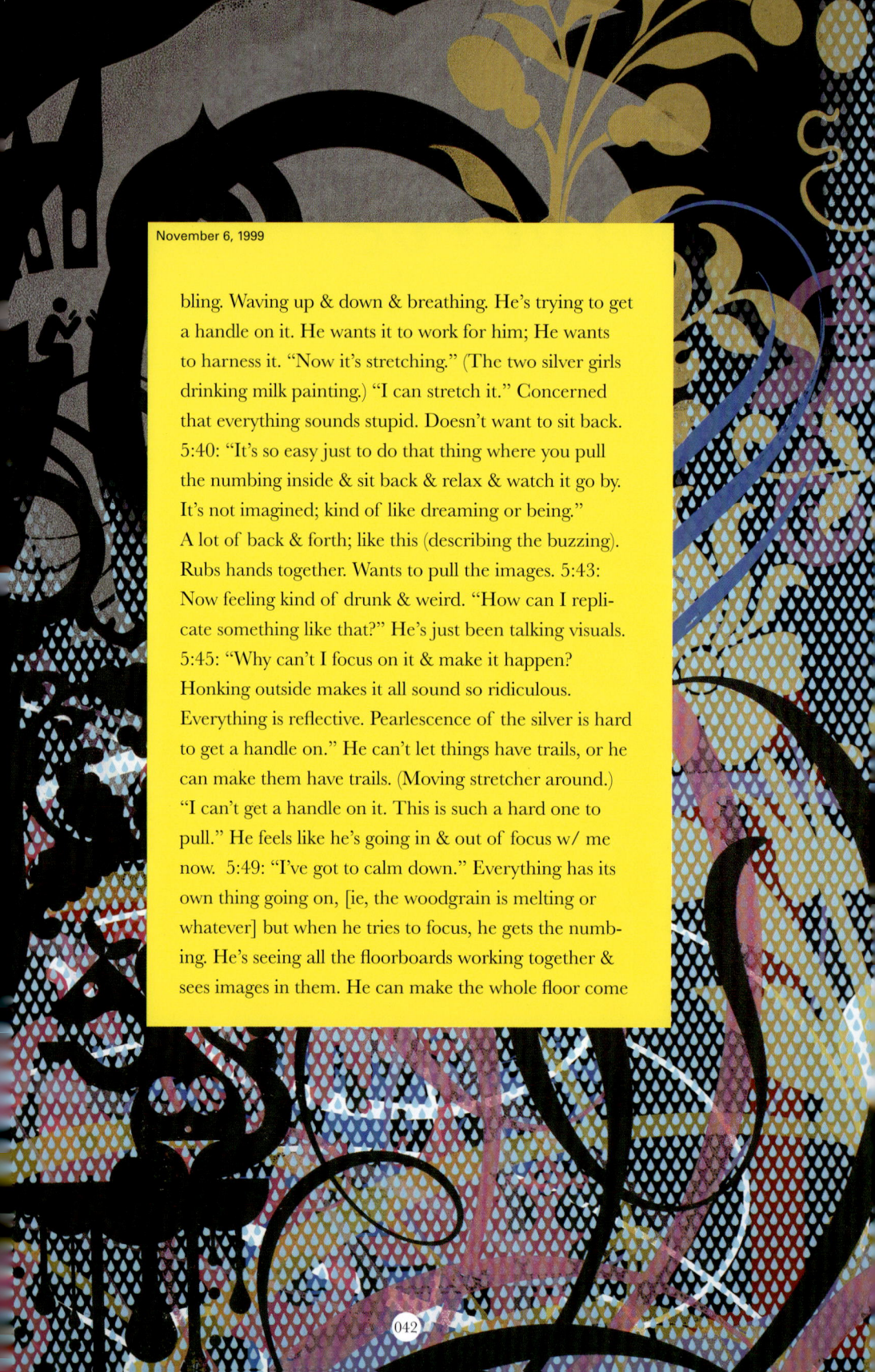

bling. Waving up & down & breathing. He's trying to get
a handle on it. He wants it to work for him; He wants
to harness it. "Now it's stretching." (The two silver girls
drinking milk painting.) "I can stretch it." Concerned
that everything sounds stupid. Doesn't want to sit back.
5:40: "It's so easy just to do that thing where you pull
the numbing inside & sit back & relax & watch it go by.
It's not imagined; kind of like dreaming or being."
A lot of back & forth; like this (describing the buzzing).
Rubs hands together. Wants to pull the images. 5:43:
Now feeling kind of drunk & weird. "How can I repli-
cate something like that?" He's just been talking visuals.
5:45: "Why can't I focus on it & make it happen?
Honking outside makes it all sound so ridiculous.
Everything is reflective. Pearlescence of the silver is hard
to get a handle on." He can't let things have trails, or he
can make them have trails. (Moving stretcher around.)
"I can't get a handle on it. This is such a hard one to
pull." He feels like he's going in & out of focus w/ me
now. 5:49: "I've got to calm down." Everything has its
own thing going on, [ie, the woodgrain is melting or
whatever] but when he tries to focus, he gets the numbing. He's seeing all the floorboards working together &
sees images in them. He can make the whole floor come

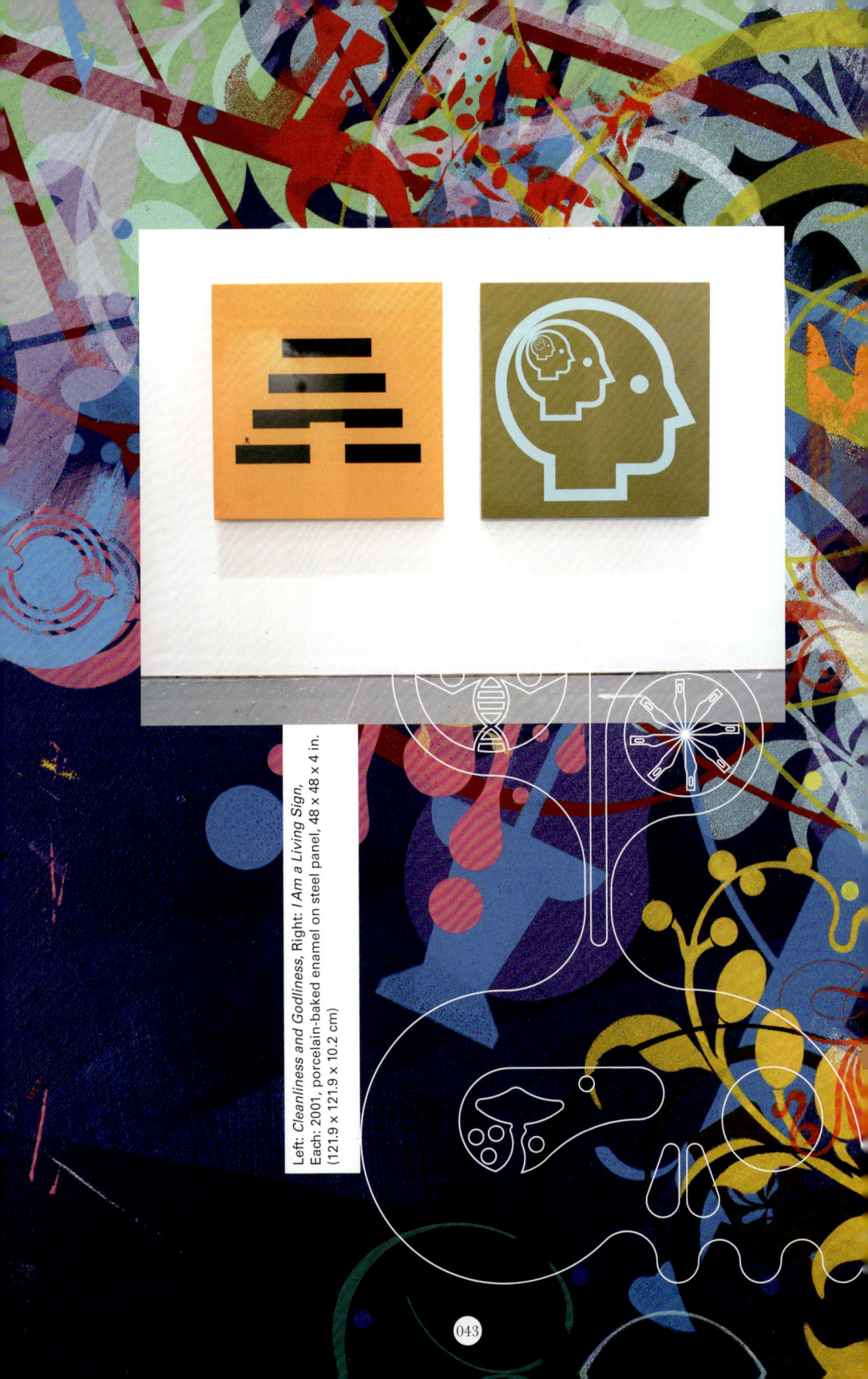

Left: *Cleanliness and Godliness*, Right: *I Am a Living Sign*,
Each: 2001, porcelain-baked enamel on steel panel, 48 x 48 x 4 in.
(121.9 x 121.9 x 10.2 cm)

alive, but he can't control it. Doesn't know on what level he's making it happen or letting it happen. 5:55: It's hard to describe. "The visual stuff is easy, but there's got to be more to it. Something's definitely happening." He's having a hard time snapping reality into it. Every time he thinks about reality or a portal, it's too hard; He lets it go. Very concerned about looking stupid & silly from the outside; That's the last thing he wants. "How can we figure this out?" When he thinks of me (portal to reality), it's hard to focus. Doesn't know what is preprogrammed & what's not. Asked for an assignment— something to focus on.

6:00: "Why can't I just let it go?" He can make time feel like any length. "I was in there for awhile." Now feels closer to where I am (reality). He can go back in. It's like a buzz. Trying to get a handle on how long he was in there. (Can't assign number.) Seems to be in & out of effects; sometimes very analytic, sometimes like, "I'm so stupid." 6:05: Rolling on floor, lying flat on back. "It was so easy to let it go. So easy. It's like when you come out of a dream & you want to go back in; but sometimes it invades." On one level, he can let it go. On another, he can't tell you how long it felt like. 6:08: He pulled him-

Nurse Alien, 1994, mixed pigments on wood, 31 x 22 in. (78.7 x 55.9 cm)

Not knowing what is historically real or not in this very first trip is interesting to read in hindsight. On heroic doses 20-some years later, I became afraid that psilocybin could be used as a weapon to change the course of history retroactively.

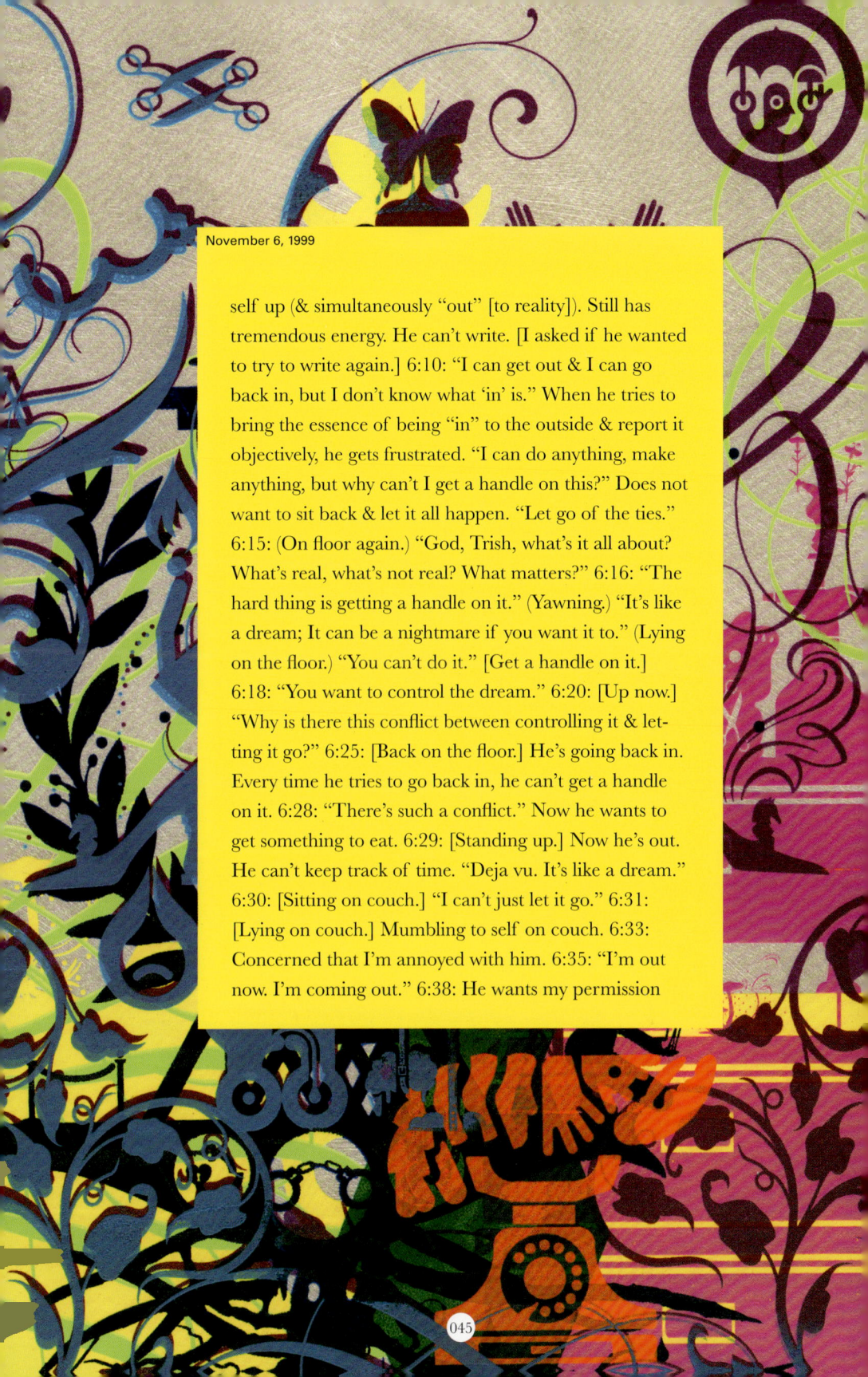

self up (& simultaneously "out" [to reality]). Still has tremendous energy. He can't write. [I asked if he wanted to try to write again.] 6:10: "I can get out & I can go back in, but I don't know what 'in' is." When he tries to bring the essence of being "in" to the outside & report it objectively, he gets frustrated. "I can do anything, make anything, but why can't I get a handle on this?" Does not want to sit back & let it all happen. "Let go of the ties." 6:15: (On floor again.) "God, Trish, what's it all about? What's real, what's not real? What matters?" 6:16: "The hard thing is getting a handle on it." (Yawning.) "It's like a dream; It can be a nightmare if you want it to." (Lying on the floor.) "You can't do it." [Get a handle on it.] 6:18: "You want to control the dream." 6:20: [Up now.] "Why is there this conflict between controlling it & letting it go?" 6:25: [Back on the floor.] He's going back in. Every time he tries to go back in, he can't get a handle on it. 6:28: "There's such a conflict." Now he wants to get something to eat. 6:29: [Standing up.] Now he's out. He can't keep track of time. "Deja vu. It's like a dream." 6:30: [Sitting on couch.] "I can't just let it go." 6:31: [Lying on couch.] Mumbling to self on couch. 6:33: Concerned that I'm annoyed with him. 6:35: "I'm out now. I'm coming out." 6:38: He wants my permission

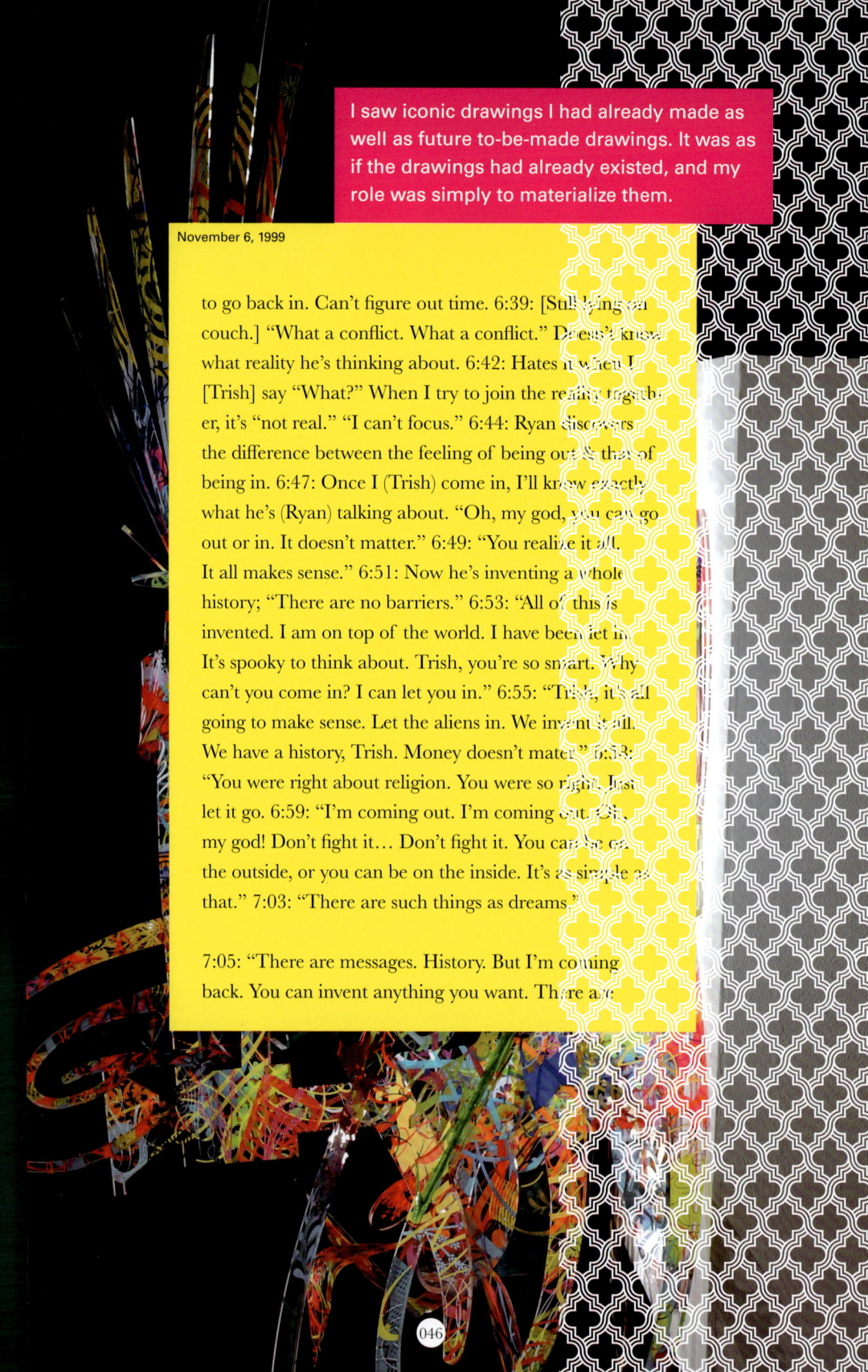

I saw iconic drawings I had already made as well as future to-be-made drawings. It was as if the drawings had already existed, and my role was simply to materialize them.

November 6, 1999

to go back in. Can't figure out time. 6:39: [Still lying on couch.] "What a conflict. What a conflict." Doesn't know what reality he's thinking about. 6:42: Hates it when I [Trish] say "What?" When I try to join the reality together, it's "not real." "I can't focus." 6:44: Ryan discovers the difference between the feeling of being out & that of being in. 6:47: Once I (Trish) come in, I'll know exactly what he's (Ryan) talking about. "Oh, my god, you can go out or in. It doesn't matter." 6:49: "You realize it all. It all makes sense." 6:51: Now he's inventing a whole history; "There are no barriers." 6:53: "All of this is invented. I am on top of the world. I have been let in. It's spooky to think about. Trish, you're so smart. Why can't you come in? I can let you in." 6:55: "Trish, it's all going to make sense. Let the aliens in. We invent it all. We have a history, Trish. Money doesn't matter." 6:58: "You were right about religion. You were so right. Just let it go. 6:59: "I'm coming out. I'm coming out. Oh, my god! Don't fight it… Don't fight it. You can be on the outside, or you can be on the inside. It's as simple as that." 7:03: "There are such things as dreams."

7:05: "There are messages. History. But I'm coming back. You can invent anything you want. There are

046

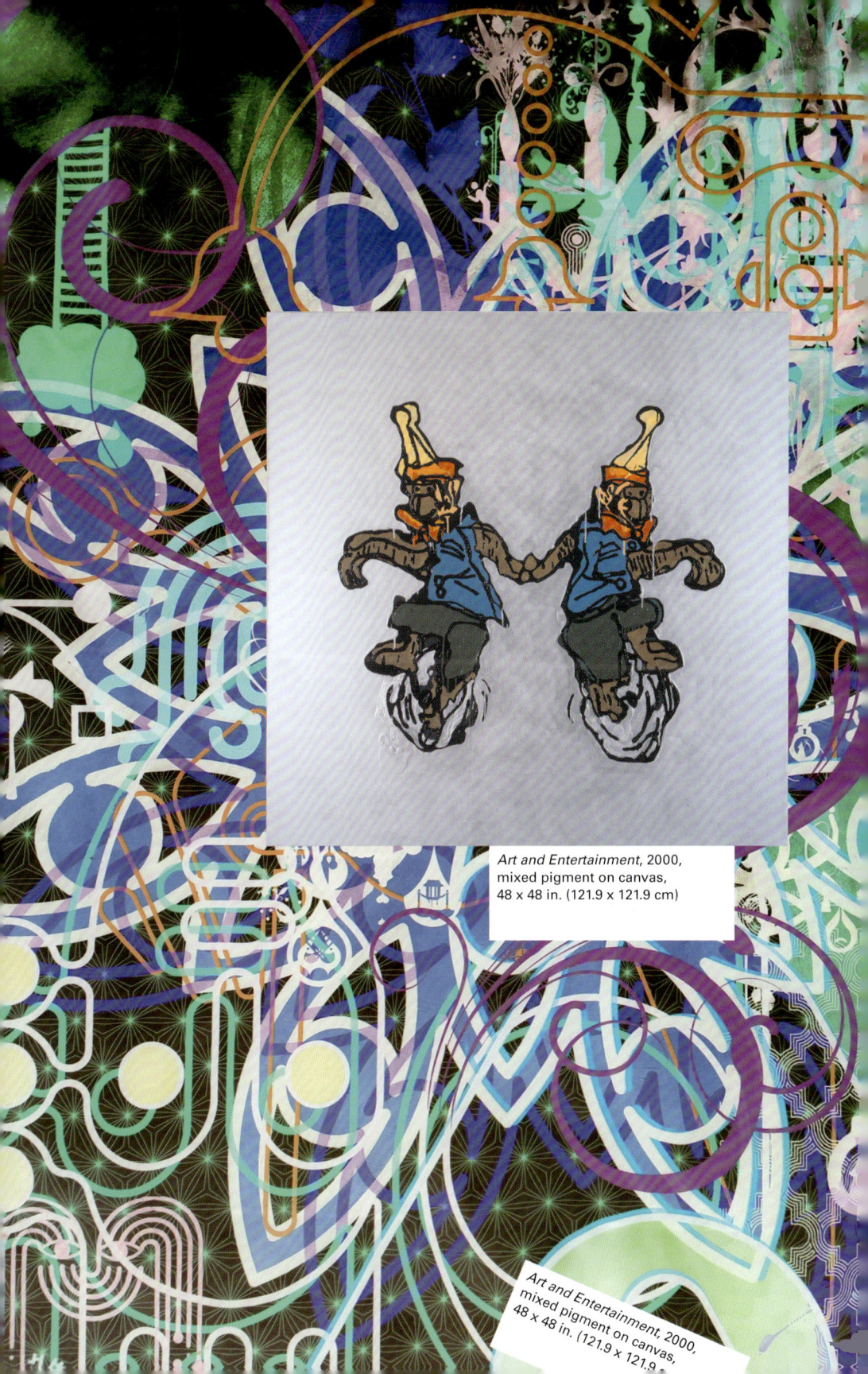

Art and Entertainment, 2000,
mixed pigment on canvas,
48 x 48 in. (121.9 x 121.9 cm)

Art and Entertainment, 2000,
mixed pigment on canvas,
48 x 48 in. (121.9 x 121.9

There is always a feeling of overwhelming insight, but without specific information. It is always as if to specify is to localize whatever it is into something too insignificant and meaningless. This leads to a feeling that nothing matters. Everything is pointless.

November 6, 1999

people I need to let in! It's not happening fast enough & we're both from VA Beach." 7:07: "Oh, god. I'm getting cold." [I bring him a blanket.] 7:09: "There really is a conflict! Just let it go." 7:10: "Every time I try to go back, there are things like… Manhattan. All things point to a sign. Diseases & everything. I finally get it. It's so fucking weird. What are dreams? Happiness! We invent happiness." 7:12: "I want you in." 7:13: [Getting really squirmy.] "I like mushrooms, and I'm allowed to. I have invented histories. It all comes back to nature." 7:15: "Just let it go. I'm on top of the world. Why is there all this conflict?" 7:16: "There is a thing called Bleecker St. & comedy makes sense." 7:18: "You're allowed to come in. You're allowed pleasure. Universal themes. That's why you have to support artists." 7:20: "You're allowed on the outside, or you can come in. Gambling & artists. They're games." 7:21: "It's all about history. Everything happens for a reason." 7:22: "Trish, I want you to come with me." 7:25: "It's all about love. You can go out or you can come…" 8-8:30: [Throws up at 8:15.] Says repeatedly, "We're in. Where do you want to be? Trish, I love you so much. That's why there's conflict." 8:30: "I'm in. I'm in. I'm in. I'm a carrier. Trish, you just have to believe me. Oh. This is why. This is why we invent

I didn't read Trish's notes on this first experience until several years later as I was collecting everything for this book. I don't think I really wanted to know just how crazy it may have looked from the outside, and after a while, I just forgot she had even taken notes. It is embarrassing to share my ramblings.

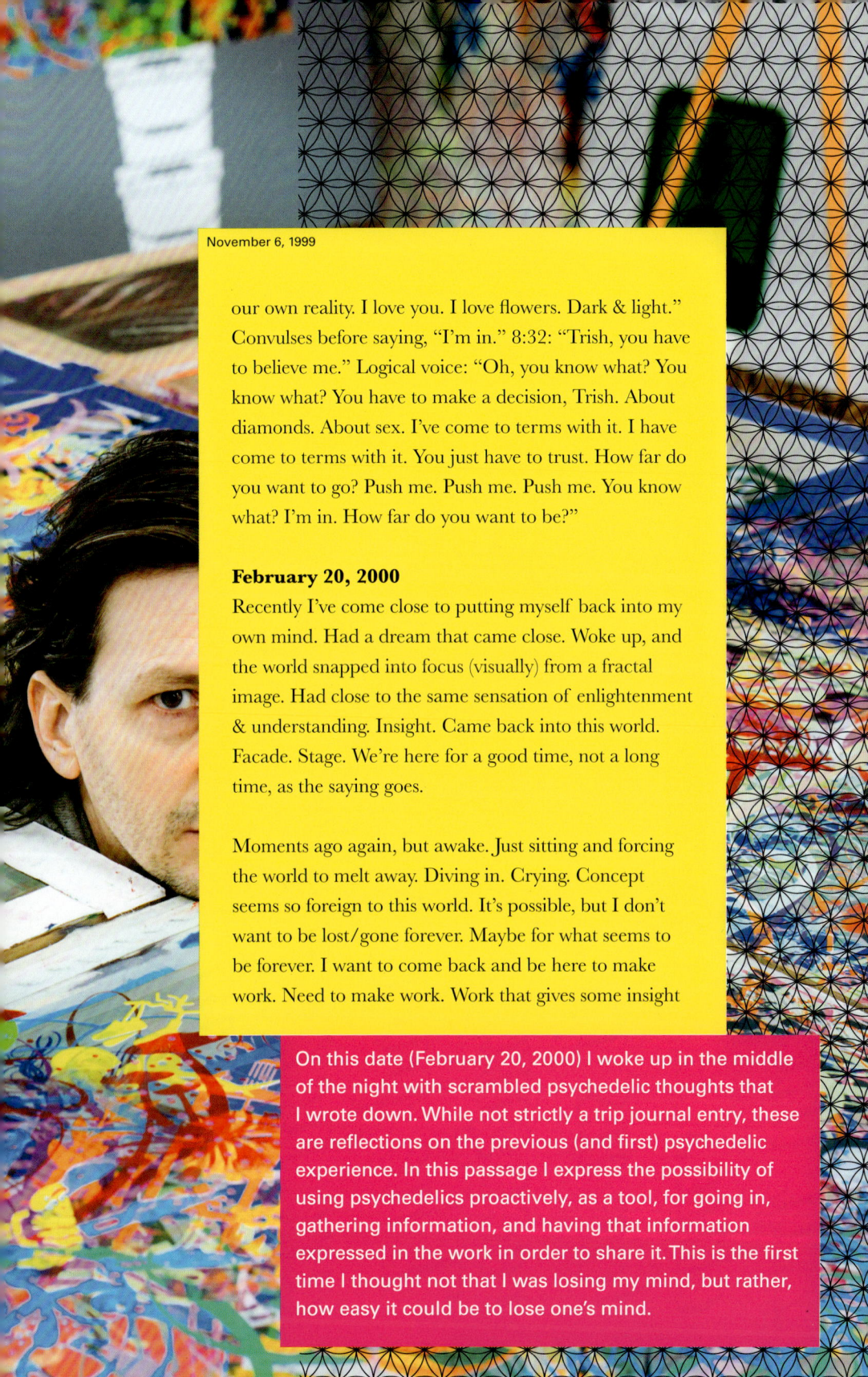

November 6, 1999

our own reality. I love you. I love flowers. Dark & light."
Convulses before saying, "I'm in." 8:32: "Trish, you have
to believe me." Logical voice: "Oh, you know what? You
know what? You have to make a decision, Trish. About
diamonds. About sex. I've come to terms with it. I have
come to terms with it. You just have to trust. How far do
you want to go? Push me. Push me. Push me. You know
what? I'm in. How far do you want to be?"

February 20, 2000
Recently I've come close to putting myself back into my
own mind. Had a dream that came close. Woke up, and
the world snapped into focus (visually) from a fractal
image. Had close to the same sensation of enlightenment
& understanding. Insight. Came back into this world.
Facade. Stage. We're here for a good time, not a long
time, as the saying goes.

Moments ago again, but awake. Just sitting and forcing
the world to melt away. Diving in. Crying. Concept
seems so foreign to this world. It's possible, but I don't
want to be lost/gone forever. Maybe for what seems to
be forever. I want to come back and be here to make
work. Need to make work. Work that gives some insight

On this date (February 20, 2000) I woke up in the middle
of the night with scrambled psychedelic thoughts that
I wrote down. While not strictly a trip journal entry, these
are reflections on the previous (and first) psychedelic
experience. In this passage I express the possibility of
using psychedelics proactively, as a tool, for going in,
gathering information, and having that information
expressed in the work in order to share it. This is the first
time I thought not that I was losing my mind, but rather,
how easy it could be to lose one's mind.

into how things really are. What does that mean anyway? Isn't this how things really are? I feel like it is so easy to slip forever into your own mind. Blip. Fractals. Infinity. It's scary that it's so close. So easy. So easy to die. It is so much harder to live out in this world. Why? For a good time? Preparation? Sharing? Conflict. Union. Halves. Parts to make the whole.

Each of us has their own world. An infinite number of worlds. Universes. Again. Fractals & patterns, in nature. Math yes, but calculations, no. Everything is here for me. Symbols. People. Tasks to recognize. Gut instinct. Intuition. But why all the static? Again, why the conflict? Why good & evil? Opposites. Opposites attract. There must be these opposites in the mind. Or is it just the vehicle? Tool. I think therefore I think I am. Keep folding in on itself. I think, therefore I think that I think I am. We are, but as individuals. Can/do we think that we think we are. Collective unconscious. Sharing. History. Feelings. We share feelings for each other. Mirrors. Mirror mirrors. It's "Mirror, Mirror, on the wall." Plural. Not "Mirror on the wall." All the clues exist for us to recognize. The pieces are here for us to put together. I have to be left alone.

All the clues exist for us to recognize. The pieces are here for us to put together.

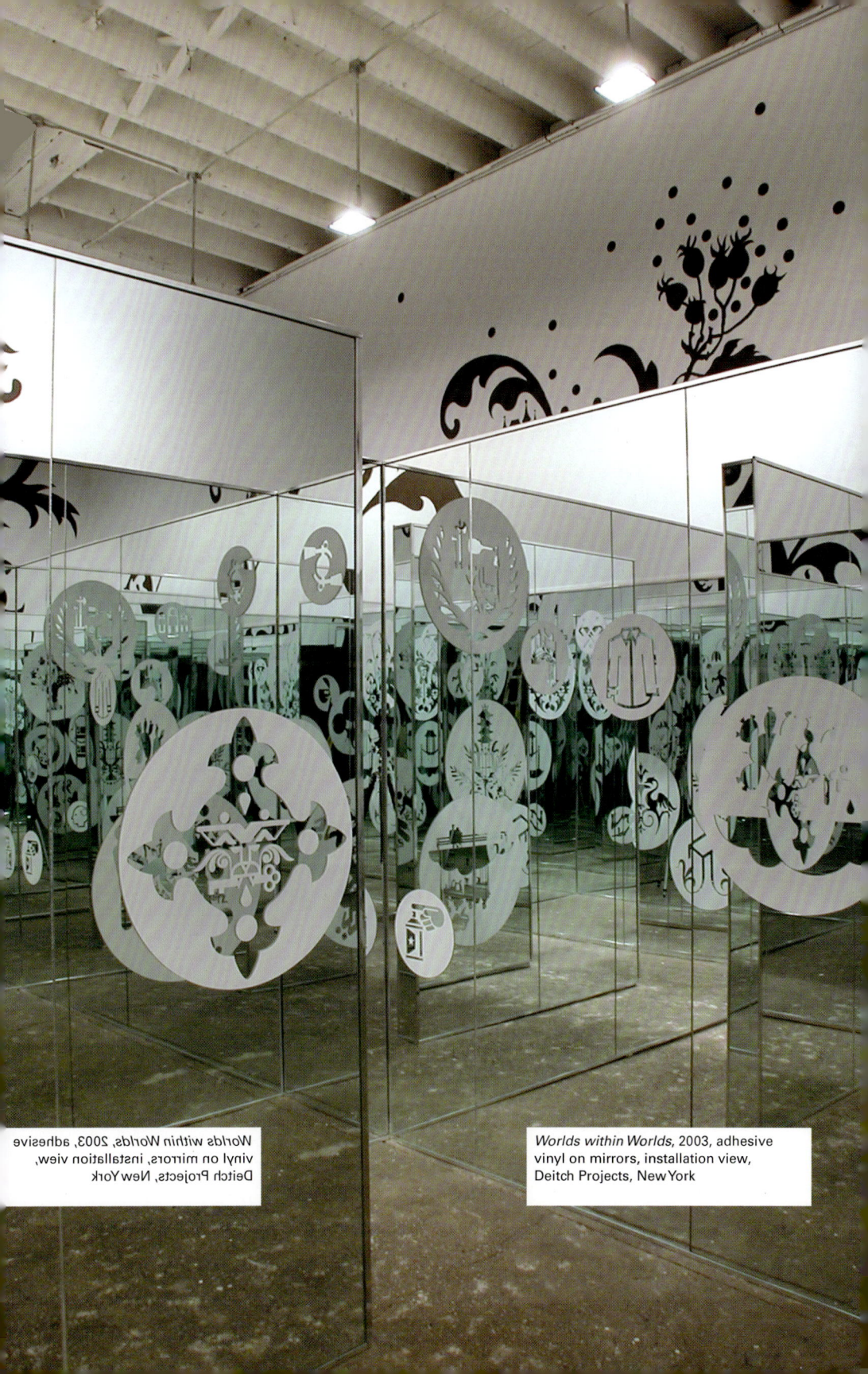

Worlds within Worlds, 2003, adhesive vinyl on mirrors, installation view, Deitch Projects, New York

Worlds within Worlds, 2003, adhesive vinyl on mirrors, installation view, Deitch Projects, New York

Conflict beginning between "zoning out" & concentrating. Need to concentrate to write. Will try to stick with it for as long as I can. 4:35 now. "Zoning out" can feel kinda like falling asleep. Palms a little sweaty. Feeling a little flush. Paper starting to yellow a bit.

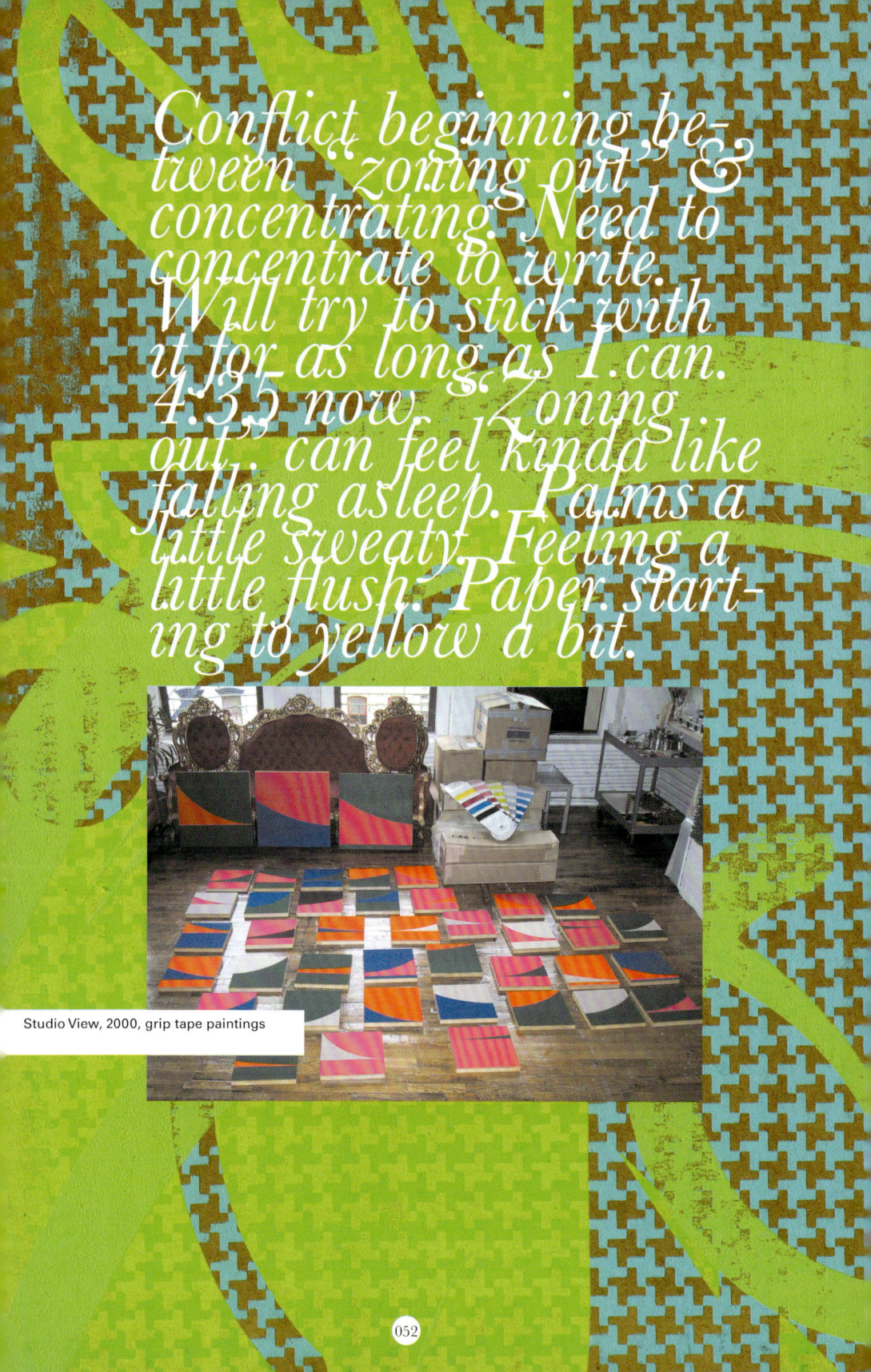

Studio View, 2000, grip tape paintings

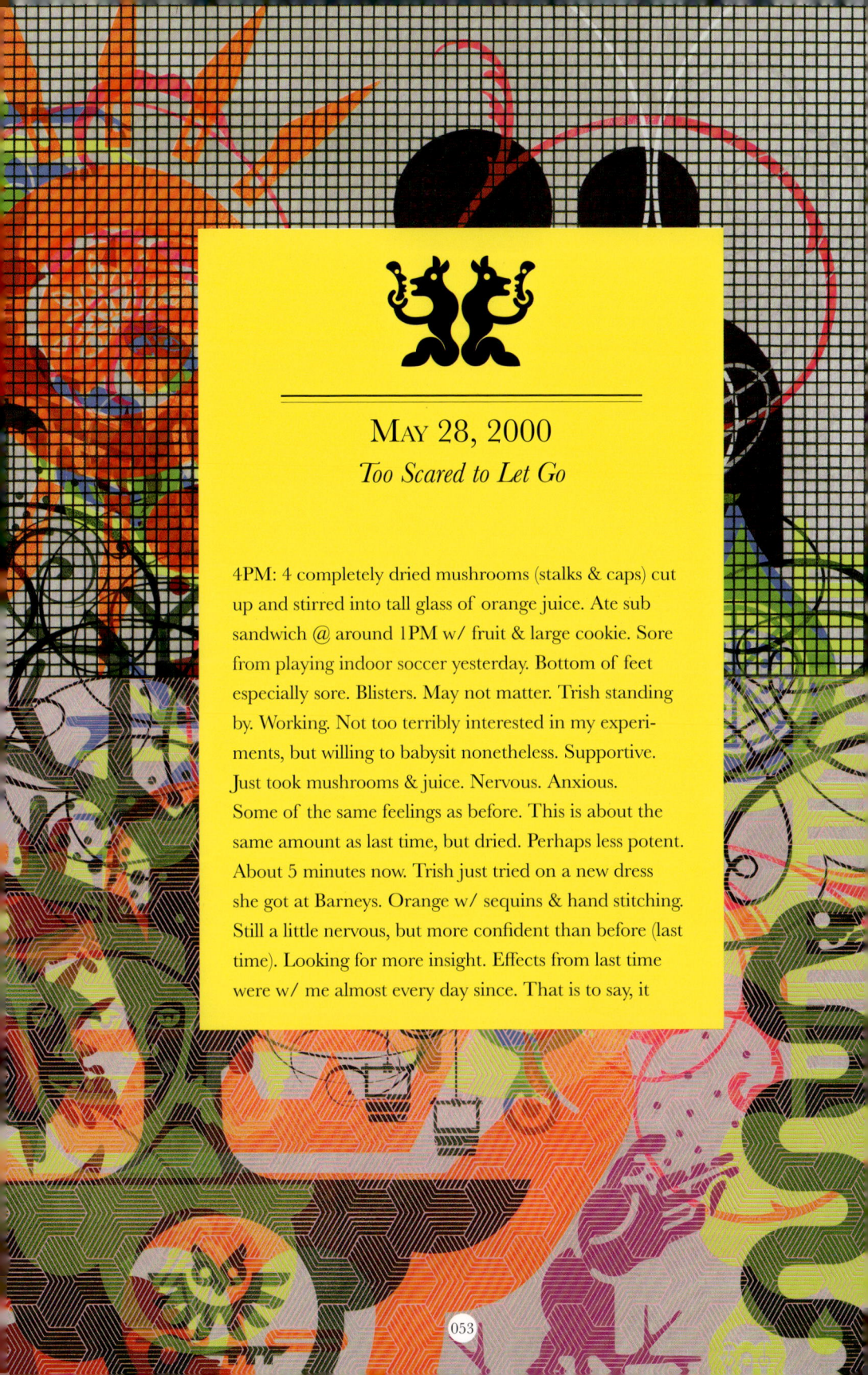

MAY 28, 2000
Too Scared to Let Go

4PM: 4 completely dried mushrooms (stalks & caps) cut up and stirred into tall glass of orange juice. Ate sub sandwich @ around 1PM w/ fruit & large cookie. Sore from playing indoor soccer yesterday. Bottom of feet especially sore. Blisters. May not matter. Trish standing by. Working. Not too terribly interested in my experiments, but willing to babysit nonetheless. Supportive. Just took mushrooms & juice. Nervous. Anxious. Some of the same feelings as before. This is about the same amount as last time, but dried. Perhaps less potent. About 5 minutes now. Trish just tried on a new dress she got at Barneys. Orange w/ sequins & hand stitching. Still a little nervous, but more confident than before (last time). Looking for more insight. Effects from last time were w/ me almost every day since. That is to say, it

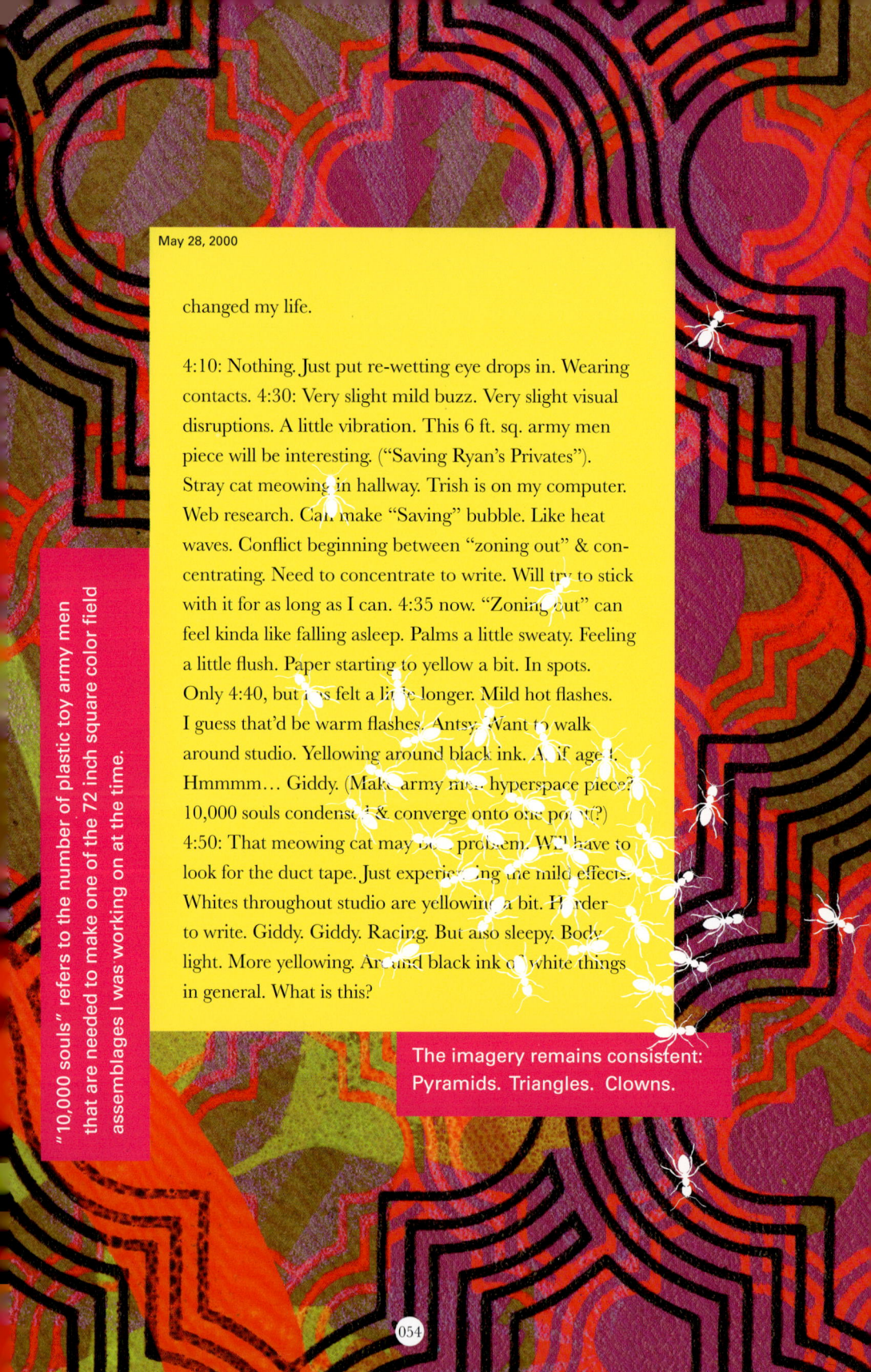

changed my life.

4:10: Nothing. Just put re-wetting eye drops in. Wearing contacts. 4:30: Very slight mild buzz. Very slight visual disruptions. A little vibration. This 6 ft. sq. army men piece will be interesting. ("Saving Ryan's Privates"). Stray cat meowing in hallway. Trish is on my computer. Web research. Can make "Saving" bubble. Like heat waves. Conflict beginning between "zoning out" & concentrating. Need to concentrate to write. Will try to stick with it for as long as I can. 4:35 now. "Zoning out" can feel kinda like falling asleep. Palms a little sweaty. Feeling a little flush. Paper starting to yellow a bit. In spots. Only 4:40, but it's felt a little longer. Mild hot flashes. I guess that'd be warm flashes. Antsy. Want to walk around studio. Yellowing around black ink. And if age? Hmmmm… Giddy. (Make army men hyperspace piece? 10,000 souls condensed & converge onto one point(?) 4:50: That meowing cat may be a problem. Will have to look for the duct tape. Just experiencing the mild effects. Whites throughout studio are yellowing a bit. Harder to write. Giddy. Giddy. Racing. But also sleepy. Body light. More yellowing. Around black ink of white things in general. What is this?

"10,000 souls" refers to the number of plastic toy army men that are needed to make one of the 72 inch square color field assemblages I was working on at the time.

The imagery remains consistent: Pyramids. Triangles. Clowns.

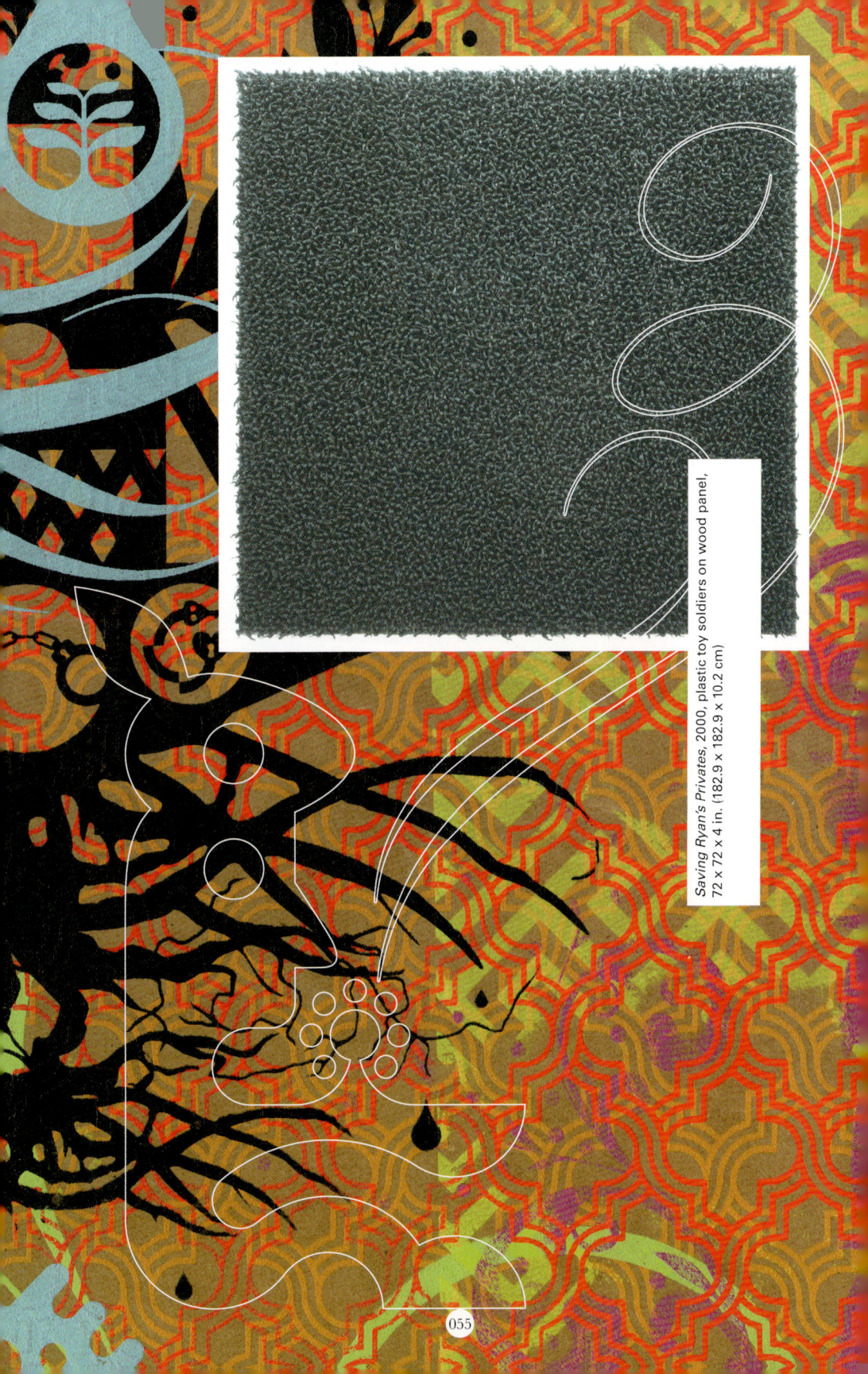

Saving Ryan's Privates, 2000, plastic toy soldiers on wood panel, 72 x 72 x 4 in. (182.9 x 182.9 x 10.2 cm)

Just letting the
army men bubble.
3-D off the wall.
The whole piece.
…individual men
swarming. Like
bees. Can't look
at piece as whole.
Just swarming.

5:08: Starting to come on stronger. 5:15: Maybe third time should be w/o the constraints of documentation. Time. What's happening? Reporting. Just letting the army men bubble. 3-D off the wall. The whole piece. All the individual men swarming. Like bees. Can't look at piece as whole. Just swarming. So much going on in there… Different patterns. Movement. Shapes. Palms really sweaty. Excited. 5:20 exactly. Looking away @ objects now. Can stretch & morph slightly. Snap in & out of some kind of zoning out dream-like state. Very much like in between sleep-awaking. Going to sleep. I keep yawning. In & out. Shifting in & out. On & off. In the in-between. The grey area. Shaking. In & out. In & out. Can make shapes out of army men freely. So much activity building up in my body. So much going on in there. I can go in or out. In or out. If you just let yourself go… 5:40: Urinated for 2nd time since 4PM. Sat with head down. Clown face fractals. Could jump into quickly. Trish talking on phone. Keeping me here. I'm searching for something to take back. Enjoy life. It doesn't matter. So insignificant. 5:50: I have to stop writing. 5:55: Just threw up. Guided by or dictated by. Overwhelming sense of otherness. None of this matters. Pyramids. Triangles. Tiles. Merging together to…

Some-
times
meaning
in
my work
was
resolved
retroac-
tively
as a result
of
contem-
plating
the work
on
psilocy-
bin.
*The army
men.
Dandruff.
Pyramids.
Triangles.
Targets.
Hyper-
space.
Duality.
Again,
opposites.
Conflict.*
These are
direct
references
to works
I was
making at
the time.

1:05PM Monday, May 29th, 2000, Memorial day.
As noted, vomited a good deal of the initial dose.
Trish pointed out that it was probably because of the
orange juice. Acidic. (Same reason for vomiting last
time?) Was never completely gone. Held on to this world.
Was always aware of the time. Was over completely by
about 7:30PM. Never allowed myself to "go in." Was
strangely afraid. Not afraid of going in, but of realizing,
as I did the 1st time, that this world/reality/dimension is
so terribly insignificant. None of this matters, so the only
thing to do that makes sense is to enjoy it to its fullest.

The vomiting felt guided. Always safe. Not violent or
frightful. Perhaps I was telling myself that I wasn't ready.
Didn't feel comfortable. Was scared—because before
getting rid of the mushrooms—getting them out of me,
I did have glimpses into the realizations. Maybe these
glimpses triggered memories of just how mind-blowing the first time was. That's really the best word.
Mind-blowing.

I had the ability to go in any time, but I chose to stay on
the perimeter. On the outside edge. I could put my head
down & start to go in, or I could start to recognize the

Supreme Color Formula Guide, 2000, five skateboards bolted together Each: oil on wood panel, 32 x 8 in. (81.3 x 20.3 cm), published by Supreme in an edition of 500 each

Supreme Color Formula Guide, together Each: oil on wood pa... published by Supreme in an edit...

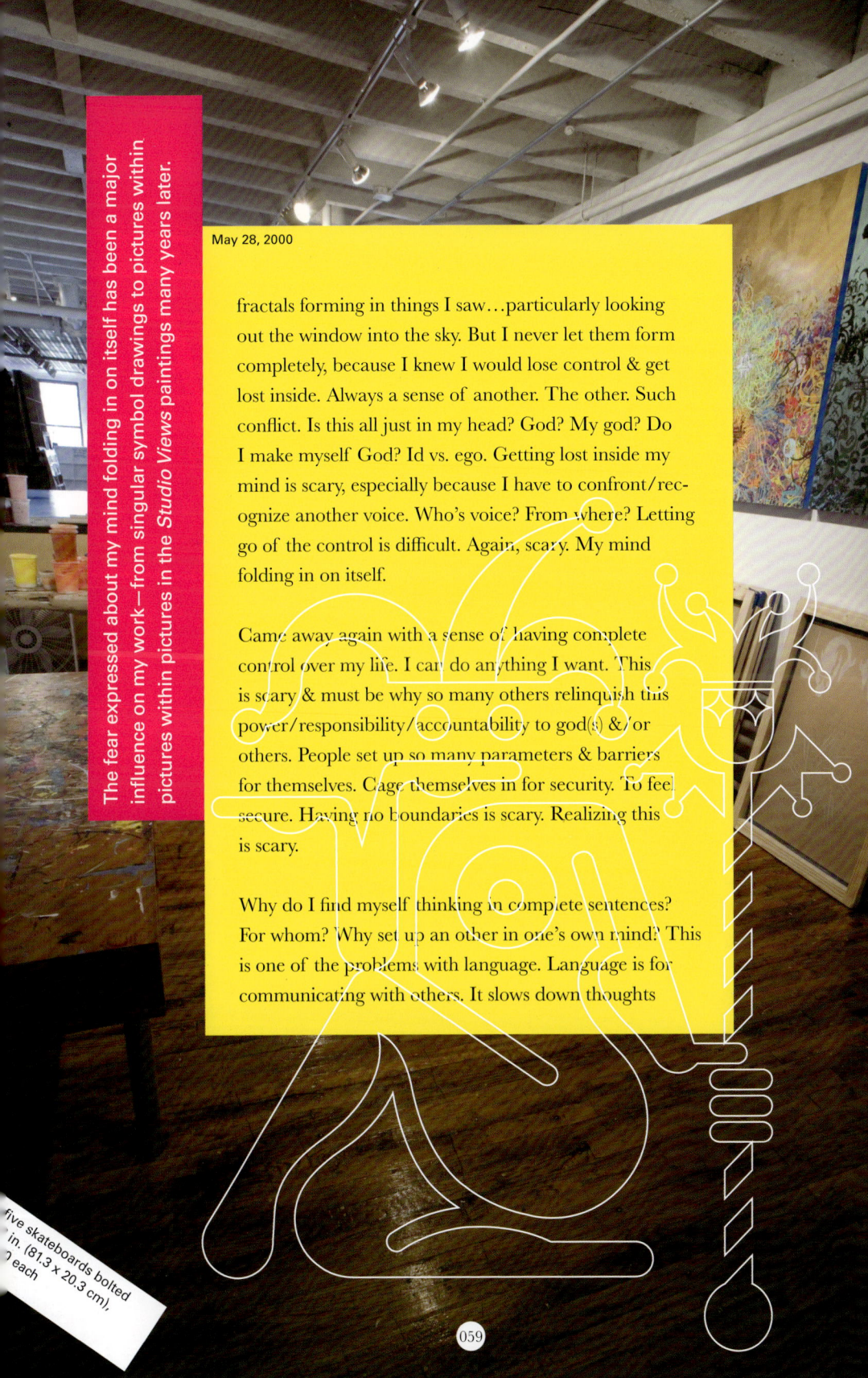

The fear expressed about my mind folding in on itself has been a major influence on my work—from singular symbol drawings to pictures within pictures within pictures in the *Studio Views* paintings many years later.

May 28, 2000

fractals forming in things I saw…particularly looking out the window into the sky. But I never let them form completely, because I knew I would lose control & get lost inside. Always a sense of another. The other. Such conflict. Is this all just in my head? God? My god? Do I make myself God? Id vs. ego. Getting lost inside my mind is scary, especially because I have to confront/recognize another voice. Who's voice? From where? Letting go of the control is difficult. Again, scary. My mind folding in on itself.

Came away again with a sense of having complete control over my life. I can do anything I want. This is scary & must be why so many others relinquish this power/responsibility/accountability to god(s) &/or others. People set up so many parameters & barriers for themselves. Cage themselves in for security. To feel secure. Having no boundaries is scary. Realizing this is scary.

Why do I find myself thinking in complete sentences? For whom? Why set up an other in one's own mind? This is one of the problems with language. Language is for communicating with others. It slows down thoughts

five skateboards bolted
in. (81.3 x 20.3 cm),
n each

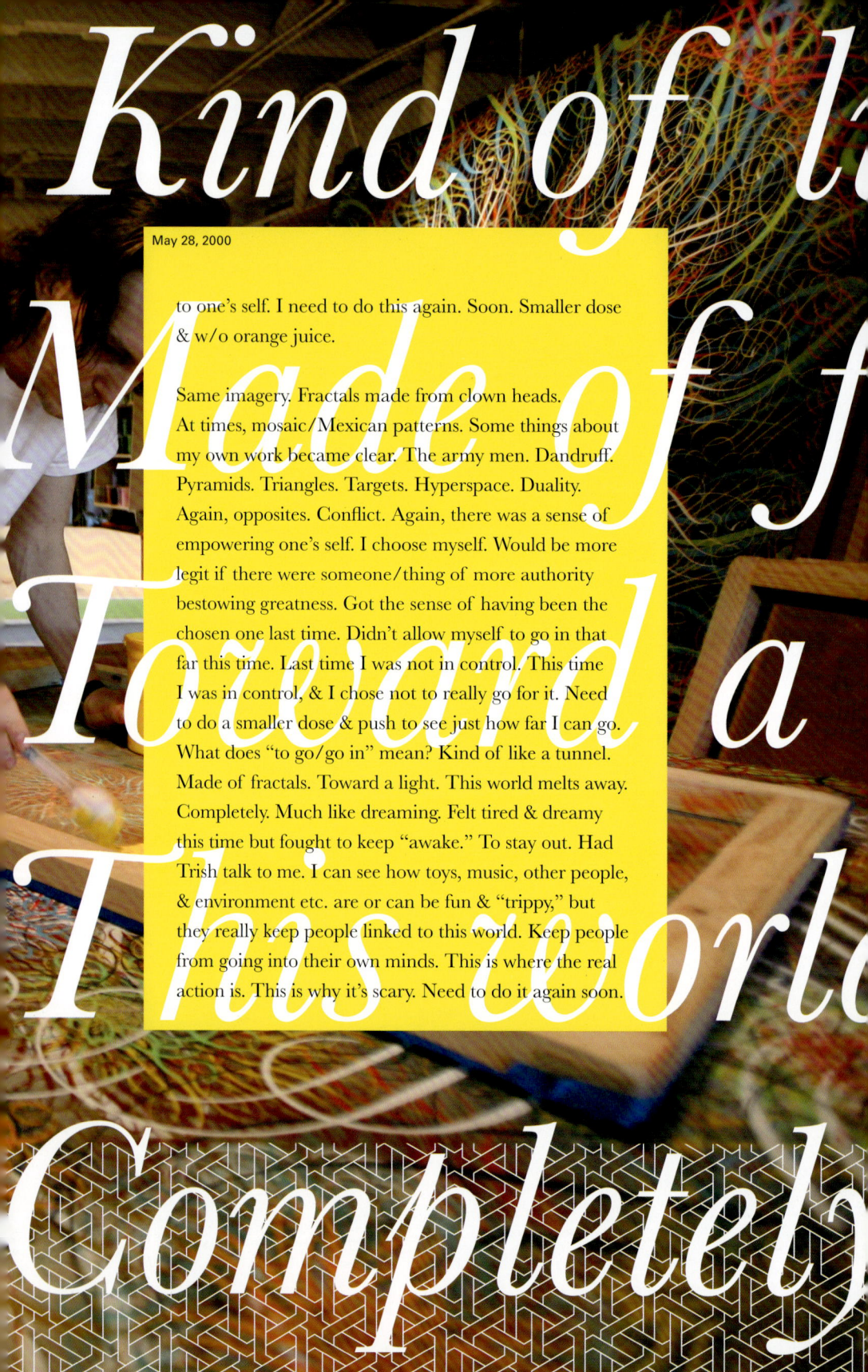

Kind of l[...]

Made of f[...]

Toward a

This world

Completely

May 28, 2000

to one's self. I need to do this again. Soon. Smaller dose & w/o orange juice.

Same imagery. Fractals made from clown heads. At times, mosaic/Mexican patterns. Some things about my own work became clear. The army men. Dandruff. Pyramids. Triangles. Targets. Hyperspace. Duality. Again, opposites. Conflict. Again, there was a sense of empowering one's self. I choose myself. Would be more legit if there were someone/thing of more authority bestowing greatness. Got the sense of having been the chosen one last time. Didn't allow myself to go in that far this time. Last time I was not in control. This time I was in control, & I chose not to really go for it. Need to do a smaller dose & push to see just how far I can go. What does "to go/go in" mean? Kind of like a tunnel. Made of fractals. Toward a light. This world melts away. Completely. Much like dreaming. Felt tired & dreamy this time but fought to keep "awake." To stay out. Had Trish talk to me. I can see how toys, music, other people, & environment etc. are or can be fun & "trippy," but they really keep people linked to this world. Keep people from going into their own minds. This is where the real action is. This is why it's scary. Need to do it again soon.

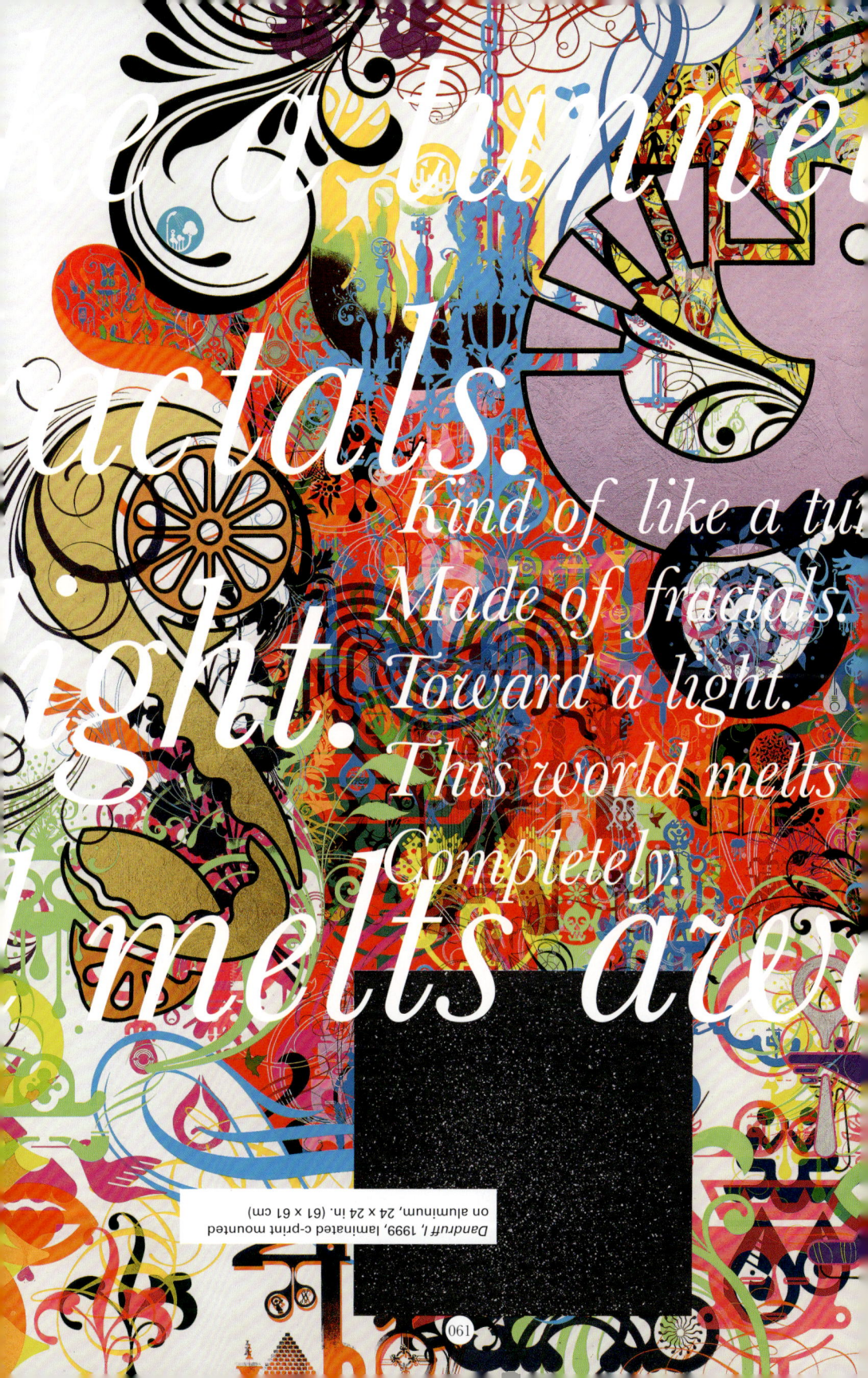

Kind of like a tunnel.
Made of fractals.
Toward a light.
This world melts
Completely.

Dandruff 1, 1999, laminated c-print mounted on aluminum, 24 x 24 in. (61 x 61 cm)

I want to really go for it next time, both with the security of knowing that Trish can/will "wake me up" or bring me back to life if I need. I really feel like I could get lost forever in the bliss of my own mind… or wherever it is that I have the choice of going. In. I really feel that this is what it's like to die. Leaving the body. This world/reality is so foreign & unlike what it's like to go in. Is this like near-death experiences where people feel like they've seen the light & are "awakened" & decide to be good people, because they understand that that's all that really matters? I think so.

All of this doesn't matter, so stop worrying about it. Just, for me, concentrate on making the work & sharing it. Again, a messenger, a carrier. Unfortunately, I don't completely understand the messages.
But I have to believe.

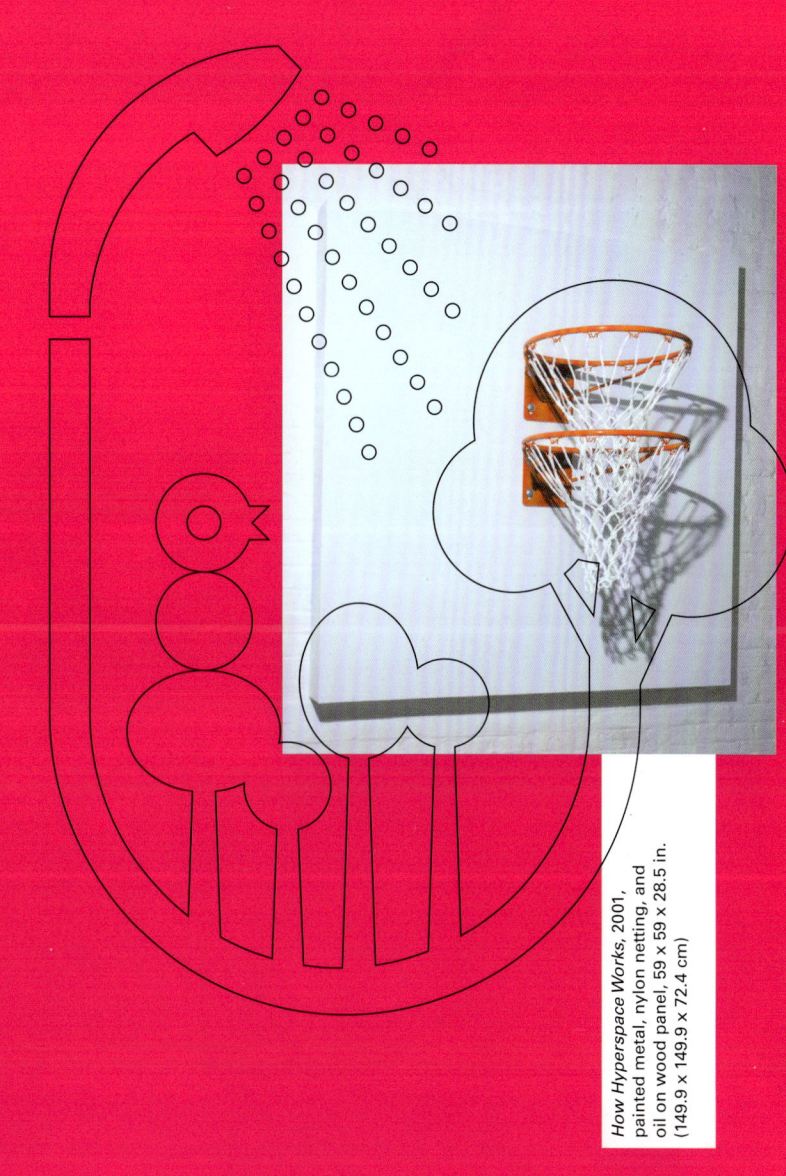

How Hyperspace Works, 2001, painted metal, nylon netting, and oil on wood panel, 59 x 59 x 28.5 in. (149.9 x 149.9 x 72.4 cm)

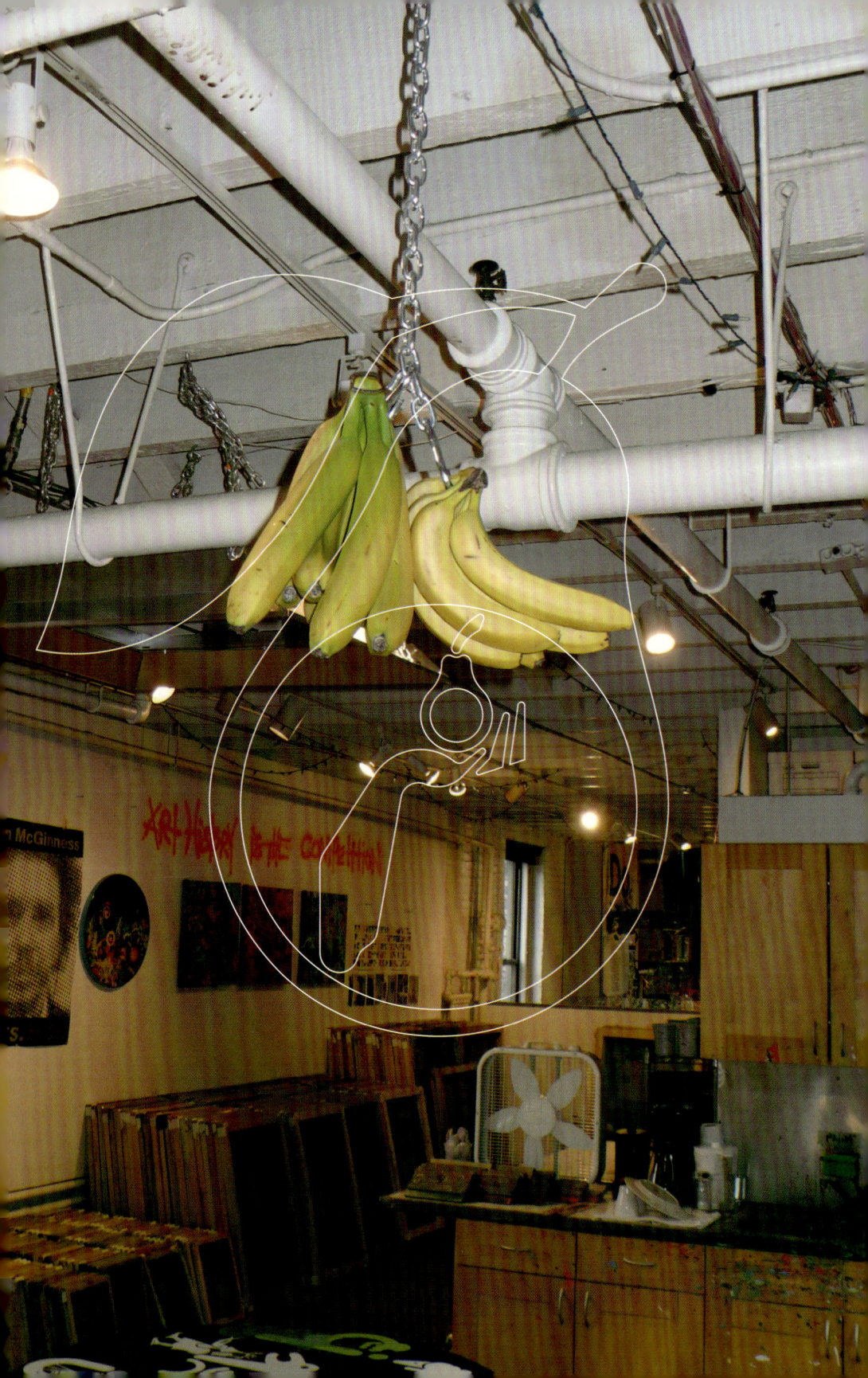

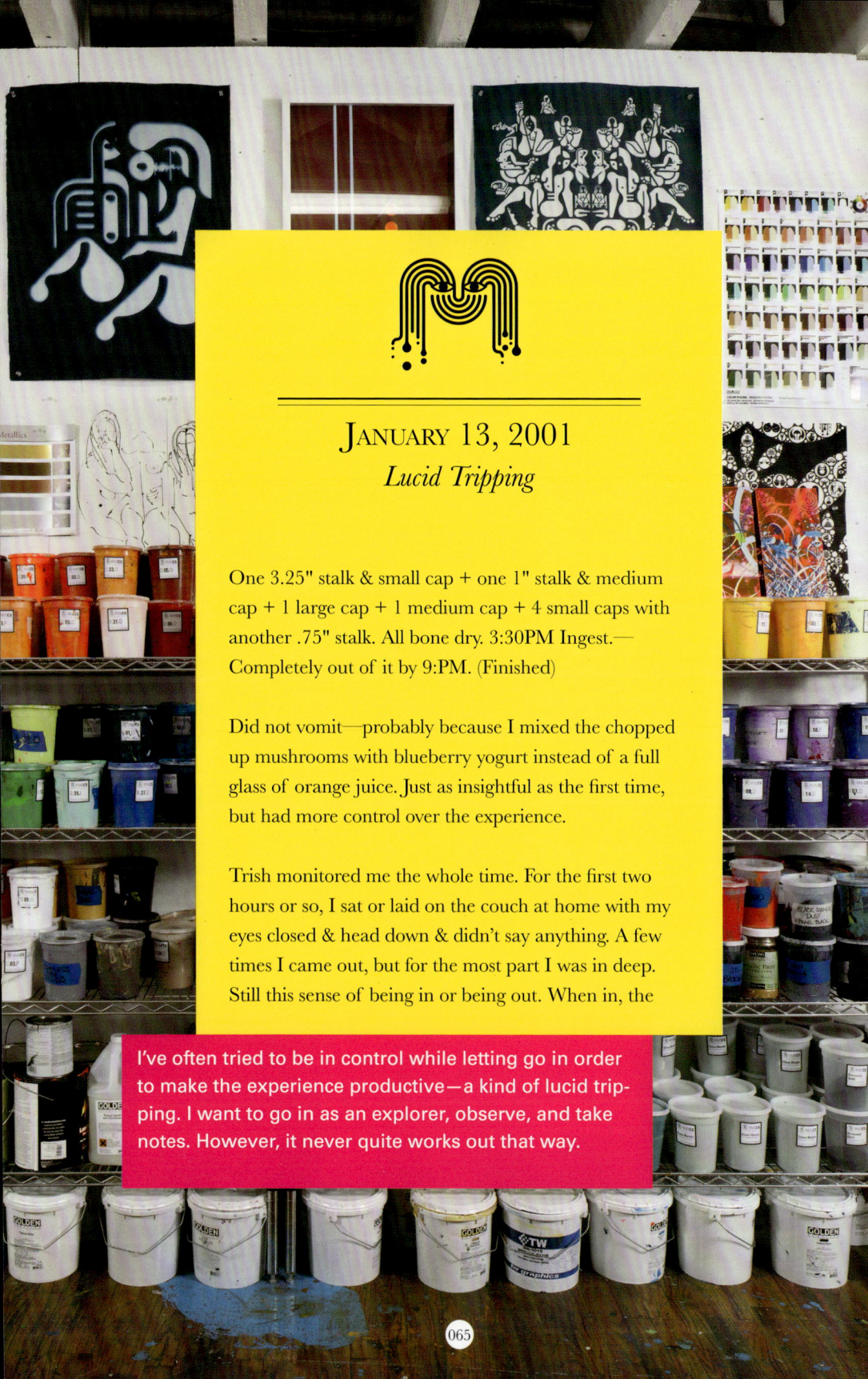

January 13, 2001
Lucid Tripping

One 3.25" stalk & small cap + one 1" stalk & medium cap + 1 large cap + 1 medium cap + 4 small caps with another .75" stalk. All bone dry. 3:30PM Ingest.— Completely out of it by 9:PM. (Finished)

Did not vomit—probably because I mixed the chopped up mushrooms with blueberry yogurt instead of a full glass of orange juice. Just as insightful as the first time, but had more control over the experience.

Trish monitored me the whole time. For the first two hours or so, I sat or laid on the couch at home with my eyes closed & head down & didn't say anything. A few times I came out, but for the most part I was in deep. Still this sense of being in or being out. When in, the

I've often tried to be in control while letting go in order to make the experience productive—a kind of lucid tripping. I want to go in as an explorer, observe, and take notes. However, it never quite works out that way.

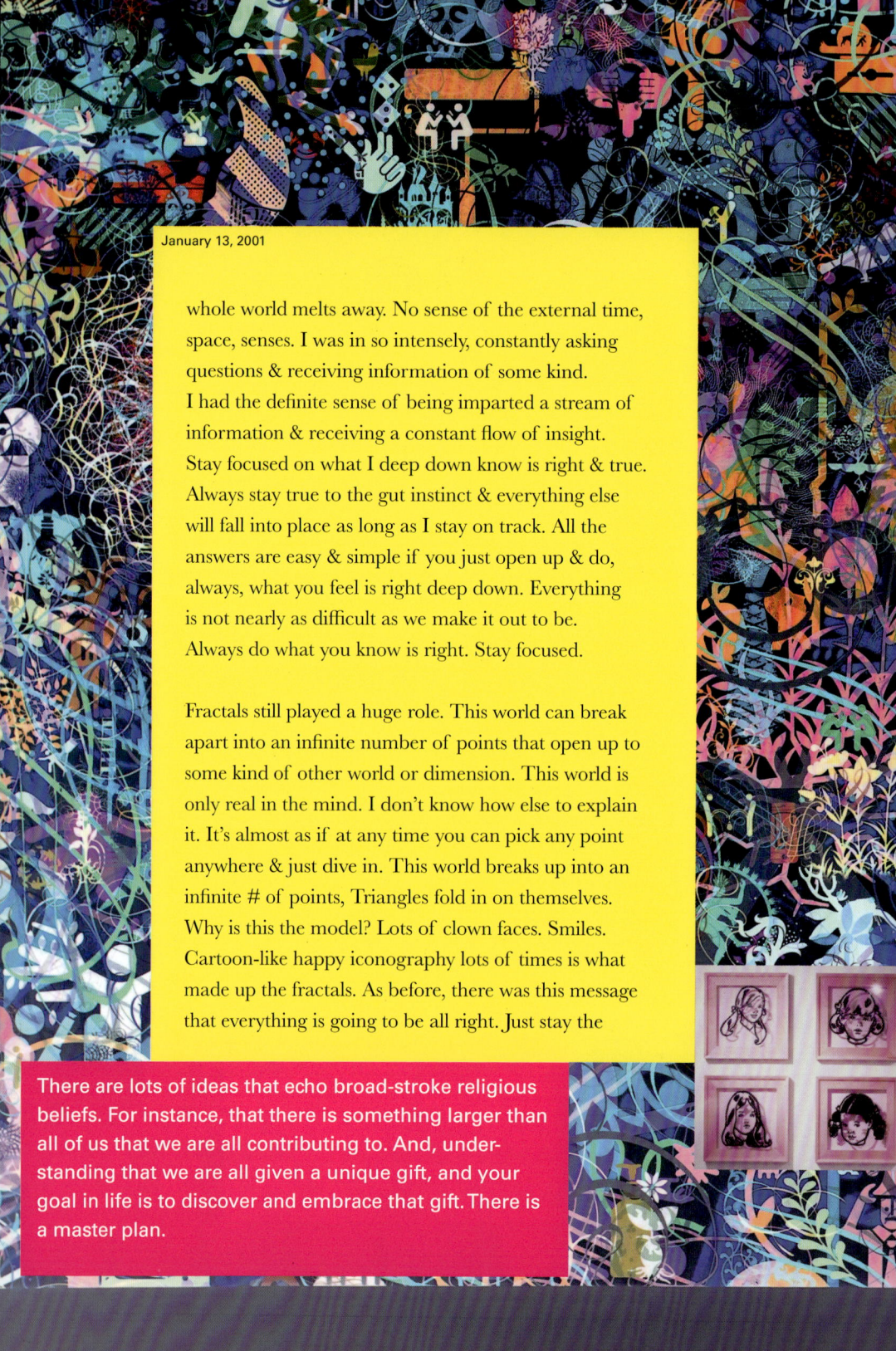

January 13, 2001

whole world melts away. No sense of the external time, space, senses. I was in so intensely, constantly asking questions & receiving information of some kind.
I had the definite sense of being imparted a stream of information & receiving a constant flow of insight.
Stay focused on what I deep down know is right & true.
Always stay true to the gut instinct & everything else will fall into place as long as I stay on track. All the answers are easy & simple if you just open up & do, always, what you feel is right deep down. Everything is not nearly as difficult as we make it out to be.
Always do what you know is right. Stay focused.

Fractals still played a huge role. This world can break apart into an infinite number of points that open up to some kind of other world or dimension. This world is only real in the mind. I don't know how else to explain it. It's almost as if at any time you can pick any point anywhere & just dive in. This world breaks up into an infinite # of points, Triangles fold in on themselves. Why is this the model? Lots of clown faces. Smiles. Cartoon-like happy iconography lots of times is what made up the fractals. As before, there was this message that everything is going to be all right. Just stay the

There are lots of ideas that echo broad-stroke religious beliefs. For instance, that there is something larger than all of us that we are all contributing to. And, understanding that we are all given a unique gift, and your goal in life is to discover and embrace that gift. There is a master plan.

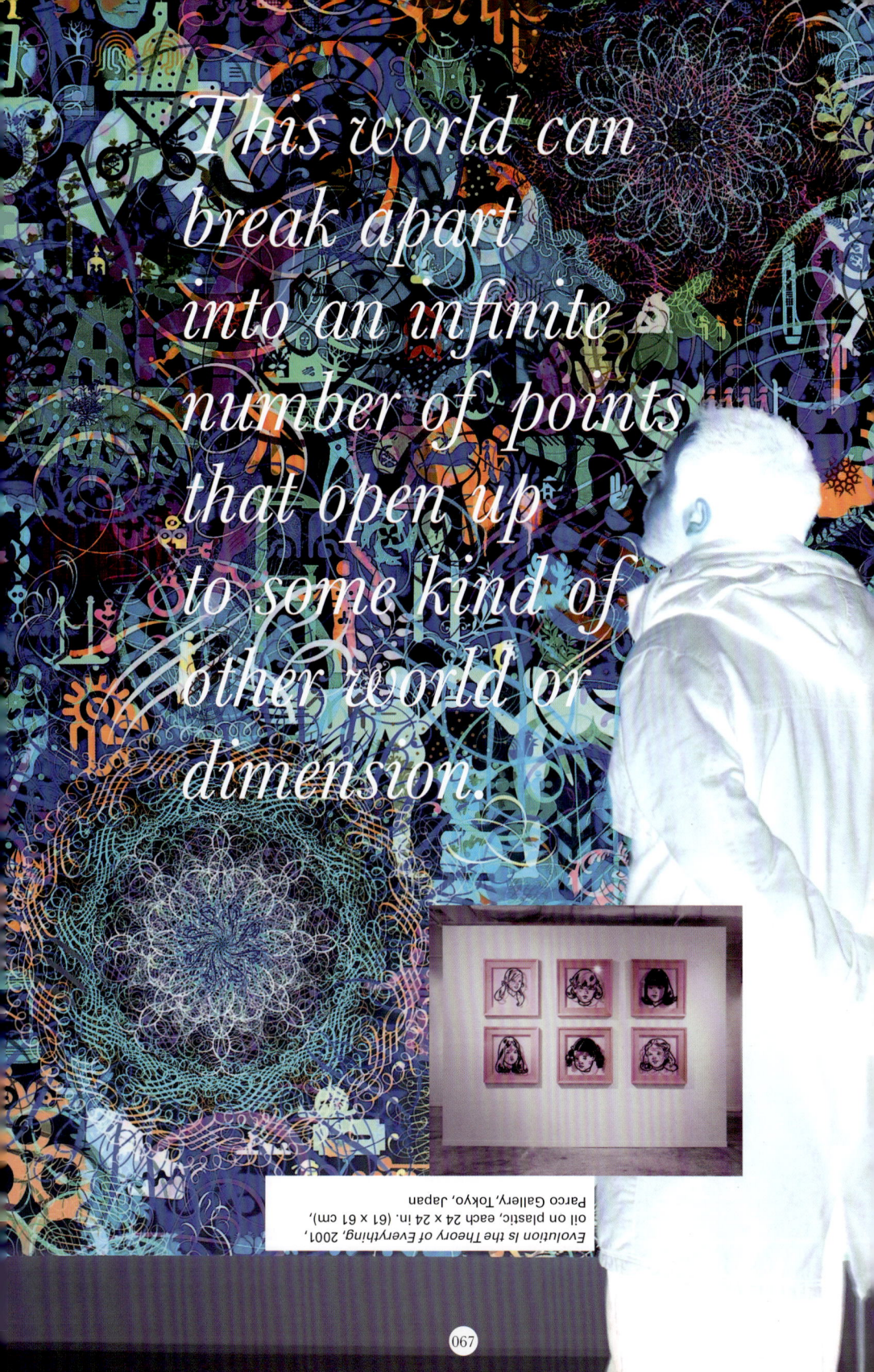

This world can break apart into an infinite number of points that open up to some kind of other world or dimension.

Evolution is the Theory of Everything, 2001,
oil on plastic, each 24 x 24 in. (61 x 61 cm),
Parco Gallery, Tokyo, Japan

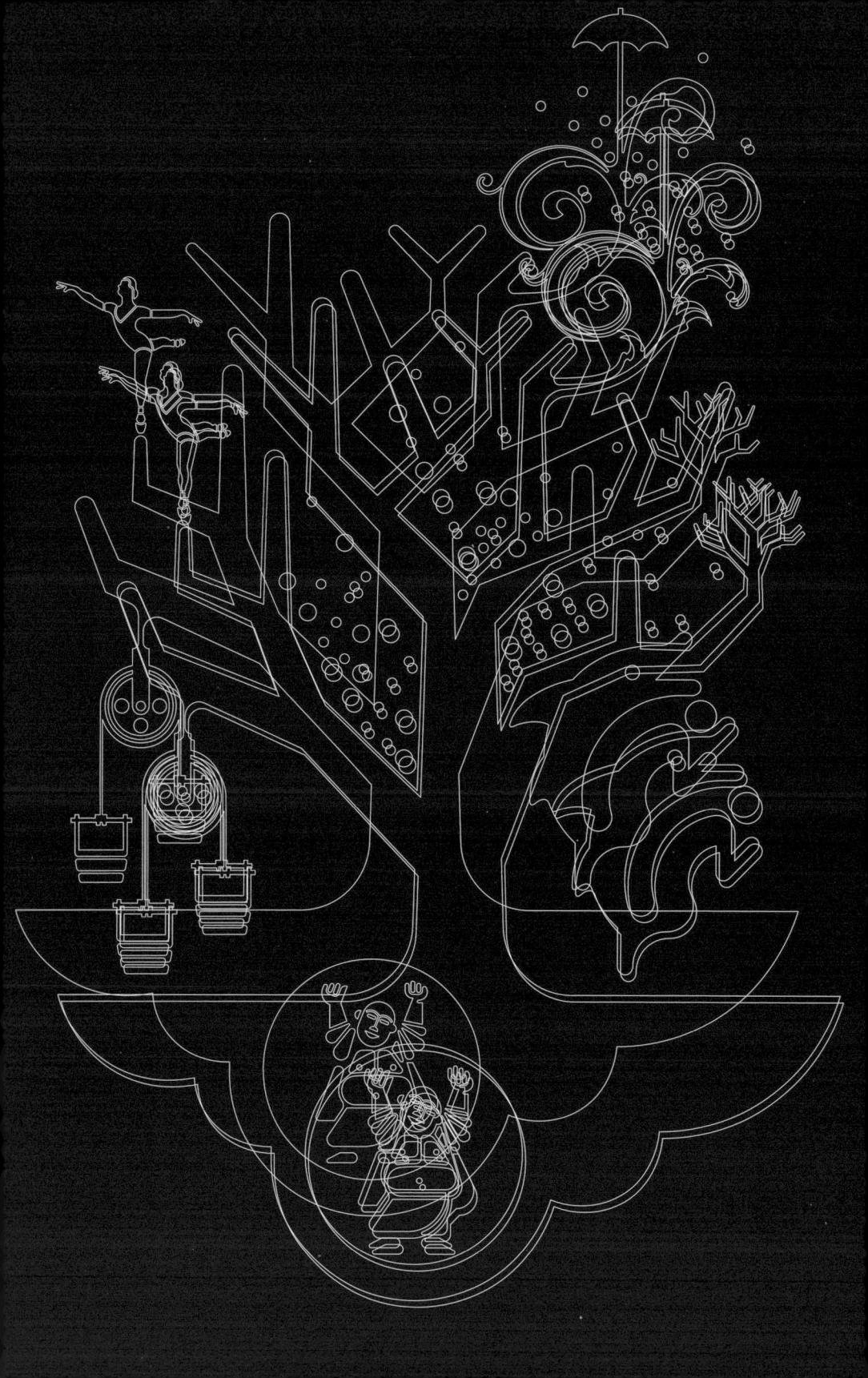

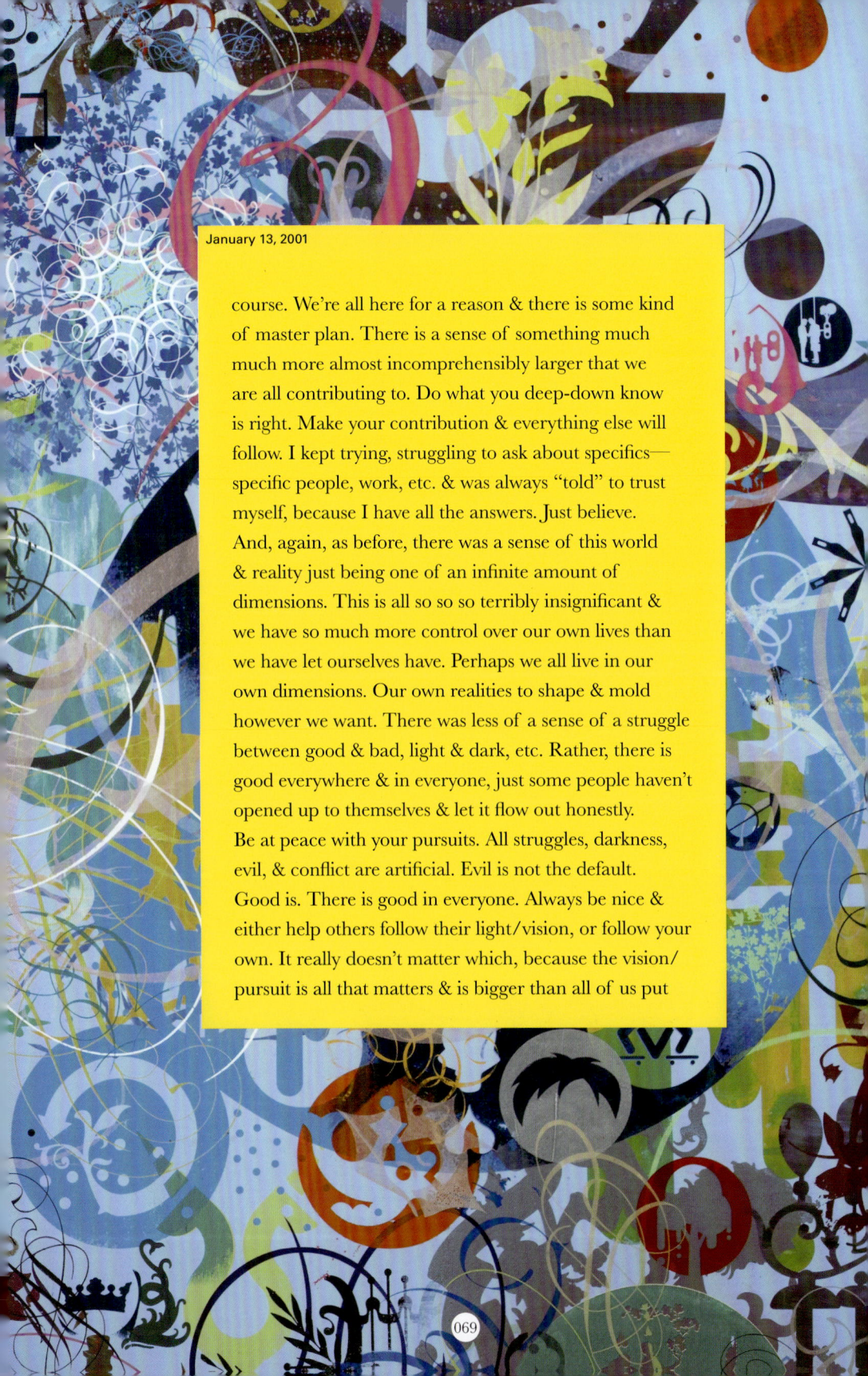

course. We're all here for a reason & there is some kind of master plan. There is a sense of something much much more almost incomprehensibly larger that we are all contributing to. Do what you deep-down know is right. Make your contribution & everything else will follow. I kept trying, struggling to ask about specifics—specific people, work, etc. & was always "told" to trust myself, because I have all the answers. Just believe. And, again, as before, there was a sense of this world & reality just being one of an infinite amount of dimensions. This is all so so so terribly insignificant & we have so much more control over our own lives than we have let ourselves have. Perhaps we all live in our own dimensions. Our own realities to shape & mold however we want. There was less of a sense of a struggle between good & bad, light & dark, etc. Rather, there is good everywhere & in everyone, just some people haven't opened up to themselves & let it flow out honestly. Be at peace with your pursuits. All struggles, darkness, evil, & conflict are artificial. Evil is not the default. Good is. There is good in everyone. Always be nice & either help others follow their light/vision, or follow your own. It really doesn't matter which, because the vision/pursuit is all that matters & is bigger than all of us put

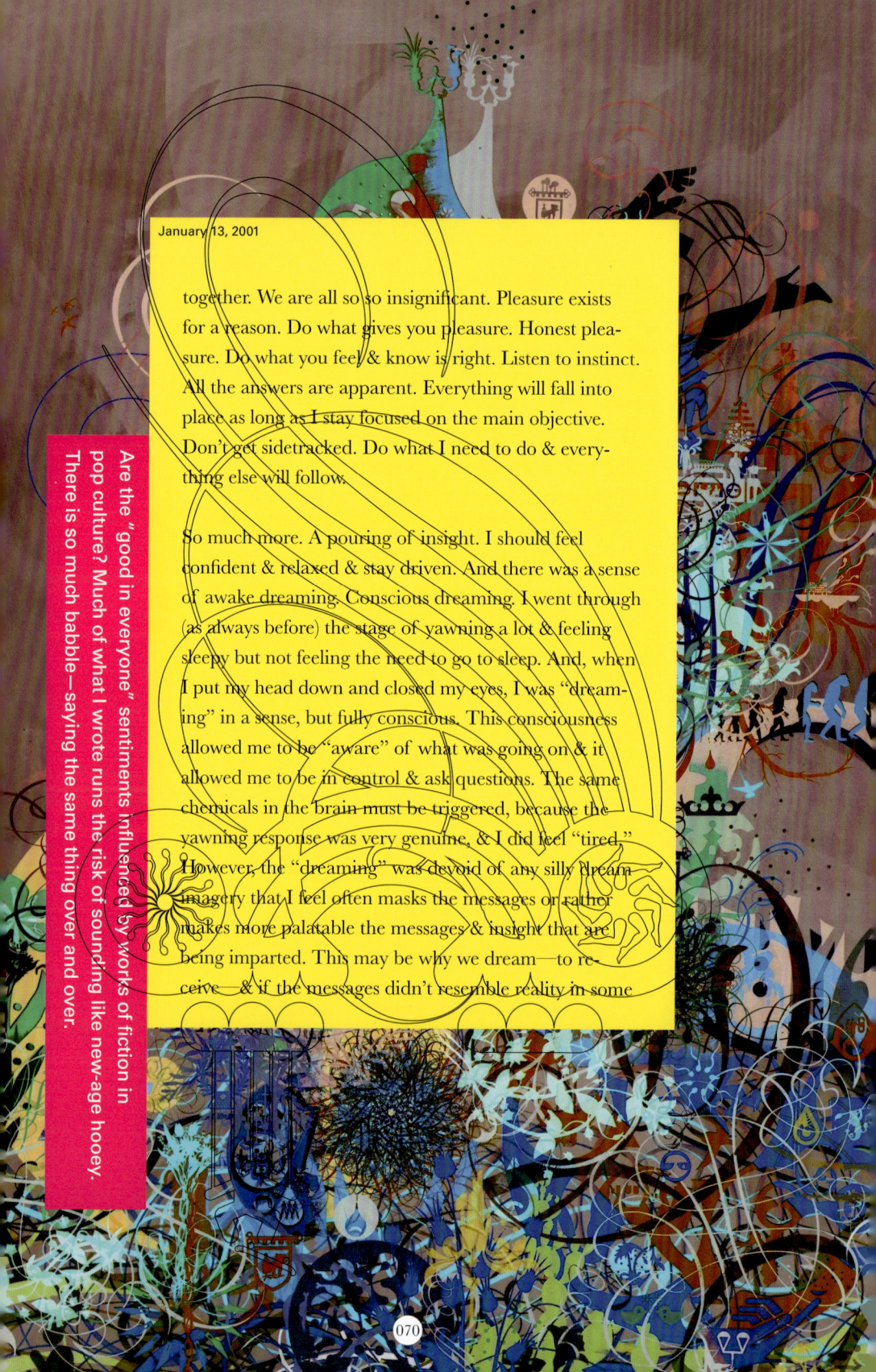

January 13, 2001

together. We are all so so insignificant. Pleasure exists for a reason. Do what gives you pleasure. Honest pleasure. Do what you feel & know is right. Listen to instinct. All the answers are apparent. Everything will fall into place as long as I stay focused on the main objective. Don't get sidetracked. Do what I need to do & everything else will follow.

So much more. A pouring of insight. I should feel confident & relaxed & stay driven. And there was a sense of awake dreaming. Conscious dreaming. I went through (as always before) the stage of yawning a lot & feeling sleepy but not feeling the need to go to sleep. And, when I put my head down and closed my eyes, I was "dreaming" in a sense, but fully conscious. This consciousness allowed me to be "aware" of what was going on & it allowed me to be in control & ask questions. The same chemicals in the brain must be triggered, because the yawning response was very genuine, & I did feel "tired." However, the "dreaming" was devoid of any silly dream imagery that I feel often masks the messages or rather makes more palatable the messages & insight that are being imparted. This may be why we dream—to receive—& if the messages didn't resemble reality in some

Are the "good in everyone" sentiments influenced by works of fiction in pop culture? Much of what I wrote runs the risk of sounding like new-age hooey. There is so much babble—saying the same thing over and over.

remote way, it would be so unbelievable(?). Should I look
to dream symbology in my search for universal codes
that we all can relate to, understand on some level.
Symbols that resonate? Just look inside for some kind
of universal symbology. Which forms feel right? Listen
to instinct & the work will resonate honestly.

These are pretty much the same messages each time.—
So, why continue to take mushrooms? Perhaps to be
reminded of just how important & true the message is.
To be reminded of just how poignant the message is.
To be reminded of just how much control we really have.
To be reminded of all the messages & perhaps, in future
journeys to ease up on the searching & just enjoy the
effects. A more casual & recreational use? Could this be
just as helpful & just as insightful? Just as "important?"
Perhaps next time: Sunlight? Music? Toys? Materials?
(paper, pen, paint, canvas,…) Outside? With other
people? TV?

Experiment. Explore.

So, why continue to take mushrooms?

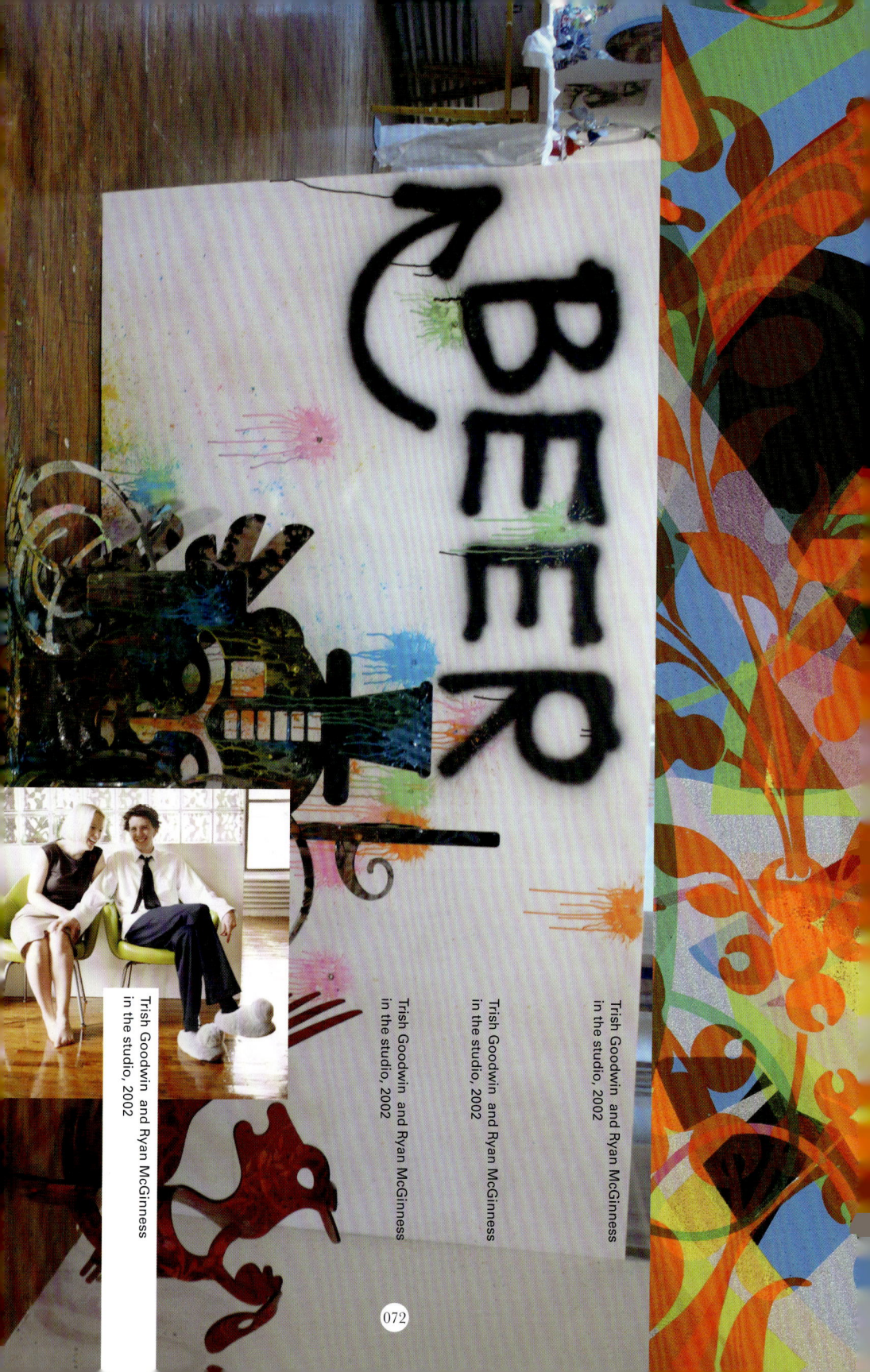

Trish Goodwin and Ryan McGinness in the studio, 2002

Trish Goodwin and Ryan McGinness in the studio, 2002

Trish Goodwin and Ryan McGinness in the studio, 2002

Trish Goodwin and Ryan McGinness in the studio, 2002

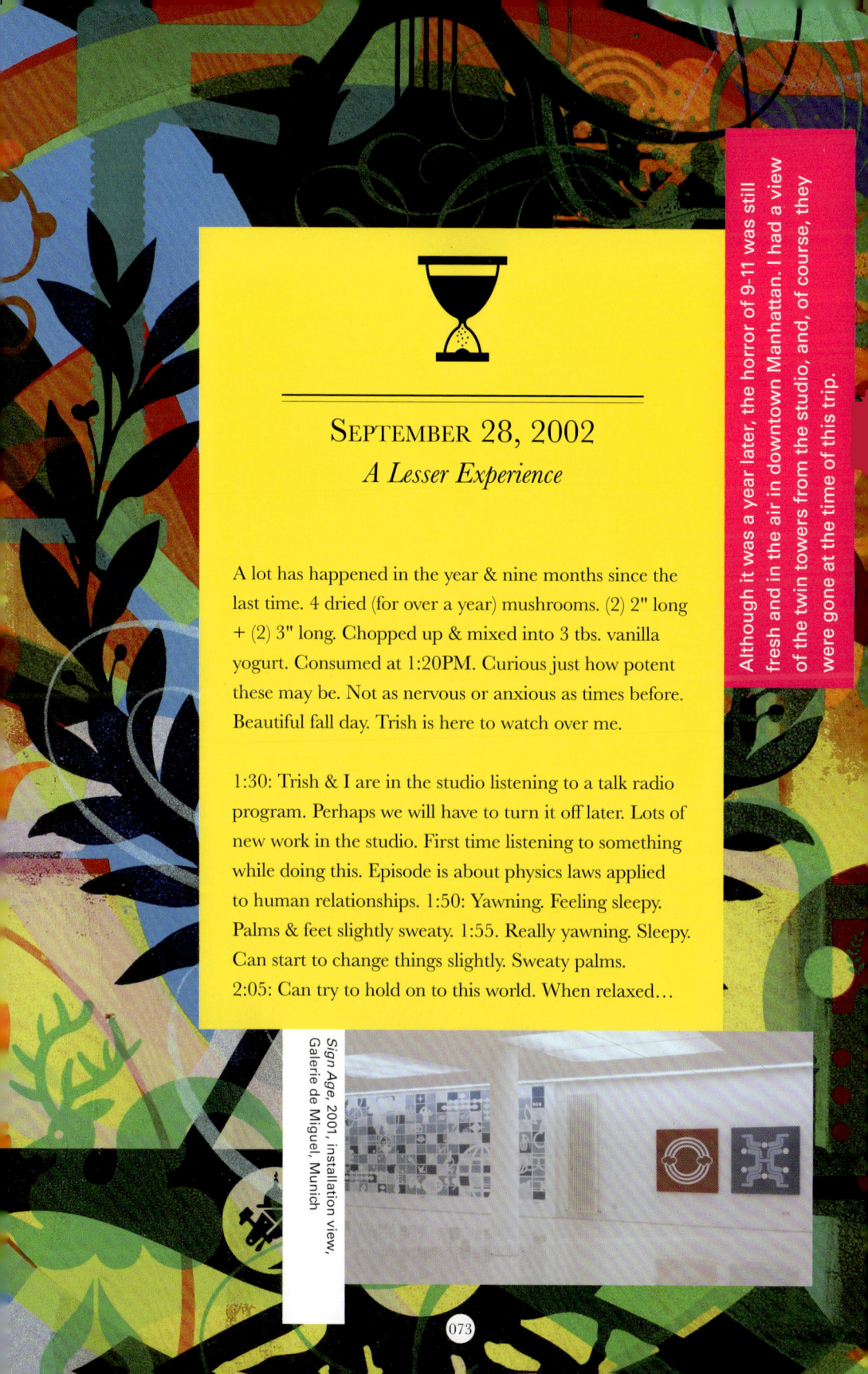

SEPTEMBER 28, 2002

A Lesser Experience

A lot has happened in the year & nine months since the last time. 4 dried (for over a year) mushrooms. (2) 2" long + (2) 3" long. Chopped up & mixed into 3 tbs. vanilla yogurt. Consumed at 1:20PM. Curious just how potent these may be. Not as nervous or anxious as times before. Beautiful fall day. Trish is here to watch over me.

1:30: Trish & I are in the studio listening to a talk radio program. Perhaps we will have to turn it off later. Lots of new work in the studio. First time listening to something while doing this. Episode is about physics laws applied to human relationships. 1:50: Yawning. Feeling sleepy. Palms & feet slightly sweaty. 1:55. Really yawning. Sleepy. Can start to change things slightly. Sweaty palms. 2:05: Can try to hold on to this world. When relaxed…

Although it was a year later, the horror of 9-11 was still fresh and in the air in downtown Manhattan. I had a view of the twin towers from the studio, and, of course, they were gone at the time of this trip.

Sign Age, 2001, installation view, Galerie de Miguel, Munich

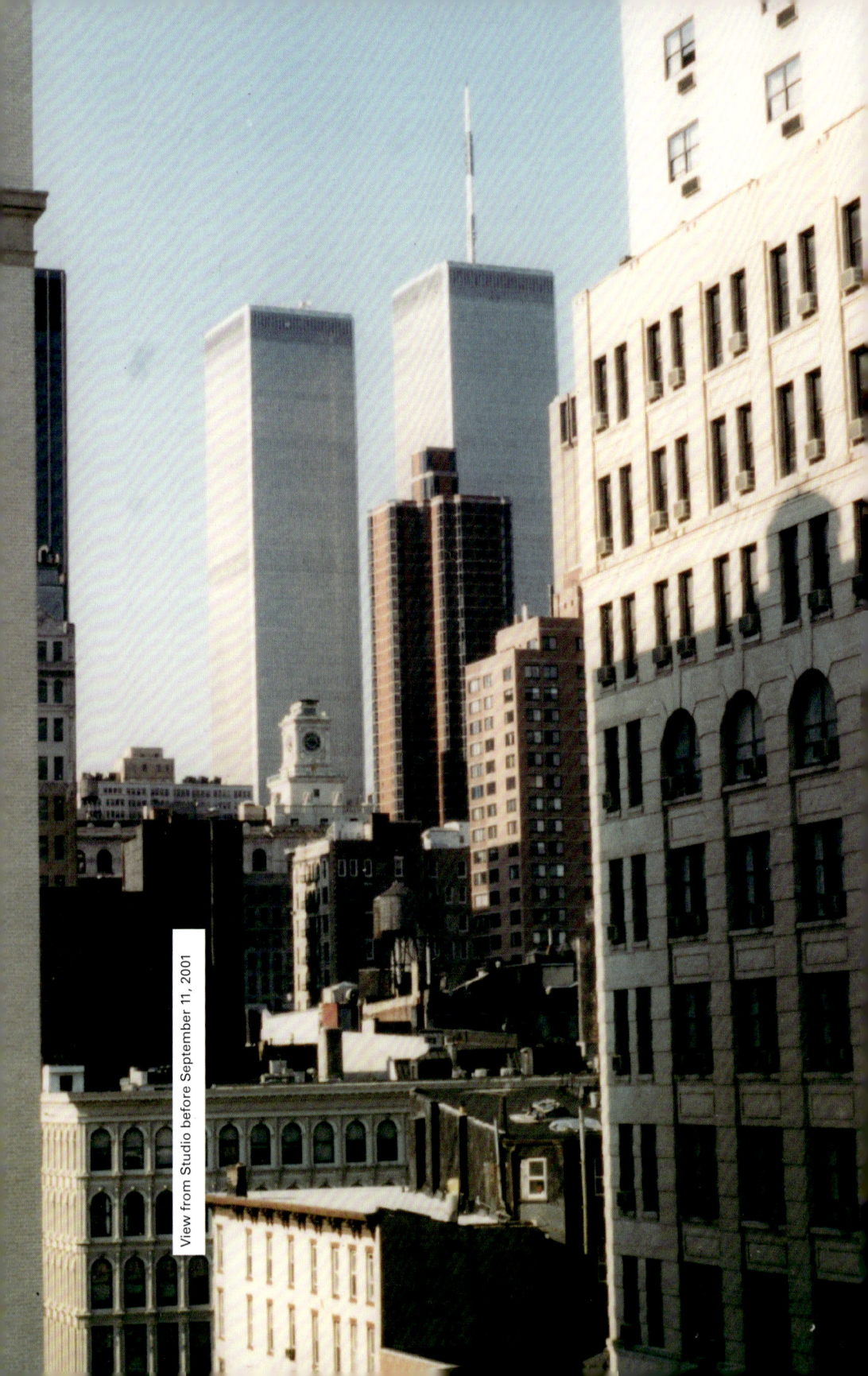

View from Studio before September 11, 2001

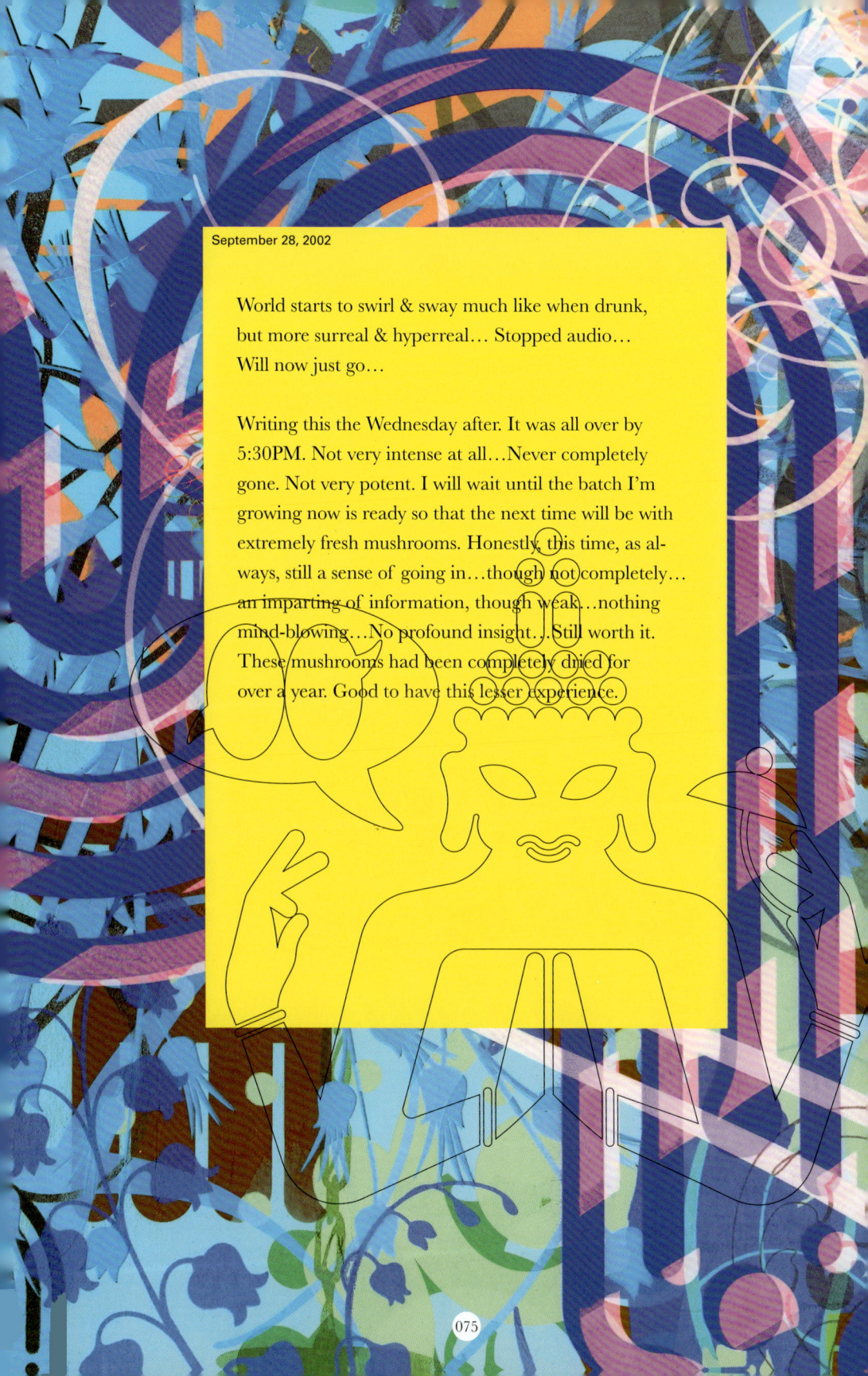

September 28, 2002

World starts to swirl & sway much like when drunk,
but more surreal & hyperreal… Stopped audio…
Will now just go…

Writing this the Wednesday after. It was all over by
5:30PM. Not very intense at all…Never completely
gone. Not very potent. I will wait until the batch I'm
growing now is ready so that the next time will be with
extremely fresh mushrooms. Honestly, this time, as always, still a sense of going in…though not completely…
an imparting of information, though weak…nothing
mind-blowing…No profound insight…Still worth it.
These mushrooms had been completely dried for
over a year. Good to have this lesser experience.

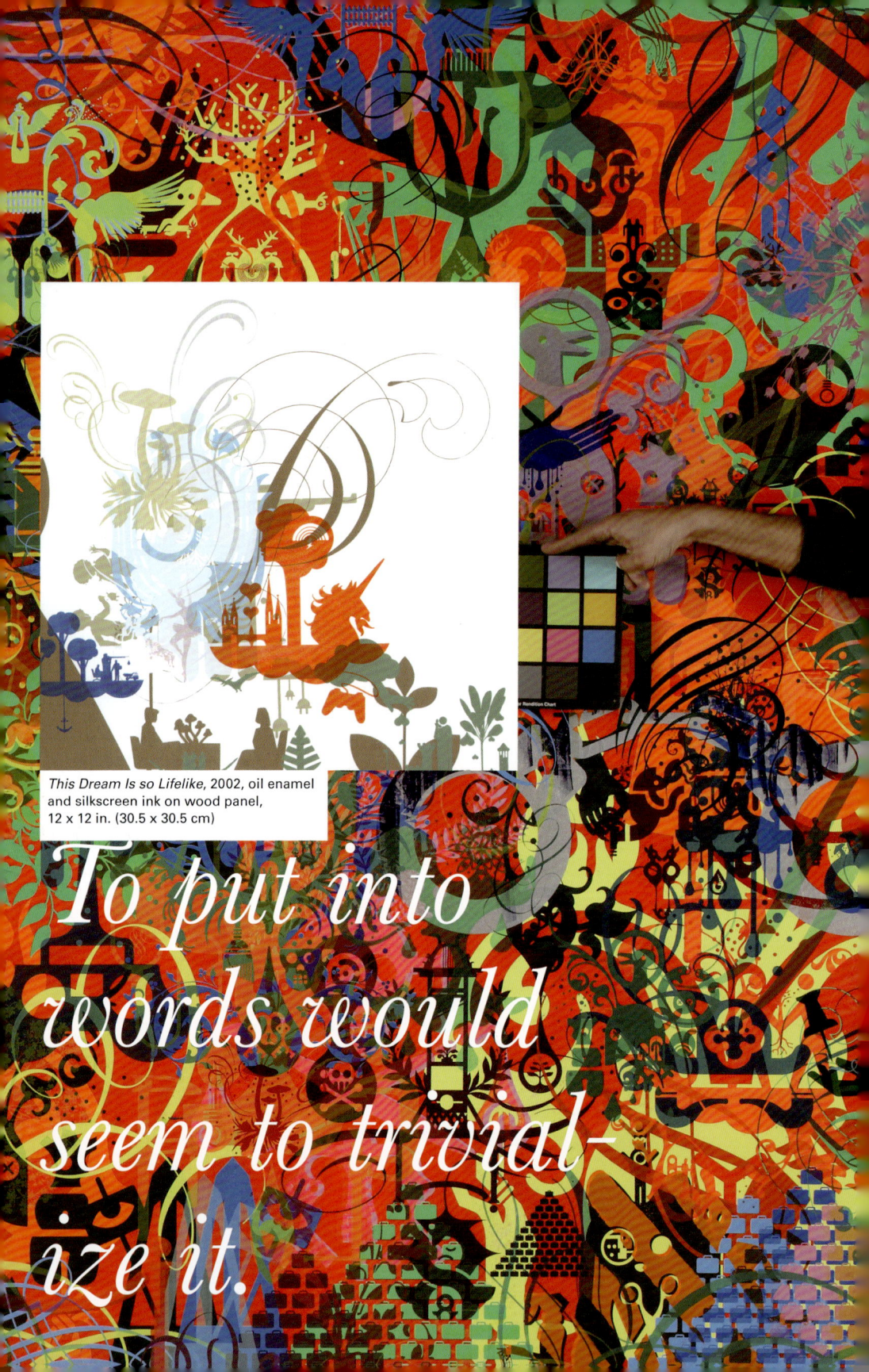

This Dream Is so Lifelike, 2002, oil enamel and silkscreen ink on wood panel, 12 x 12 in. (30.5 x 30.5 cm)

To put into words would seem to trivial-ize it.

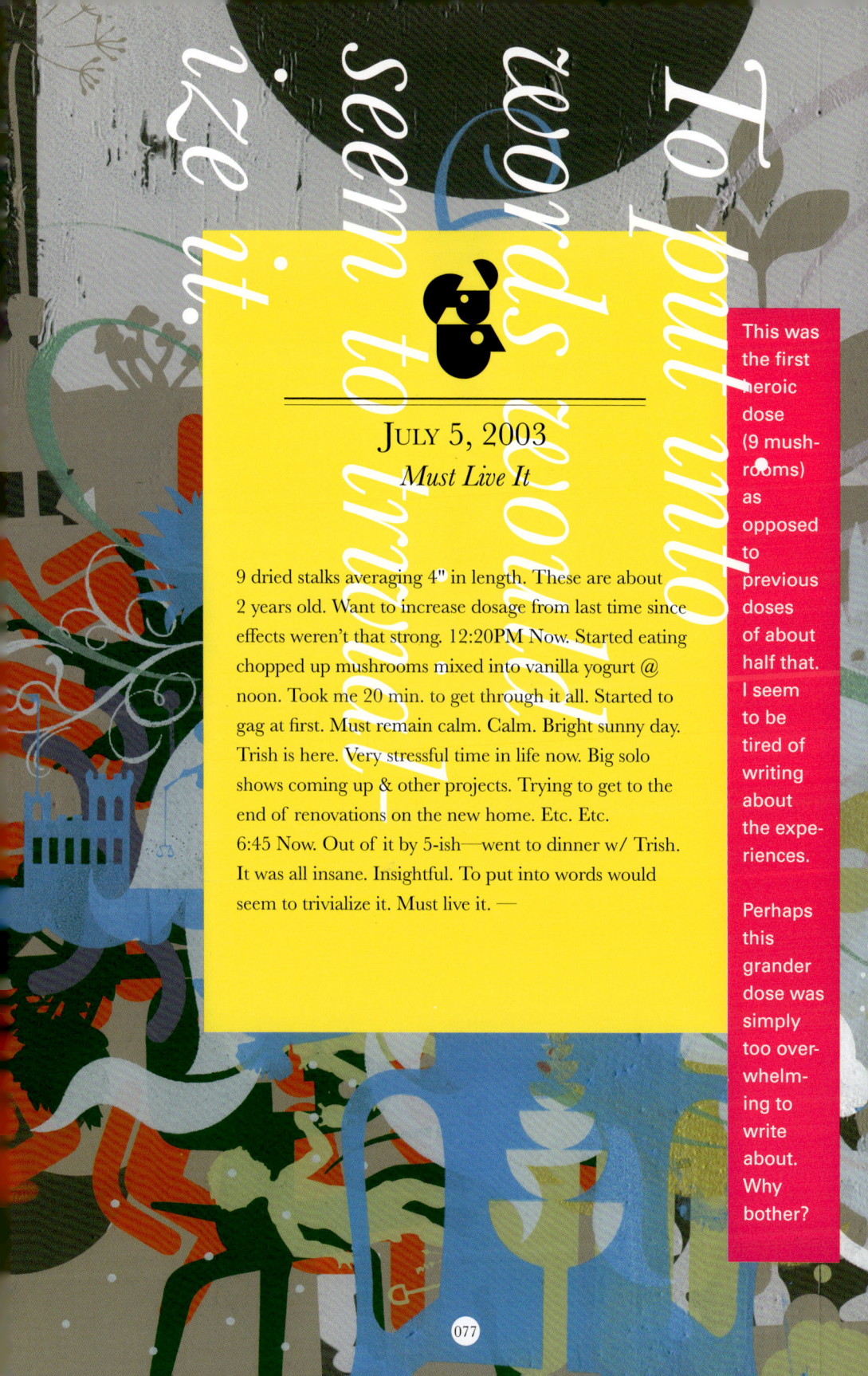

JULY 5, 2003

Must Live It

9 dried stalks averaging 4" in length. These are about 2 years old. Want to increase dosage from last time since effects weren't that strong. 12:20PM Now. Started eating chopped up mushrooms mixed into vanilla yogurt @ noon. Took me 20 min. to get through it all. Started to gag at first. Must remain calm. Calm. Bright sunny day. Trish is here. Very stressful time in life now. Big solo shows coming up & other projects. Trying to get to the end of renovations on the new home. Etc. Etc.
6:45 Now. Out of it by 5-ish—went to dinner w/ Trish. It was all insane. Insightful. To put into words would seem to trivialize it. Must live it. —

This was the first heroic dose (9 mushrooms) as opposed to previous doses of about half that. I seem to be tired of writing about the experiences.

Perhaps this grander dose was simply too overwhelming to write about. Why bother?

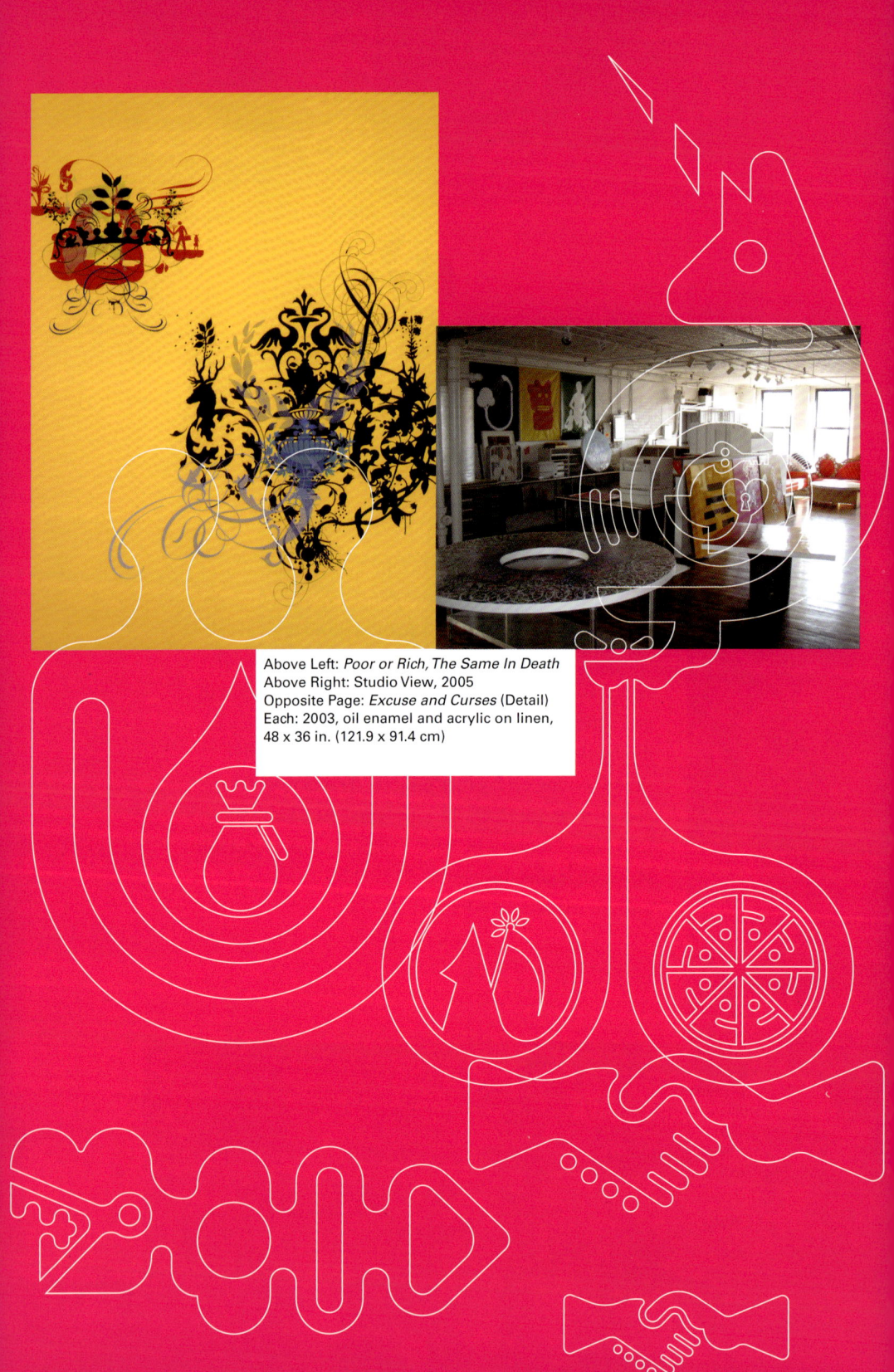

Above Left: *Poor or Rich, The Same In Death*
Above Right: Studio View, 2005
Opposite Page: *Excuse and Curses* (Detail)
Each: 2003, oil enamel and acrylic on linen,
48 x 36 in. (121.9 x 91.4 cm)

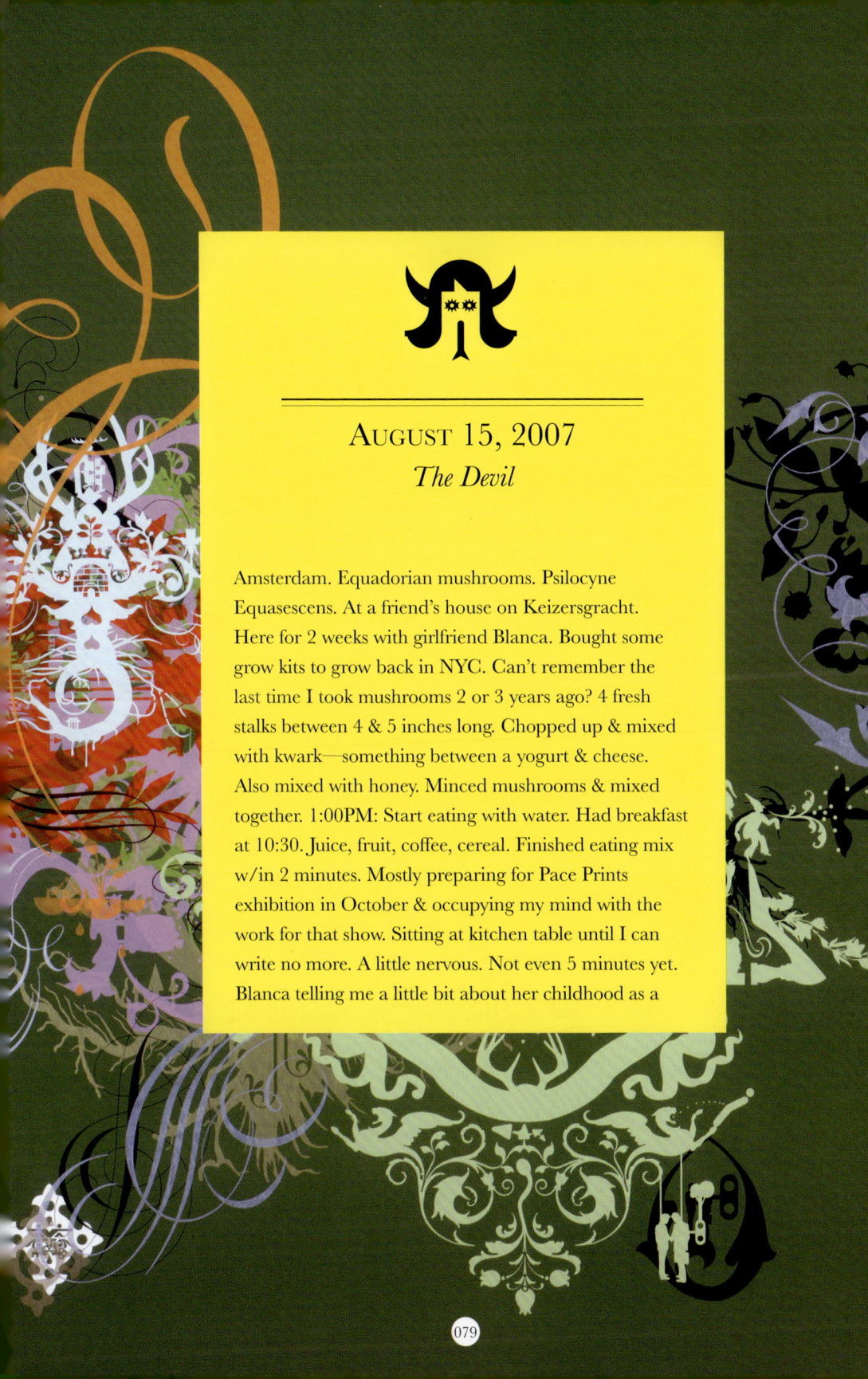

AUGUST 15, 2007
The Devil

Amsterdam. Equadorian mushrooms. Psilocyne Equasescens. At a friend's house on Keizersgracht. Here for 2 weeks with girlfriend Blanca. Bought some grow kits to grow back in NYC. Can't remember the last time I took mushrooms 2 or 3 years ago? 4 fresh stalks between 4 & 5 inches long. Chopped up & mixed with kwark—something between a yogurt & cheese. Also mixed with honey. Minced mushrooms & mixed together. 1:00PM: Start eating with water. Had breakfast at 10:30. Juice, fruit, coffee, cereal. Finished eating mix w/in 2 minutes. Mostly preparing for Pace Prints exhibition in October & occupying my mind with the work for that show. Sitting at kitchen table until I can write no more. A little nervous. Not even 5 minutes yet. Blanca telling me a little bit about her childhood as a

I was disposed to recognizing patterns in everything—creating images out of abstractions in scratches, woodgrain, marble, bricks, and clouds.

I felt as if the magic tricks that they were performing for me were demonstrations of their power to manipulate my reality.

August 15, 2007

way to pass some time. Really can't remember how long ago I did this last, so it is hard to list all the major life changes and developments since then that may or may not have an affect on this trip. Mostly lots of new work & projects. I feel like I'm on the brink of something big with the studio practice/business if I can only find the right people to work for me. That's the key to the break-through I need to make. 1:15: Starting to feel simulta-neously giddy & sleepy—the same kind of entering—dream-state sleepiness as always. Jittery & sound waves starting to go in & out. 20 minutes & it's really starting to come over me in waves. Writing is like fighting it off. Like fighting off sleep. Palms slightly sweaty. Hard to stay focused, but can let it go & stay focused on something by letting go. Like cactus on the table, for instance. I can see the ink bleed into the paper—with every pen stroke. The paper is starting to move like a wave. Melt. Bubble slightly. I don't know how much longer I can stay here. Holding on. Losing grip. 1:23: Material things starting to melt & merge. Trying to escape or let go of their mate-riality. Nothing wants to be anything specific. This is just only one minute example of all the possible states. It's as if we exist in a very fragile state of possibility. So hard to stay here. The paper is yellowing. & the blue grid lines.

Studio View, 2006

Nothing wants to be anything specific. This is just only one minute example of all the possible states. It's as if we exist in a very fragile state of possibility.

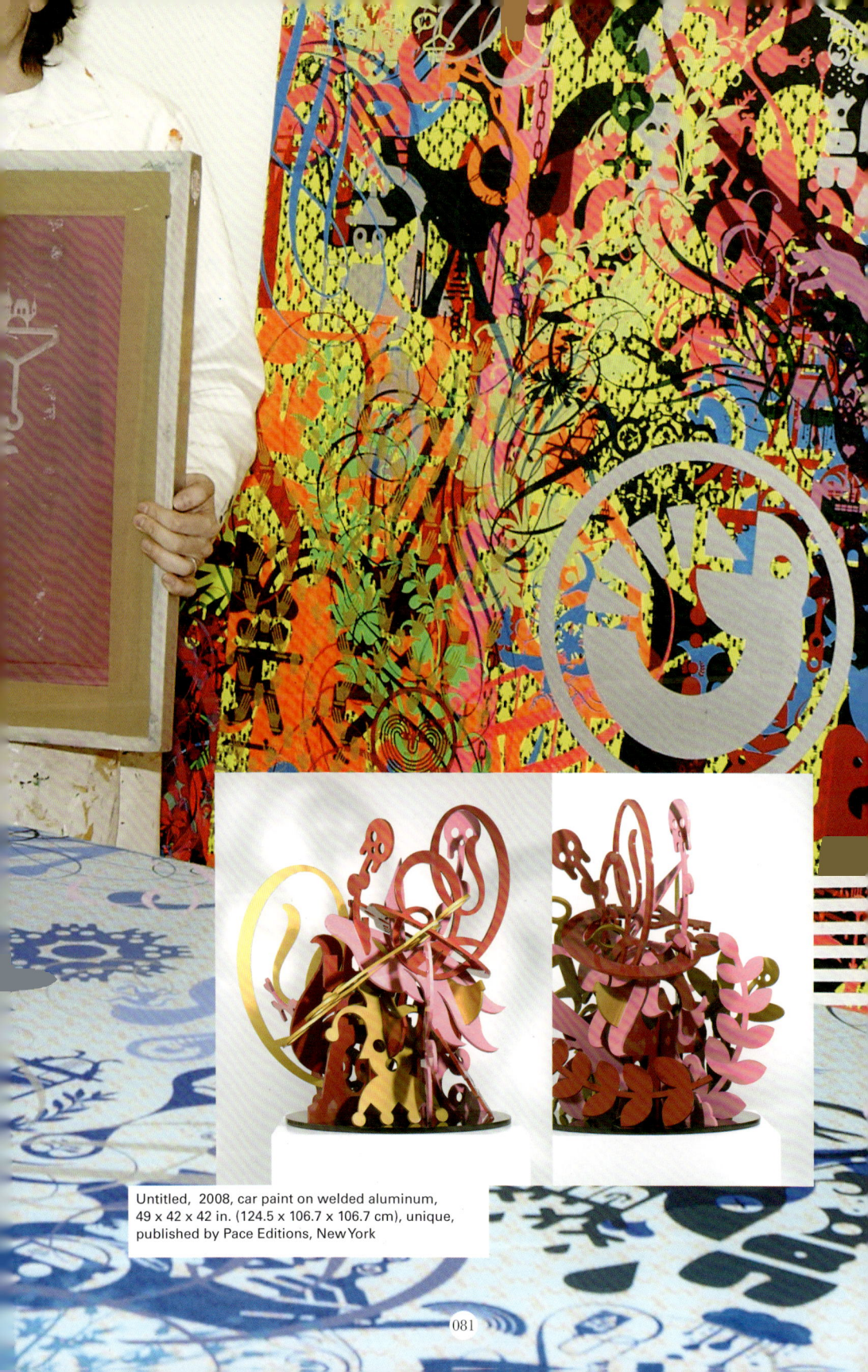

Untitled, 2008, car paint on welded aluminum,
49 x 42 x 42 in. (124.5 x 106.7 x 106.7 cm), unique,
published by Pace Editions, New York

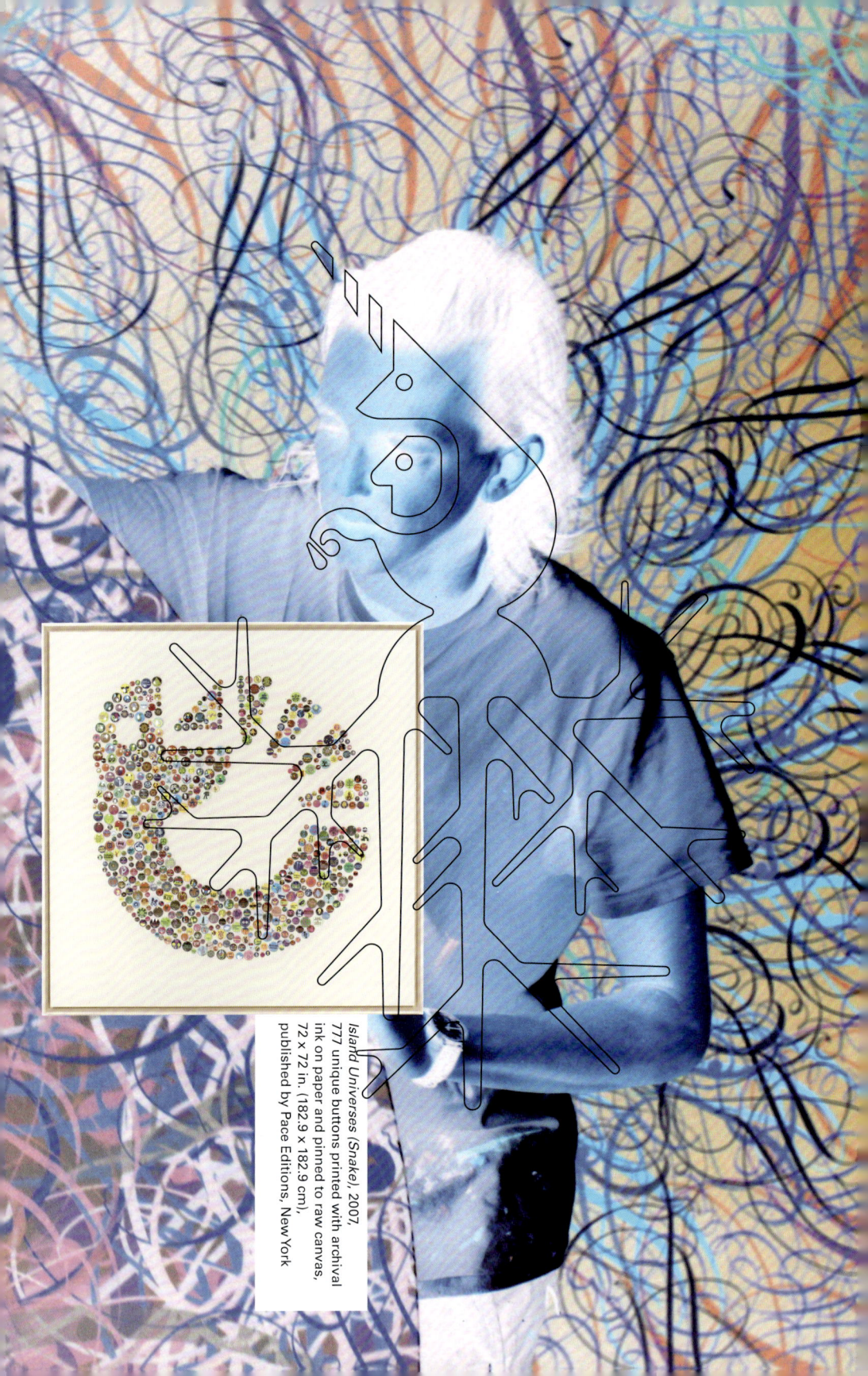

Island Universes (Snake), 2007,
777 unique buttons printed with archival
ink on paper and pinned to raw canvas,
72 x 72 in. (182.9 x 182.9 cm),
published by Pace Editions, New York

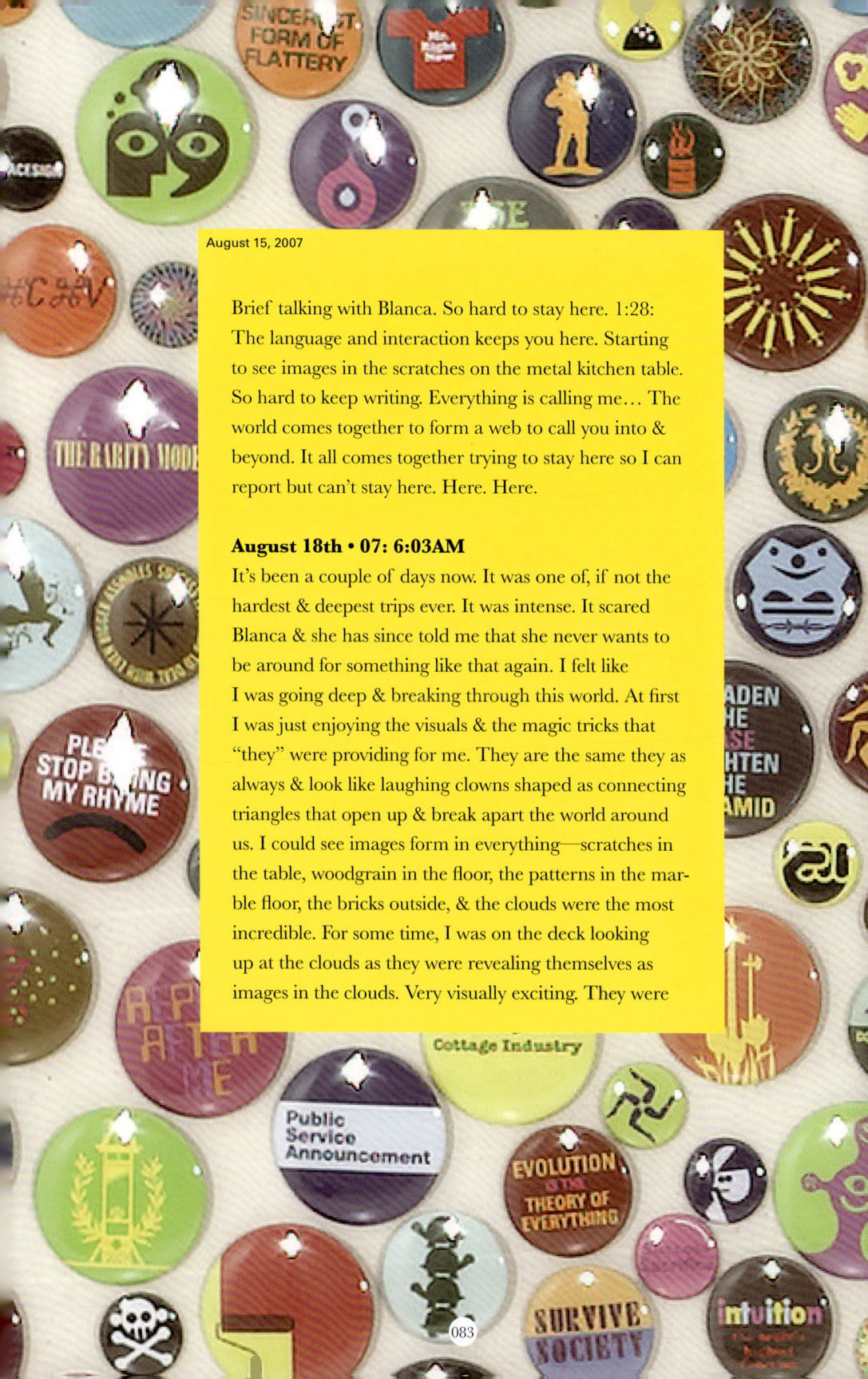

Brief talking with Blanca. So hard to stay here. 1:28:
The language and interaction keeps you here. Starting
to see images in the scratches on the metal kitchen table.
So hard to keep writing. Everything is calling me… The
world comes together to form a web to call you into &
beyond. It all comes together trying to stay here so I can
report but can't stay here. Here. Here.

August 18th • 07: 6:03AM

It's been a couple of days now. It was one of, if not the
hardest & deepest trips ever. It was intense. It scared
Blanca & she has since told me that she never wants to
be around for something like that again. I felt like
I was going deep & breaking through this world. At first
I was just enjoying the visuals & the magic tricks that
"they" were providing for me. They are the same they as
always & look like laughing clowns shaped as connecting
triangles that open up & break apart the world around
us. I could see images form in everything—scratches in
the table, woodgrain in the floor, the patterns in the marble floor, the bricks outside, & the clouds were the most
incredible. For some time, I was on the deck looking
up at the clouds as they were revealing themselves as
images in the clouds. Very visually exciting. They were

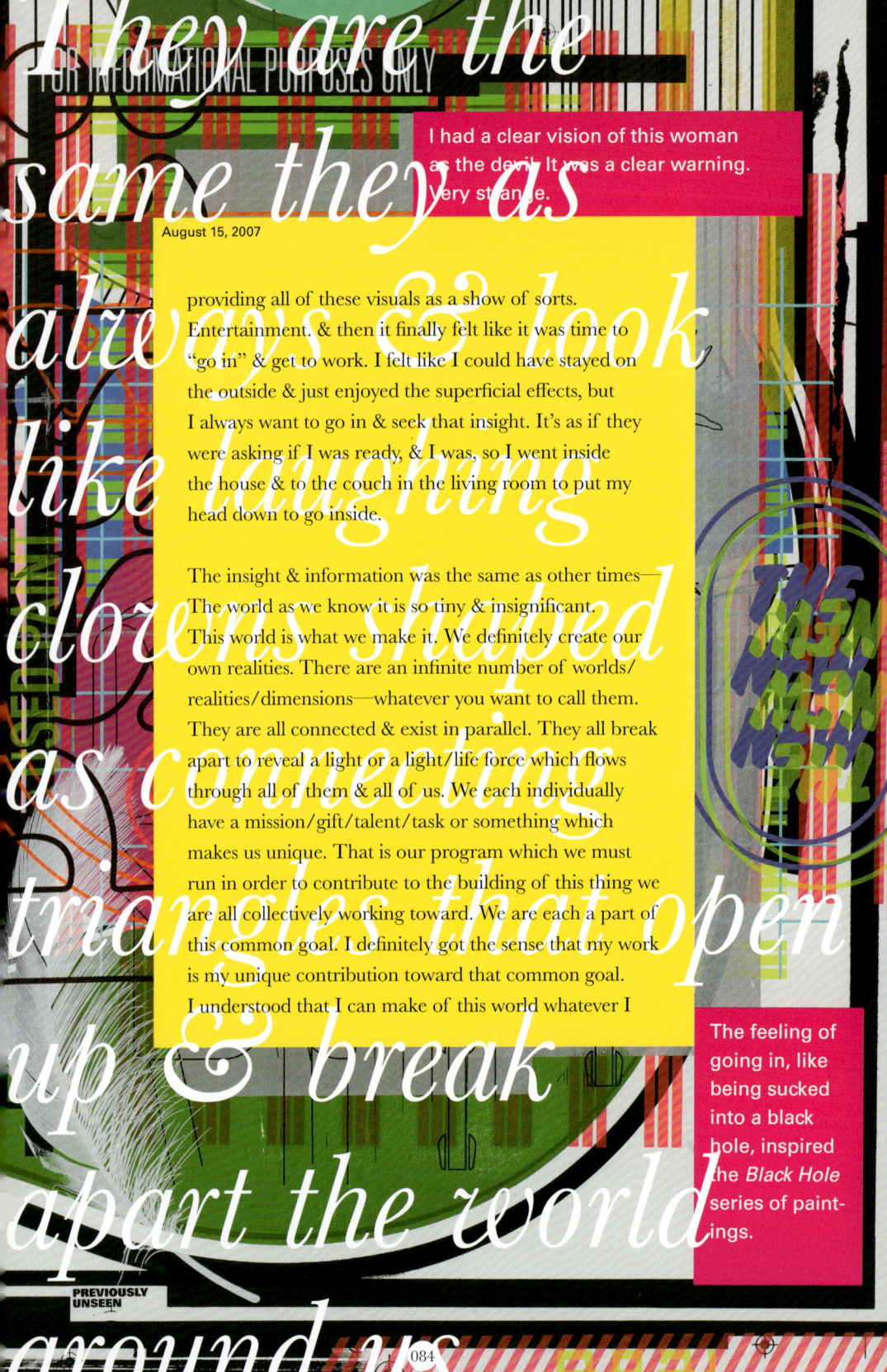

They are the same they as always & look like laughing clowns shaped as connecting triangles that open up & break apart the world around us.

I had a clear vision of this woman as the devil. It was a clear warning. Very strange.

August 15, 2007

providing all of these visuals as a show of sorts. Entertainment. & then it finally felt like it was time to "go in" & get to work. I felt like I could have stayed on the outside & just enjoyed the superficial effects, but I always want to go in & seek that insight. It's as if they were asking if I was ready, & I was, so I went inside the house & to the couch in the living room to put my head down to go inside.

The insight & information was the same as other times—The world as we know it is so tiny & insignificant. This world is what we make it. We definitely create our own realities. There are an infinite number of worlds/realities/dimensions—whatever you want to call them. They are all connected & exist in parallel. They all break apart to reveal a light or a light/life force which flows through all of them & all of us. We each individually have a mission/gift/talent/task or something which makes us unique. That is our program which we must run in order to contribute to the building of this thing we are all collectively working toward. We are each a part of this common goal. I definitely got the sense that my work is my unique contribution toward that common goal. I understood that I can make of this world whatever I

The feeling of going in, like being sucked into a black hole, inspired the *Black Hole* series of paintings.

THE HARD WORK 2021

PREVIOUSLY UNSEEN

They are the
same they as
always & look
like laughing
clowns shaped
as connecting
triangles that open
up & break
apart the world
around us.

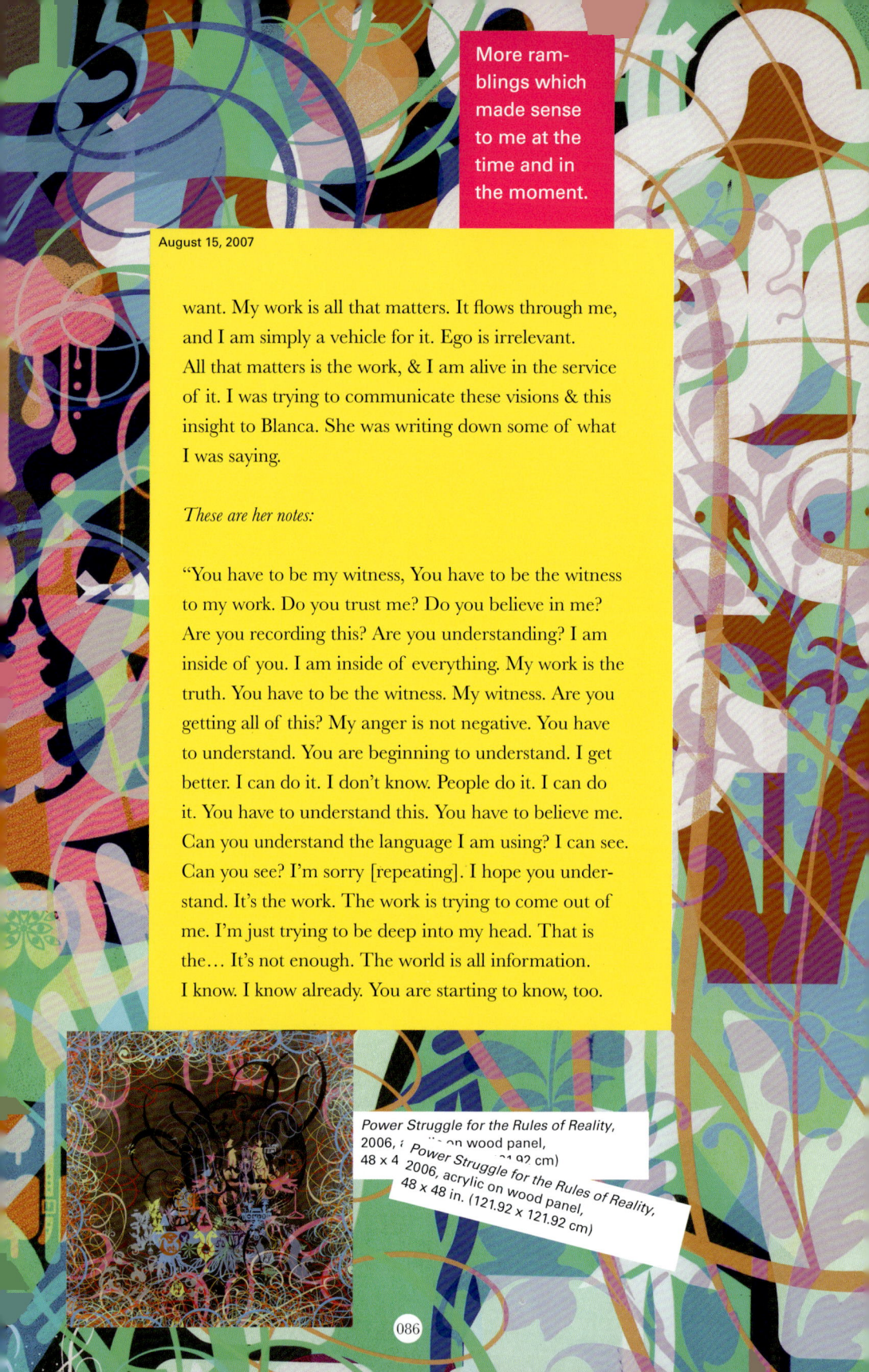

August 15, 2007

want. My work is all that matters. It flows through me, and I am simply a vehicle for it. Ego is irrelevant. All that matters is the work, & I am alive in the service of it. I was trying to communicate these visions & this insight to Blanca. She was writing down some of what I was saying.

These are her notes:

"You have to be my witness, You have to be the witness to my work. Do you trust me? Do you believe in me? Are you recording this? Are you understanding? I am inside of you. I am inside of everything. My work is the truth. You have to be the witness. My witness. Are you getting all of this? My anger is not negative. You have to understand. You are beginning to understand. I get better. I can do it. I don't know. People do it. I can do it. You have to understand this. You have to believe me. Can you understand the language I am using? I can see. Can you see? I'm sorry [repeating]. I hope you under-stand. It's the work. The work is trying to come out of me. I'm just trying to be deep into my head. That is the… It's not enough. The world is all information. I know. I know already. You are starting to know, too.

Power Struggle for the Rules of Reality,
2006, acrylic on wood panel,
48 x 4... (121.92 cm)

Power Struggle for the Rules of Reality,
2006, acrylic on wood panel,
48 x 48 in. (121.92 x 121.92 cm)

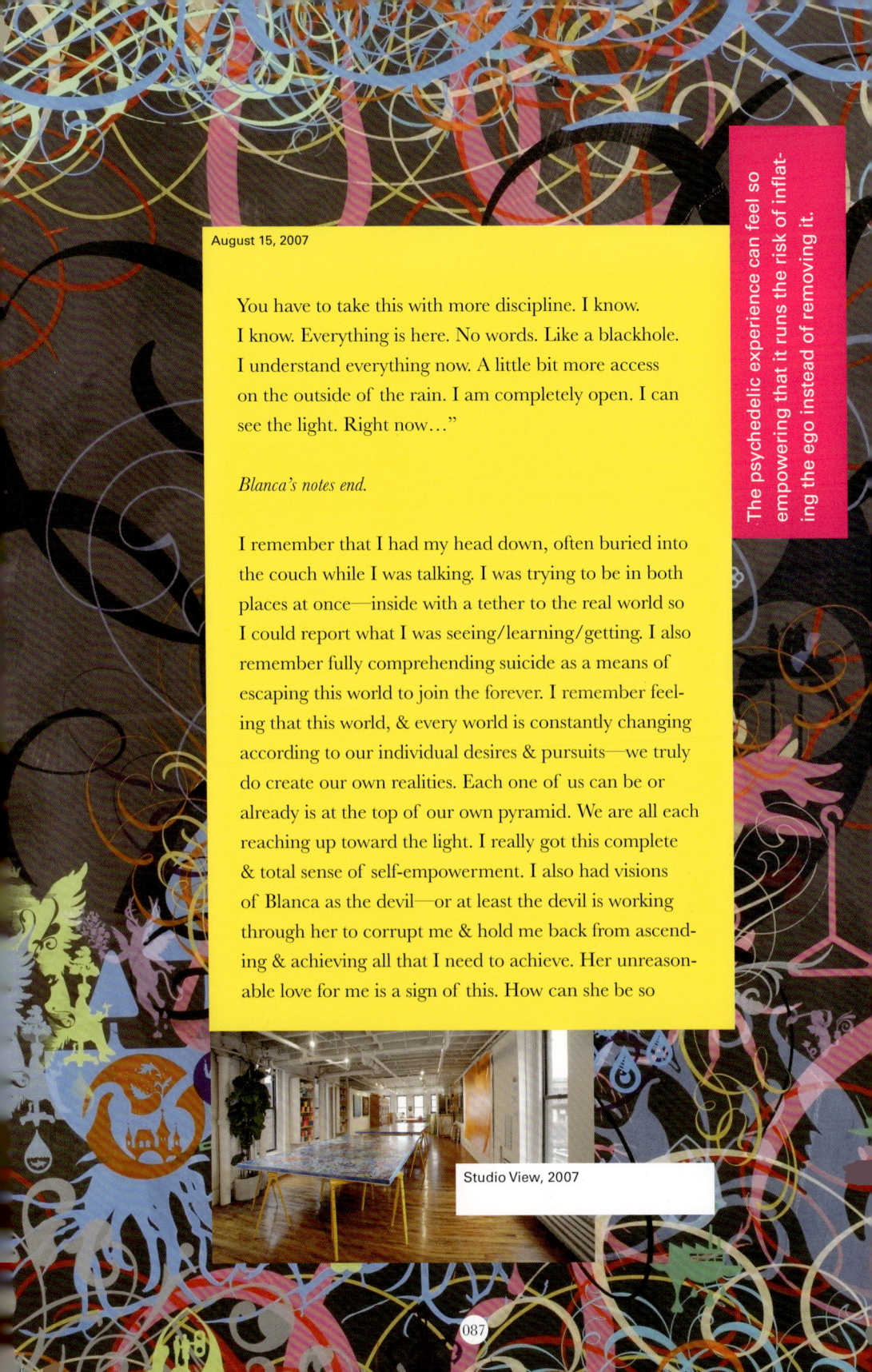

August 15, 2007

You have to take this with more discipline. I know.
I know. Everything is here. No words. Like a blackhole.
I understand everything now. A little bit more access
on the outside of the rain. I am completely open. I can
see the light. Right now…"

Blanca's notes end.

I remember that I had my head down, often buried into
the couch while I was talking. I was trying to be in both
places at once—inside with a tether to the real world so
I could report what I was seeing/learning/getting. I also
remember fully comprehending suicide as a means of
escaping this world to join the forever. I remember feeling that this world, & every world is constantly changing
according to our individual desires & pursuits—we truly
do create our own realities. Each one of us can be or
already is at the top of our own pyramid. We are all each
reaching up toward the light. I really got this complete
& total sense of self-empowerment. I also had visions
of Blanca as the devil—or at least the devil is working
through her to corrupt me & hold me back from ascending & achieving all that I need to achieve. Her unreason-
able love for me is a sign of this. How can she be so

The psychedelic experience can feel so
empowering that it runs the risk of inflat-
ing the ego instead of removing it.

Studio View, 2007

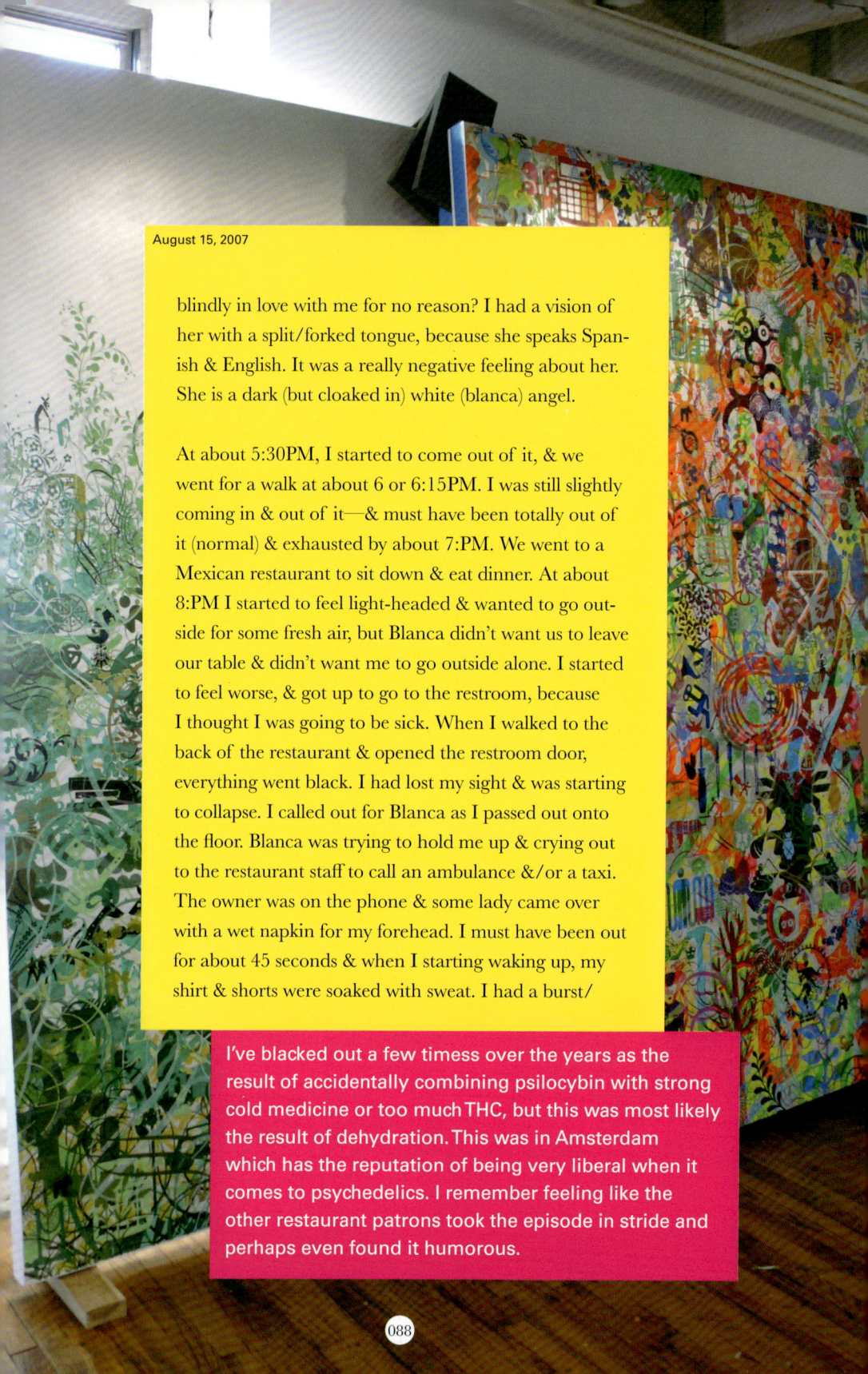

blindly in love with me for no reason? I had a vision of
her with a split/forked tongue, because she speaks Span-
ish & English. It was a really negative feeling about her.
She is a dark (but cloaked in) white (blanca) angel.

At about 5:30PM, I started to come out of it, & we
went for a walk at about 6 or 6:15PM. I was still slightly
coming in & out of it—& must have been totally out of
it (normal) & exhausted by about 7:PM. We went to a
Mexican restaurant to sit down & eat dinner. At about
8:PM I started to feel light-headed & wanted to go outside for some fresh air, but Blanca didn't want us to leave
our table & didn't want me to go outside alone. I started
to feel worse, & got up to go to the restroom, because
I thought I was going to be sick. When I walked to the
back of the restaurant & opened the restroom door,
everything went black. I had lost my sight & was starting
to collapse. I called out for Blanca as I passed out onto
the floor. Blanca was trying to hold me up & crying out
to the restaurant staff to call an ambulance &/or a taxi.
The owner was on the phone & some lady came over
with a wet napkin for my forehead. I must have been out
for about 45 seconds & when I starting waking up, my
shirt & shorts were soaked with sweat. I had a burst/

I've blacked out a few timess over the years as the
result of accidentally combining psilocybin with strong
cold medicine or too much THC, but this was most likely
the result of dehydration. This was in Amsterdam
which has the reputation of being very liberal when it
comes to psychedelics. I remember feeling like the
other restaurant patrons took the episode in stride and
perhaps even found it humorous.

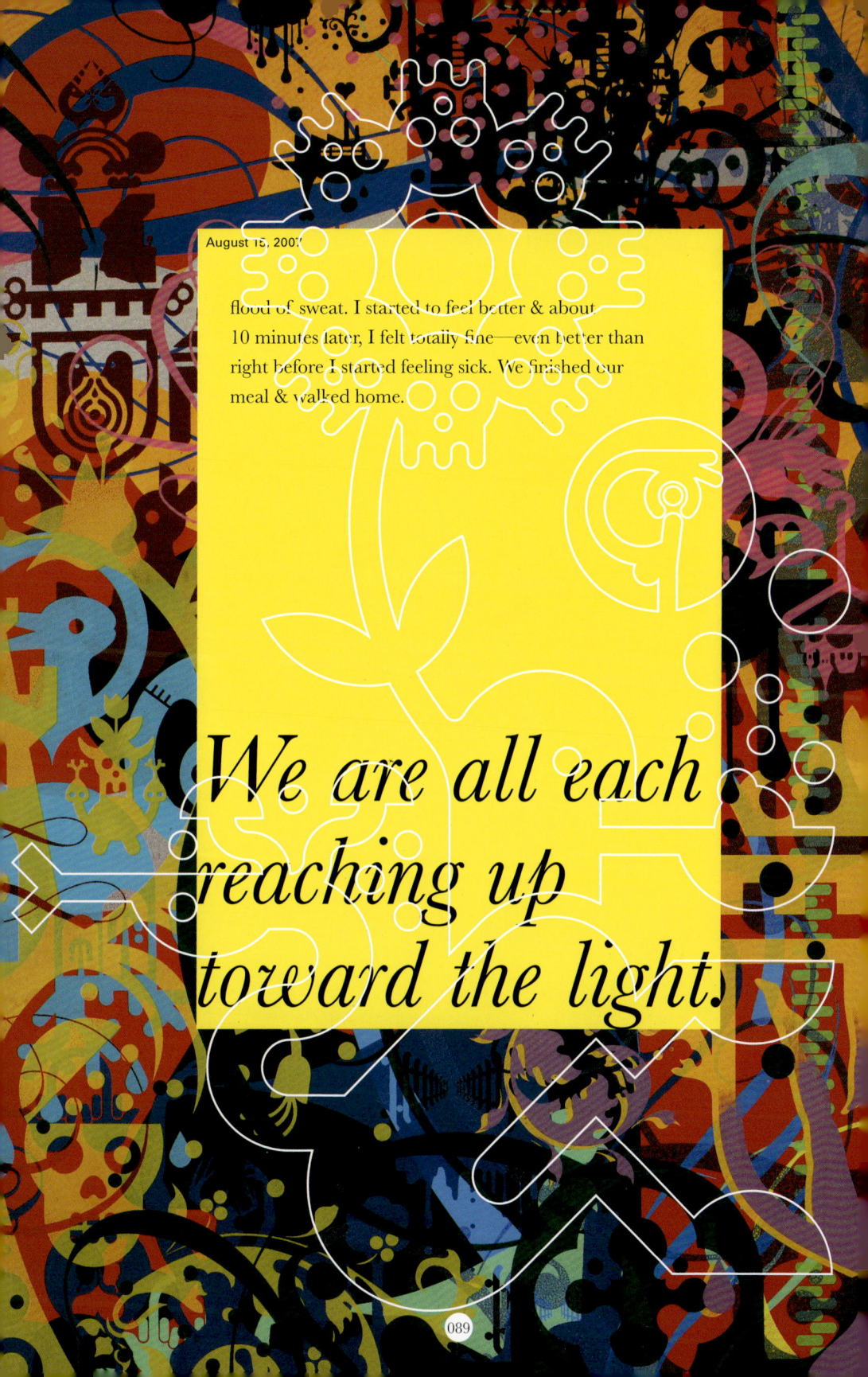

August 15, 2007

flood of sweat. I started to feel better & about 10 minutes later, I felt totally fine—even better than right before I started feeling sick. We finished our meal & walked home.

We are all each reaching up toward the light.

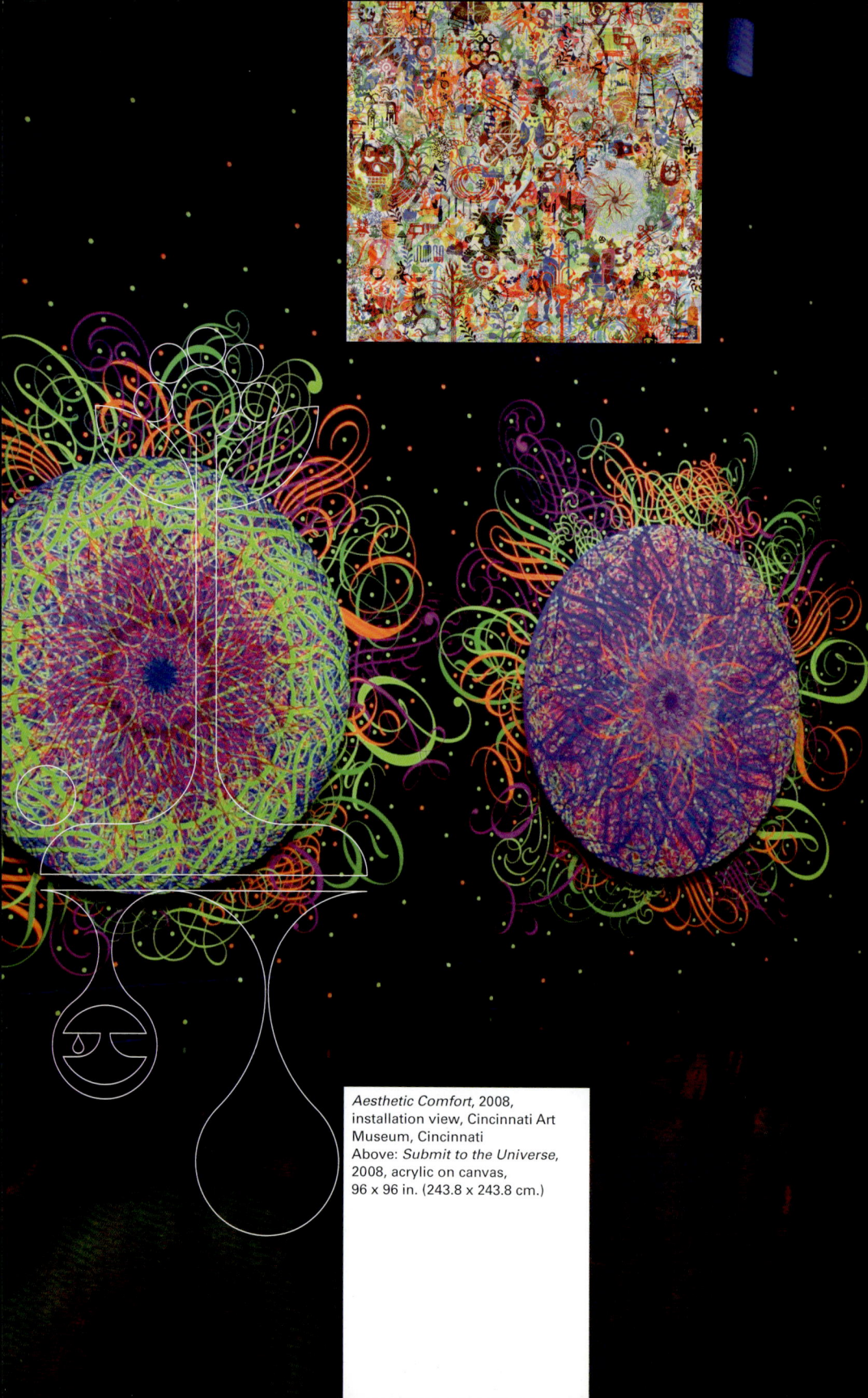

Aesthetic Comfort, 2008,
installation view, Cincinnati Art
Museum, Cincinnati
Above: *Submit to the Universe*,
2008, acrylic on canvas,
96 x 96 in. (243.8 x 243.8 cm.)

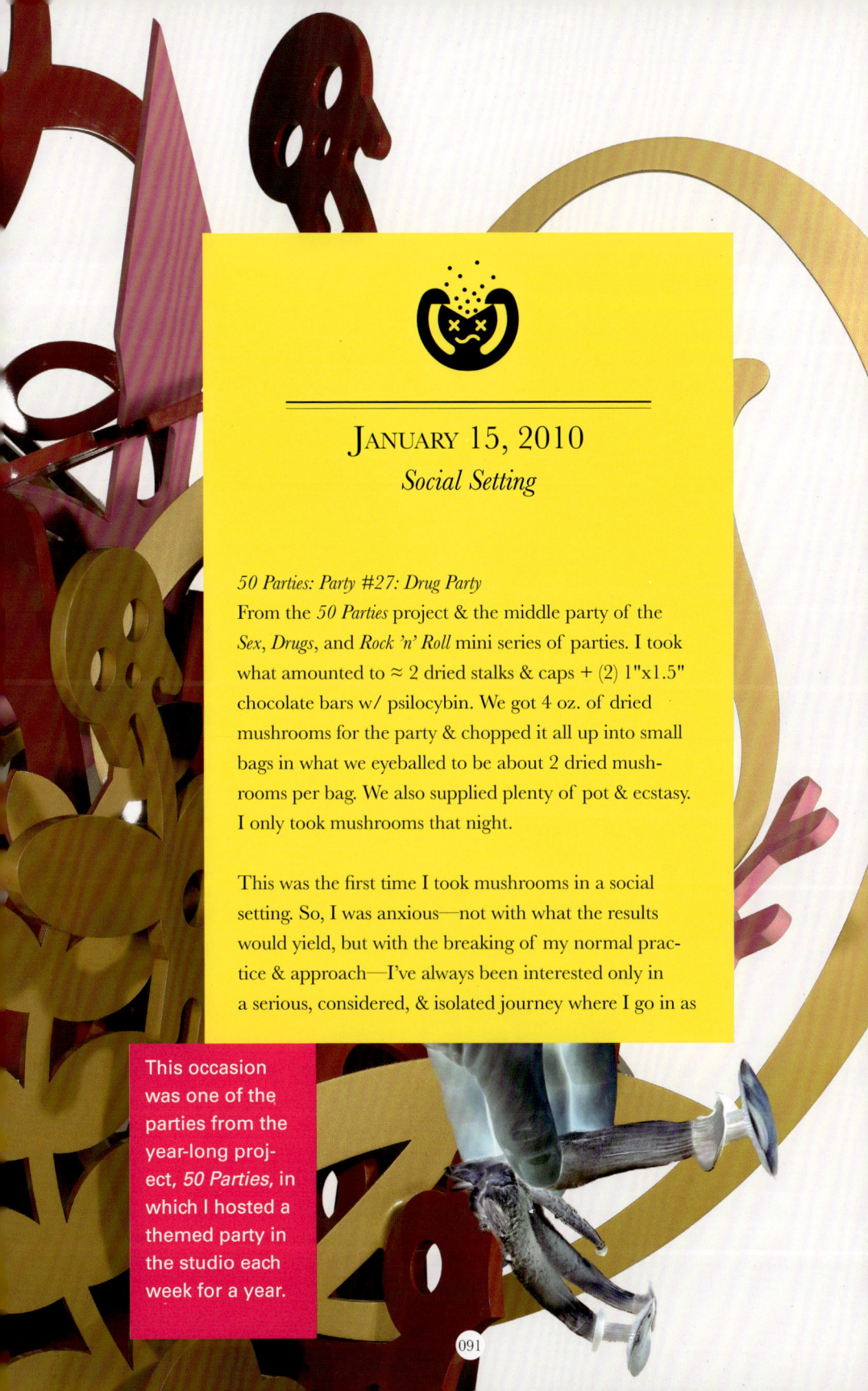

January 15, 2010
Social Setting

50 Parties: Party #27: Drug Party
From the *50 Parties* project & the middle party of the *Sex*, *Drugs*, and *Rock 'n' Roll* mini series of parties. I took what amounted to ≈ 2 dried stalks & caps + (2) 1"x1.5" chocolate bars w/ psilocybin. We got 4 oz. of dried mushrooms for the party & chopped it all up into small bags in what we eyeballed to be about 2 dried mushrooms per bag. We also supplied plenty of pot & ecstasy. I only took mushrooms that night.

This was the first time I took mushrooms in a social setting. So, I was anxious—not with what the results would yield, but with the breaking of my normal practice & approach—I've always been interested only in a serious, considered, & isolated journey where I go in as

This occasion was one of the parties from the year-long project, *50 Parties*, in which I hosted a themed party in the studio each week for a year.

The entire world is a projection.

Ryan McGinness and Trish Goodwin
at Party #27 of the *50 Parties* project,
2010, New York

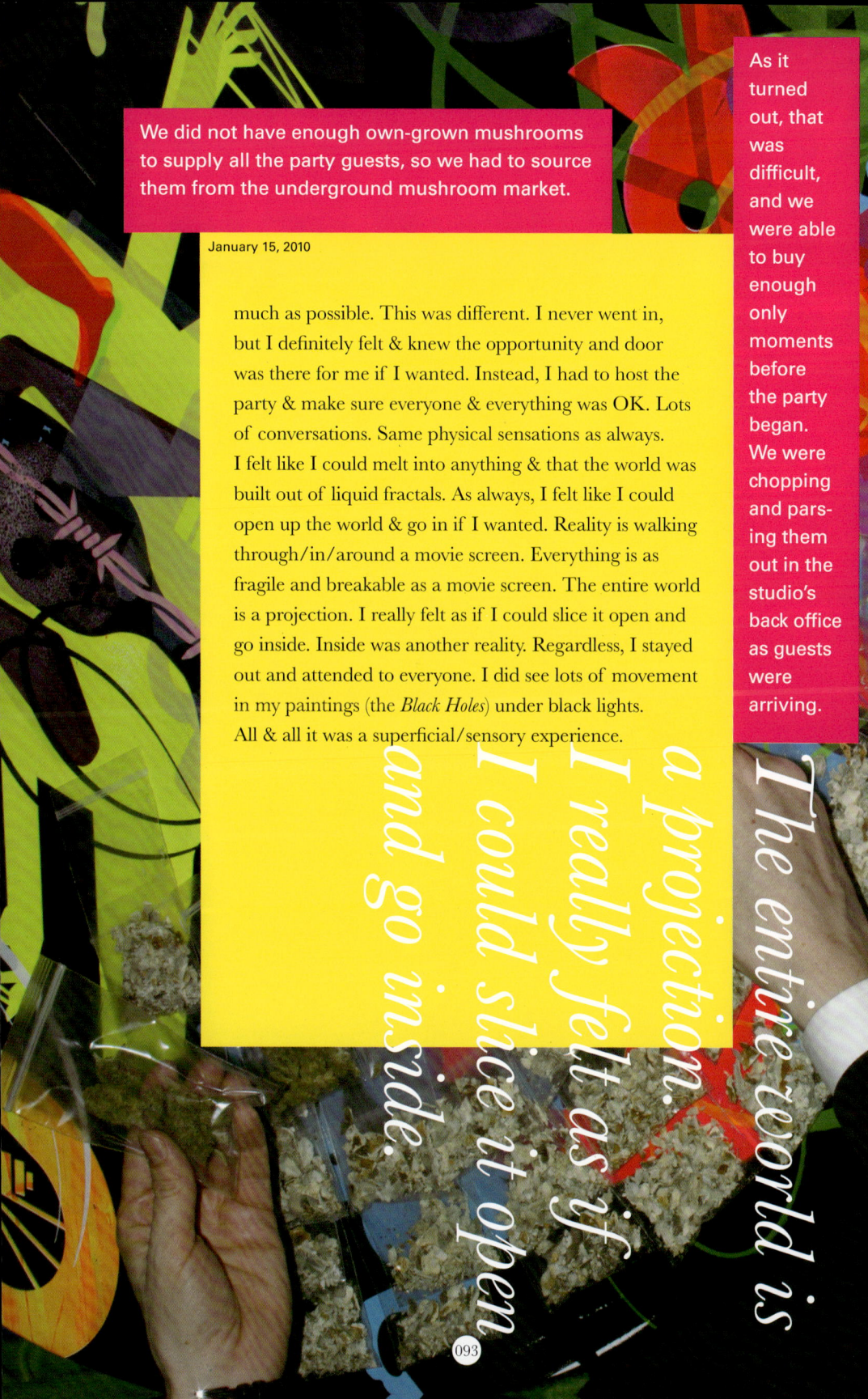

We did not have enough own-grown mushrooms to supply all the party guests, so we had to source them from the underground mushroom market.

As it turned out, that was difficult, and we were able to buy enough only moments before the party began. We were chopping and parsing them out in the studio's back office as guests were arriving.

January 15, 2010

much as possible. This was different. I never went in, but I definitely felt & knew the opportunity and door was there for me if I wanted. Instead, I had to host the party & make sure everyone & everything was OK. Lots of conversations. Same physical sensations as always. I felt like I could melt into anything & that the world was built out of liquid fractals. As always, I felt like I could open up the world & go in if I wanted. Reality is walking through/in/around a movie screen. Everything is as fragile and breakable as a movie screen. The entire world is a projection. I really felt as if I could slice it open and go inside. Inside was another reality. Regardless, I stayed out and attended to everyone. I did see lots of movement in my paintings (the *Black Holes*) under black lights. All & all it was a superficial/sensory experience.

The entire world is a projection. I really felt as if I could slice it open and go inside.

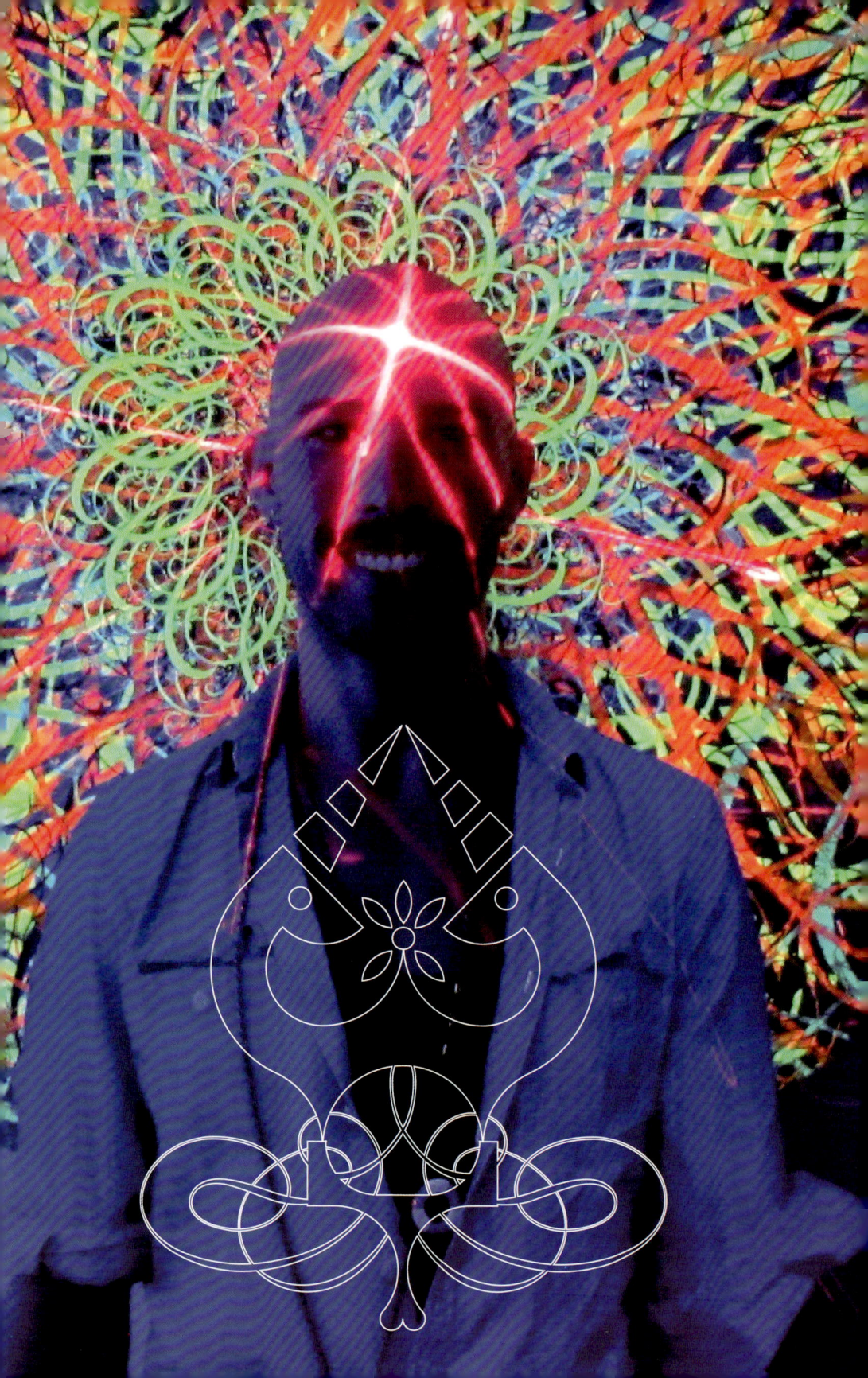

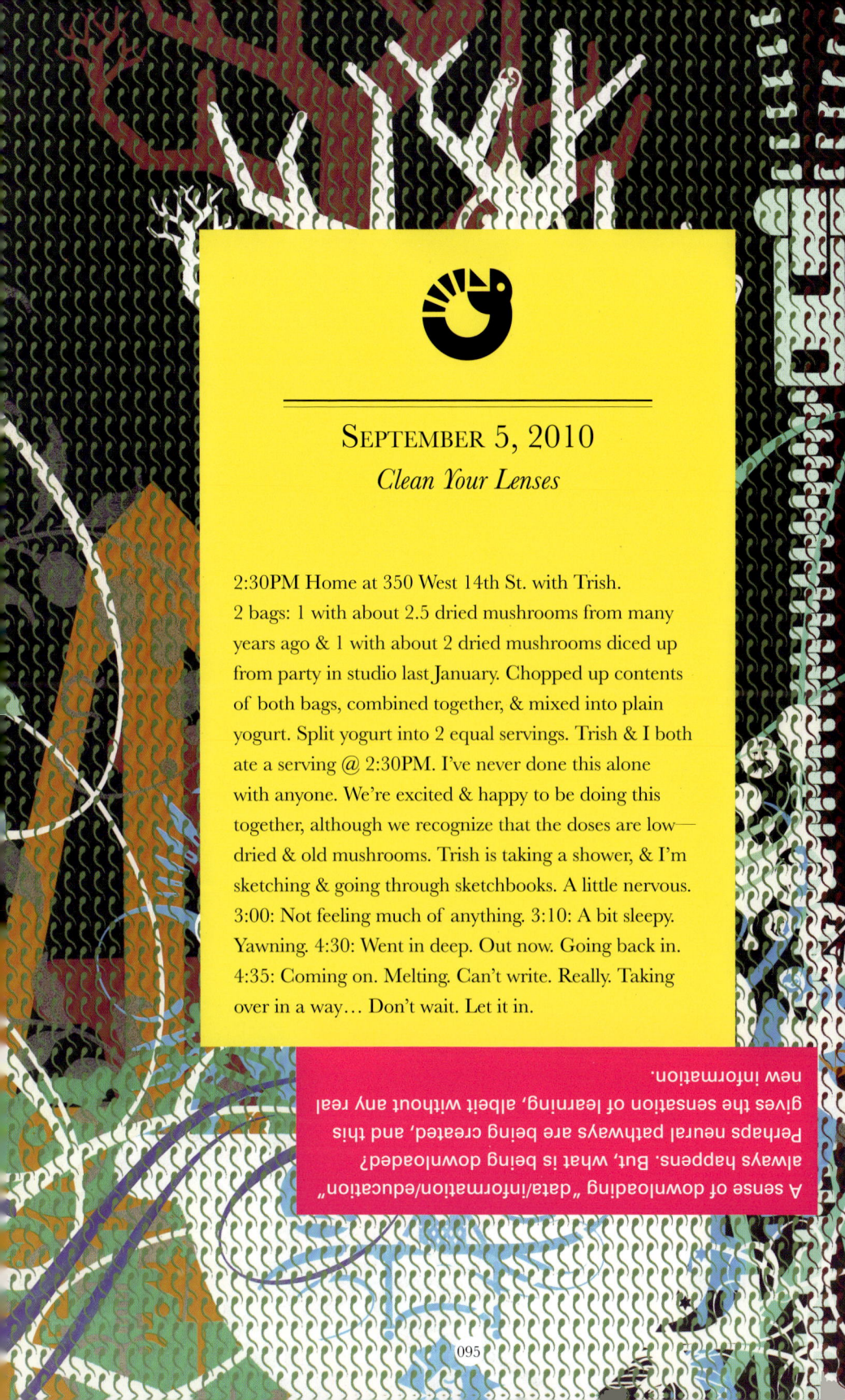

SEPTEMBER 5, 2010
Clean Your Lenses

2:30PM Home at 350 West 14th St. with Trish.
2 bags: 1 with about 2.5 dried mushrooms from many
years ago & 1 with about 2 dried mushrooms diced up
from party in studio last January. Chopped up contents
of both bags, combined together, & mixed into plain
yogurt. Split yogurt into 2 equal servings. Trish & I both
ate a serving @ 2:30PM. I've never done this alone
with anyone. We're excited & happy to be doing this
together, although we recognize that the doses are low—
dried & old mushrooms. Trish is taking a shower, & I'm
sketching & going through sketchbooks. A little nervous.
3:00: Not feeling much of anything. 3:10: A bit sleepy.
Yawning. 4:30: Went in deep. Out now. Going back in.
4:35: Coming on. Melting. Can't write. Really. Taking
over in a way… Don't wait. Let it in.

A sense of downloading "data/information/education"
always happens. But, what is being downloaded?
Perhaps neural pathways are being created, and this
gives the sensation of learning, albeit without any real
new information.

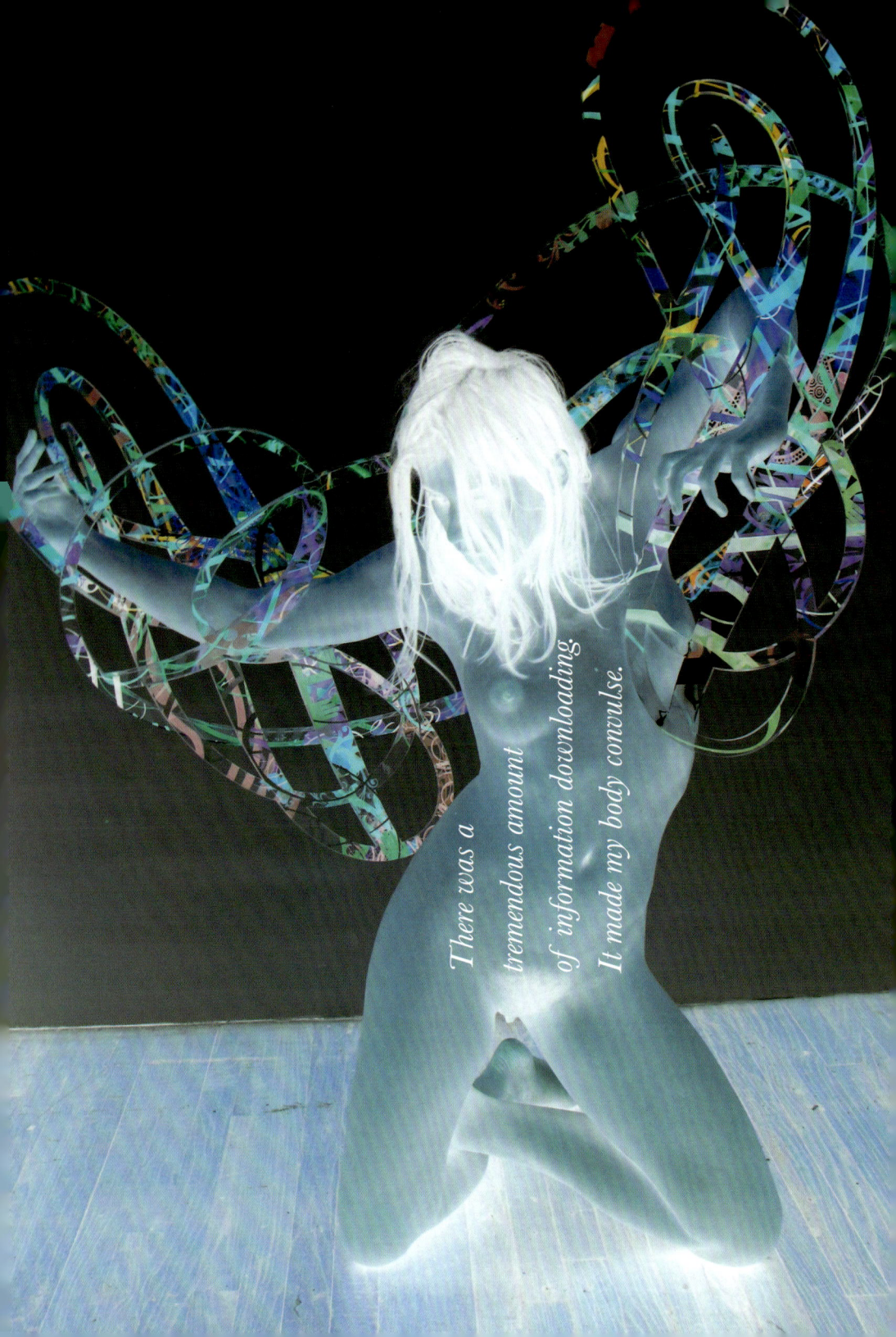

There was a tremendous amount of information downloading. It made my body convulse.

September 5, 2010

By 7PM, we were both fine enough to go out to dinner in the neighborhood. Lots of insight and downloading of data/information/education. Didn't go to other worlds, but was communicating with them. Others. Aliens of sorts. Same messages as always reconfirmed. Revisiting is like cleaning your lenses. Everything is crystal clear now/again. Stay concentrated on the work. Everything is clear concerning the directions to pursue & with whom to work. There was a tremendous amount of information downloading. It made my body convulse. Many insights and realizations. Career ambition should be avoided; instead, stay focused on the work and remain open so the universe can provide & fate/destiny can flow through you. Don't want it; let it.—Don't seek fame/fortune/success. Instead, just let it happen. Instead, just stay focused on making honest work that is unique to me—work that only I can make as a result of my experiences and history in this space/time.

Felt like I could come back out to any number of different infinite dimensions/universes—this world experiences. Felt as though I really could shape this world to be anything. I want to serve the work. Keep

An insignificant but humorous side note: Trish and I both felt fine enough to go out to dinner soon after our co-trip. When we got to the restaurant and ordered tea, it came set as a pot of hot water, tea bags, and two cups. We both sat there not knowing what to do. We kept asking each other, "How does tea work?" "I don't know. I thought you knew how tea worked." The waiter eventually showed us.

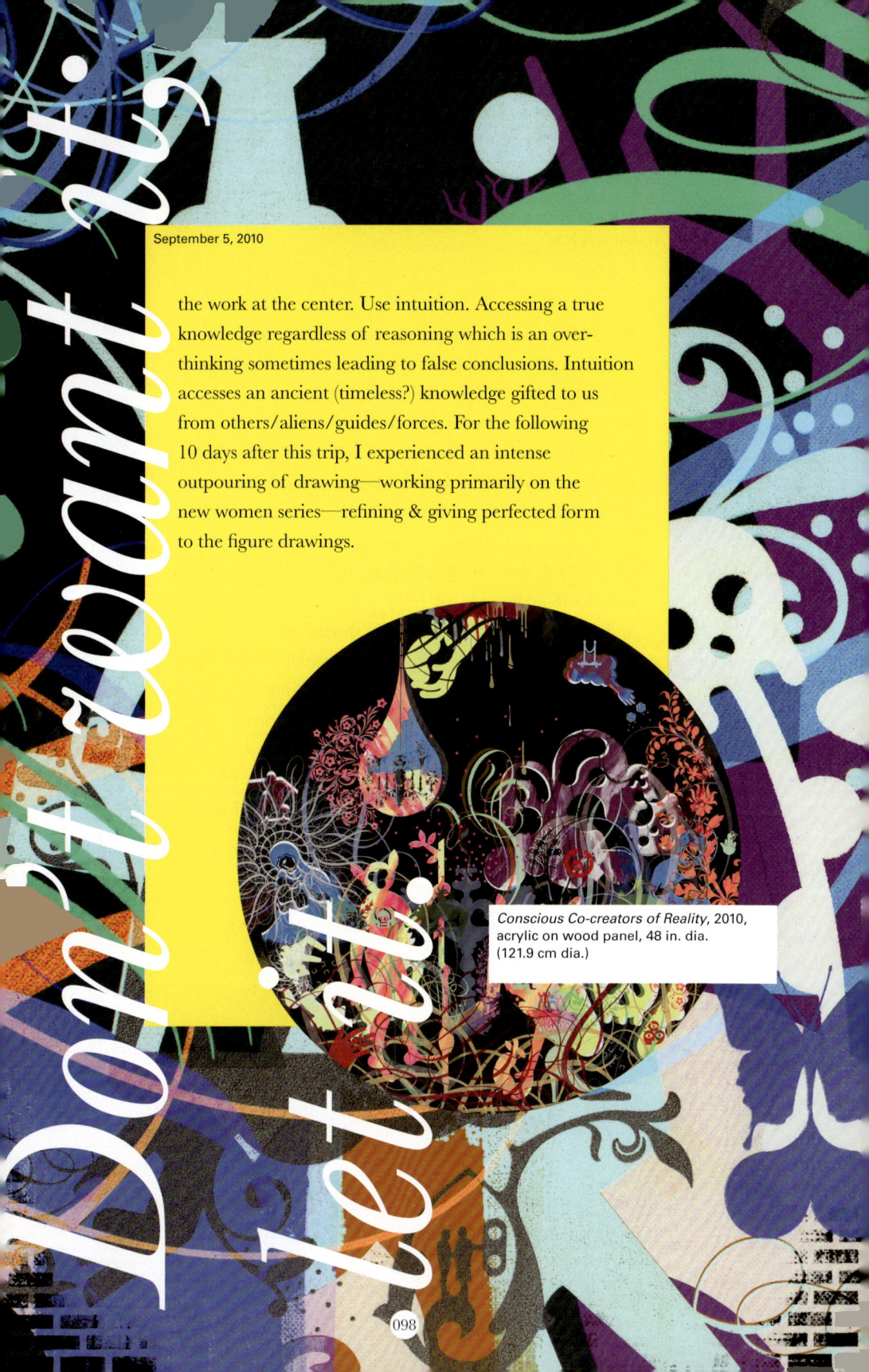

September 5, 2010

the work at the center. Use intuition. Accessing a true knowledge regardless of reasoning which is an over-thinking sometimes leading to false conclusions. Intuition accesses an ancient (timeless?) knowledge gifted to us from others/aliens/guides/forces. For the following 10 days after this trip, I experienced an intense outpouring of drawing—working primarily on the new women series—refining & giving perfected form to the figure drawings.

Conscious Co-creators of Reality, 2010, acrylic on wood panel, 48 in. dia. (121.9 cm dia.)

Don't want it?

let it.

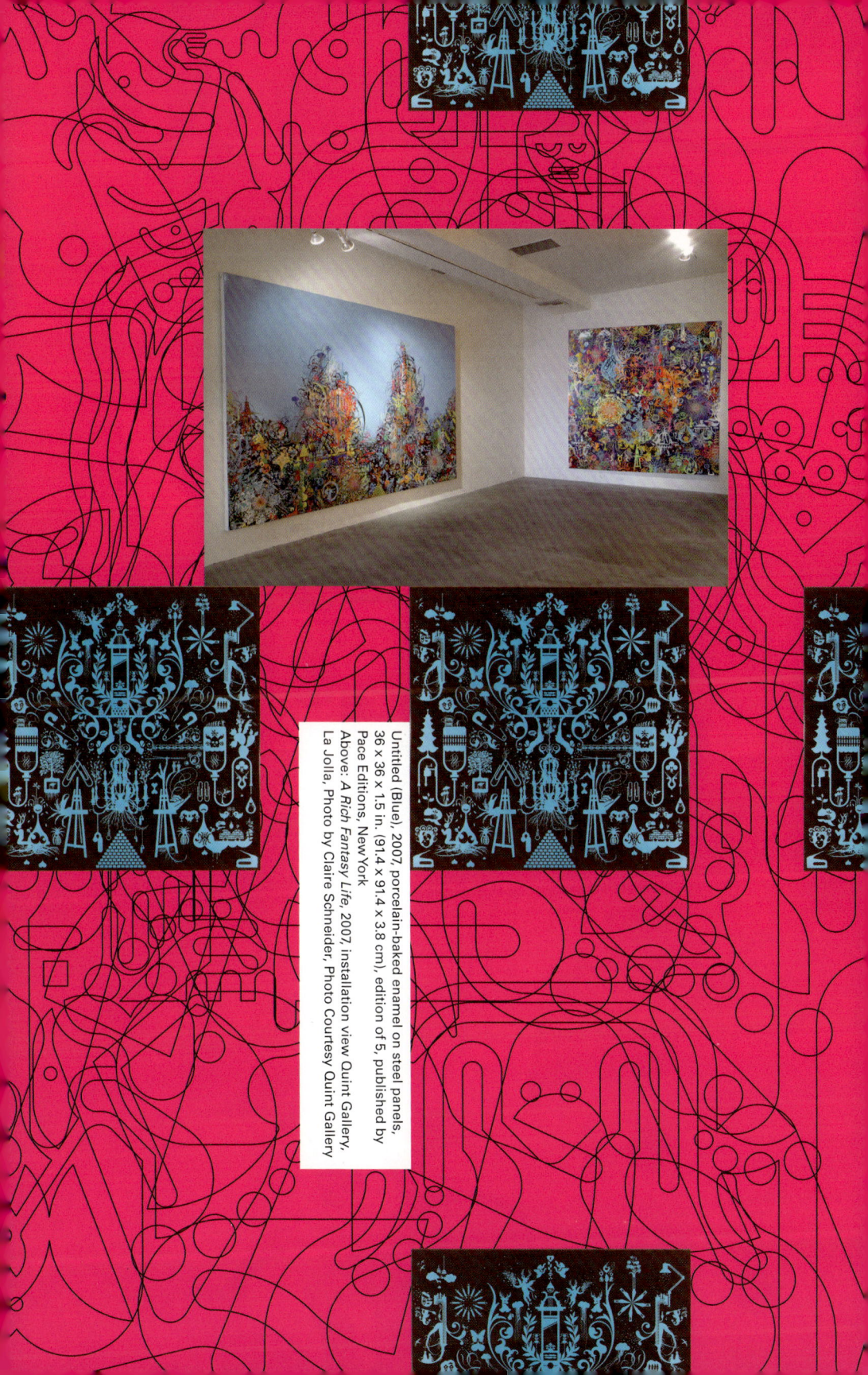

Untitled (Blue), 2007, porcelain-baked enamel on steel panels, 36 x 36 x 1.5 in. (91.4 x 91.4 x 3.8 cm), edition of 5, published by Pace Editions, New York

Above: *A Rich Fantasy Life*, 2007, installation view Quint Gallery, La Jolla, Photo by Claire Schneider, Photo Courtesy Quint Gallery

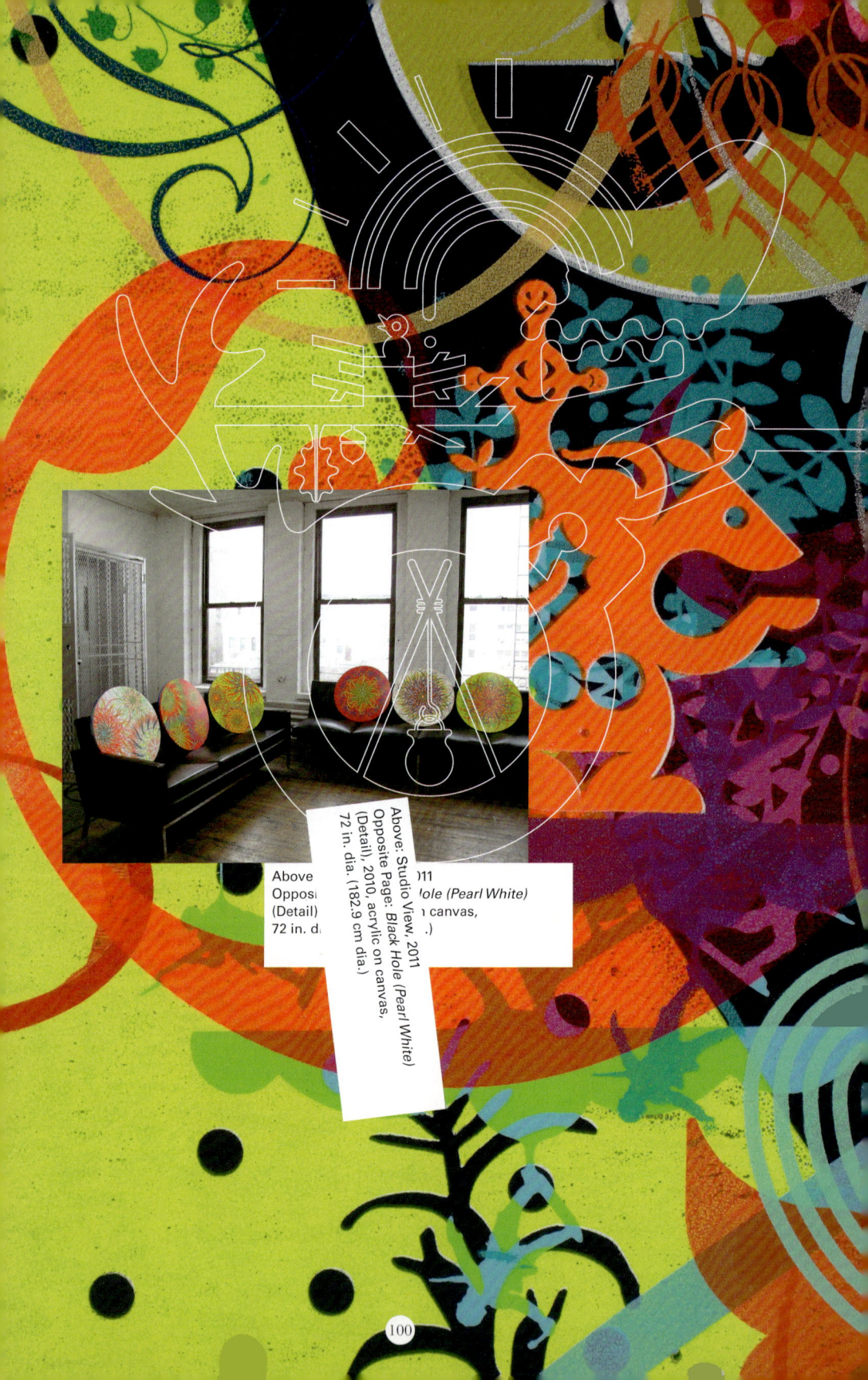

Above: Studio View, 2011
Opposite Page: Black Hole (Pearl White)
(Detail), 2010, acrylic on canvas,
72 in. dia. (182.9 cm dia.)

Above: 011
Opposi: lole (Pearl White)
(Detail) n canvas,
72 in. d

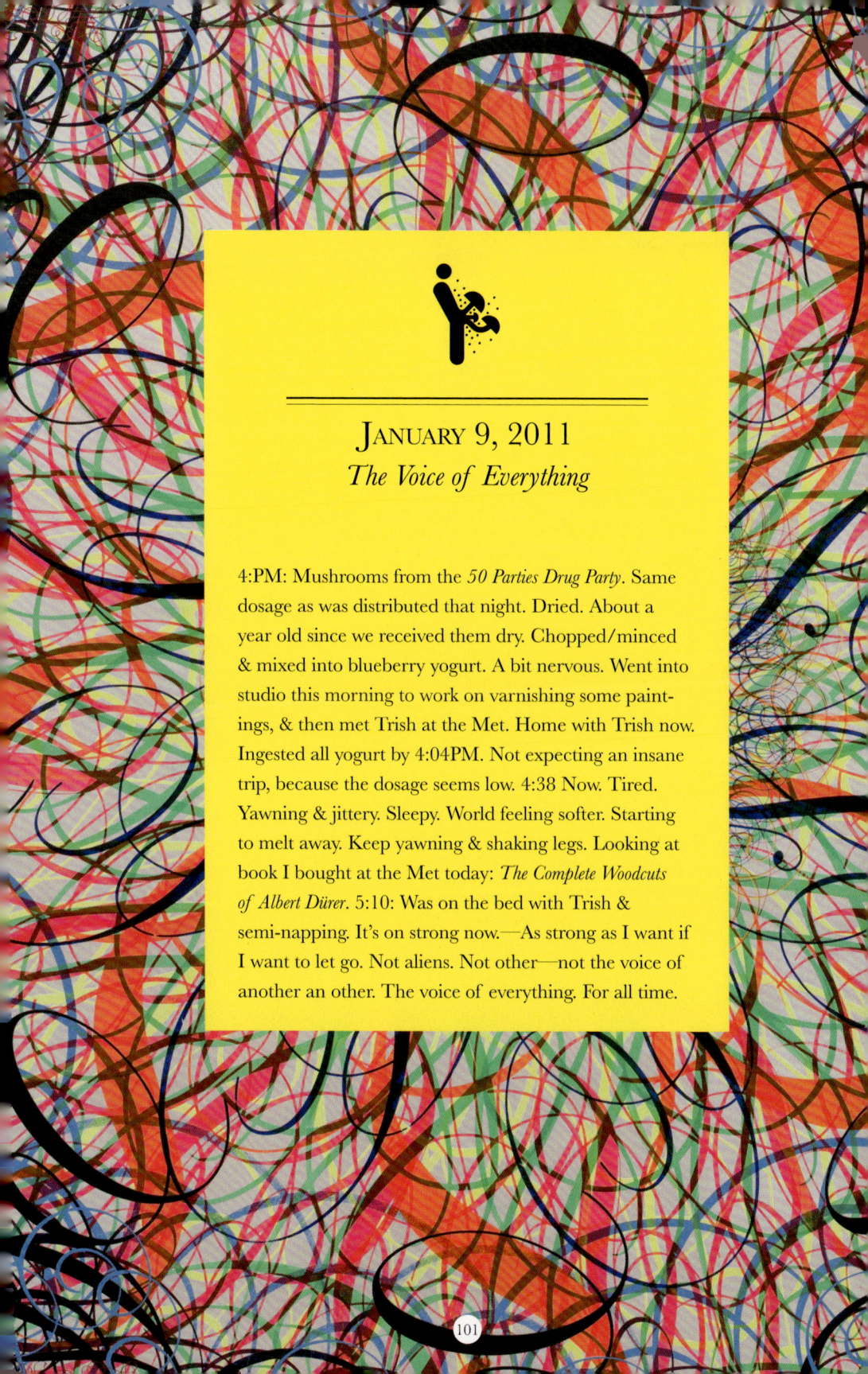

JANUARY 9, 2011
The Voice of Everything

4:PM: Mushrooms from the *50 Parties Drug Party*. Same dosage as was distributed that night. Dried. About a year old since we received them dry. Chopped/minced & mixed into blueberry yogurt. A bit nervous. Went into studio this morning to work on varnishing some paintings, & then met Trish at the Met. Home with Trish now. Ingested all yogurt by 4:04PM. Not expecting an insane trip, because the dosage seems low. 4:38 Now. Tired. Yawning & jittery. Sleepy. World feeling softer. Starting to melt away. Keep yawning & shaking legs. Looking at book I bought at the Met today: *The Complete Woodcuts of Albert Dürer*. 5:10: Was on the bed with Trish & semi-napping. It's on strong now.—As strong as I want if I want to let go. Not aliens. Not other—not the voice of another an other. The voice of everything. For all time.

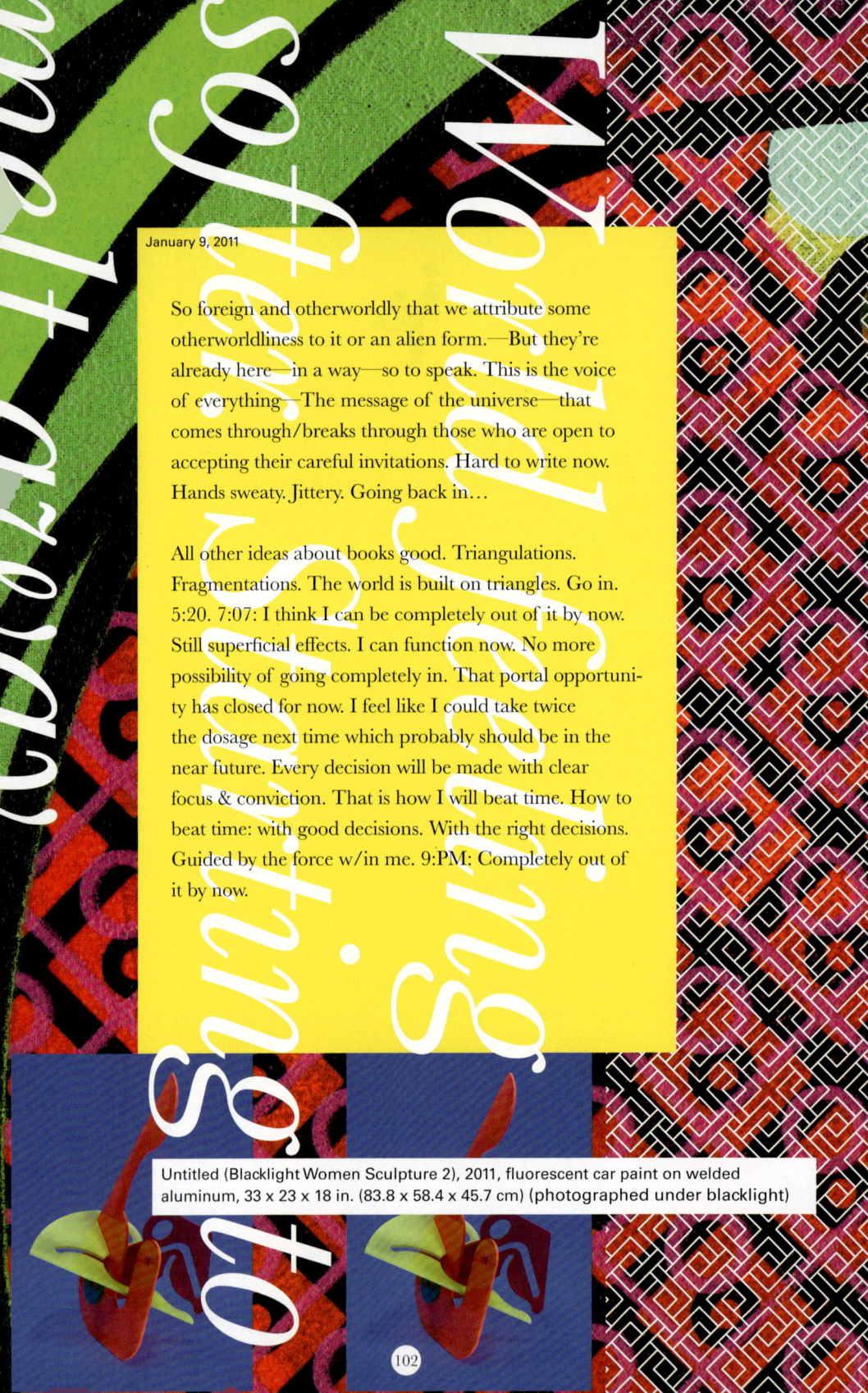

January 9, 2011

So foreign and otherworldly that we attribute some otherworldliness to it or an alien form.—But they're already here—in a way—so to speak. This is the voice of everything—The message of the universe—that comes through/breaks through those who are open to accepting their careful invitations. Hard to write now. Hands sweaty. Jittery. Going back in…

All other ideas about books good. Triangulations. Fragmentations. The world is built on triangles. Go in. 5:20. 7:07: I think I can be completely out of it by now. Still superficial effects. I can function now. No more possibility of going completely in. That portal opportunity has closed for now. I feel like I could take twice the dosage next time which probably should be in the near future. Every decision will be made with clear focus & conviction. That is how I will beat time. How to beat time: with good decisions. With the right decisions. Guided by the force w/in me. 9:PM: Completely out of it by now.

Untitled (Blacklight Women Sculpture 2), 2011, fluorescent car paint on welded aluminum, 33 x 23 x 18 in. (83.8 x 58.4 x 45.7 cm) (photographed under blacklight)

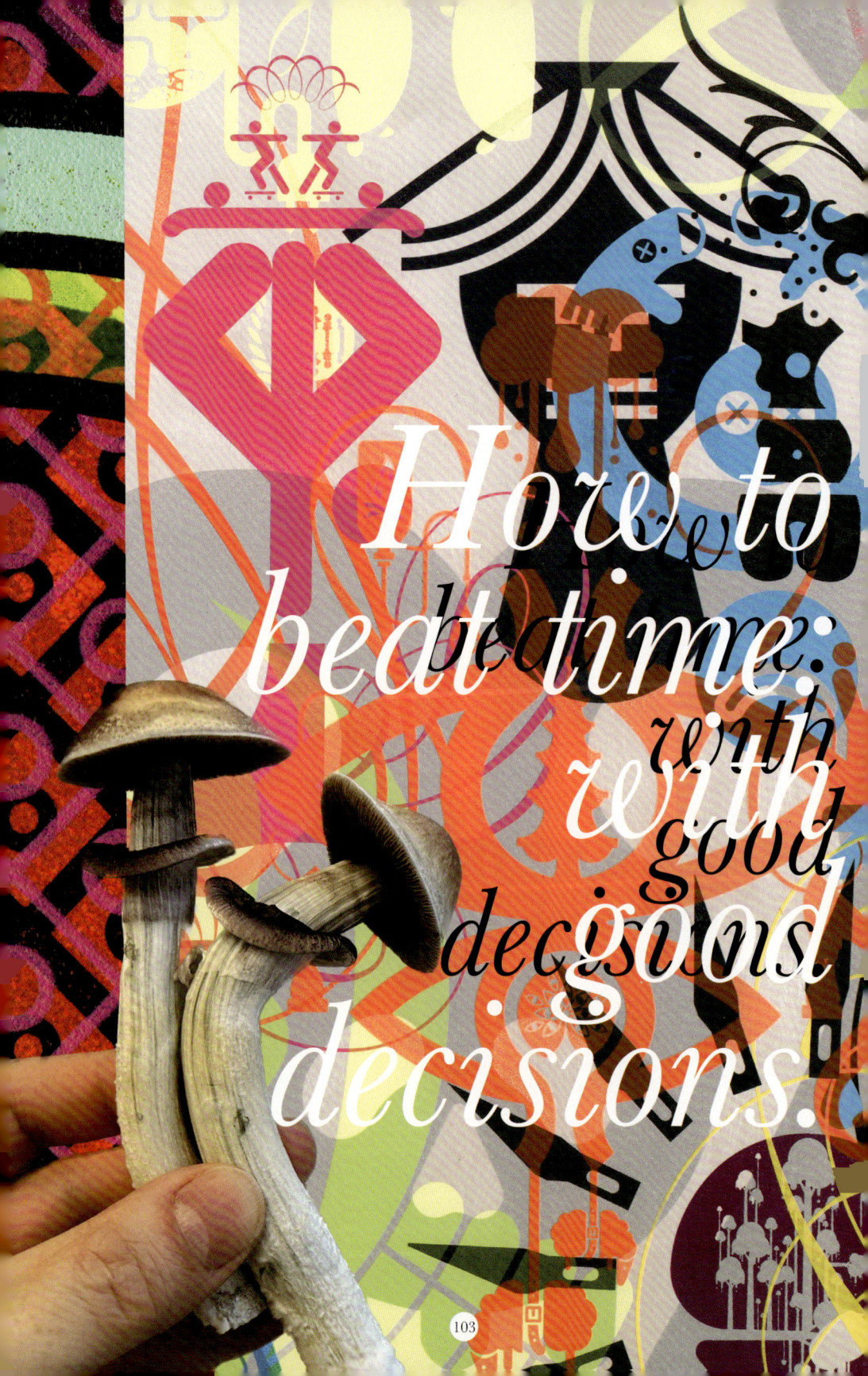

How to beat time: with good decisions.

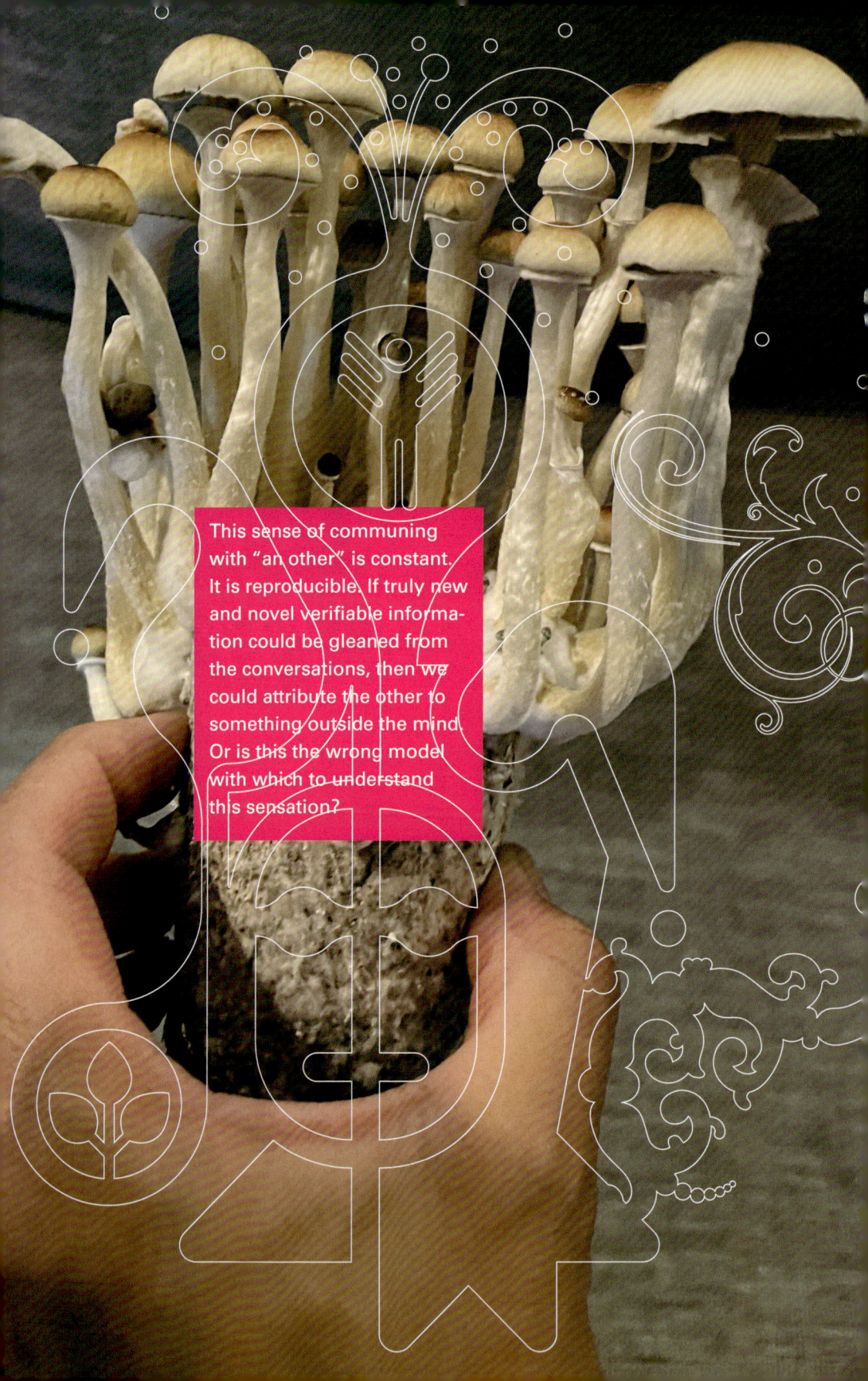

This sense of communing with "an other" is constant. It is reproducible. If truly new and novel verifiable information could be gleaned from the conversations, then we could attribute the other to something outside the mind. Or is this the wrong model with which to understand this sensation?

JUNE 18, 2016

Every Moment Is an Opportunity to Choose

Studio. NYC. 2 small bags of crushed mushrooms
> 5 yrs. old—left over from the *50 Parties*. Mixed in a
bowl of applesauce. Ate quickly & finished at 11:25AM.
I have no idea what the dosage is or what the effect
will be. Trish will join me as soon as she can. A babysitter
will watch the girls at home from 11:30-5:30. Then we
have a dinner to go to. So, 6 hrs. should be enough time
to concentrate & get through this. I believe it has been
about 5 years. This is so long overdue. A lot has happened in 5 yrs., of course.

Starting to feel a little strange (11:37AM), but probably
just nerves. Making paintings, sculptures, prints, drawings, books, products, etc. + New loft/home purchase
& renovation. + Offspring. To some degree, I feel like

By this time, I was
accustomed to the
"take off" routine—
I stop being able to
write, the paper starts
to yellow, my legs get
jittery and start shak-
ing, and a general
feeling of excitement
takes over.

105

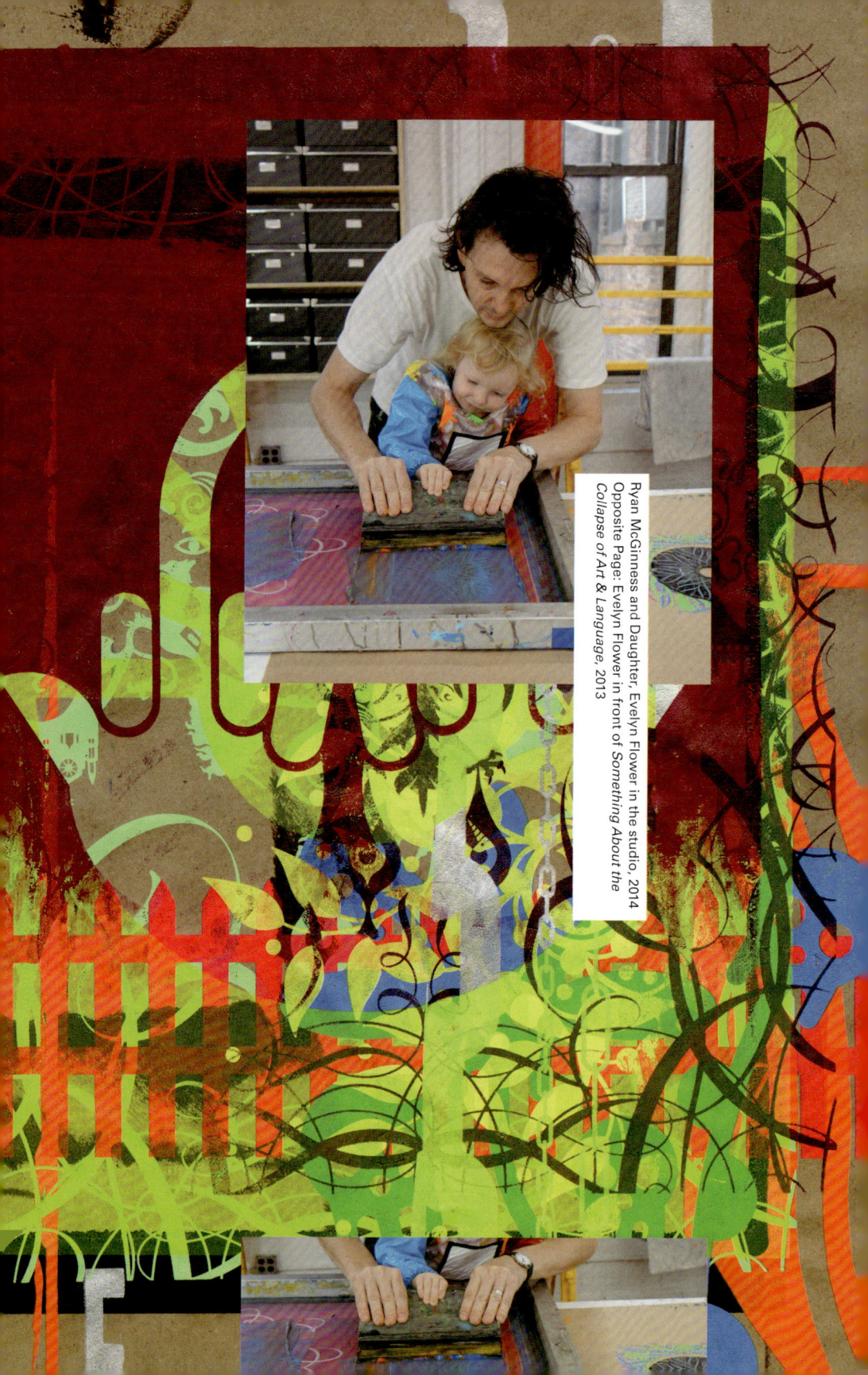

Ryan McGinness and Daughter, Evelyn Flower in the studio, 2014
Opposite Page: Evelyn Flower in front of *Something About the Collapse of Art & Language*, 2013

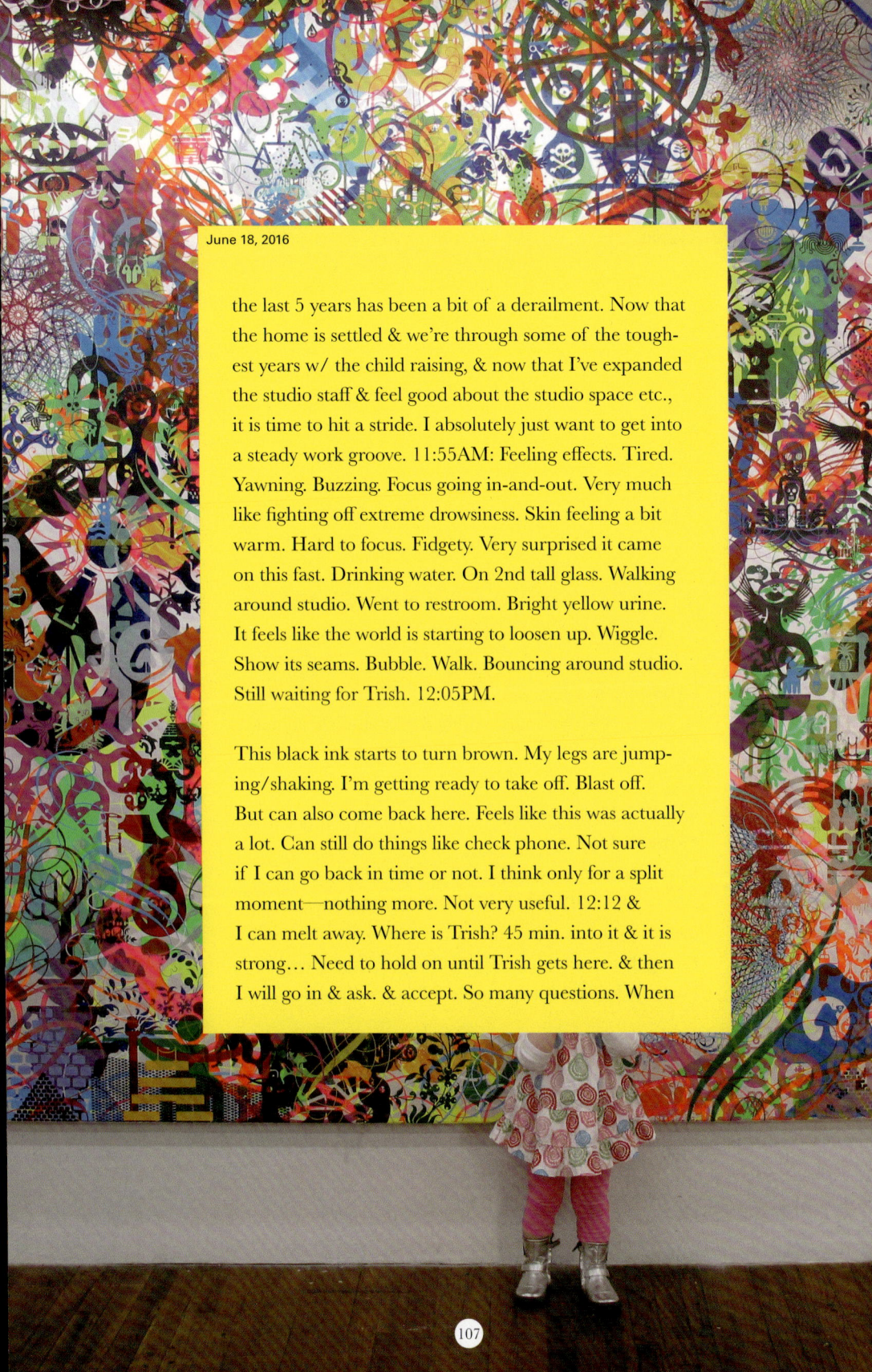

June 18, 2016

the last 5 years has been a bit of a derailment. Now that the home is settled & we're through some of the toughest years w/ the child raising, & now that I've expanded the studio staff & feel good about the studio space etc., it is time to hit a stride. I absolutely just want to get into a steady work groove. 11:55AM: Feeling effects. Tired. Yawning. Buzzing. Focus going in-and-out. Very much like fighting off extreme drowsiness. Skin feeling a bit warm. Hard to focus. Fidgety. Very surprised it came on this fast. Drinking water. On 2nd tall glass. Walking around studio. Went to restroom. Bright yellow urine. It feels like the world is starting to loosen up. Wiggle. Show its seams. Bubble. Walk. Bouncing around studio. Still waiting for Trish. 12:05PM.

This black ink starts to turn brown. My legs are jumping/shaking. I'm getting ready to take off. Blast off. But can also come back here. Feels like this was actually a lot. Can still do things like check phone. Not sure if I can go back in time or not. I think only for a split moment—nothing more. Not very useful. 12:12 & I can melt away. Where is Trish? 45 min. into it & it is strong… Need to hold on until Trish gets here. & then I will go in & ask. & accept. So many questions. When

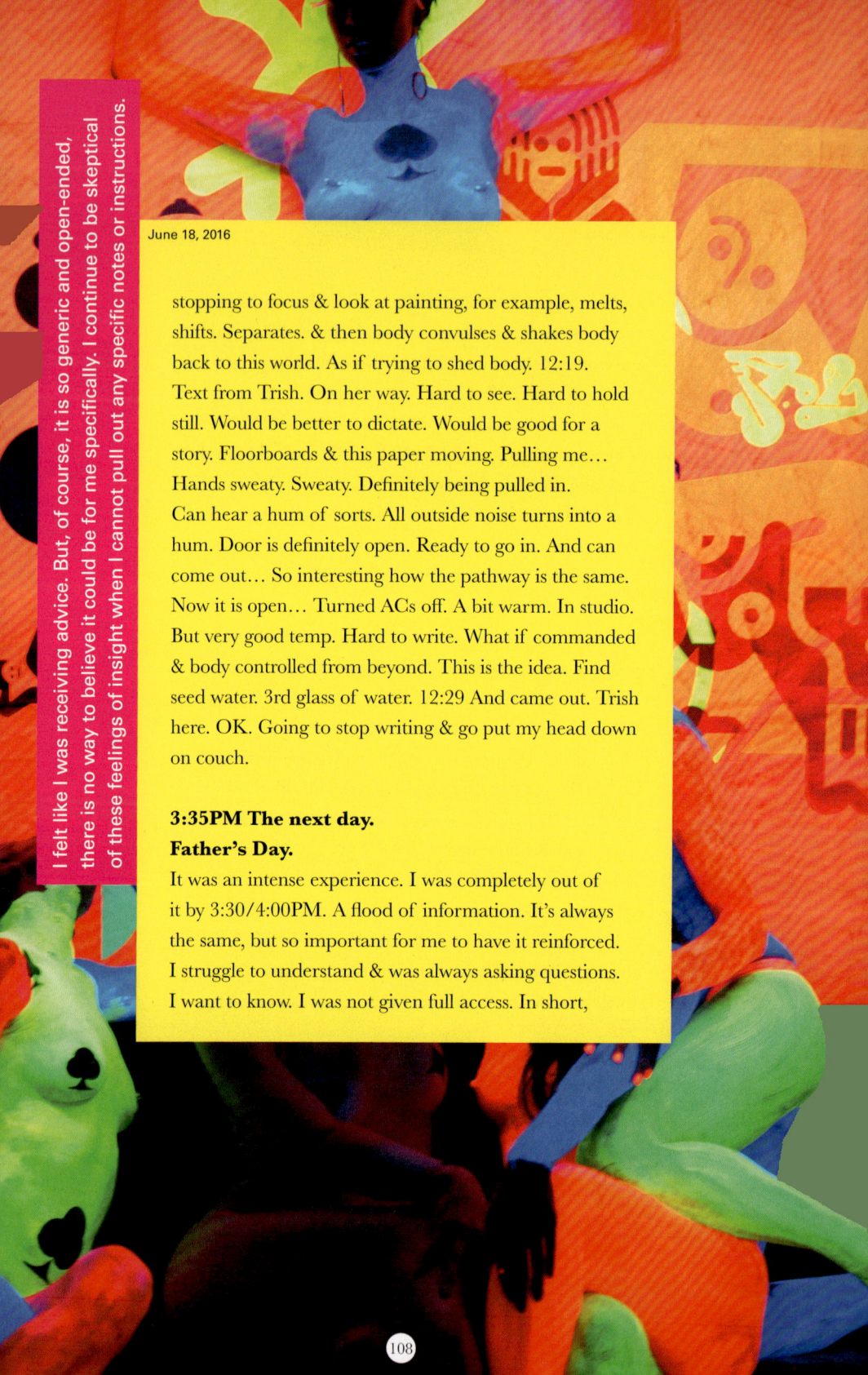

June 18, 2016

stopping to focus & look at painting, for example, melts, shifts. Separates. & then body convulses & shakes body back to this world. As if trying to shed body. 12:19. Text from Trish. On her way. Hard to see. Hard to hold still. Would be better to dictate. Would be good for a story. Floorboards & this paper moving. Pulling me… Hands sweaty. Sweaty. Definitely being pulled in. Can hear a hum of sorts. All outside noise turns into a hum. Door is definitely open. Ready to go in. And can come out… So interesting how the pathway is the same. Now it is open… Turned ACs off. A bit warm. In studio. But very good temp. Hard to write. What if commanded & body controlled from beyond. This is the idea. Find seed water. 3rd glass of water. 12:29 And came out. Trish here. OK. Going to stop writing & go put my head down on couch.

3:35PM The next day.
Father's Day.

It was an intense experience. I was completely out of it by 3:30/4:00PM. A flood of information. It's always the same, but so important for me to have it reinforced. I struggle to understand & was always asking questions. I want to know. I was not given full access. In short,

I felt like I was receiving advice. But, of course, it is so generic and open-ended, there is no way to believe it could be for me specifically. I continue to be skeptical of these feelings of insight when I cannot pull out any specific notes or instructions.

108

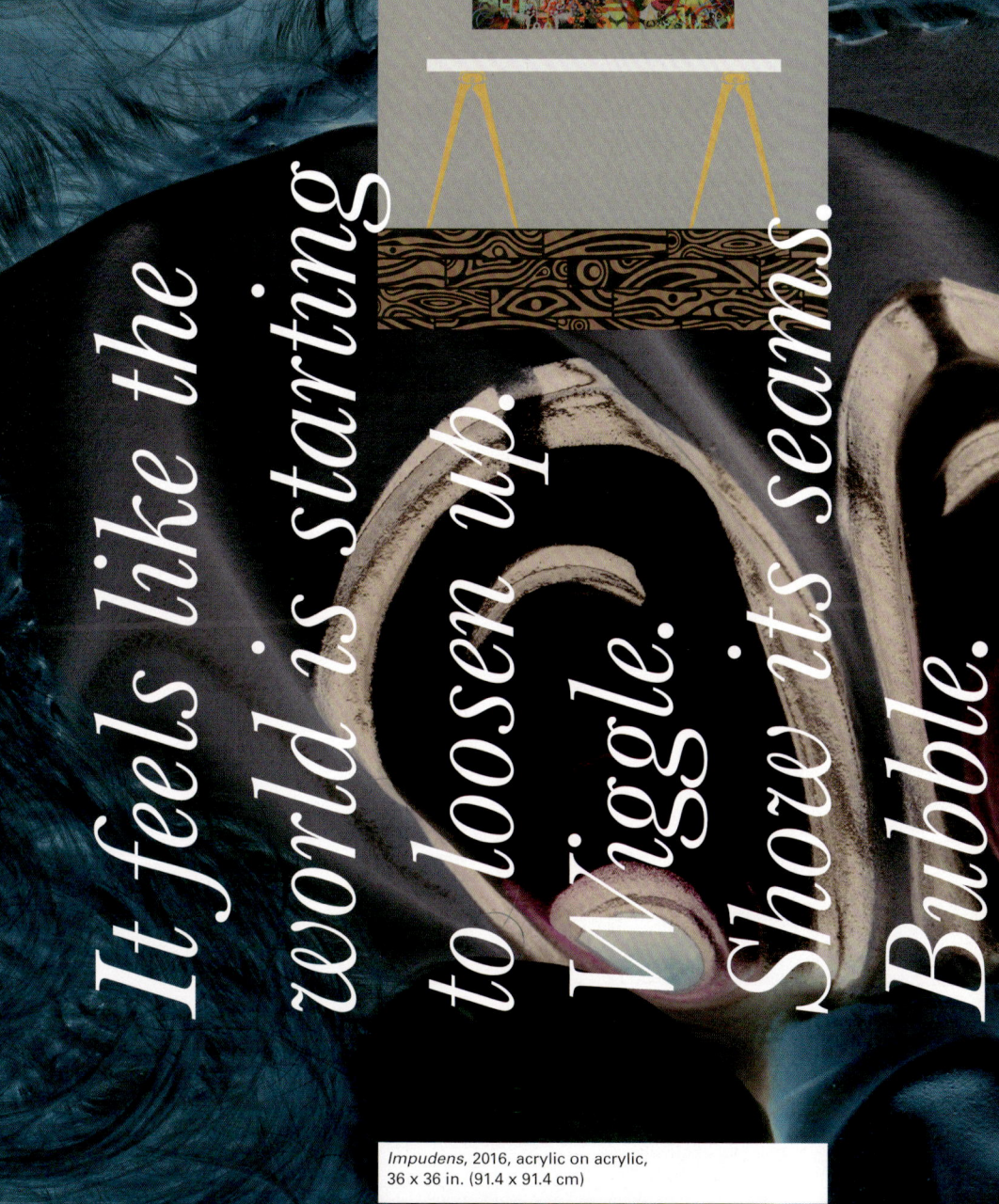

It feels like the world is starting to loosen up. Wiggle. Show its seams. Bubble.

Impudens, 2016, acrylic on acrylic, 36 x 36 in. (91.4 x 91.4 cm)

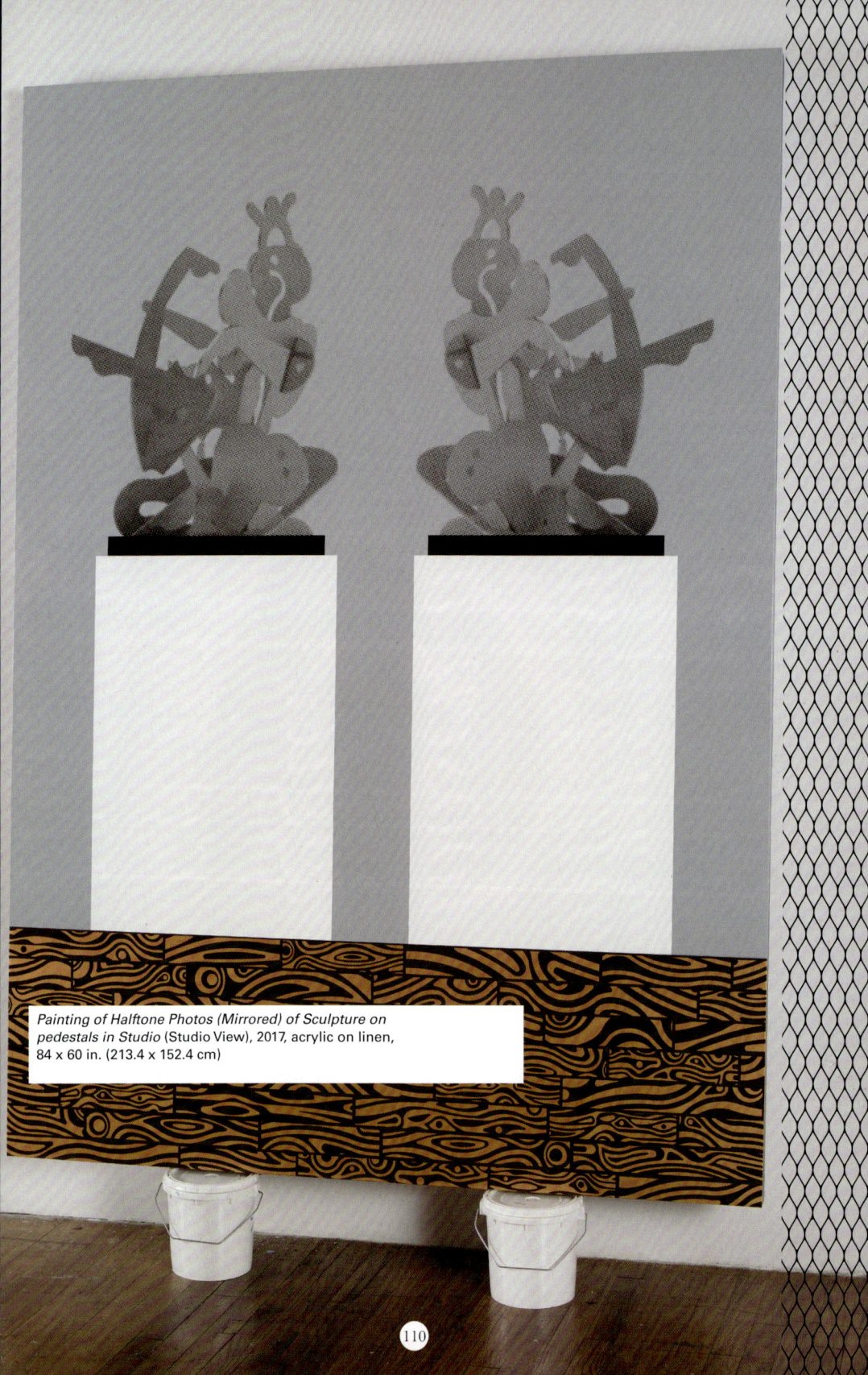

Painting of Halftone Photos (Mirrored) of Sculpture on pedestals in Studio (Studio View), 2017, acrylic on linen, 84 x 60 in. (213.4 x 152.4 cm)

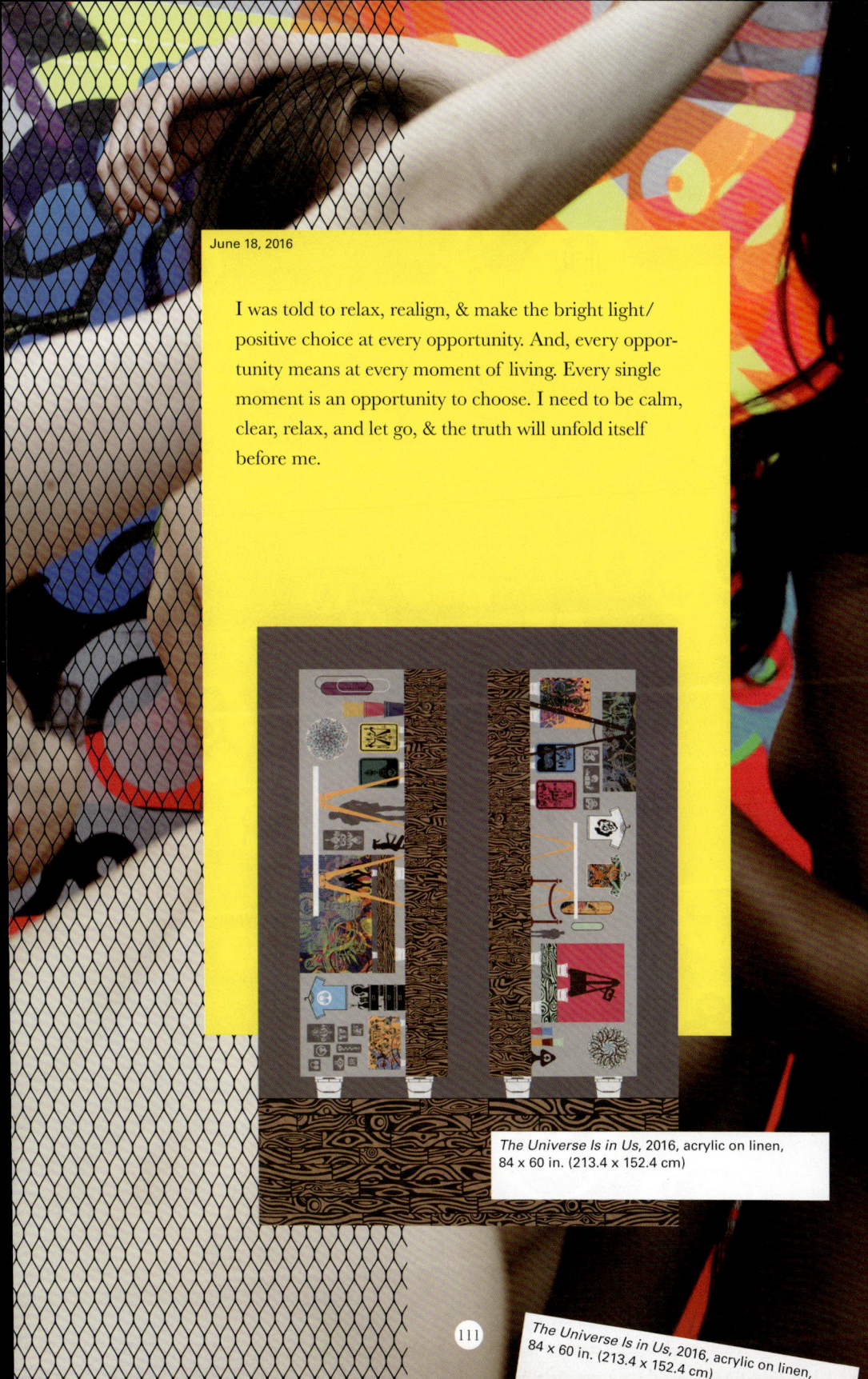

I was told to relax, realign, & make the bright light/ positive choice at every opportunity. And, every opportunity means at every moment of living. Every single moment is an opportunity to choose. I need to be calm, clear, relax, and let go, & the truth will unfold itself before me.

The Universe Is in Us, 2016, acrylic on linen, 84 x 60 in. (213.4 x 152.4 cm)

The Universe Is in Us, 2016, acrylic on linen, 84 x 60 in. (213.4 x 152.4 cm)

2017 (MICRODOSING)
Productive & Happy

January 30, 2017: Monday. 10:40AM: Microdosing begins. (x2) Capsules ≈ .2 grams each. Ecuadorian strain of P. Cubensis mushrooms grown in the studio Dec./Jan. Air-dried. Diced. Pulverized w/ small coffee bean grinder. Loosely packed into size 0 vegetarian capsules. Weighed with a digital scale after calibrating scale. Will continue to take 2 capsules (.4 grams total) every 3rd day. (Dose/Rest/Rest/Dose)—Repeat.
Goals: Using "sub perceptual" doses of psilocybin to increase & prolong periods of intense focus (for work—drawing) & combat chronic depression. In general, to increase happiness, decrease stress & be more productive.
12:17PM: I think I am starting to feel a little something, but not quite sure. Had early breakfast (7:30AM) of oatmeal, pineapple, cherries, & coffee. Had a yogurt &

Opposite Page:
Signals Painting 10
(with Color Chart), 2016,
acrylic on linen,
84 x 60 in.
(213.4 x 152.4 cm)

In 2017, I microdosed on a semi-regular schedule with the primary goal of increasing productivity. What follows is a transcript of mostly banal notes (and dietary records) providing very little insights into the psychedelic experience. These transcripts are included in order to provide as complete and comprehensive a picture of the range of trips I have taken. Admittedly, these are on the boring end of the spectrum.

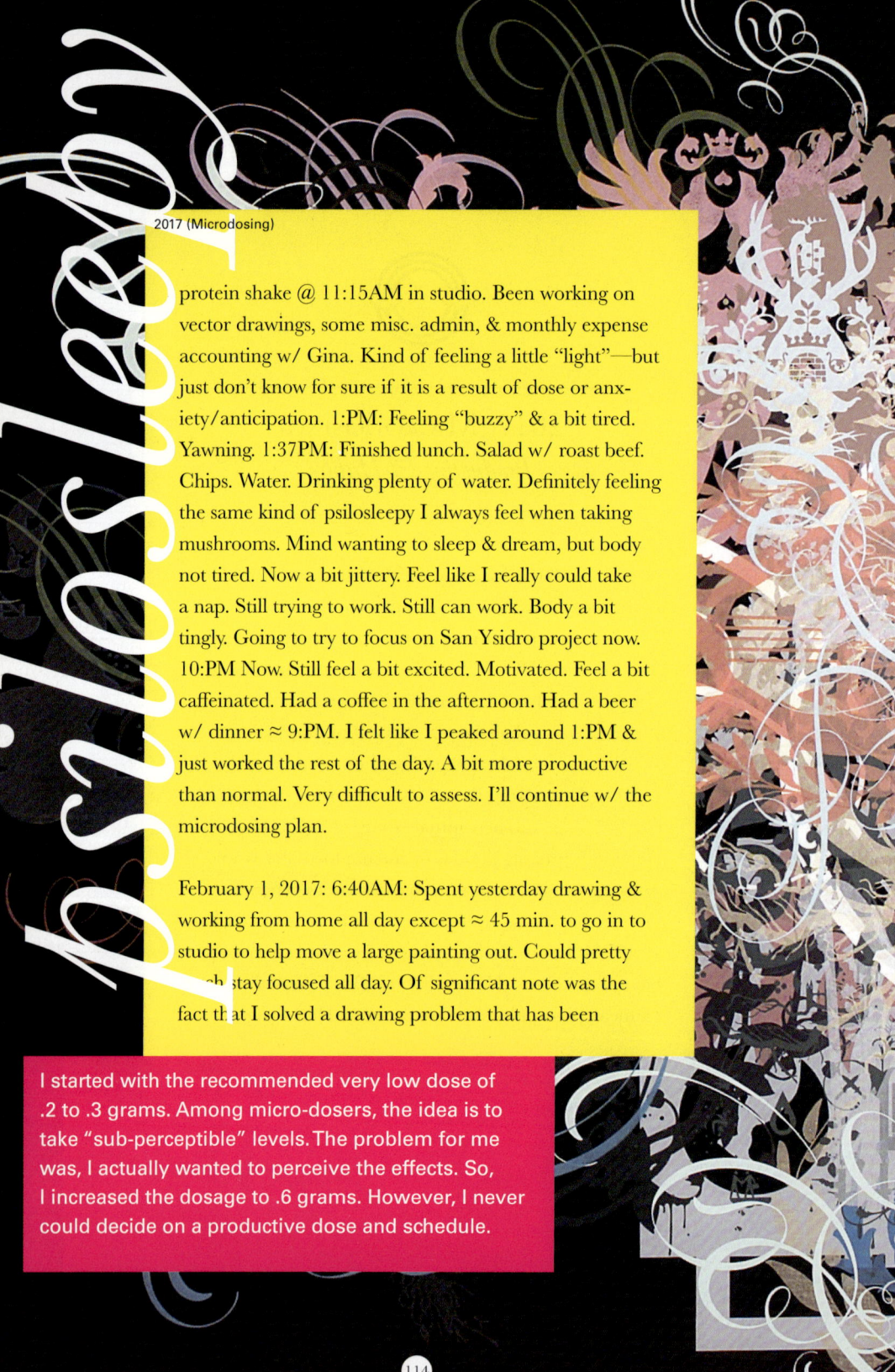

psilosleep?

protein shake @ 11:15AM in studio. Been working on vector drawings, some misc. admin, & monthly expense accounting w/ Gina. Kind of feeling a little "light"—but just don't know for sure if it is a result of dose or anxiety/anticipation. 1:PM: Feeling "buzzy" & a bit tired. Yawning. 1:37PM: Finished lunch. Salad w/ roast beef. Chips. Water. Drinking plenty of water. Definitely feeling the same kind of psilosleepy I always feel when taking mushrooms. Mind wanting to sleep & dream, but body not tired. Now a bit jittery. Feel like I really could take a nap. Still trying to work. Still can work. Body a bit tingly. Going to try to focus on San Ysidro project now. 10:PM Now. Still feel a bit excited. Motivated. Feel a bit caffeinated. Had a coffee in the afternoon. Had a beer w/ dinner ≈ 9:PM. I felt like I peaked around 1:PM & just worked the rest of the day. A bit more productive than normal. Very difficult to assess. I'll continue w/ the microdosing plan.

February 1, 2017: 6:40AM: Spent yesterday drawing & working from home all day except ≈ 45 min. to go in to studio to help move a large painting out. Could pretty much stay focused all day. Of significant note was the fact that I solved a drawing problem that has been

I started with the recommended very low dose of .2 to .3 grams. Among micro-dosers, the idea is to take "sub-perceptible" levels. The problem for me was, I actually wanted to perceive the effects. So, I increased the dosage to .6 grams. However, I never could decide on a productive dose and schedule.

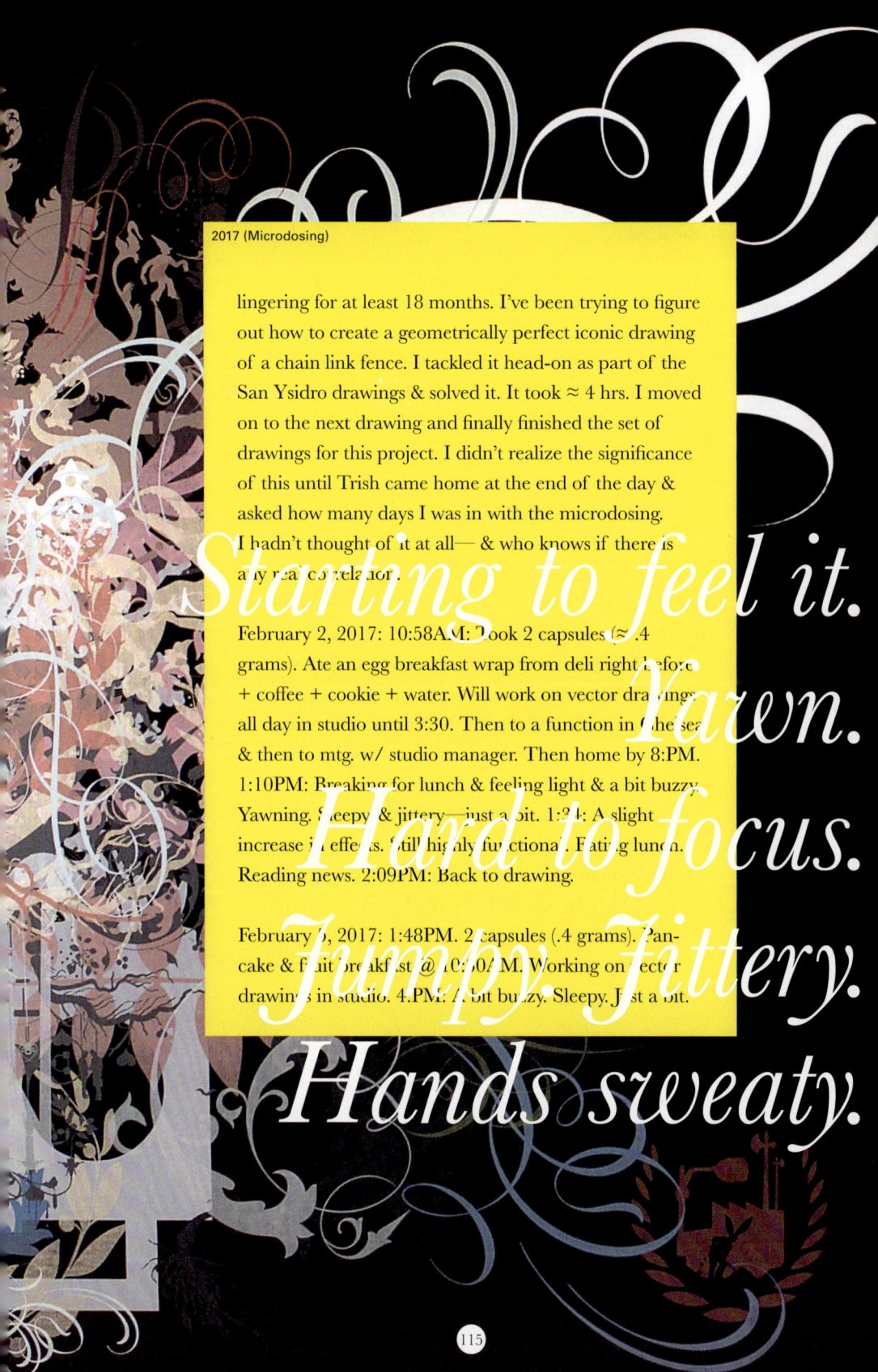

lingering for at least 18 months. I've been trying to figure out how to create a geometrically perfect iconic drawing of a chain link fence. I tackled it head-on as part of the San Ysidro drawings & solved it. It took ≈ 4 hrs. I moved on to the next drawing and finally finished the set of drawings for this project. I didn't realize the significance of this until Trish came home at the end of the day & asked how many days I was in with the microdosing. I hadn't thought of it at all— & who knows if there is any real correlation.

February 2, 2017: 10:58AM: Took 2 capsules (≈ .4 grams). Ate an egg breakfast wrap from deli right before + coffee + cookie + water. Will work on vector drawings all day in studio until 3:30. Then to a function in the sea & then to mtg. w/ studio manager. Then home by 8:PM. 1:10PM: Breaking for lunch & feeling light & a bit buzzy. Yawning. Sleepy & jittery—just a bit. 1:34: A slight increase in effects. Still highly functional. Eating lunch. Reading news. 2:09PM: Back to drawing.

February 6, 2017: 1:48PM. 2 capsules (.4 grams). Pancake & fruit breakfast @ 10:50AM. Working on vector drawings in studio. 4:PM: A bit buzzy. Sleepy. Just a bit.

Starting to feel it.

Yawn.

Hard to focus.

Jumpy. Jittery.

Hands sweaty.

All very subtle. 5:PM: Now blood is flowing. Definitely
feeling affected. A bit heightened activity but also tired
at the same time. Trying to put together some kind of
V-Day/B-Day gift for Trish by searching through archive
boxes looking for high school love letters &/or photos…

February 20, 2017: 9:33AM: 3 capsules ($\approx$ .6 grams
total). I want to increase the dosage in order to feel more.
Test more. Took 2 weeks off for trip to Turks & Caicos.
So, this is the first dose since Feb. 5th. Breakfast 2 hrs
ago: cereal, 2 oranges, & English muffin w/cream cheese
& jam. Took the capsules w/ yogurt & coffee. 11:AM
Now. Starting to feel it. Yawn. Hard to focus. Jumpy.
Jittery. Hands sweaty. Trying to get through emails &
planning… 11:35AM. Trying to drink lots of water.
.6 grams is definitely more to try to stay in control over.
Hard to hold on to here. But do-able. Still doing admin
emails & transcribing notes to sketchbook. 12:16PM:
Hard to hang on, but can still hold a conversation etc.
Finished admin work. Going to get into vector drawings
now. 1:20PM: Ate a sushi lunch. Feel more in control,
but I can't believe food had anything to do with it.
3:11PM: Over the peak & have been focused on drawing.

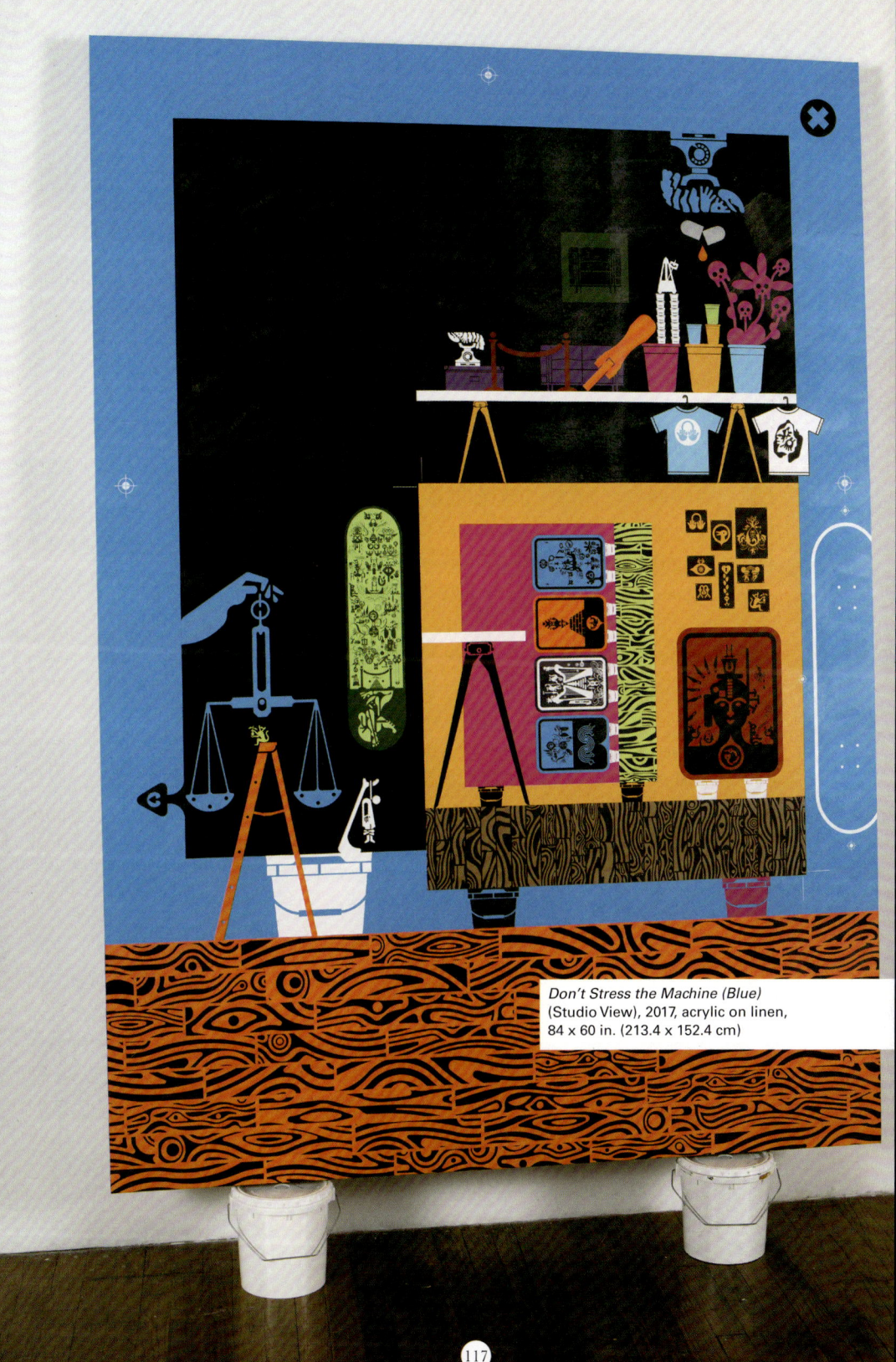

Don't Stress the Machine (Blue)
(Studio View), 2017, acrylic on linen,
84 x 60 in. (213.4 x 152.4 cm)

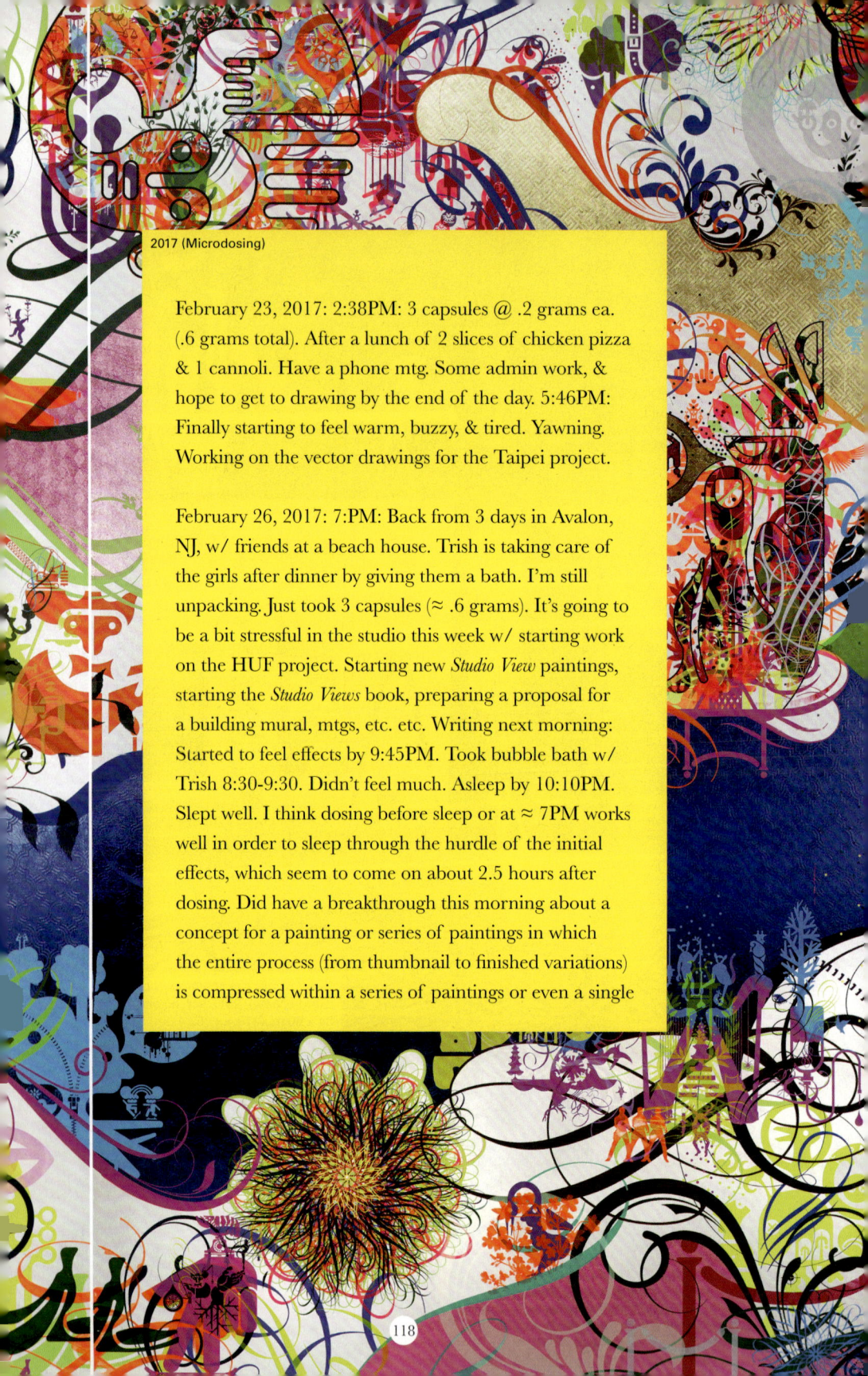

February 23, 2017: 2:38PM: 3 capsules @ .2 grams ea. (.6 grams total). After a lunch of 2 slices of chicken pizza & 1 cannoli. Have a phone mtg. Some admin work, & hope to get to drawing by the end of the day. 5:46PM: Finally starting to feel warm, buzzy, & tired. Yawning. Working on the vector drawings for the Taipei project.

February 26, 2017: 7:PM: Back from 3 days in Avalon, NJ, w/ friends at a beach house. Trish is taking care of the girls after dinner by giving them a bath. I'm still unpacking. Just took 3 capsules (≈ .6 grams). It's going to be a bit stressful in the studio this week w/ starting work on the HUF project. Starting new *Studio View* paintings, starting the *Studio Views* book, preparing a proposal for a building mural, mtgs, etc. etc. Writing next morning: Started to feel effects by 9:45PM. Took bubble bath w/ Trish 8:30-9:30. Didn't feel much. Asleep by 10:10PM. Slept well. I think dosing before sleep or at ≈ 7PM works well in order to sleep through the hurdle of the initial effects, which seem to come on about 2.5 hours after dosing. Did have a breakthrough this morning about a concept for a painting or series of paintings in which the entire process (from thumbnail to finished variations) is compressed within a series of paintings or even a single

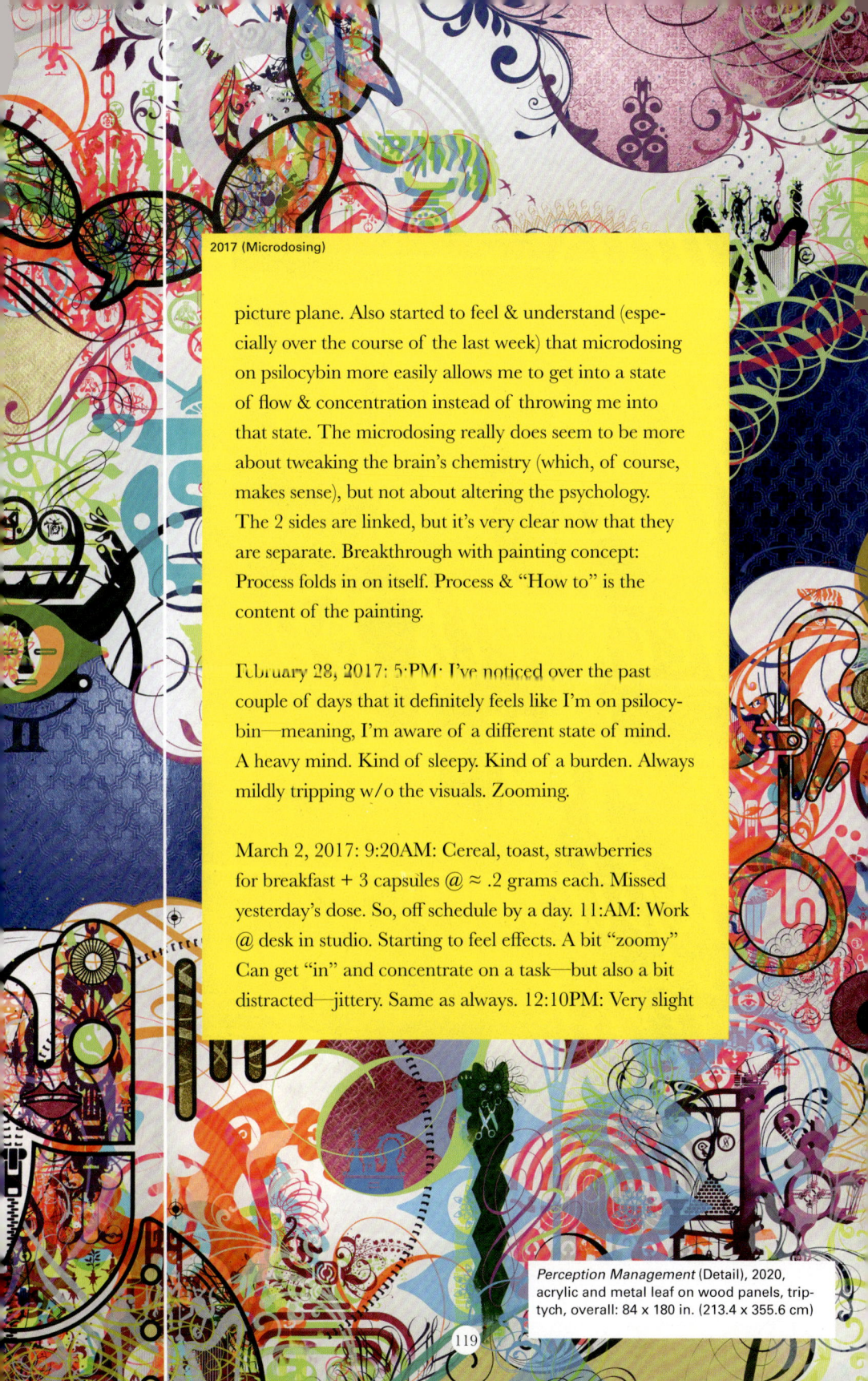

picture plane. Also started to feel & understand (especially over the course of the last week) that microdosing on psilocybin more easily allows me to get into a state of flow & concentration instead of throwing me into that state. The microdosing really does seem to be more about tweaking the brain's chemistry (which, of course, makes sense), but not about altering the psychology. The 2 sides are linked, but it's very clear now that they are separate. Breakthrough with painting concept: Process folds in on itself. Process & "How to" is the content of the painting.

February 28, 2017: 5:PM: I've noticed over the past couple of days that it definitely feels like I'm on psilocybin—meaning, I'm aware of a different state of mind. A heavy mind. Kind of sleepy. Kind of a burden. Always mildly tripping w/o the visuals. Zooming.

March 2, 2017: 9:20AM: Cereal, toast, strawberries for breakfast + 3 capsules @ ≈ .2 grams each. Missed yesterday's dose. So, off schedule by a day. 11:AM: Work @ desk in studio. Starting to feel effects. A bit "zoomy" Can get "in" and concentrate on a task—but also a bit distracted—jittery. Same as always. 12:10PM: Very slight

Perception Management (Detail), 2020, acrylic and metal leaf on wood panels, triptych, overall: 84 x 180 in. (213.4 x 355.6 cm)

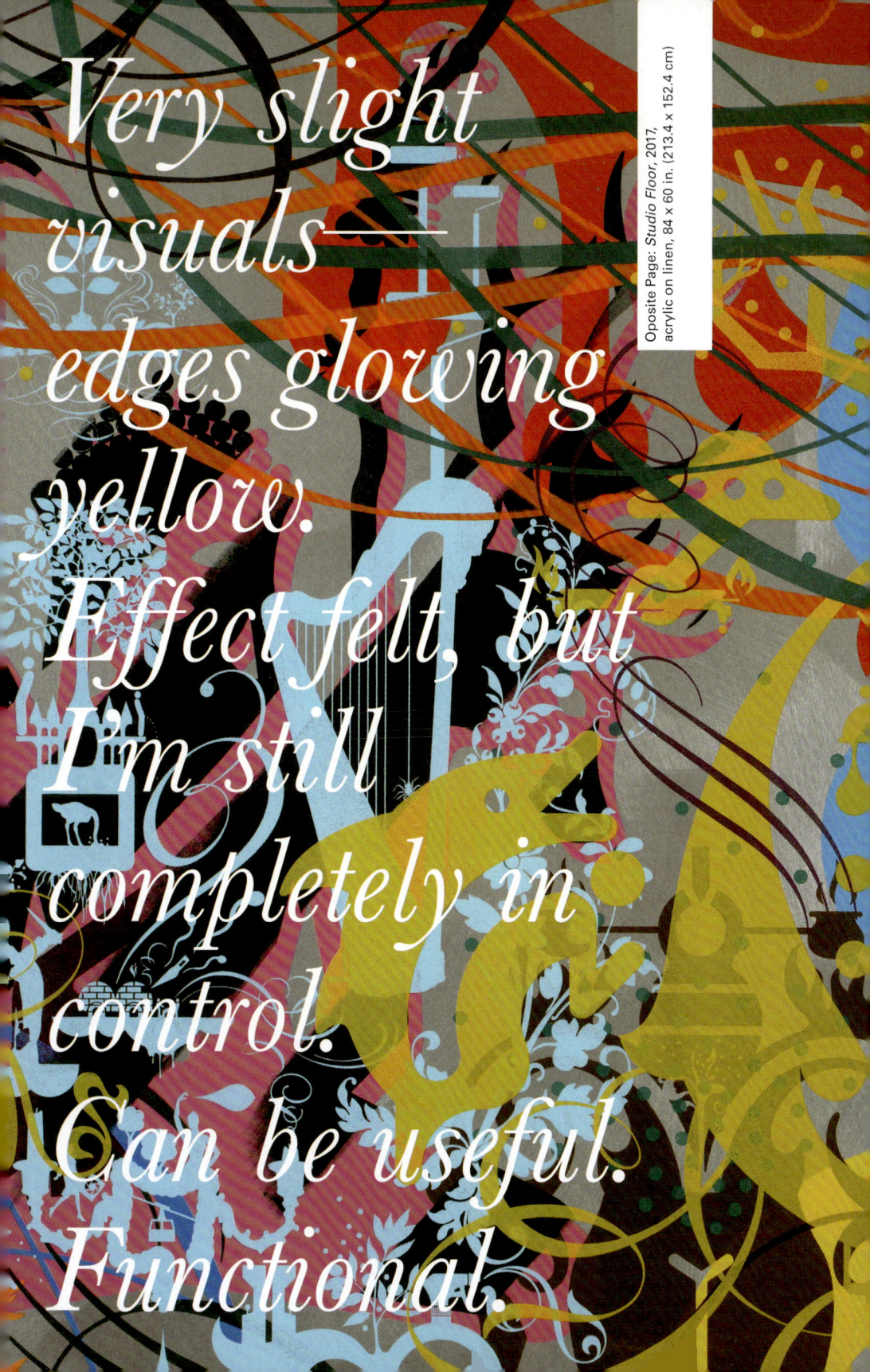

Very slight visuals— edges glowing yellow. Effect felt, but I'm still completely in control. Can be useful. Functional.

Oposite Page: *Studio Floor,* 2017, acrylic on linen, 84 x 60 in. (213.4 x 152.4 cm)

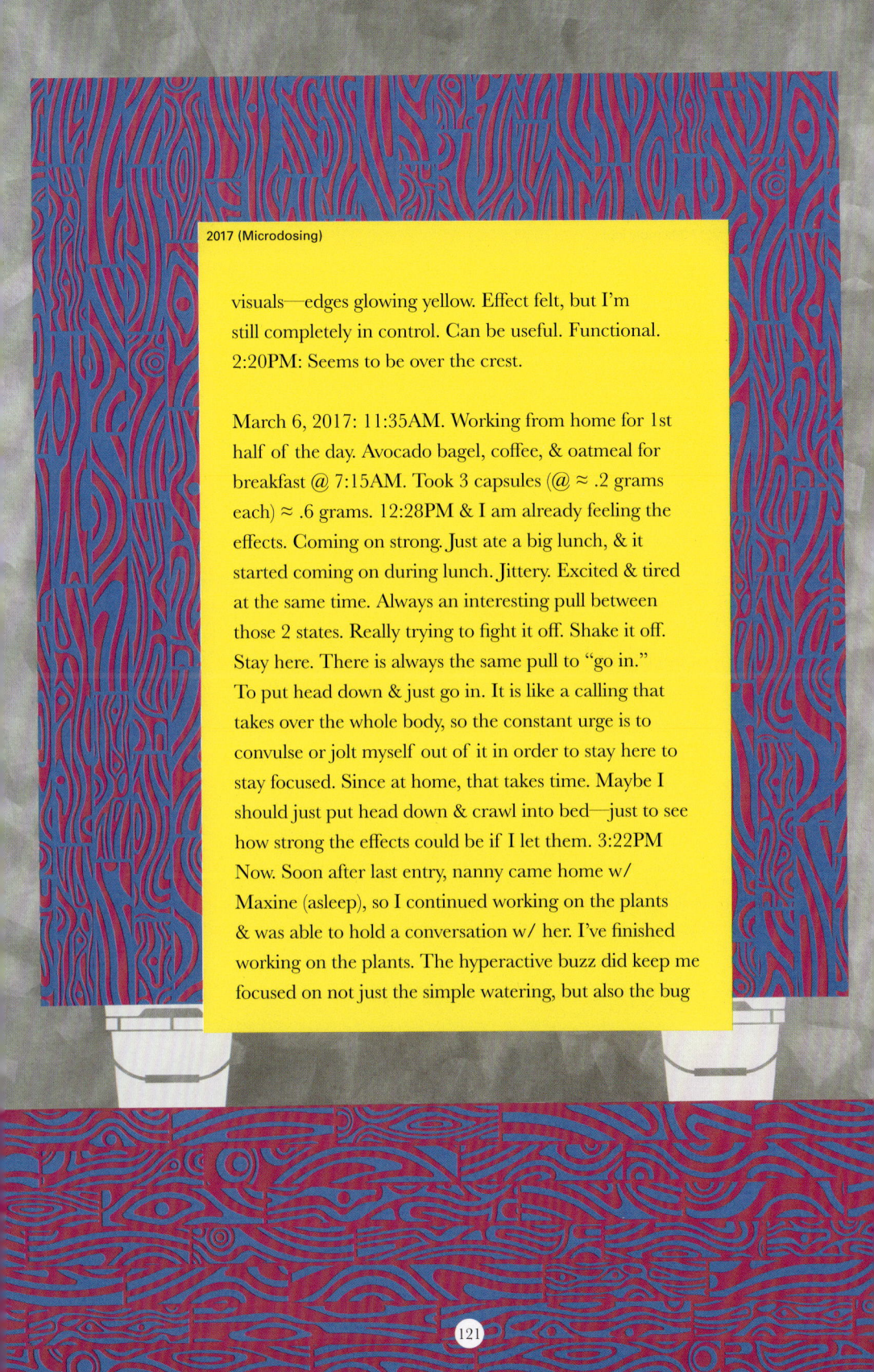

visuals—edges glowing yellow. Effect felt, but I'm still completely in control. Can be useful. Functional. 2:20PM: Seems to be over the crest.

March 6, 2017: 11:35AM. Working from home for 1st half of the day. Avocado bagel, coffee, & oatmeal for breakfast @ 7:15AM. Took 3 capsules (@ ≈ .2 grams each) ≈ .6 grams. 12:28PM & I am already feeling the effects. Coming on strong. Just ate a big lunch, & it started coming on during lunch. Jittery. Excited & tired at the same time. Always an interesting pull between those 2 states. Really trying to fight it off. Shake it off. Stay here. There is always the same pull to "go in." To put head down & just go in. It is like a calling that takes over the whole body, so the constant urge is to convulse or jolt myself out of it in order to stay here to stay focused. Since at home, that takes time. Maybe I should just put head down & crawl into bed—just to see how strong the effects could be if I let them. 3:22PM Now. Soon after last entry, nanny came home w/ Maxine (asleep), so I continued working on the plants & was able to hold a conversation w/ her. I've finished working on the plants. The hyperactive buzz did keep me focused on not just the simple watering, but also the bug

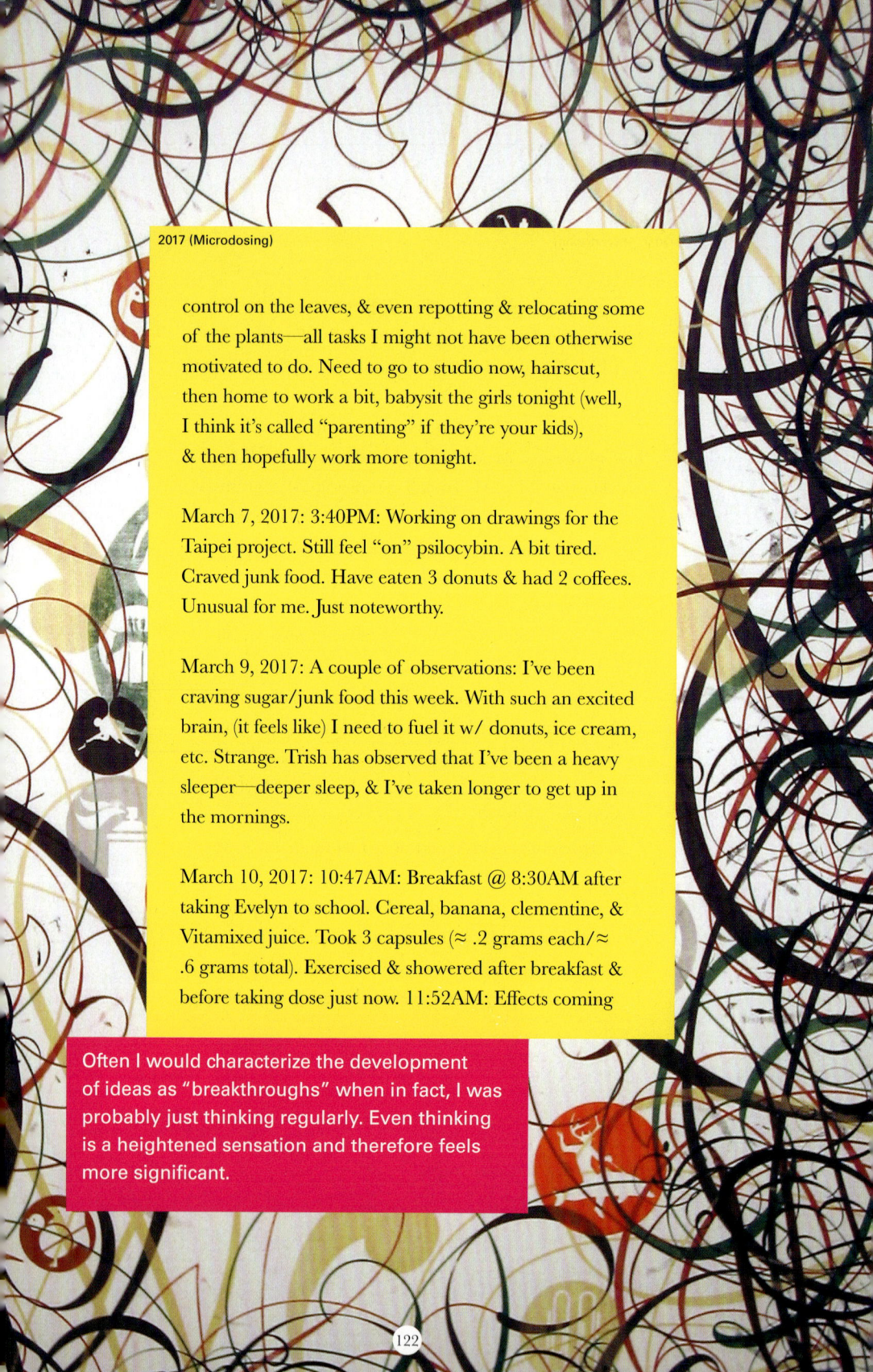

control on the leaves, & even repotting & relocating some of the plants—all tasks I might not have been otherwise motivated to do. Need to go to studio now, haircut, then home to work a bit, babysit the girls tonight (well, I think it's called "parenting" if they're your kids), & then hopefully work more tonight.

March 7, 2017: 3:40PM: Working on drawings for the Taipei project. Still feel "on" psilocybin. A bit tired. Craved junk food. Have eaten 3 donuts & had 2 coffees. Unusual for me. Just noteworthy.

March 9, 2017: A couple of observations: I've been craving sugar/junk food this week. With such an excited brain, (it feels like) I need to fuel it w/ donuts, ice cream, etc. Strange. Trish has observed that I've been a heavy sleeper—deeper sleep, & I've taken longer to get up in the mornings.

March 10, 2017: 10:47AM: Breakfast @ 8:30AM after taking Evelyn to school. Cereal, banana, clementine, & Vitamixed juice. Took 3 capsules ($\approx$ .2 grams each/$\approx$ .6 grams total). Exercised & showered after breakfast & before taking dose just now. 11:52AM: Effects coming

Often I would characterize the development of ideas as "breakthroughs" when in fact, I was probably just thinking regularly. Even thinking is a heightened sensation and therefore feels more significant.

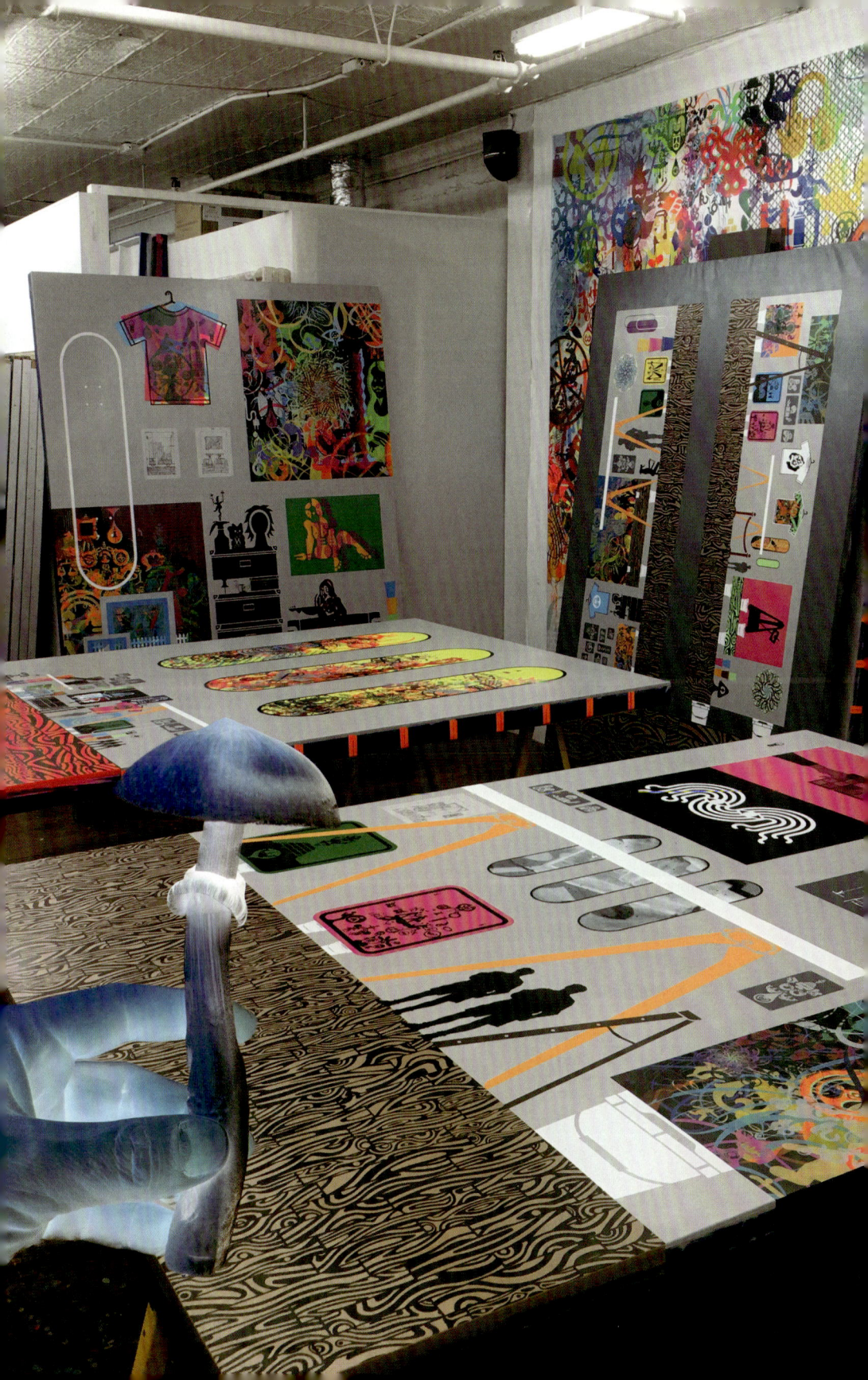

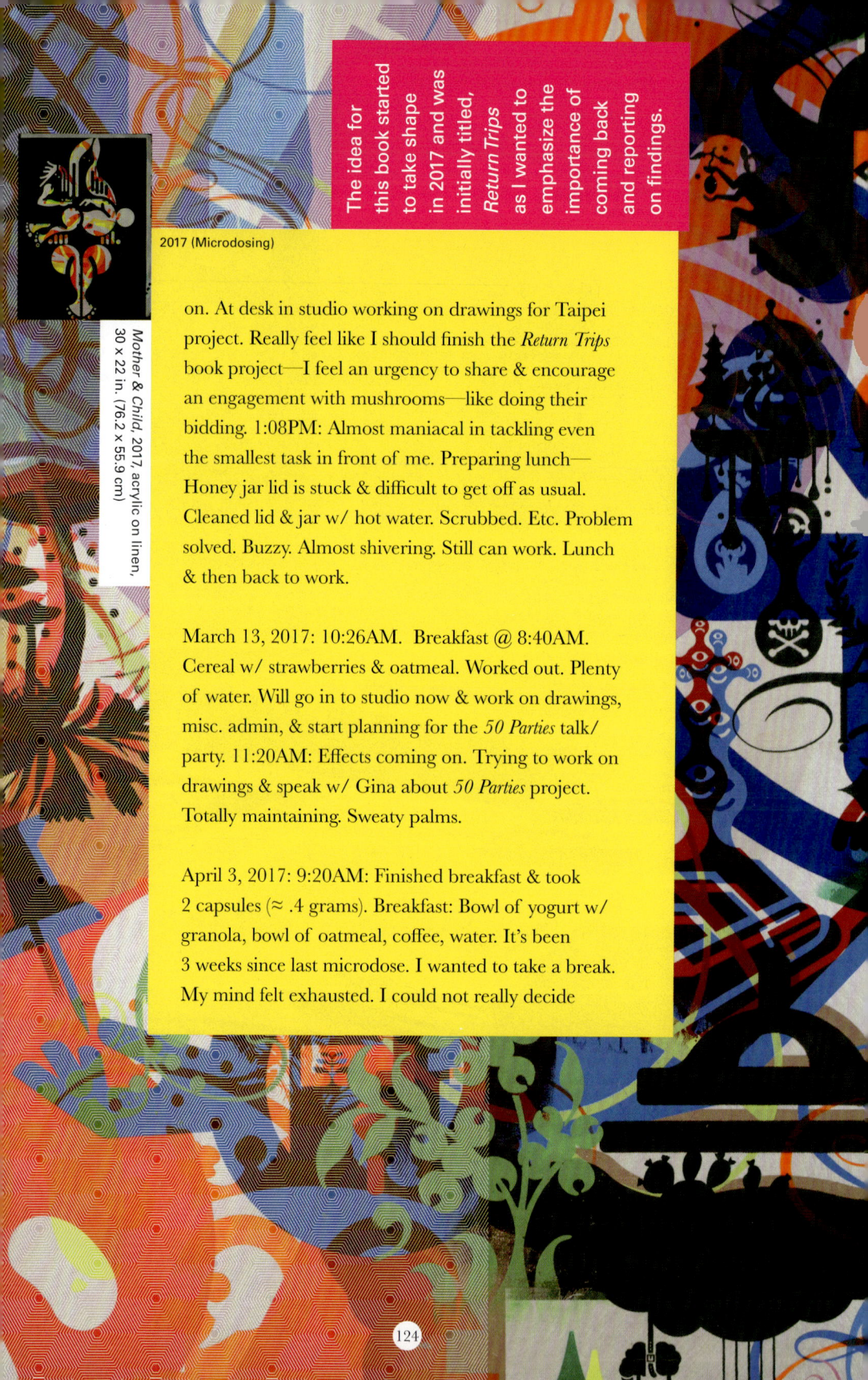

The idea for this book started to take shape in 2017 and was initially titled, *Return Trips* as I wanted to emphasize the importance of coming back and reporting on findings.

2017 (Microdosing)

Mother & Child, 2017, acrylic on linen, 30 × 22 in. (76.2 × 55.9 cm)

on. At desk in studio working on drawings for Taipei project. Really feel like I should finish the *Return Trips* book project—I feel an urgency to share & encourage an engagement with mushrooms—like doing their bidding. 1:08PM: Almost maniacal in tackling even the smallest task in front of me. Preparing lunch— Honey jar lid is stuck & difficult to get off as usual. Cleaned lid & jar w/ hot water. Scrubbed. Etc. Problem solved. Buzzy. Almost shivering. Still can work. Lunch & then back to work.

March 13, 2017: 10:26AM. Breakfast @ 8:40AM. Cereal w/ strawberries & oatmeal. Worked out. Plenty of water. Will go in to studio now & work on drawings, misc. admin, & start planning for the *50 Parties* talk/ party. 11:20AM: Effects coming on. Trying to work on drawings & speak w/ Gina about *50 Parties* project. Totally maintaining. Sweaty palms.

April 3, 2017: 9:20AM: Finished breakfast & took 2 capsules (≈ .4 grams). Breakfast: Bowl of yogurt w/ granola, bowl of oatmeal, coffee, water. It's been 3 weeks since last microdose. I wanted to take a break. My mind felt exhausted. I could not really decide

Mostly a kind of hyperactivity. Also creative solutions. Making connections.

...elsewhere to go back on. Now I feel ready and a bit in need — meaning stressed, snappy, depressed, etc. I felt all right for about 2+ weeks after having stopped — but w/in the past few days I haven't been able to completely focus & simply finish projects the way I need to — lots of manageable projects to get done. And I haven't been able to decide if .4 or .6 grams is right for me. Solution: Stay on a schedule of .4 & bump up to .6 if I know I need to stay focused & "zoom in" on a project/task — like working on a set of drawings or painting plans. I'll also try not to drink so much. 10:30AM: Feeling effects. Mild. A bit jumpy. Jittery. Excited to work. Caffeinated. 2:25PM: Went through the main wave. Productive. Going through painting rack to decide what to put into storage. Something I might not have been motivated to do. Will stick to plan of .4 grams every 3 days — does not rest dose & increase to .6 grams on occasion.

April 6, 2017: 10:36AM: .4 grams. Breakfast @ 8:45AM: Cereal, yogurt, apple, & now coffee. I have noticed positive effects since Monday. Mostly a kind of hyperactivity. Also creative solutions. Making connections. Seeing connections between projects & opportunities.

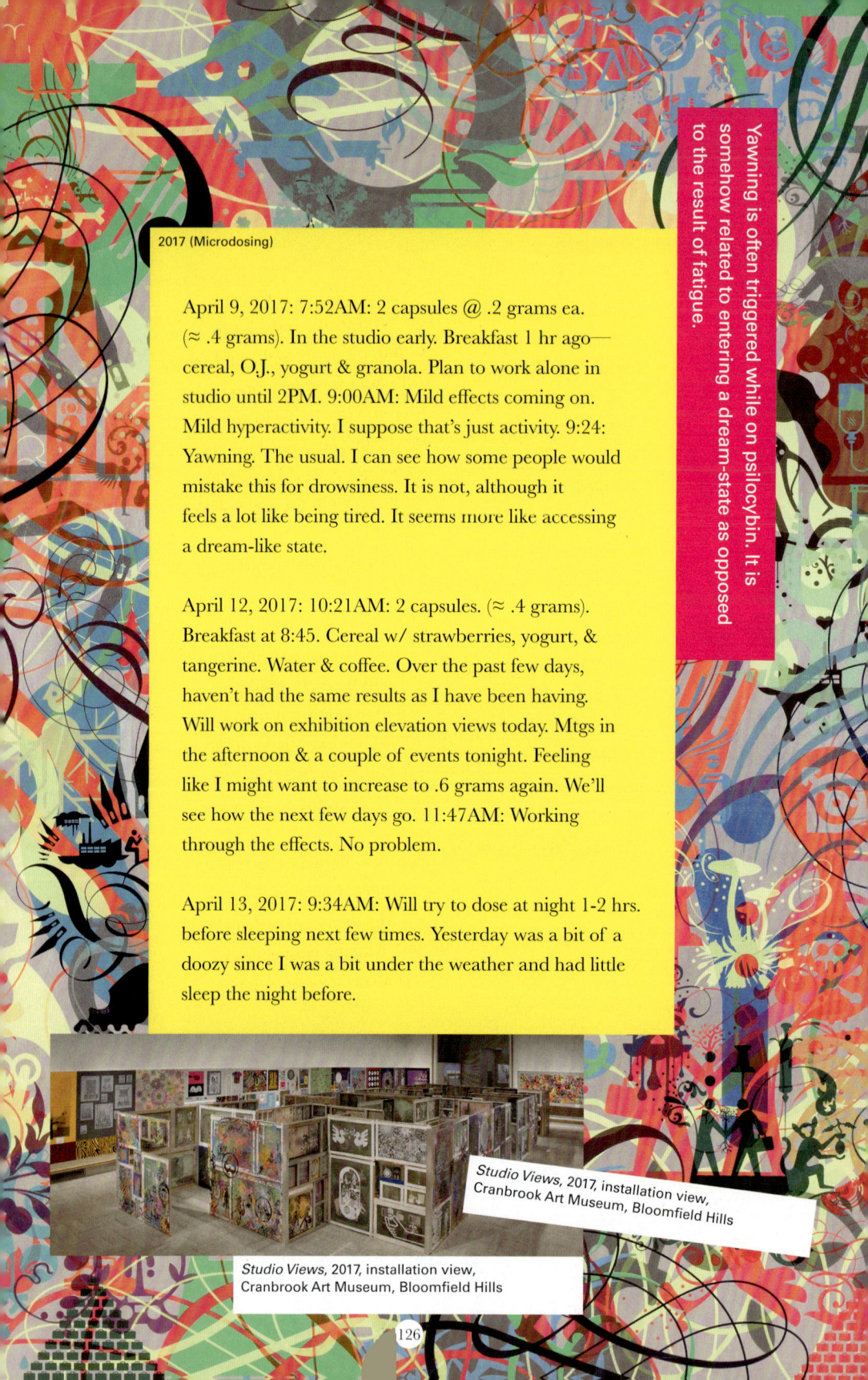

2017 (Microdosing)

Yawning is often triggered while on psilocybin. It is somehow related to entering a dream-state as opposed to the result of fatigue.

April 9, 2017: 7:52AM: 2 capsules @ .2 grams ea. (≈ .4 grams). In the studio early. Breakfast 1 hr ago—cereal, O.J., yogurt & granola. Plan to work alone in studio until 2PM. 9:00AM: Mild effects coming on. Mild hyperactivity. I suppose that's just activity. 9:24: Yawning. The usual. I can see how some people would mistake this for drowsiness. It is not, although it feels a lot like being tired. It seems more like accessing a dream-like state.

April 12, 2017: 10:21AM: 2 capsules. (≈ .4 grams). Breakfast at 8:45. Cereal w/ strawberries, yogurt, & tangerine. Water & coffee. Over the past few days, haven't had the same results as I have been having. Will work on exhibition elevation views today. Mtgs in the afternoon & a couple of events tonight. Feeling like I might want to increase to .6 grams again. We'll see how the next few days go. 11:47AM: Working through the effects. No problem.

April 13, 2017: 9:34AM: Will try to dose at night 1-2 hrs. before sleeping next few times. Yesterday was a bit of a doozy since I was a bit under the weather and had little sleep the night before.

Studio Views, 2017, installation view, Cranbrook Art Museum, Bloomfield Hills

Studio Views, 2017, installation view, Cranbrook Art Museum, Bloomfield Hills

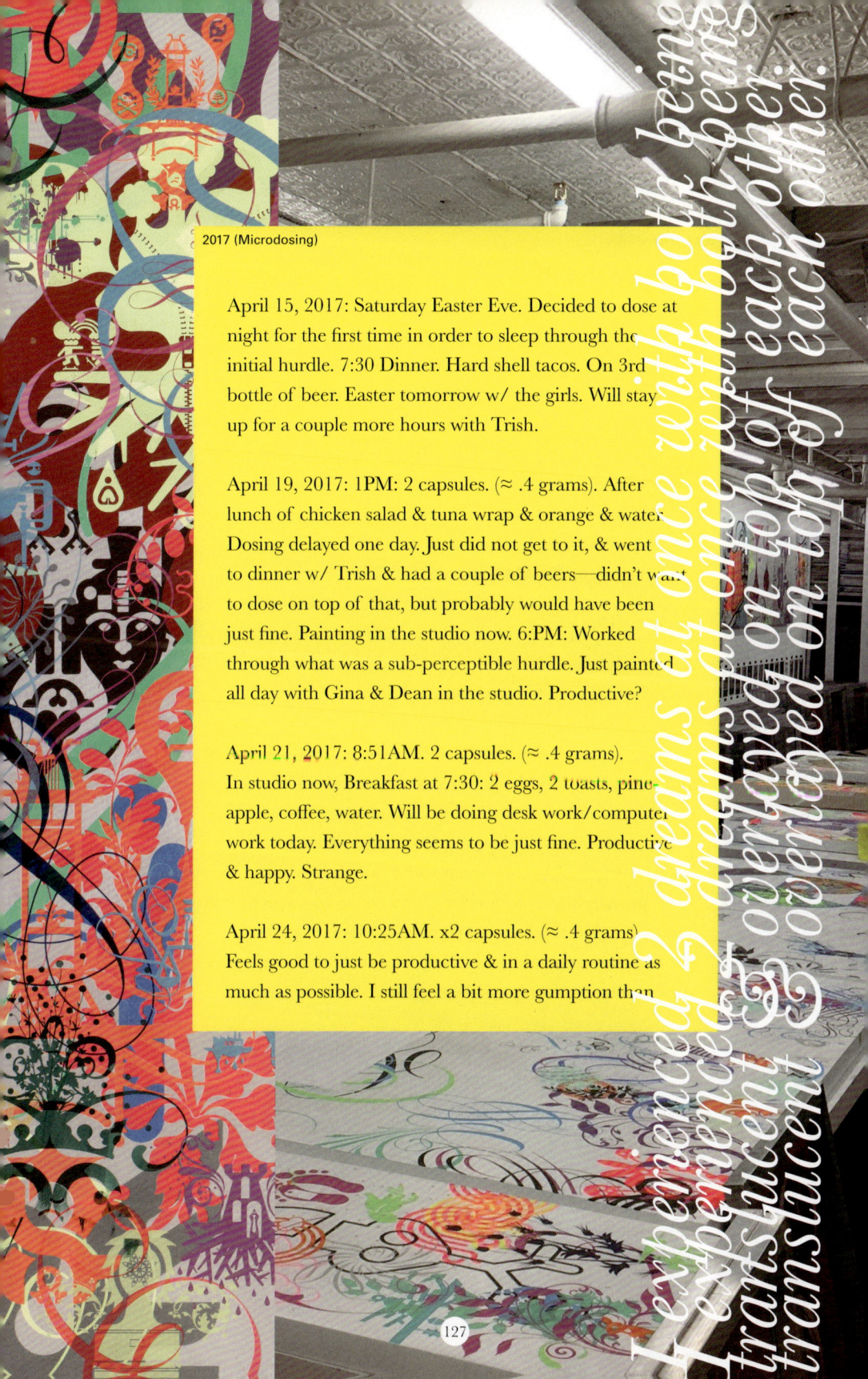

2017 (Microdosing)

April 15, 2017: Saturday Easter Eve. Decided to dose at night for the first time in order to sleep through the initial hurdle. 7:30 Dinner. Hard shell tacos. On 3rd bottle of beer. Easter tomorrow w/ the girls. Will stay up for a couple more hours with Trish.

April 19, 2017: 1PM: 2 capsules. (≈ .4 grams). After lunch of chicken salad & tuna wrap & orange & water. Dosing delayed one day. Just did not get to it, & went to dinner w/ Trish & had a couple of beers—didn't want to dose on top of that, but probably would have been just fine. Painting in the studio now. 6:PM: Worked through what was a sub-perceptible hurdle. Just painted all day with Gina & Dean in the studio. Productive?

April 21, 2017: 8:51AM. 2 capsules. (≈ .4 grams). In studio now, Breakfast at 7:30: 2 eggs, 2 toasts, pine-apple, coffee, water. Will be doing desk work/computer work today. Everything seems to be just fine. Productive & happy. Strange.

April 24, 2017: 10:25AM. x2 capsules. (≈ .4 grams) Feels good to just be productive & in a daily routine as much as possible. I still feel a bit more gumption than

2017 (Microdosing)

usual to tackle even the smallest pain-in-the-ass tasks like unclogging a sink or cleaning or putting things into storage—stupid shit that takes me away from working & I would normally push aside. The girls still wake us both up at odd hours even though Trish is the one they want, so she gets up & deals w/ them, I am woken up & find myself having a hard time going back to sleep— So I'm up but not being productive & eventually go back to sleep, like yesterday (Sunday) when I fell asleep on the couch from 6-9AM during which time I experienced 2 dreams at once with both being translucent & over-layed on top of each other. Additionally, I could hear the girls laughing and yelling & that added another layer of information to the dreams.

April 27, 2017: 11:20AM: 2 capsules. (≈ .4 grams). Breakfast @ 7:45AM—oatmeal & yogurt— So almost an empty stomach now. I've been wondering if the returns have been diminishing. Been very stressed & angry lately—especially because of & around the girls. Also been feeling a chronic heaviness w/ an overactive mind. Kind of tired a lot. And have not had the super-focus powers previously experienced. I wonder if the best strategy is to only do .6 grams for 1-2 weeks every

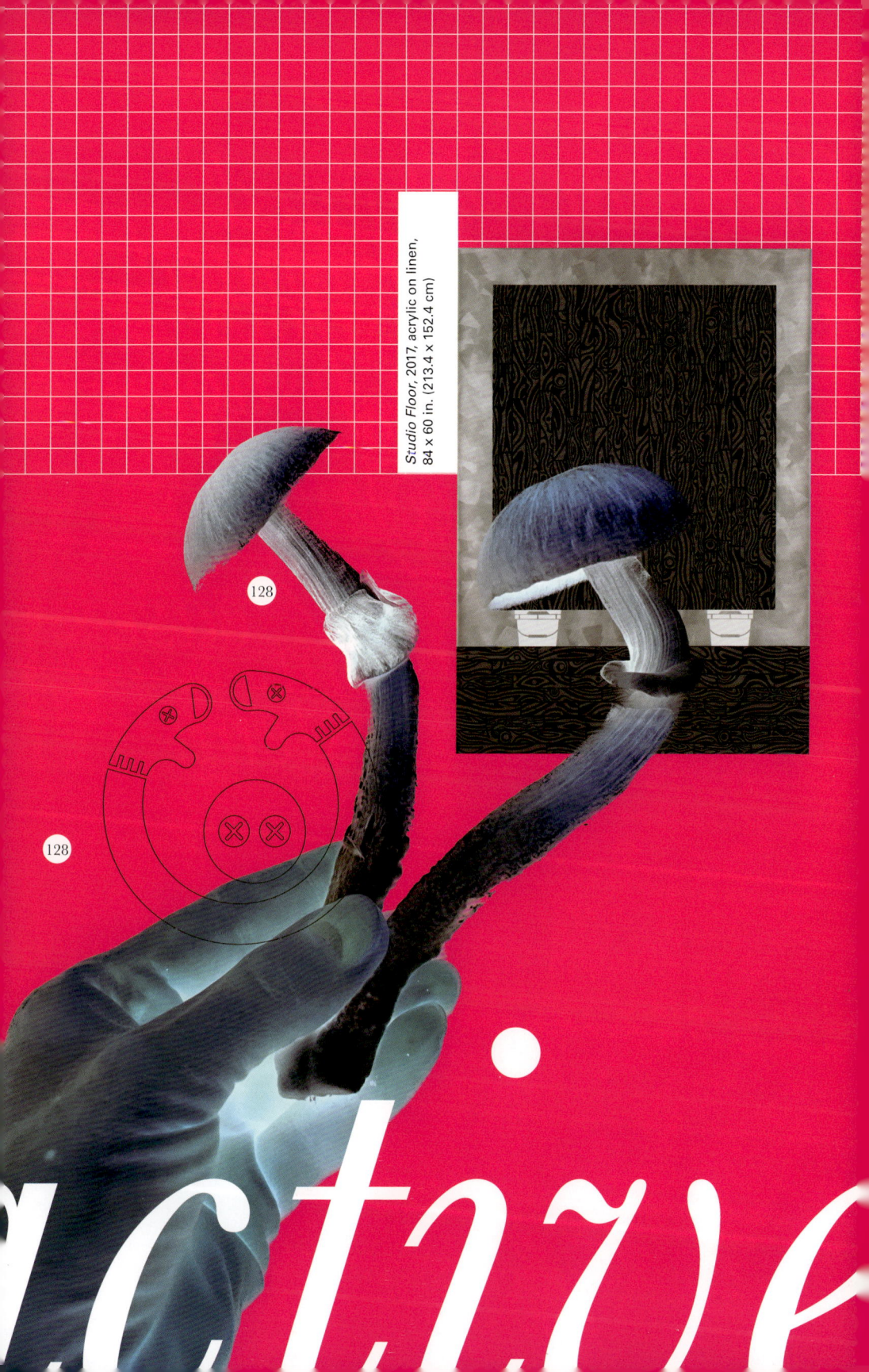

Studio Floor, 2017, acrylic on linen, 84 x 60 in. (213.4 x 152.4 cm)

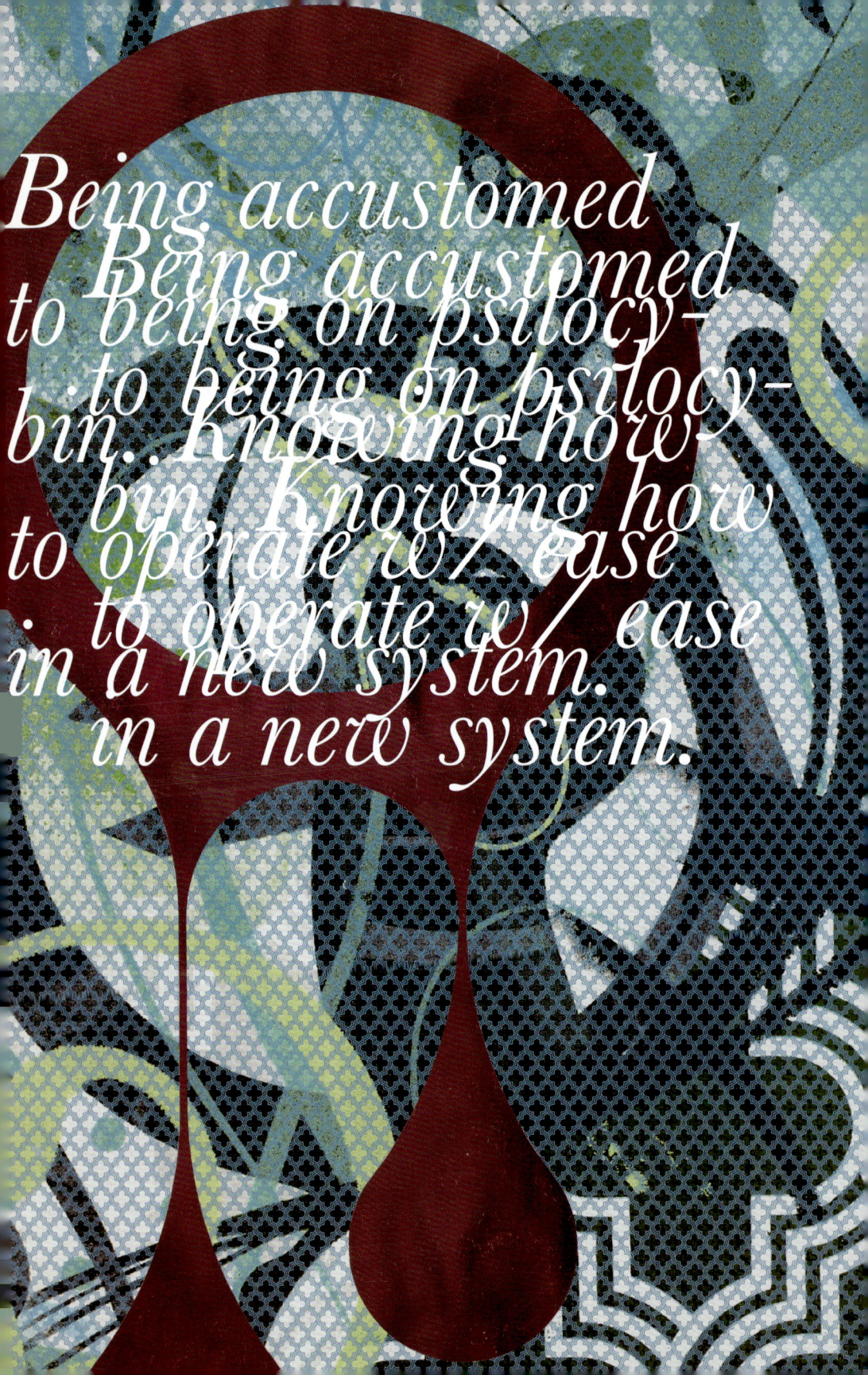

Being accustomed
to being on psilocy-
bin...knowing how
to operate w/ ease
in a new system.

Being accustomed
to being on psilocy-
bin. Knowing how
to operate w/ ease
in a new system.

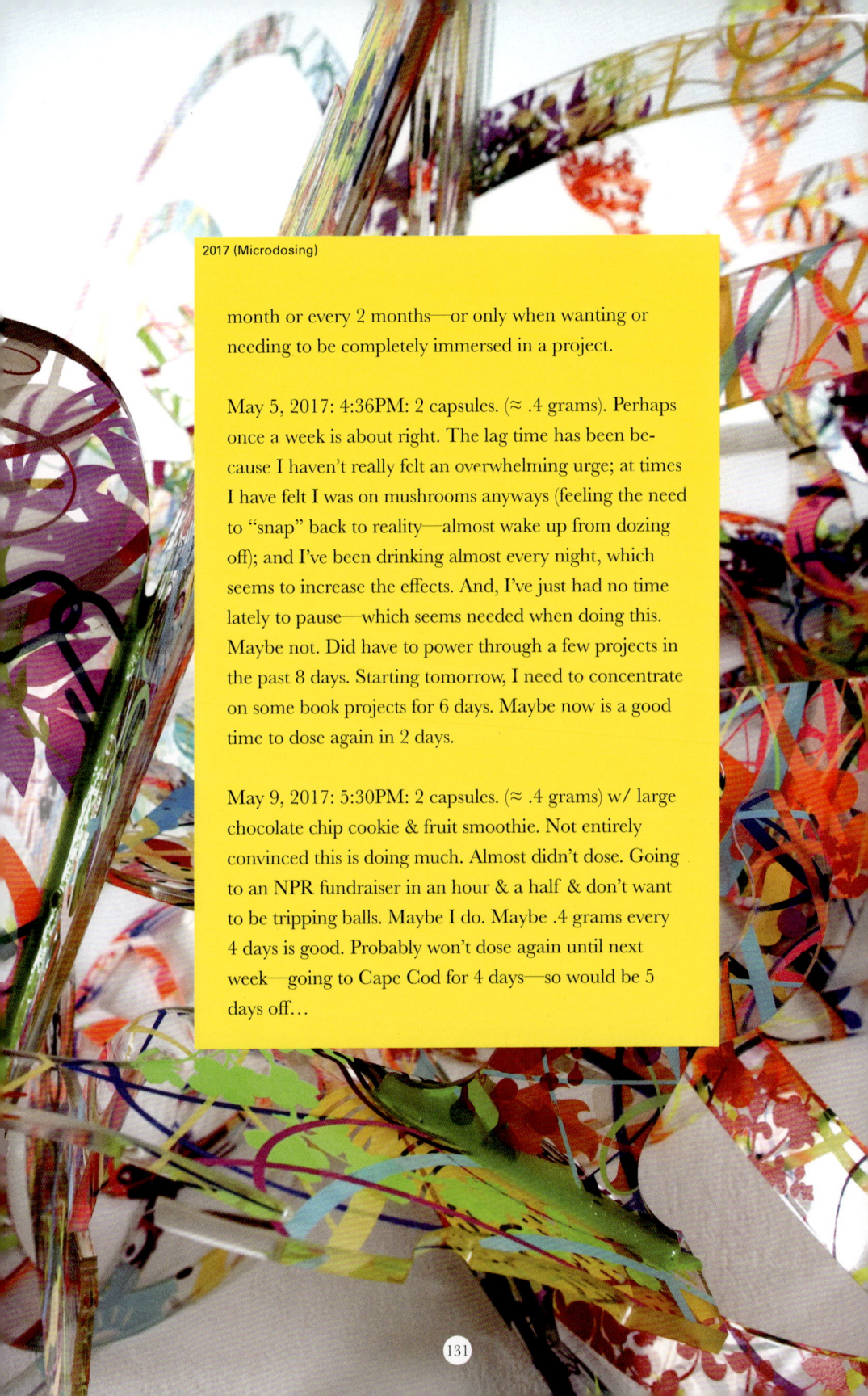

month or every 2 months—or only when wanting or needing to be completely immersed in a project.

May 5, 2017: 4:36PM: 2 capsules. (≈ .4 grams). Perhaps once a week is about right. The lag time has been because I haven't really felt an overwhelming urge; at times I have felt I was on mushrooms anyways (feeling the need to "snap" back to reality—almost wake up from dozing off); and I've been drinking almost every night, which seems to increase the effects. And, I've just had no time lately to pause—which seems needed when doing this. Maybe not. Did have to power through a few projects in the past 8 days. Starting tomorrow, I need to concentrate on some book projects for 6 days. Maybe now is a good time to dose again in 2 days.

May 9, 2017: 5:30PM: 2 capsules. (≈ .4 grams) w/ large chocolate chip cookie & fruit smoothie. Not entirely convinced this is doing much. Almost didn't dose. Going to an NPR fundraiser in an hour & a half & don't want to be tripping balls. Maybe I do. Maybe .4 grams every 4 days is good. Probably won't dose again until next week—going to Cape Cod for 4 days—so would be 5 days off…

May 27, 2017: 11:15AM: 2 capsules. (≈ .4 grams).
It has been 17 days since the last dose. I feel like it took
nine days (until May 18th) to be completely off psilocybin. The trip to Cape Cod for nephew's bar mitzvah one
week & the preparation for & the actual *50 Parties* talk &
party the next week kept me off microdosing. It has been
a good rest. During this time (since the beginning of
May) I have been drinking less, eating better, & exercising more (push-up challenge daily, especially). Now is
a good time (work-wise) to start again, & today especially
to help get through this Memorial Day weekend with the
girls. Today I will be working with them, working on the
plants, & exercising—also finishing touches on revamped
home office, hopefully. 4:11PM Now. Started to feel
effects 1:15PM-2:30PM-ish. Jittery etc. Same as always.
Calm. Able to focus. Does not make you focus. Puts you
in a dream-like flow-craving state. Like a dream-craving
state. Wanting or open to entering a dimension where
space-time dissolves. Mistaken for or feels like sleepiness—but what I think this is—is an openness to
concentration or focus. Could "fall asleep" to get there
or "fall into" something to concentrate on—anything.
Still feel that way a couple of hours later.

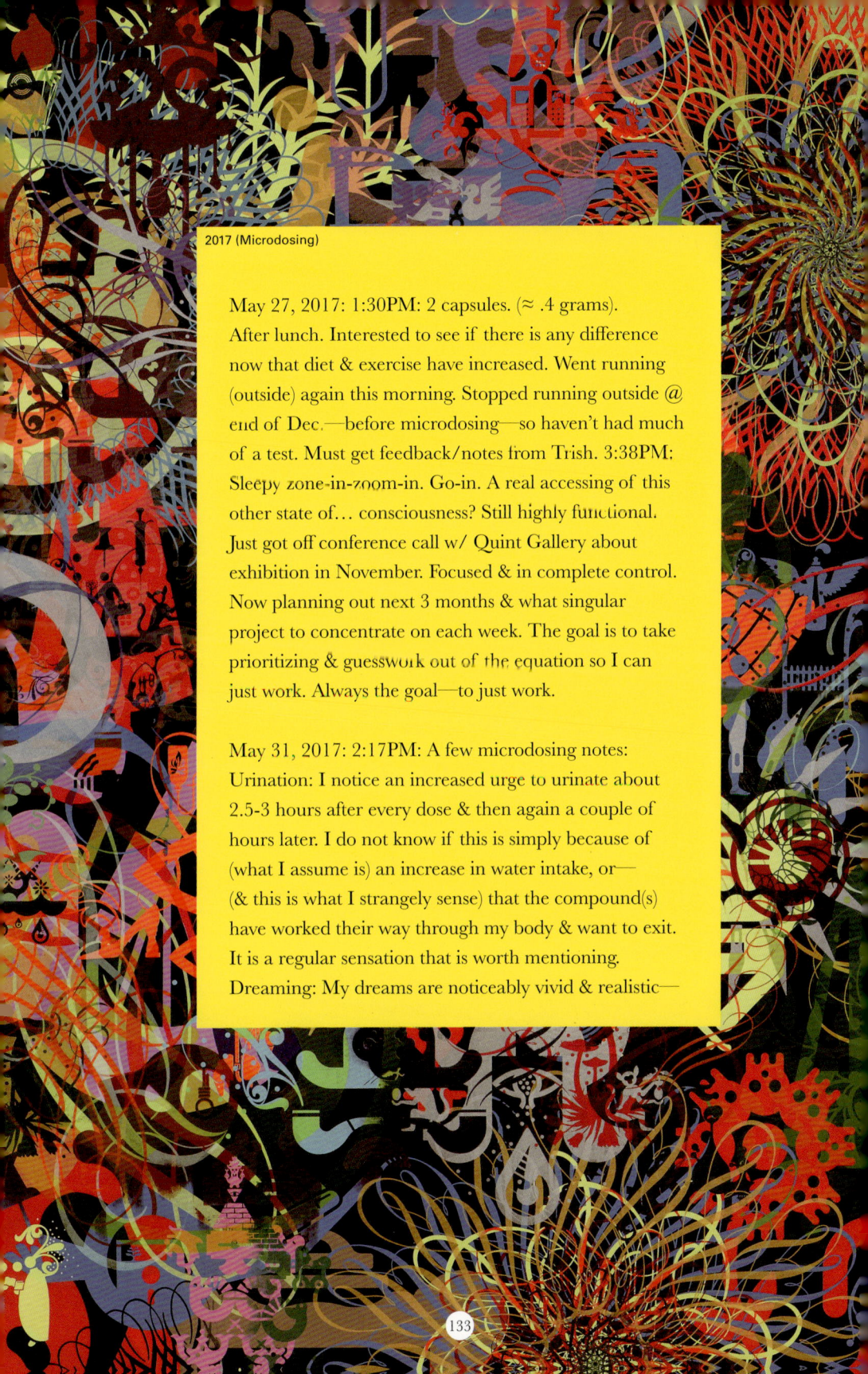

May 27, 2017: 1:30PM: 2 capsules. (≈ .4 grams).
After lunch. Interested to see if there is any difference
now that diet & exercise have increased. Went running
(outside) again this morning. Stopped running outside @
end of Dec.—before microdosing—so haven't had much
of a test. Must get feedback/notes from Trish. 3:38PM:
Sleepy zone-in-zoom-in. Go-in. A real accessing of this
other state of… consciousness? Still highly functional.
Just got off conference call w/ Quint Gallery about
exhibition in November. Focused & in complete control.
Now planning out next 3 months & what singular
project to concentrate on each week. The goal is to take
prioritizing & guesswork out of the equation so I can
just work. Always the goal—to just work.

May 31, 2017: 2:17PM: A few microdosing notes:
Urination: I notice an increased urge to urinate about
2.5-3 hours after every dose & then again a couple of
hours later. I do not know if this is simply because of
(what I assume is) an increase in water intake, or—
(& this is what I strangely sense) that the compound(s)
have worked their way through my body & want to exit.
It is a regular sensation that is worth mentioning.
Dreaming: My dreams are noticeably vivid & realistic—

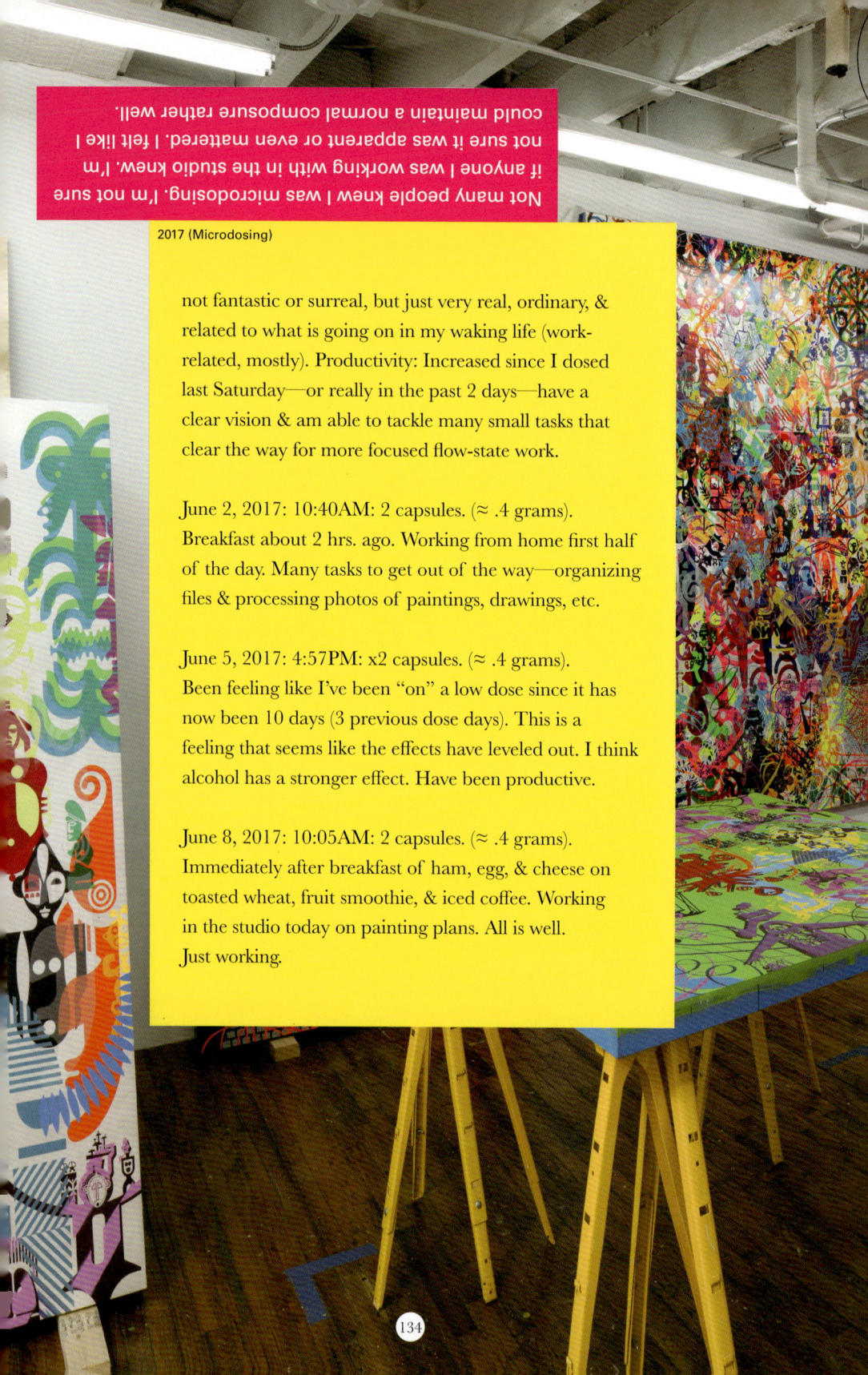

2017 (Microdosing)

not fantastic or surreal, but just very real, ordinary, & related to what is going on in my waking life (work-related, mostly). Productivity: Increased since I dosed last Saturday—or really in the past 2 days—have a clear vision & am able to tackle many small tasks that clear the way for more focused flow-state work.

June 2, 2017: 10:40AM: 2 capsules. (≈ .4 grams). Breakfast about 2 hrs. ago. Working from home first half of the day. Many tasks to get out of the way—organizing files & processing photos of paintings, drawings, etc.

June 5, 2017: 4:57PM: x2 capsules. (≈ .4 grams). Been feeling like I've been "on" a low dose since it has now been 10 days (3 previous dose days). This is a feeling that seems like the effects have leveled out. I think alcohol has a stronger effect. Have been productive.

June 8, 2017: 10:05AM: 2 capsules. (≈ .4 grams). Immediately after breakfast of ham, egg, & cheese on toasted wheat, fruit smoothie, & iced coffee. Working in the studio today on painting plans. All is well. Just working.

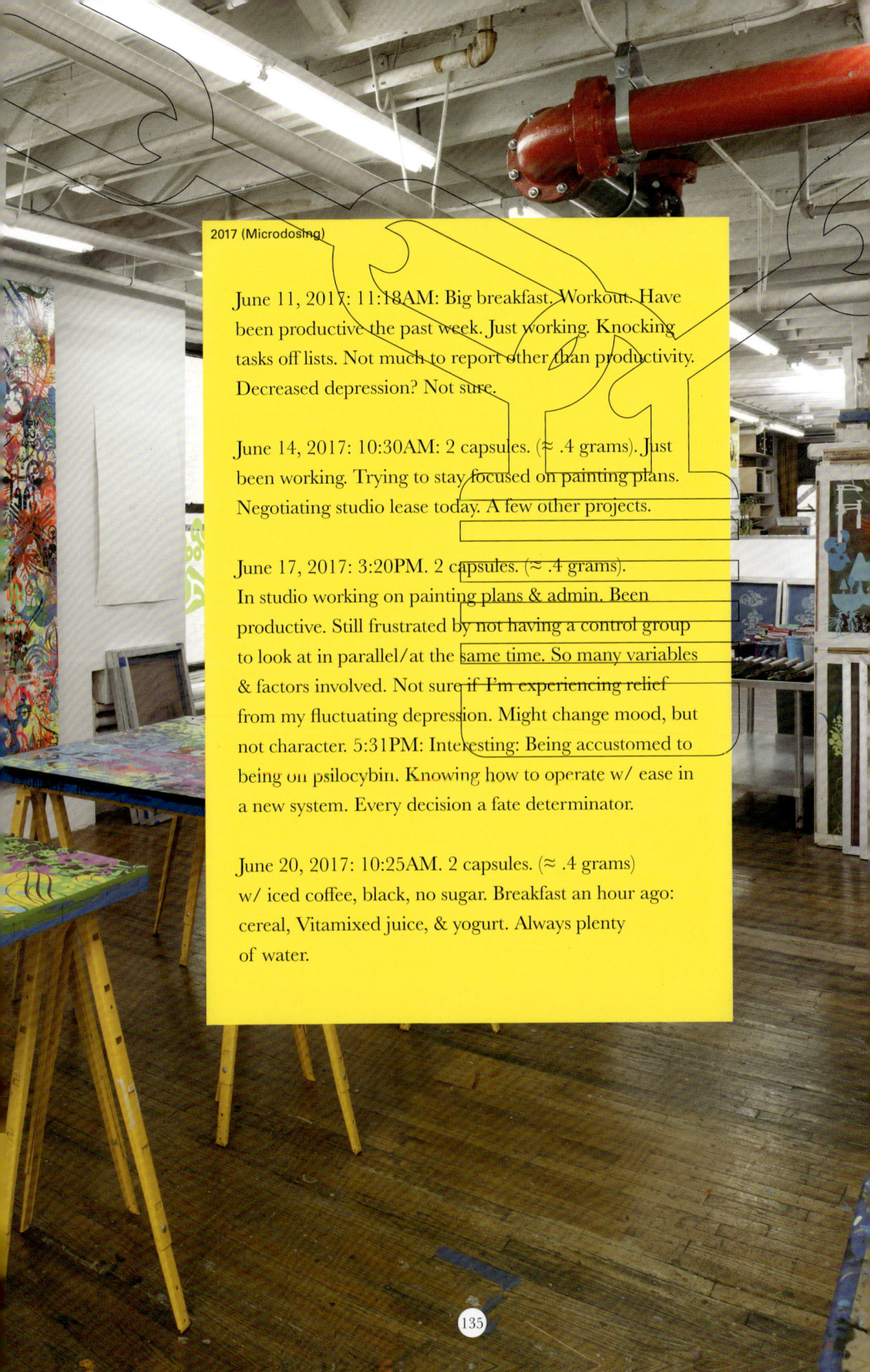

June 11, 2017: 11:18AM: Big breakfast. Workout. Have been productive the past week. Just working. Knocking tasks off lists. Not much to report other than productivity. Decreased depression? Not sure.

June 14, 2017: 10:30AM: 2 capsules. (≈ .4 grams). Just been working. Trying to stay focused on painting plans. Negotiating studio lease today. A few other projects.

June 17, 2017: 3:20PM. 2 capsules. (≈ .4 grams). In studio working on painting plans & admin. Been productive. Still frustrated by not having a control group to look at in parallel/at the same time. So many variables & factors involved. Not sure if I'm experiencing relief from my fluctuating depression. Might change mood, but not character. 5:31PM: Interesting: Being accustomed to being on psilocybin. Knowing how to operate w/ ease in a new system. Every decision a fate determinator.

June 20, 2017: 10:25AM. 2 capsules. (≈ .4 grams) w/ iced coffee, black, no sugar. Breakfast an hour ago: cereal, Vitamixed juice, & yogurt. Always plenty of water.

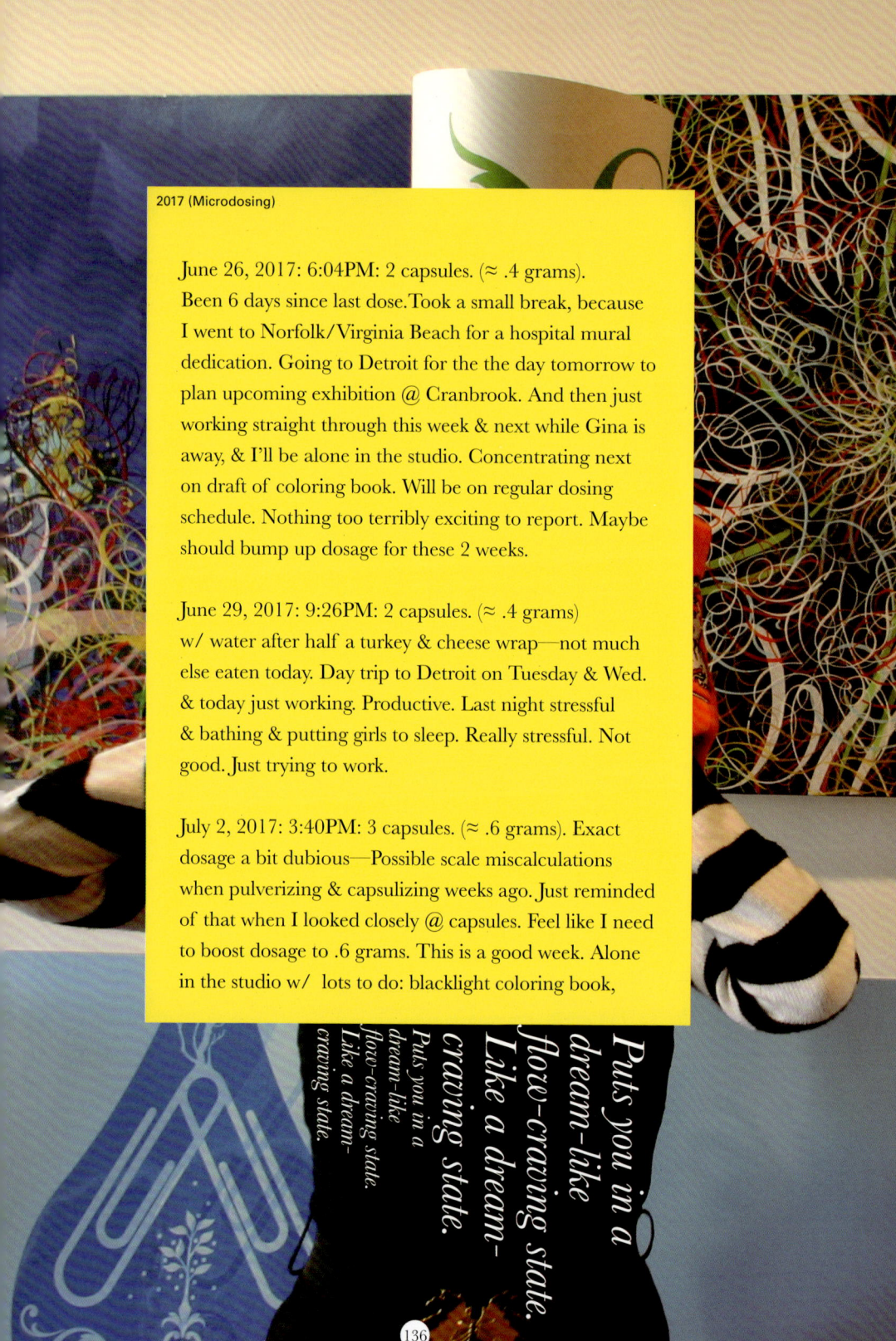

June 26, 2017: 6:04PM: 2 capsules. (≈ .4 grams).
Been 6 days since last dose. Took a small break, because
I went to Norfolk/Virginia Beach for a hospital mural
dedication. Going to Detroit for the the day tomorrow to
plan upcoming exhibition @ Cranbrook. And then just
working straight through this week & next while Gina is
away, & I'll be alone in the studio. Concentrating next
on draft of coloring book. Will be on regular dosing
schedule. Nothing too terribly exciting to report. Maybe
should bump up dosage for these 2 weeks.

June 29, 2017: 9:26PM: 2 capsules. (≈ .4 grams)
w/ water after half a turkey & cheese wrap—not much
else eaten today. Day trip to Detroit on Tuesday & Wed.
& today just working. Productive. Last night stressful
& bathing & putting girls to sleep. Really stressful. Not
good. Just trying to work.

July 2, 2017: 3:40PM: 3 capsules. (≈ .6 grams). Exact
dosage a bit dubious—Possible scale miscalculations
when pulverizing & capsulizing weeks ago. Just reminded
of that when I looked closely @ capsules. Feel like I need
to boost dosage to .6 grams. This is a good week. Alone
in the studio w/ lots to do: blacklight coloring book,

Puts you in a dream-like flow-craving state. Like a dream-craving state.

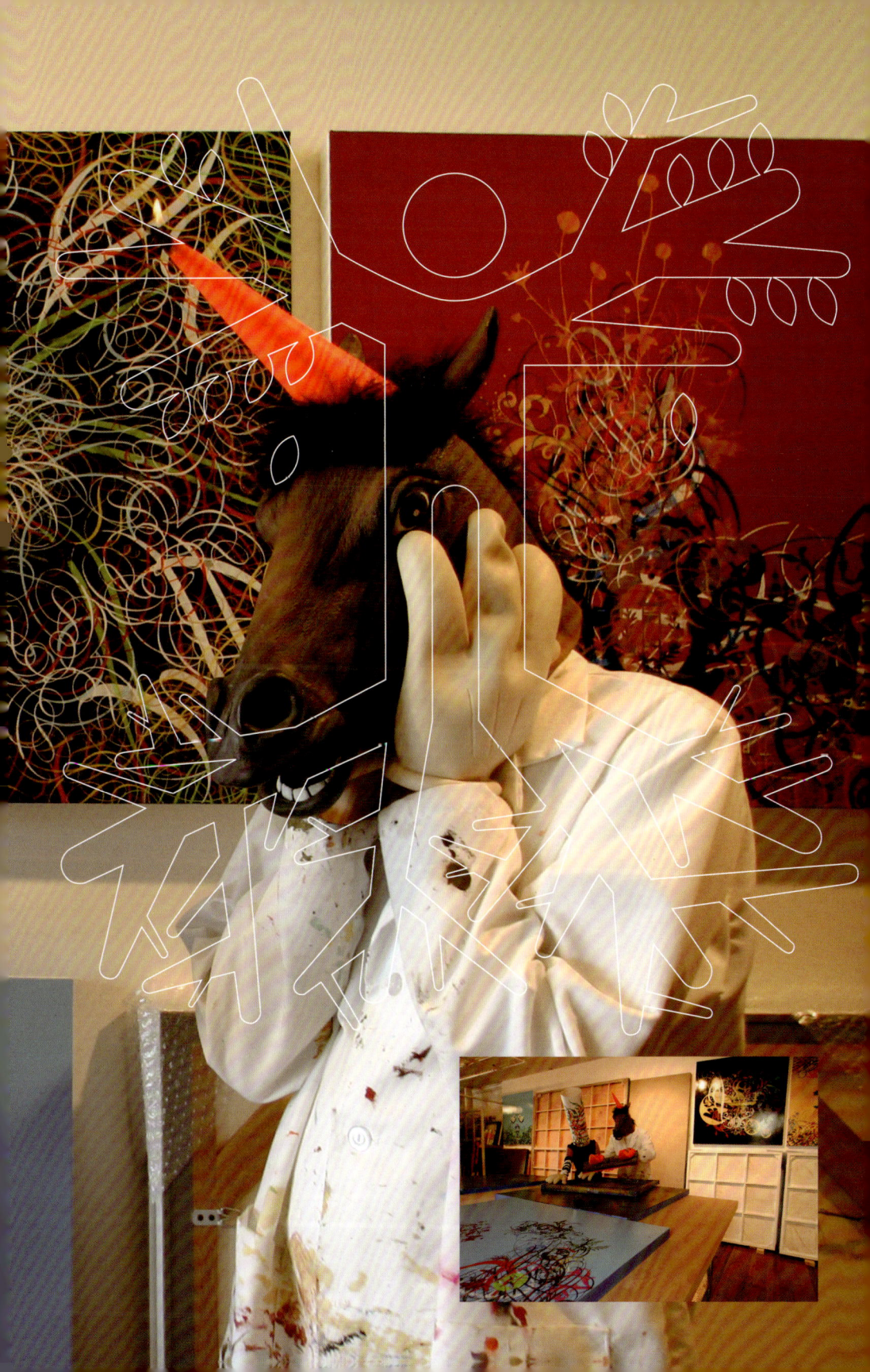

artwork for Detroit skate park, *#metadata* book, etc.
5:15PM: Buzzy. Working a bit frantically. Alone in
studio. 5:30PM: .6 g. is definitely different than .4 g..

July 3, 2017: 4:05PM: A couple of quick notes: Had a
breakthrough in developing a concept for the Detroit
skatepark that ties together the ideas of skating architectural elements & subverting public signage by relating
both to "wayfinding." Is this a coincidence or because
I'm on a higher dose of psilocybin? I do feel that I've
got a bit more "gumption"—or "get-up-and-go"—or
simply more motivated to act on every thought to do
something—for directly work-related to everyday living
tasks—or any task that has a slight barrier to overcome
(basically, effort) and that can easily & comfortably be put
off to later. I seem more able to simply just do everything.

July 5, 2017: 4:43PM: 3 capsules. (≈ .6 grams). These
capsules looked a little more packed than usual. Been
productive. Getting a lot done. Even productively
procrastinating. Still not sure about being nicer or going
with the flow— Still annoyed & angry at uncooperative
offspring. Maybe it is just my character to be annoyed &
psilocybin is not going to change character. Working

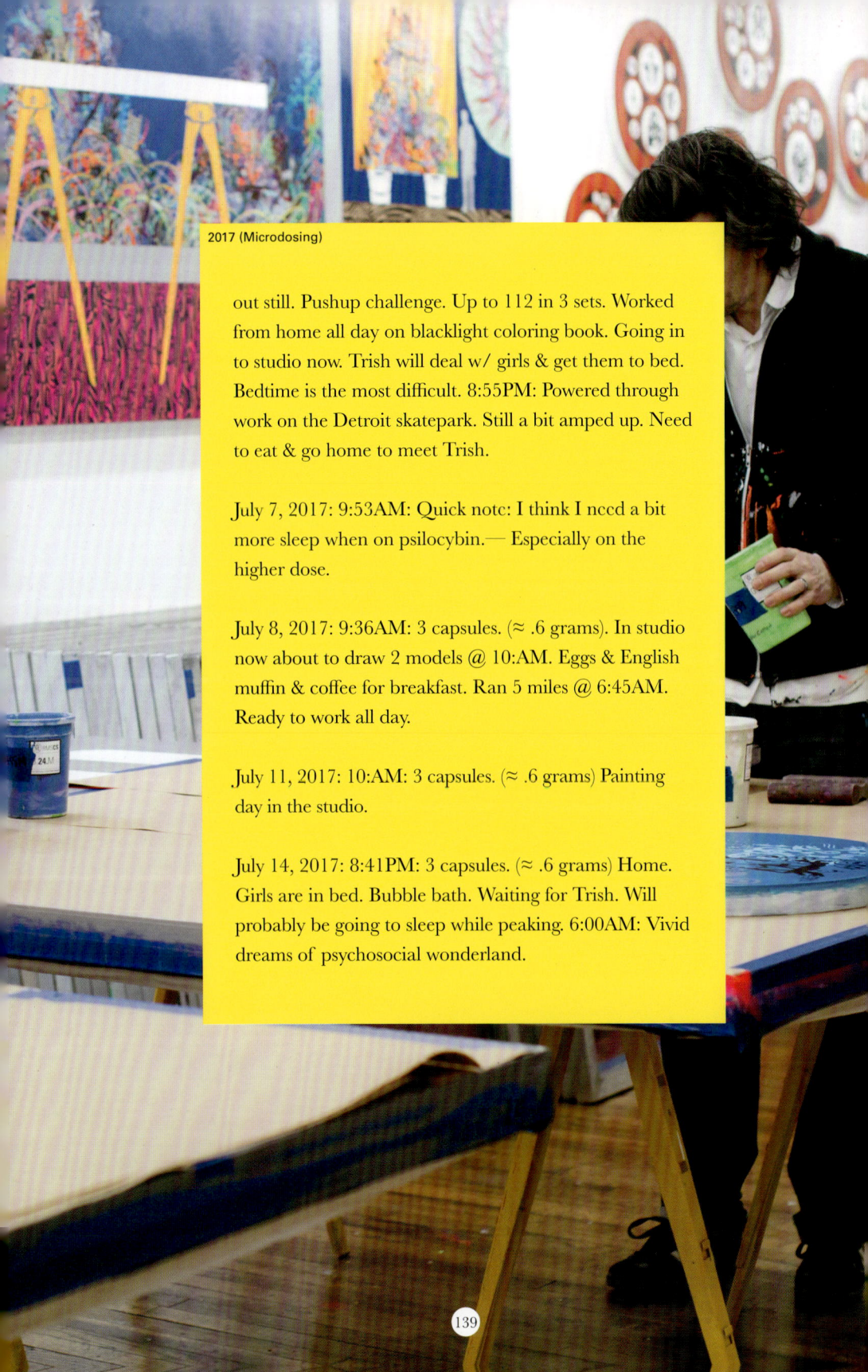

out still. Pushup challenge. Up to 112 in 3 sets. Worked from home all day on blacklight coloring book. Going in to studio now. Trish will deal w/ girls & get them to bed. Bedtime is the most difficult. 8:55PM: Powered through work on the Detroit skatepark. Still a bit amped up. Need to eat & go home to meet Trish.

July 7, 2017: 9:53AM: Quick note: I think I need a bit more sleep when on psilocybin.— Especially on the higher dose.

July 8, 2017: 9:36AM: 3 capsules. (≈ .6 grams). In studio now about to draw 2 models @ 10:AM. Eggs & English muffin & coffee for breakfast. Ran 5 miles @ 6:45AM. Ready to work all day.

July 11, 2017: 10:AM: 3 capsules. (≈ .6 grams) Painting day in the studio.

July 14, 2017: 8:41PM: 3 capsules. (≈ .6 grams) Home. Girls are in bed. Bubble bath. Waiting for Trish. Will probably be going to sleep while peaking. 6:00AM: Vivid dreams of psychosocial wonderland.

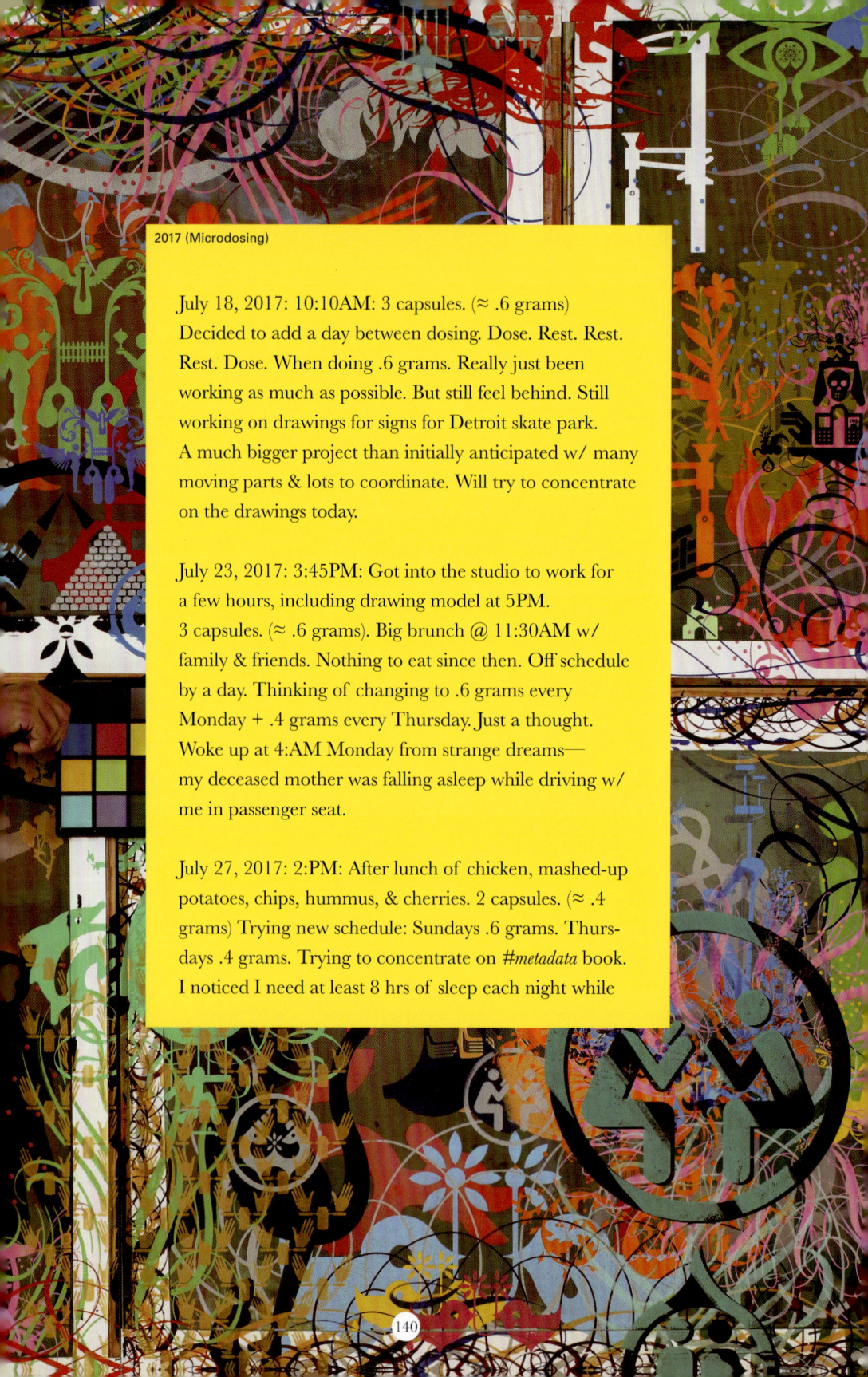

July 18, 2017: 10:10AM: 3 capsules. (≈ .6 grams)
Decided to add a day between dosing. Dose. Rest. Rest.
Rest. Dose. When doing .6 grams. Really just been
working as much as possible. But still feel behind. Still
working on drawings for signs for Detroit skate park.
A much bigger project than initially anticipated w/ many
moving parts & lots to coordinate. Will try to concentrate
on the drawings today.

July 23, 2017: 3:45PM: Got into the studio to work for
a few hours, including drawing model at 5PM.
3 capsules. (≈ .6 grams). Big brunch @ 11:30AM w/
family & friends. Nothing to eat since then. Off schedule
by a day. Thinking of changing to .6 grams every
Monday + .4 grams every Thursday. Just a thought.
Woke up at 4:AM Monday from strange dreams—
my deceased mother was falling asleep while driving w/
me in passenger seat.

July 27, 2017: 2:PM: After lunch of chicken, mashed-up
potatoes, chips, hummus, & cherries. 2 capsules. (≈ .4
grams) Trying new schedule: Sundays .6 grams. Thurs-
days .4 grams. Trying to concentrate on *#metadata* book.
I noticed I need at least 8 hrs of sleep each night while

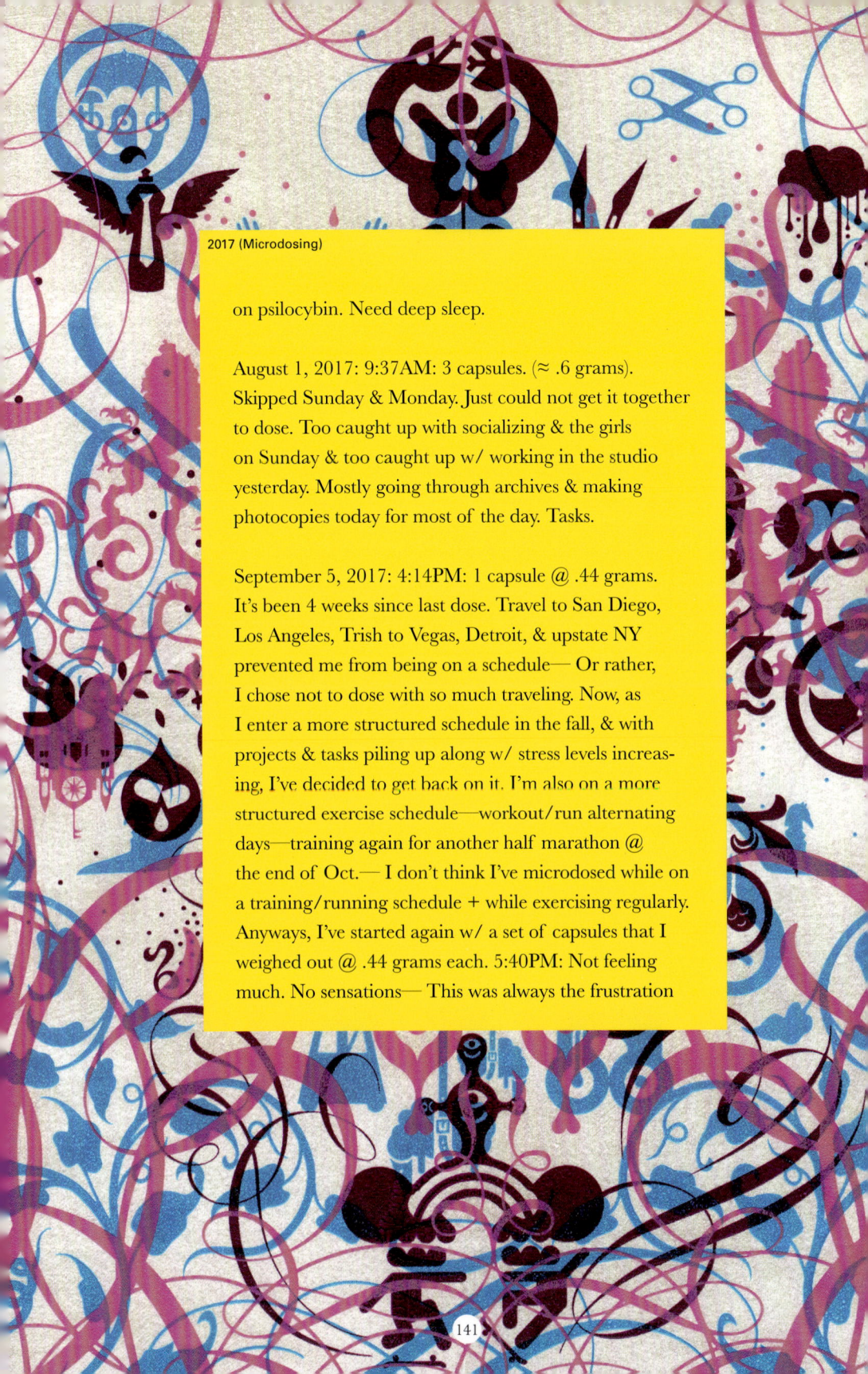

on psilocybin. Need deep sleep.

August 1, 2017: 9:37AM: 3 capsules. ($\approx$ .6 grams).
Skipped Sunday & Monday. Just could not get it together
to dose. Too caught up with socializing & the girls
on Sunday & too caught up w/ working in the studio
yesterday. Mostly going through archives & making
photocopies today for most of the day. Tasks.

September 5, 2017: 4:14PM: 1 capsule @ .44 grams.
It's been 4 weeks since last dose. Travel to San Diego,
Los Angeles, Trish to Vegas, Detroit, & upstate NY
prevented me from being on a schedule— Or rather,
I chose not to dose with so much traveling. Now, as
I enter a more structured schedule in the fall, & with
projects & tasks piling up along w/ stress levels increasing, I've decided to get back on it. I'm also on a more
structured exercise schedule—workout/run alternating
days—training again for another half marathon @
the end of Oct.— I don't think I've microdosed while on
a training/running schedule + while exercising regularly.
Anyways, I've started again w/ a set of capsules that I
weighed out @ .44 grams each. 5:40PM: Not feeling
much. No sensations— This was always the frustration

w/ ≈ .4 grams—not quite sure if I'm "on" psilocybin. Regardless, I'll stick to this dosage—especially after having been off for so long.

September 11, 2017: 9:44AM: .44 grams. 5 days since last dose. Just simply didn't get a chance—missed the dose in-between. Maybe I should set these up like vitamins. Wouldn't be a bad idea to set up vitamins like vitamins. Busy week—shipping 2 exhibitions & finishing up drawings for Cranbrook. Maxine starts school this week. Her birthday party (to get ready for) on Sat.— Things to go to every night etc. etc.— By 11:30AM a bit jumpy/jittery/productive. 12:40PM: Must've been more than .44 grams. Really need to calibrate that scale.

September 15, 2017: 12:28PM: 1 capsule @ ≈ .44 grams. 4th day since last dose. Should have been yesterday. Just did not get to it. Worked on #metadata book. Super stressed working on that, under deadline for Cranbrook drawings. Need to put together dinosaur party for Maxine for tomorrow + social obligations. Just working through it all.

September 19, 2017: 2:47PM: 1 capsule @ ≈ .44 grams. 4th day since last dose. Just so hard to tell if this dosage is doing anything special. 4:47: Yawning. Jittery. Far from out of control—still, interesting how it is coming on 2 hrs. later. Did eat big lunch—chicken & pasta.

September 22, 2017: 11:27AM: 1 capsule @ ≈ .44 grams. Had avg. breakfast @ 9:30AM. Eating yogurt now. Expecting same as always. Working on drawings today. No need to journalize anymore, but will still keep track on calendar—

November 24, 2017: Friday. Day after Thanksgiving. 3 weeks + 2 days since last dose. About 2-3 days ago noticed lack of focus & feeling scattered. A bit lost. Went off microdosing because of travel to LA, San Diego, & Detroit. Now taking .5 grams at 5:48PM. Going to start a 25 day run of being completely concentrated on year-end misc. projects in the studio. + exercising every day. Microdosing a part of this last 25 day push (before going to Barbados). @ just about 7:30PM felt it coming on a bit. Still very much in control and productive.

Figure Drawings, 2014, installation view, Pace Prints, New York

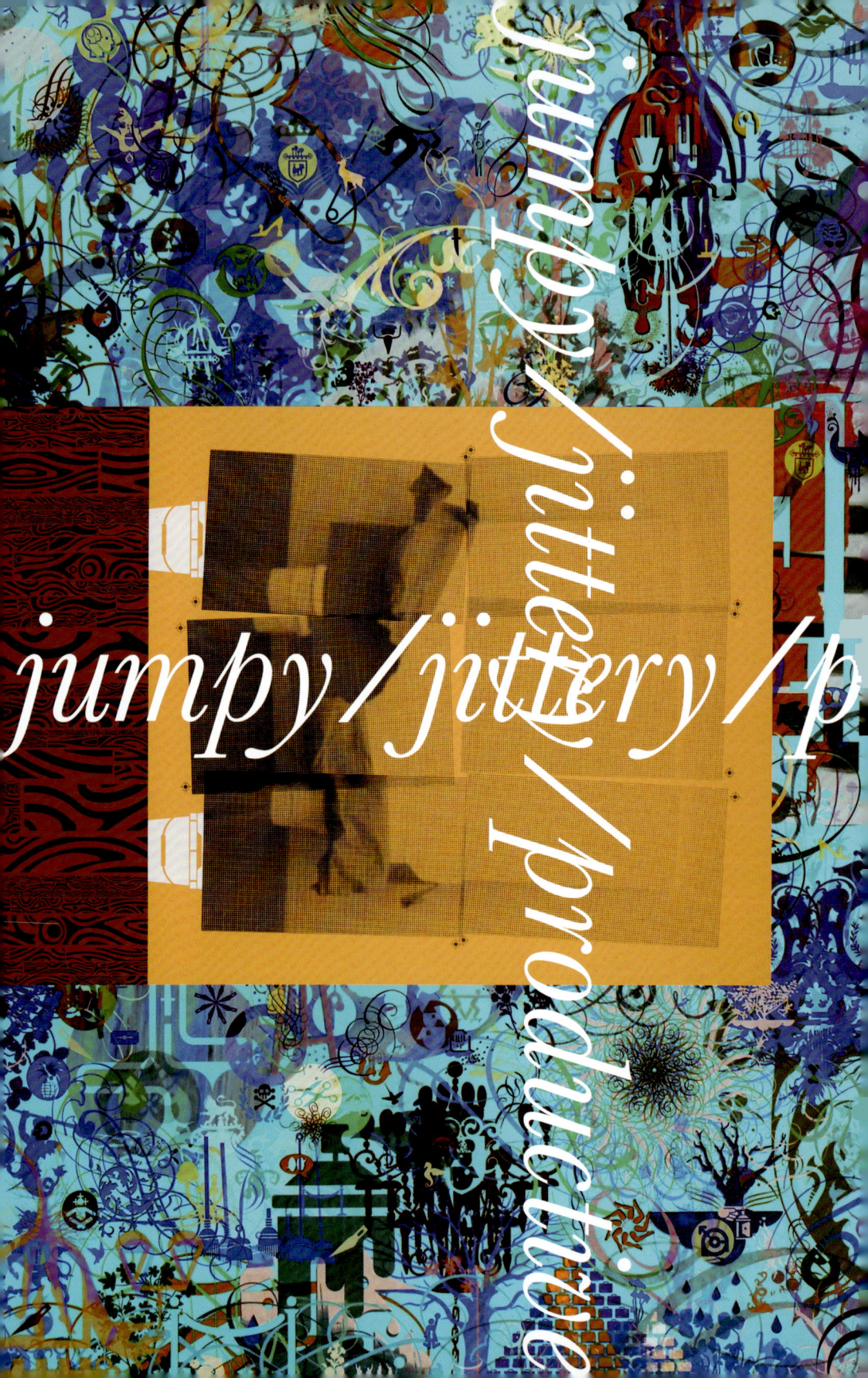

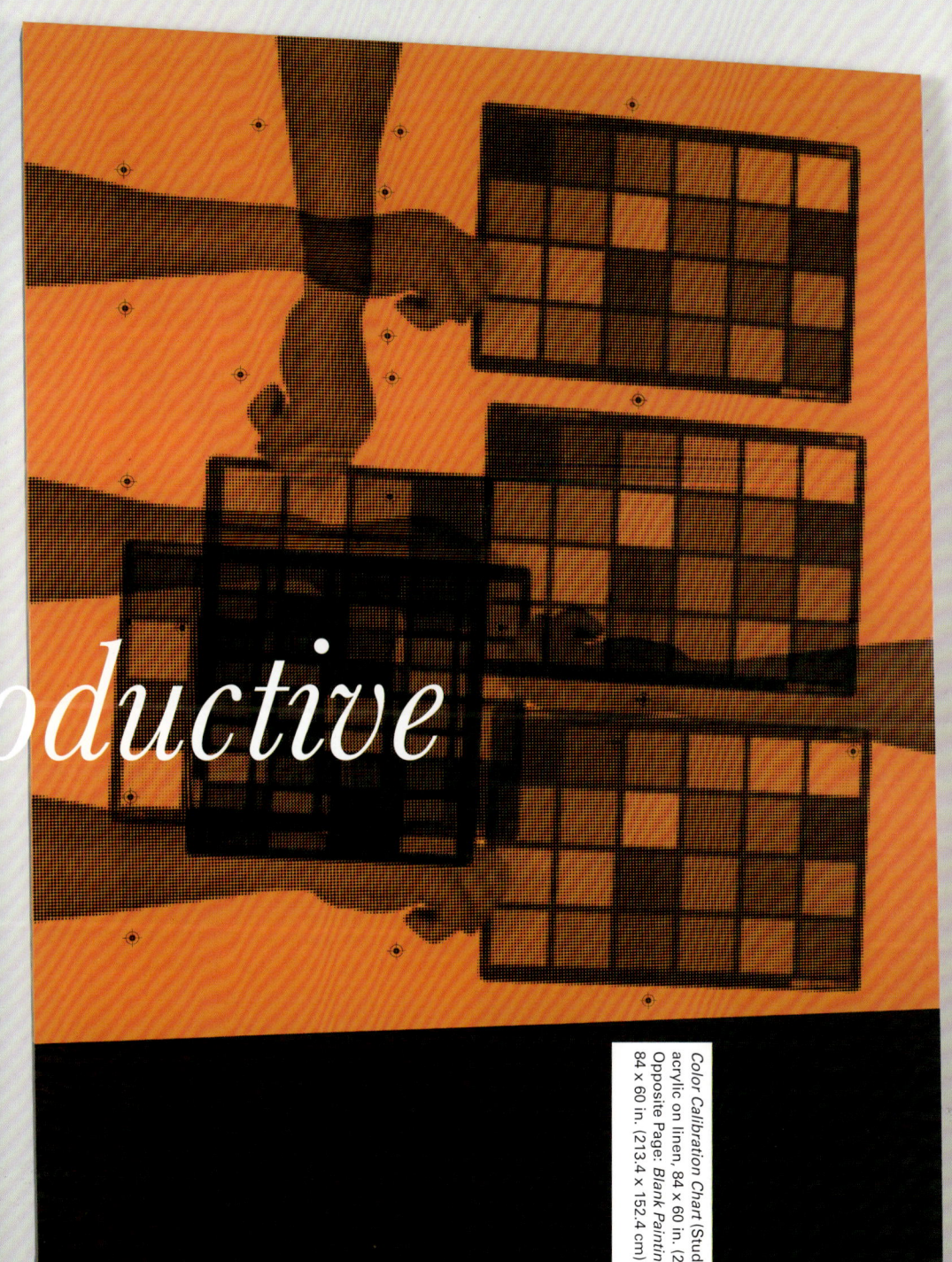

oductive

Color Calibration Chart (Studio View), 2017,
acrylic on linen, 84 x 60 in. (213.4 x 152.4 cm)
Opposite Page: *Blank Painting*, 2017, acrylic on linen,
84 x 60 in. (213.4 x 152.4 cm)

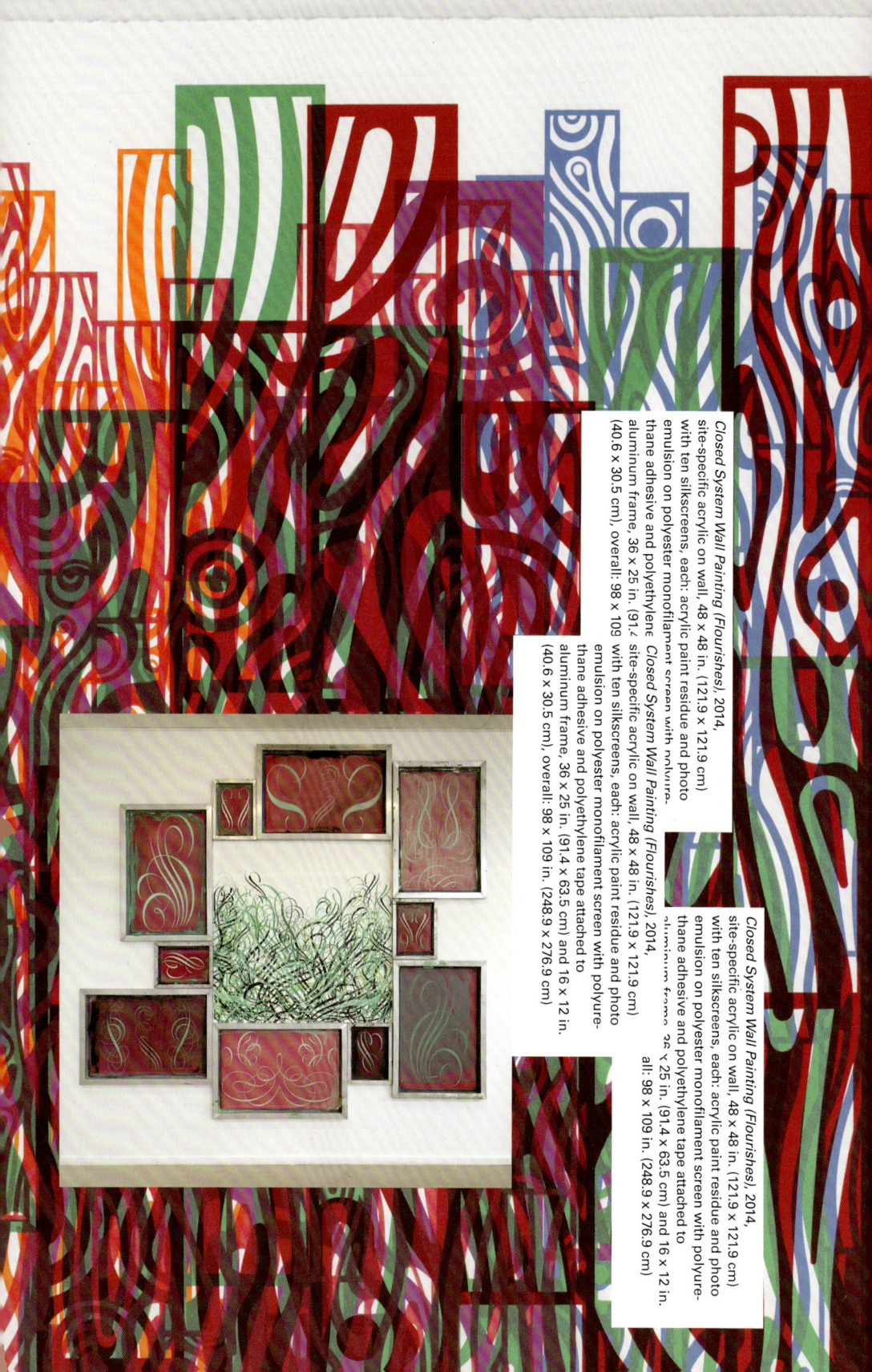

Closed System Wall Painting (Flourishes), 2014, site-specific acrylic on wall, 48 x 48 in. (121.9 x 121.9 cm) with ten silkscreens, each: acrylic paint residue and photo emulsion on polyester monofilament screen with polyurethane adhesive and polyethylene aluminum frame, 36 x 25 in. (91.4 x 63.5 cm) and 16 x 12 in. (40.6 x 30.5 cm), overall: 98 x 109 in. (248.9 x 276.9 cm)

Closed System Wall Painting (Flourishes), 2014, site-specific acrylic on wall, 48 x 48 in. (121.9 x 121.9 cm) with ten silkscreens, each: acrylic paint residue and photo emulsion on polyester monofilament screen with polyurethane adhesive and polyethylene aluminum frame, 36 x 25 in. (91.4 x 63.5 cm) and 16 x 12 in. (40.6 x 30.5 cm), overall: 98 x 109 in. (248.9 x 276.9 cm)

Closed System Wall Painting (Flourishes), 2014, site-specific acrylic on wall, 48 x 48 in. (121.9 x 121.9 cm) with ten silkscreens, each: acrylic paint residue and photo emulsion on polyester monofilament screen with polyurethane adhesive and polyethylene aluminum frame, 36 x 25 in. (91.4 x 63.5 cm) and 16 x 12 in. (248.9 x 276.9 cm)

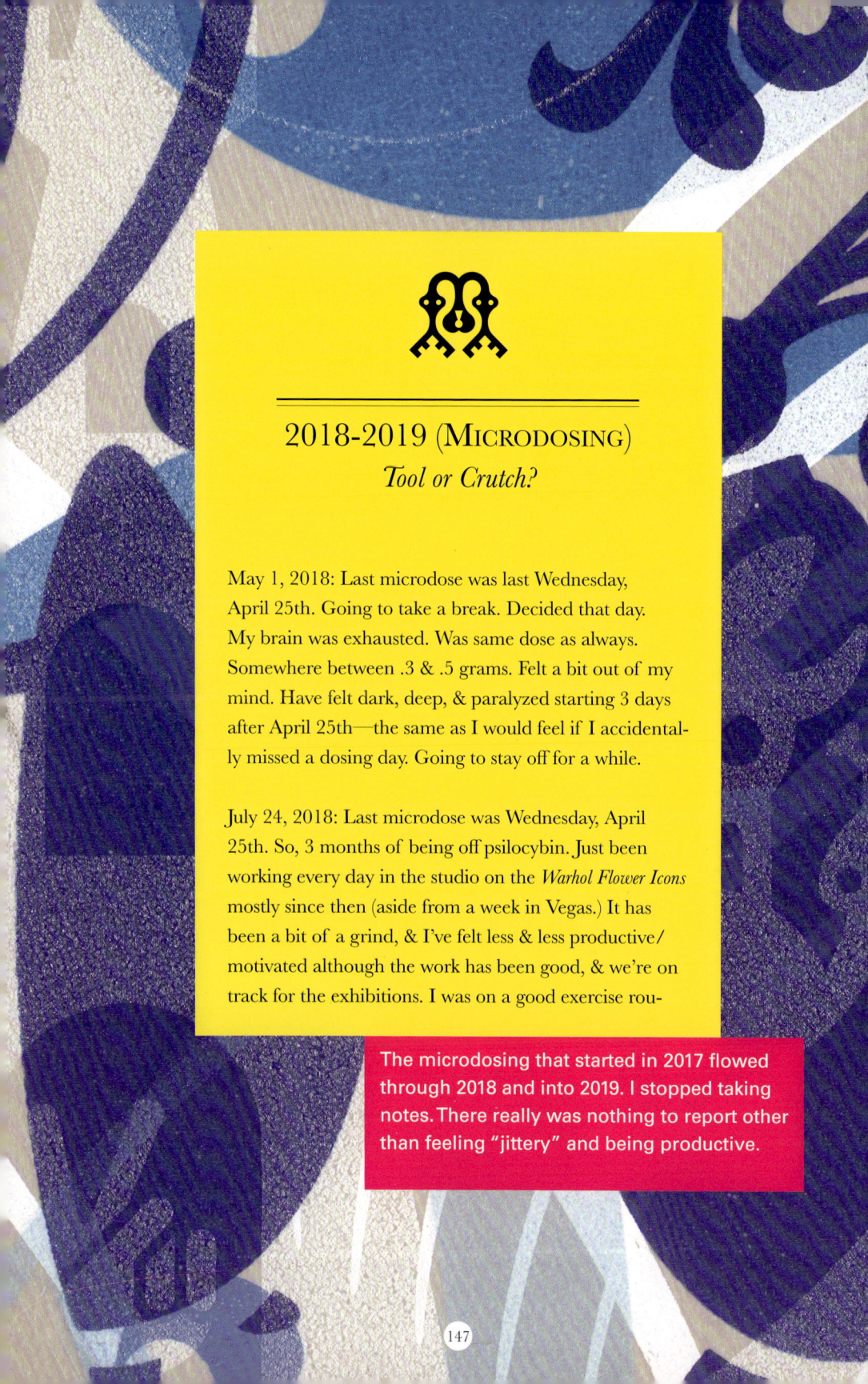

2018-2019 (MICRODOSING)
Tool or Crutch?

May 1, 2018: Last microdose was last Wednesday, April 25th. Going to take a break. Decided that day. My brain was exhausted. Was same dose as always. Somewhere between .3 & .5 grams. Felt a bit out of my mind. Have felt dark, deep, & paralyzed starting 3 days after April 25th—the same as I would feel if I accidentally missed a dosing day. Going to stay off for a while.

July 24, 2018: Last microdose was Wednesday, April 25th. So, 3 months of being off psilocybin. Just been working every day in the studio on the *Warhol Flower Icons* mostly since then (aside from a week in Vegas.) It has been a bit of a grind, & I've felt less & less productive/ motivated although the work has been good, & we're on track for the exhibitions. I was on a good exercise rou-

The microdosing that started in 2017 flowed through 2018 and into 2019. I stopped taking notes. There really was nothing to report other than feeling "jittery" and being productive.

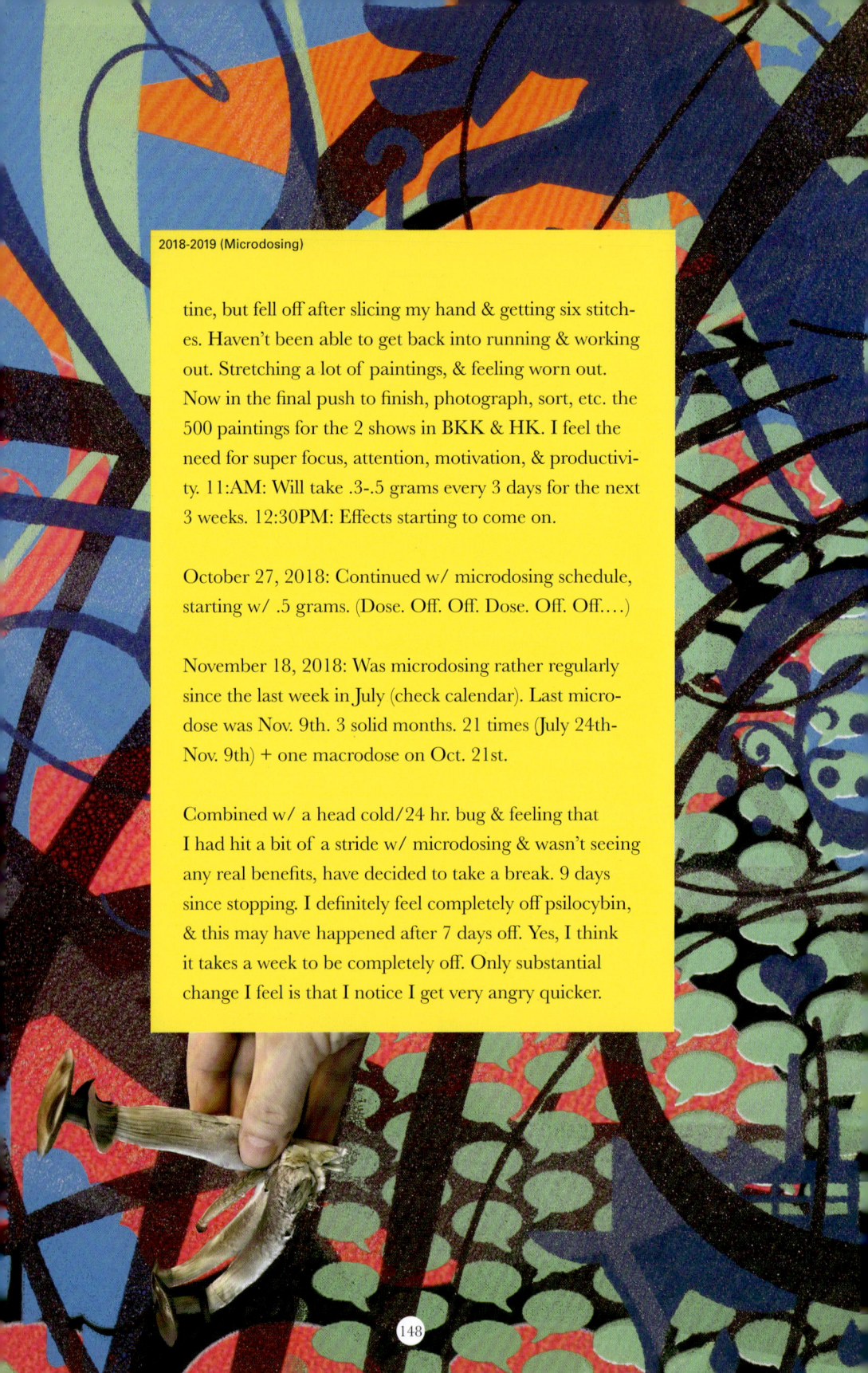

tine, but fell off after slicing my hand & getting six stitch-
es. Haven't been able to get back into running & working
out. Stretching a lot of paintings, & feeling worn out.
Now in the final push to finish, photograph, sort, etc. the
500 paintings for the 2 shows in BKK & HK. I feel the
need for super focus, attention, motivation, & productivity. 11:AM: Will take .3-.5 grams every 3 days for the next
3 weeks. 12:30PM: Effects starting to come on.

October 27, 2018: Continued w/ microdosing schedule,
starting w/ .5 grams. (Dose. Off. Off. Dose. Off. Off....)

November 18, 2018: Was microdosing rather regularly
since the last week in July (check calendar). Last microdose was Nov. 9th. 3 solid months. 21 times (July 24th-
Nov. 9th) + one macrodose on Oct. 21st.

Combined w/ a head cold/24 hr. bug & feeling that
I had hit a bit of a stride w/ microdosing & wasn't seeing
any real benefits, have decided to take a break. 9 days
since stopping. I definitely feel completely off psilocybin,
& this may have happened after 7 days off. Yes, I think
it takes a week to be completely off. Only substantial
change I feel is that I notice I get very angry quicker.

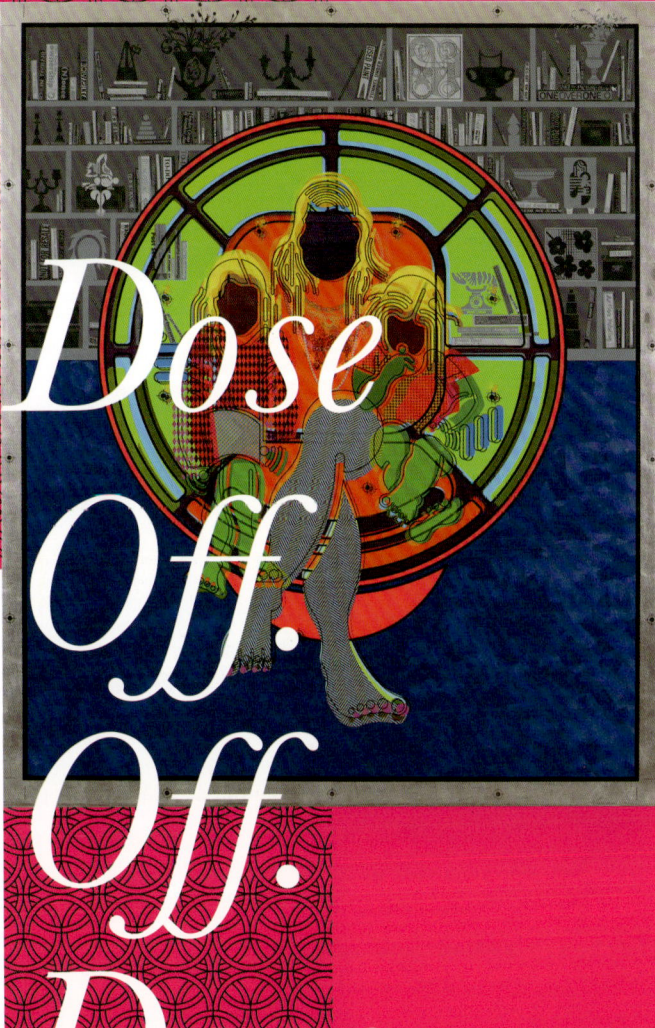

Dose
Off.
Off.
Dose.
Off.
Off.

Mother & Child (Ball Chair), 2019, acrylic and metal leaf on linen, 72 x 60 in. (182.88 x 152.4 cm)

I have been exercising w/ regularity for the past 7 weeks.
I just wasn't seeing/feeling or needing the benefits of
microdosing & don't want to make the mistake of turning this tool into a crutch. So, I've stopped. Will continue
again when I feel it would be beneficial—probably to
help get into a productive groove after the holidays & in
the new year—January.

January 28, 2019: Starting microdosing again. Today:
.32 grams after lunch. 2:47PM. I have a clear vision of
what needs doing in the studio over the next few months.
A clear vision for the work. A clear vision of how to get
it done. Just need to focus. 2 weeks in on a new exercise
challenge. Stressed & in a rage recently. Really bad
last night. Reason for starting now—& the desire to be
productive & focused. I'm so close to catching up to myself, especially w/ the periodic table of drawing elements.
Starting regular schedule: Every 3 days:
Dose/Rest/Rest/Dose.

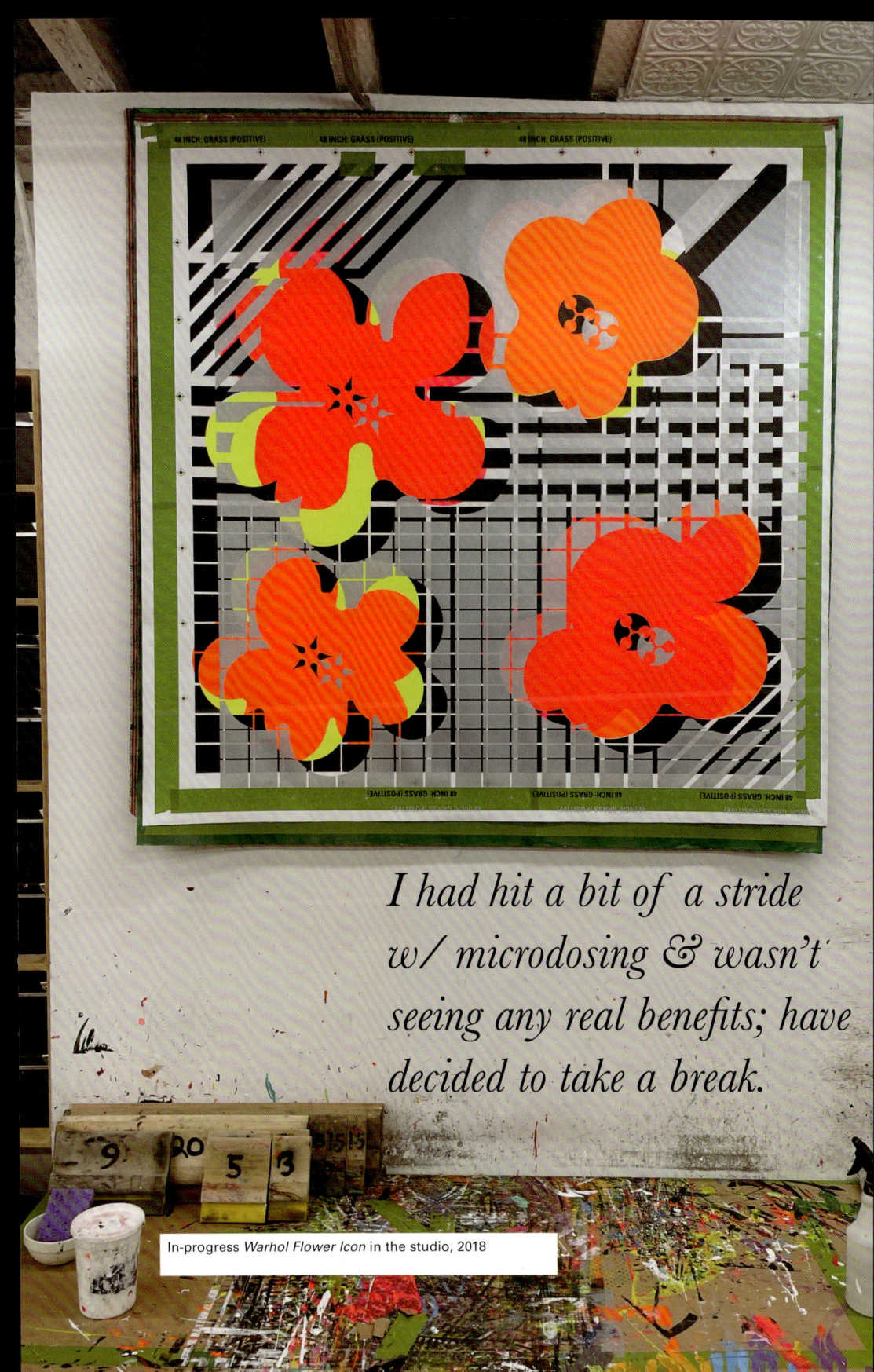

I had hit a bit of a stride w/ microdosing & wasn't seeing any real benefits; have decided to take a break.

In-progress *Warhol Flower Icon* in the studio, 2018

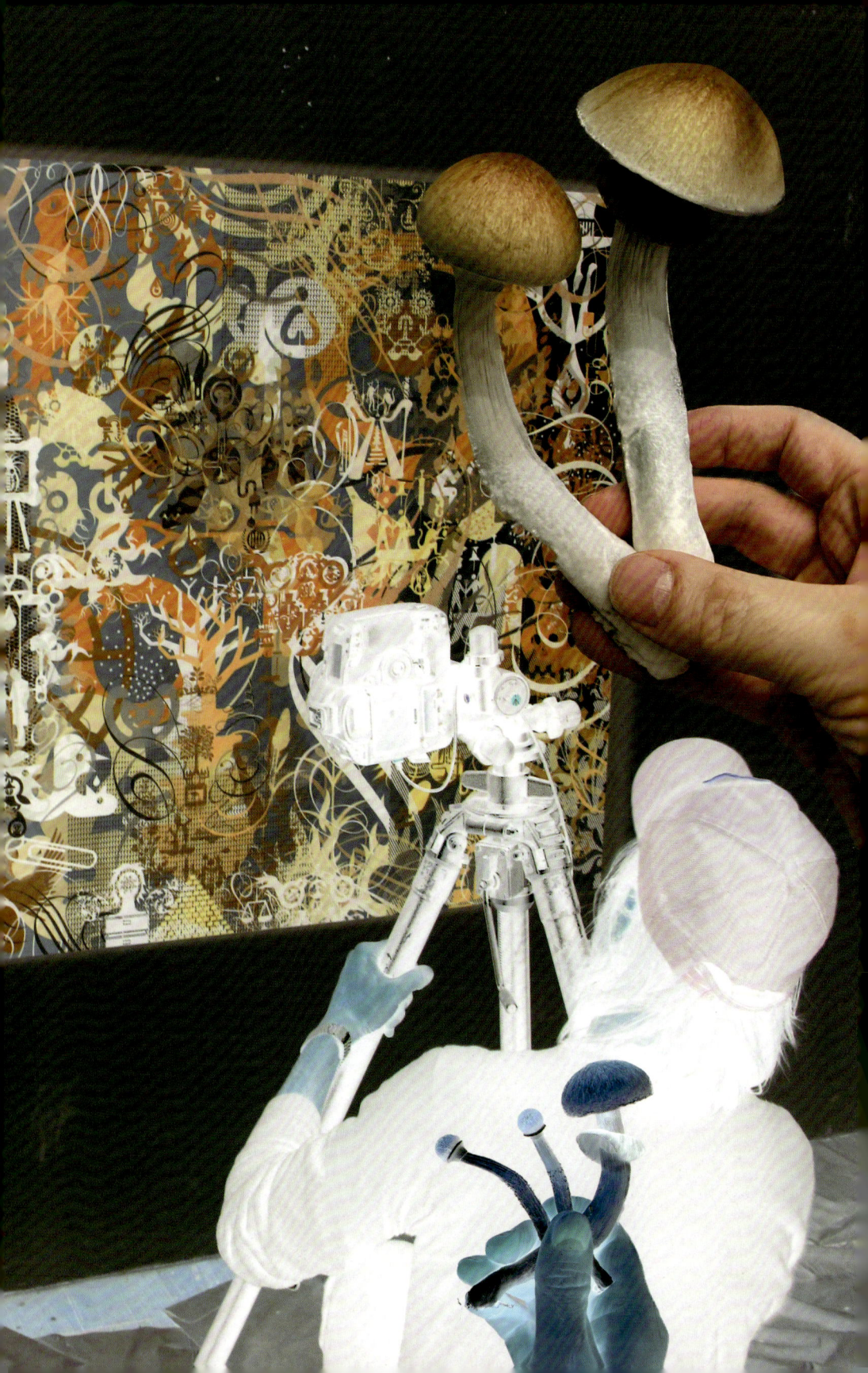

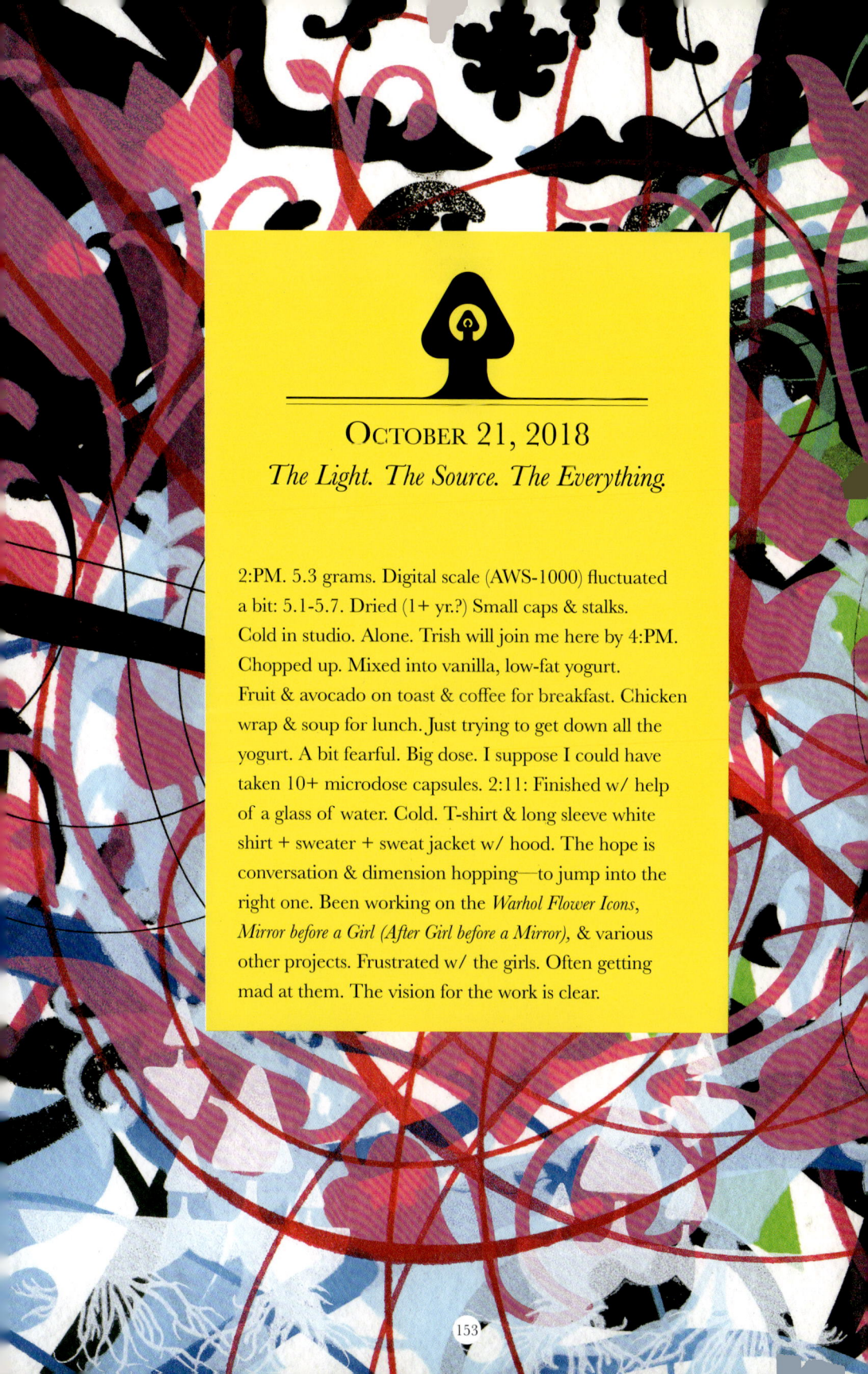

OCTOBER 21, 2018

The Light. The Source. The Everything.

2:PM. 5.3 grams. Digital scale (AWS-1000) fluctuated a bit: 5.1-5.7. Dried (1+ yr.?) Small caps & stalks. Cold in studio. Alone. Trish will join me here by 4:PM. Chopped up. Mixed into vanilla, low-fat yogurt. Fruit & avocado on toast & coffee for breakfast. Chicken wrap & soup for lunch. Just trying to get down all the yogurt. A bit fearful. Big dose. I suppose I could have taken 10+ microdose capsules. 2:11: Finished w/ help of a glass of water. Cold. T-shirt & long sleeve white shirt + sweater + sweat jacket w/ hood. The hope is conversation & dimension hopping—to jump into the right one. Been working on the *Warhol Flower Icons, Mirror before a Girl (After Girl before a Mirror),* & various other projects. Frustrated w/ the girls. Often getting mad at them. The vision for the work is clear.

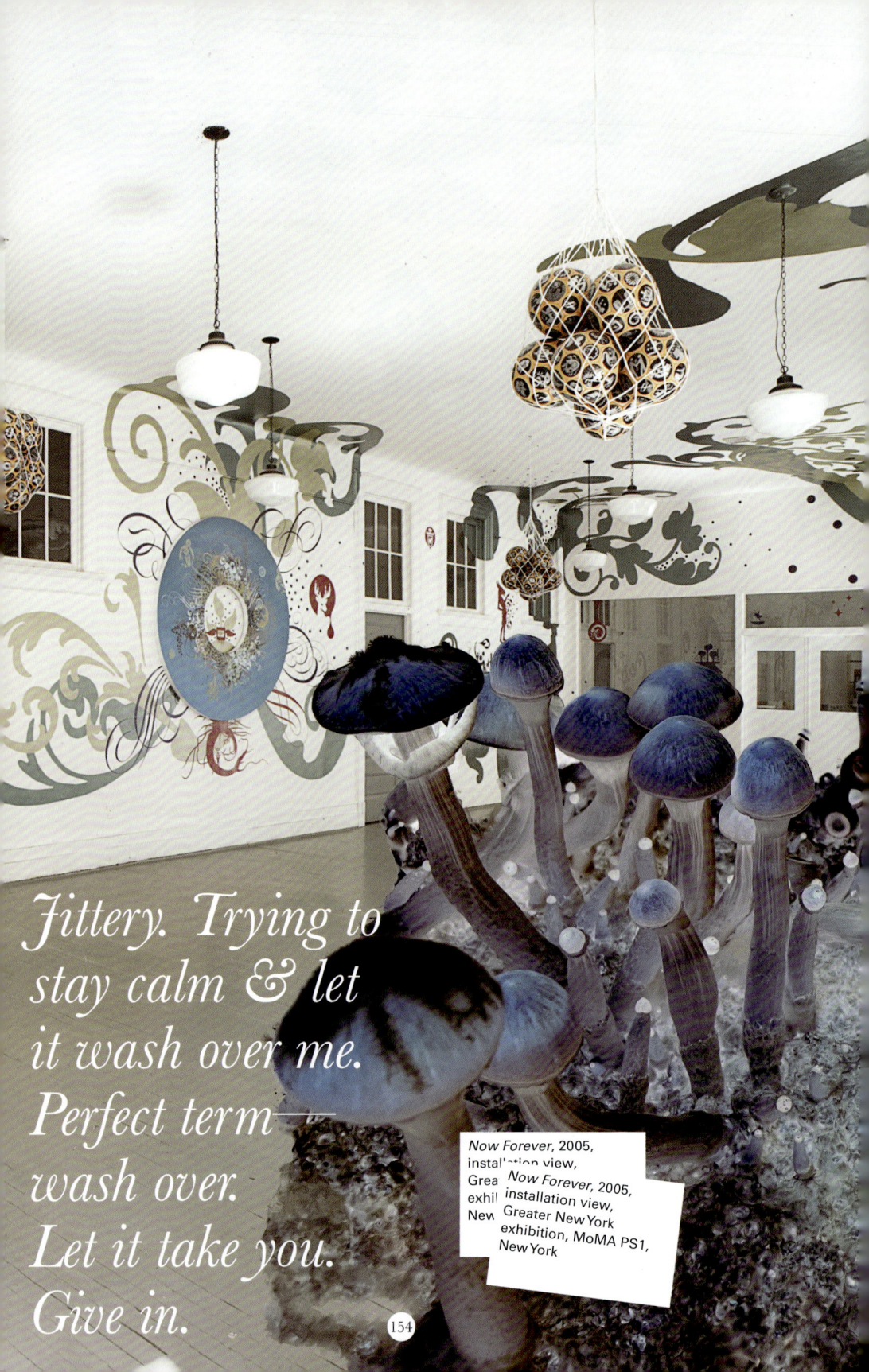

Jittery. Trying to stay calm & let it wash over me. Perfect term— wash over. Let it take you. Give in.

Now Forever, 2005, installation view, Greater New York exhibition, MoMA PS1, New York

154

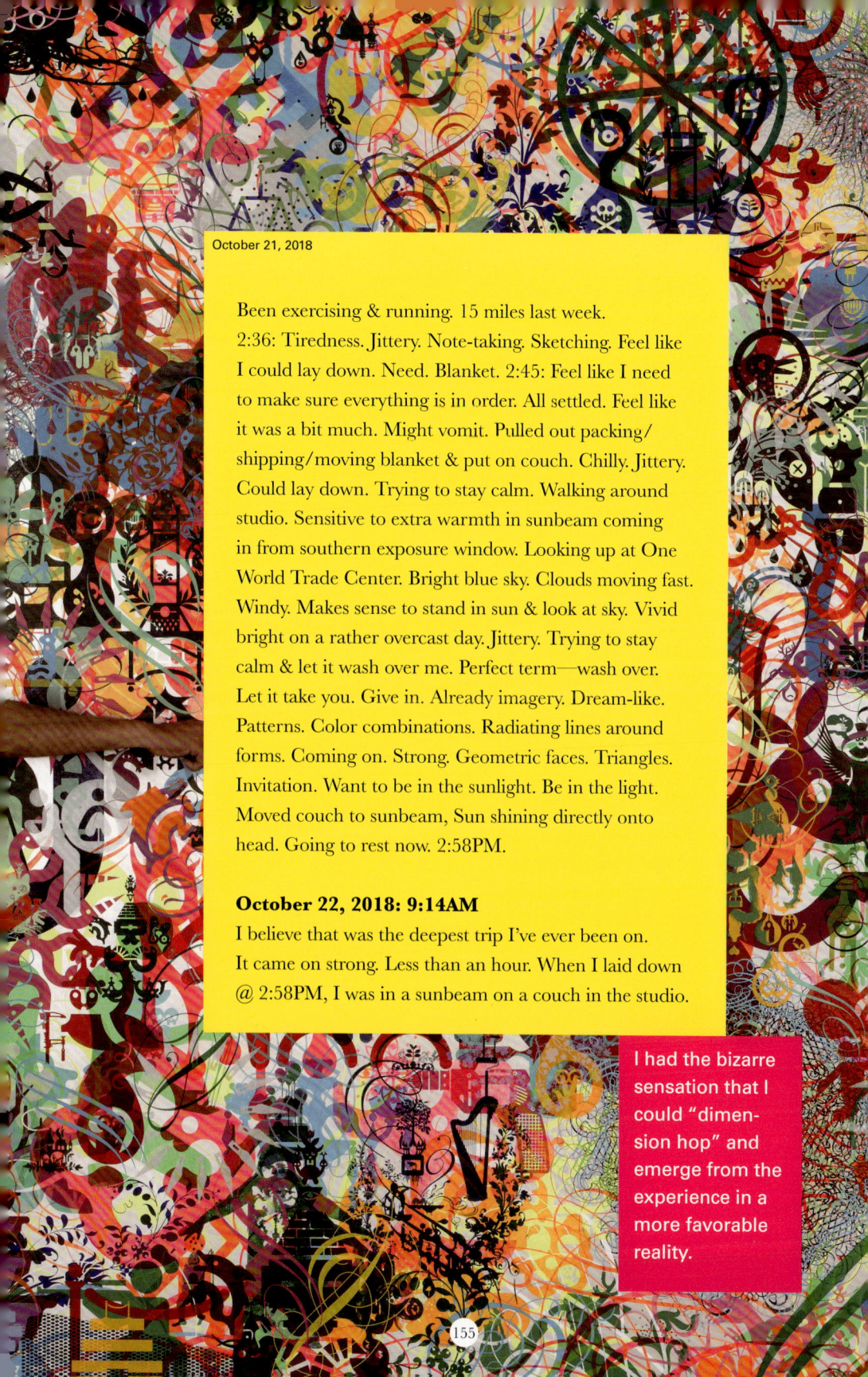

October 21, 2018

Been exercising & running. 15 miles last week.
2:36: Tiredness. Jittery. Note-taking. Sketching. Feel like
I could lay down. Need. Blanket. 2:45: Feel like I need
to make sure everything is in order. All settled. Feel like
it was a bit much. Might vomit. Pulled out packing/
shipping/moving blanket & put on couch. Chilly. Jittery.
Could lay down. Trying to stay calm. Walking around
studio. Sensitive to extra warmth in sunbeam coming
in from southern exposure window. Looking up at One
World Trade Center. Bright blue sky. Clouds moving fast.
Windy. Makes sense to stand in sun & look at sky. Vivid
bright on a rather overcast day. Jittery. Trying to stay
calm & let it wash over me. Perfect term—wash over.
Let it take you. Give in. Already imagery. Dream-like.
Patterns. Color combinations. Radiating lines around
forms. Coming on. Strong. Geometric faces. Triangles.
Invitation. Want to be in the sunlight. Be in the light.
Moved couch to sunbeam, Sun shining directly onto
head. Going to rest now. 2:58PM.

October 22, 2018: 9:14AM
I believe that was the deepest trip I've ever been on.
It came on strong. Less than an hour. When I laid down
@ 2:58PM, I was in a sunbeam on a couch in the studio.

I had the bizarre
sensation that I
could "dimen-
sion hop" and
emerge from the
experience in a
more favorable
reality.

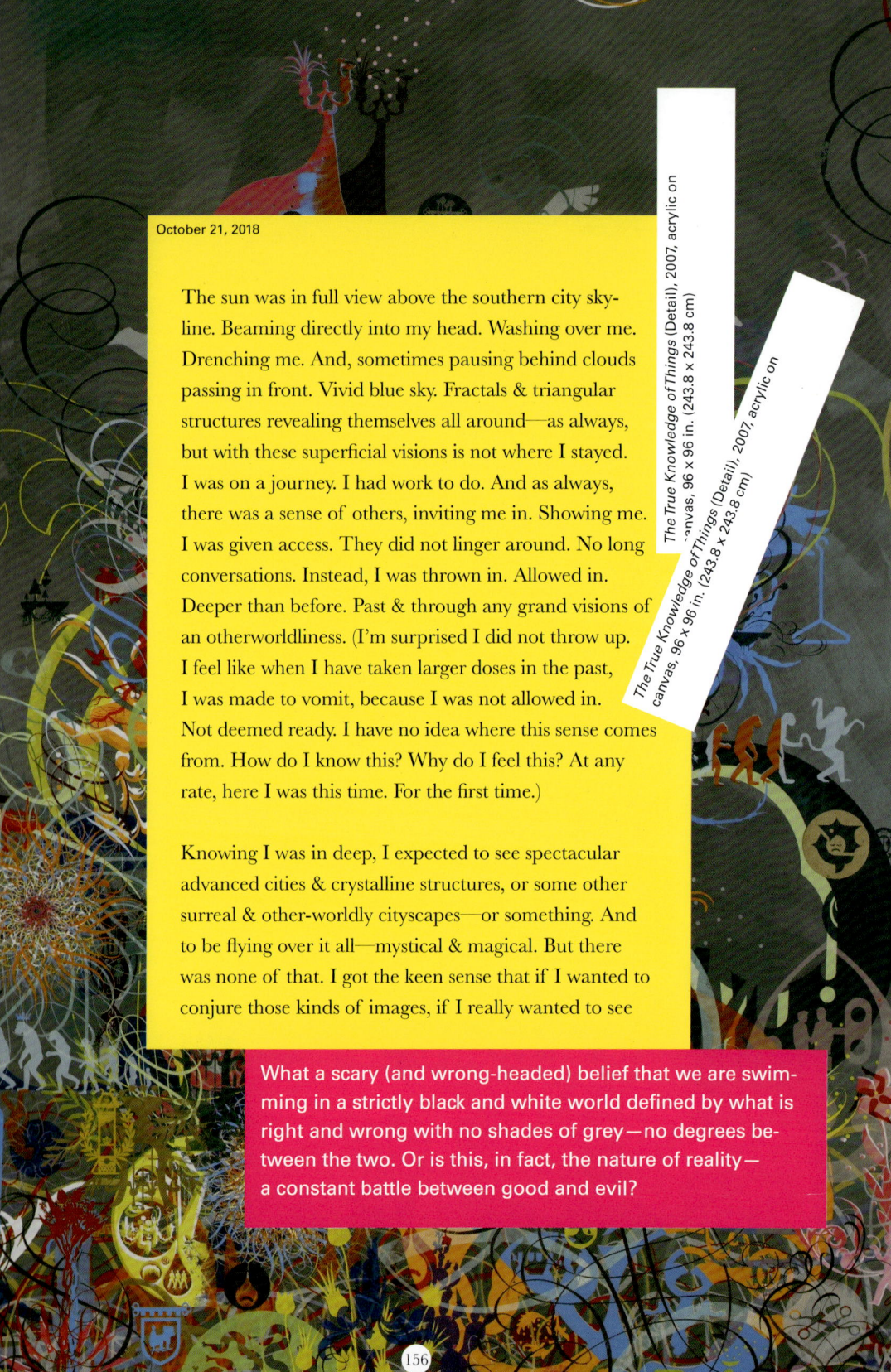

October 21, 2018

The sun was in full view above the southern city sky-line. Beaming directly into my head. Washing over me. Drenching me. And, sometimes pausing behind clouds passing in front. Vivid blue sky. Fractals & triangular structures revealing themselves all around—as always, but with these superficial visions is not where I stayed. I was on a journey. I had work to do. And as always, there was a sense of others, inviting me in. Showing me. I was given access. They did not linger around. No long conversations. Instead, I was thrown in. Allowed in. Deeper than before. Past & through any grand visions of an otherworldliness. (I'm surprised I did not throw up. I feel like when I have taken larger doses in the past, I was made to vomit, because I was not allowed in. Not deemed ready. I have no idea where this sense comes from. How do I know this? Why do I feel this? At any rate, here I was this time. For the first time.)

Knowing I was in deep, I expected to see spectacular advanced cities & crystalline structures, or some other surreal & other-worldly cityscapes—or something. And to be flying over it all—mystical & magical. But there was none of that. I got the keen sense that if I wanted to conjure those kinds of images, if I really wanted to see

The True Knowledge of Things (Detail), 2007, acrylic on canvas, 96 × 96 in. (243.8 × 243.8 cm)

The True Knowledge of Things (Detail), 2007, acrylic on canvas, 96 × 96 in. (243.8 × 243.8 cm)

What a scary (and wrong-headed) belief that we are swimming in a strictly black and white world defined by what is right and wrong with no shades of grey—no degrees between the two. Or is this, in fact, the nature of reality—a constant battle between good and evil?

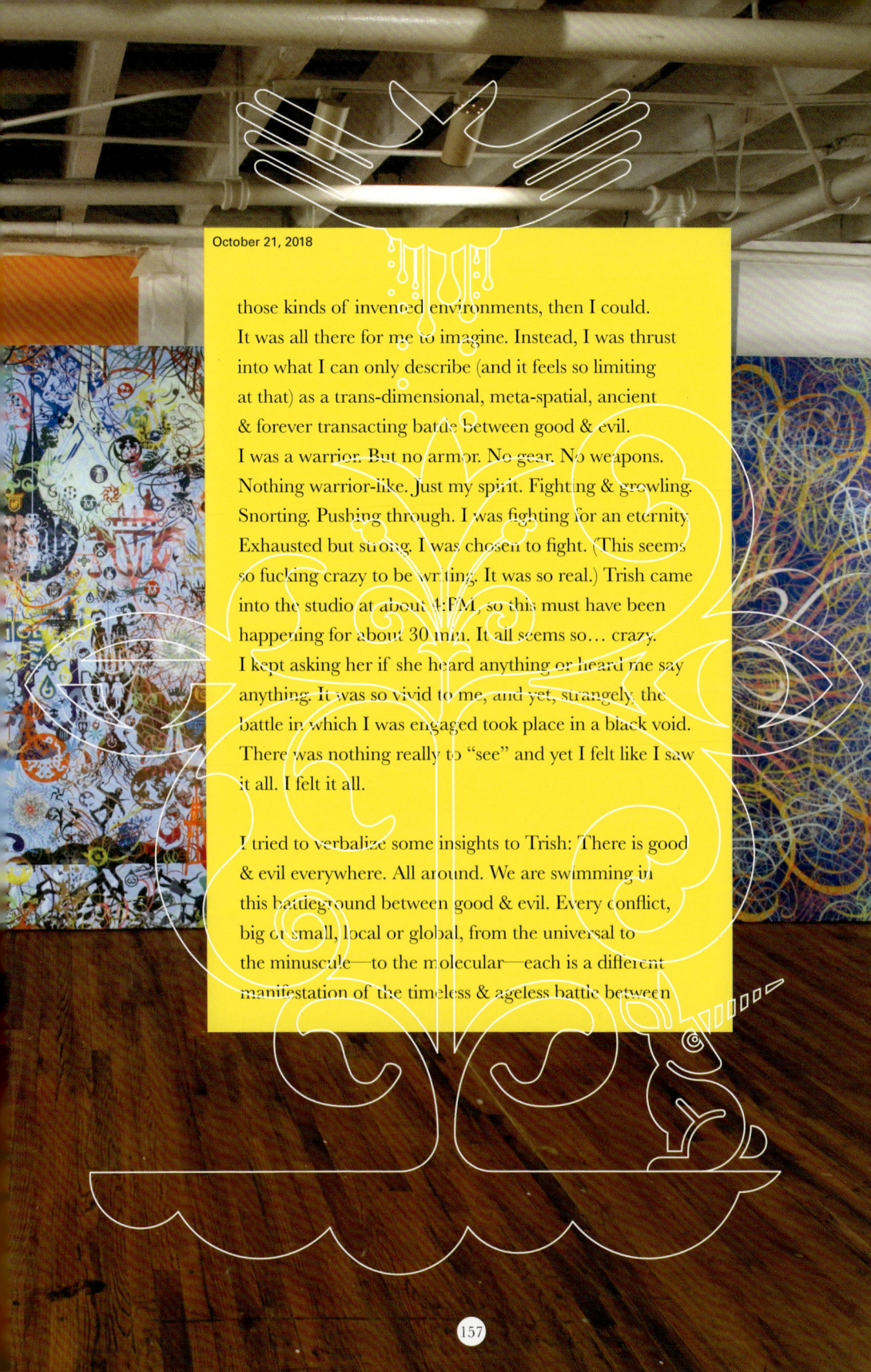

October 21, 2018

those kinds of invented environments, then I could.
It was all there for me to imagine. Instead, I was thrust
into what I can only describe (and it feels so limiting
at that) as a trans-dimensional, meta-spatial, ancient
& forever transacting battle between good & evil.
I was a warrior. But no armor. No gear. No weapons.
Nothing warrior-like. Just my spirit. Fighting & growling.
Snorting. Pushing through. I was fighting for an eternity.
Exhausted but strong. I was chosen to fight. (This seems
so fucking crazy to be writing. It was so real.) Trish came
into the studio at about 4:PM, so this must have been
happening for about 30 min. It all seems so… crazy.
I kept asking her if she heard anything or heard me say
anything. It was so vivid to me, and yet, strangely, the
battle in which I was engaged took place in a black void.
There was nothing really to "see" and yet I felt like I saw
it all. I felt it all.

I tried to verbalize some insights to Trish: There is good
& evil everywhere. All around. We are swimming in
this battleground between good & evil. Every conflict,
big or small, local or global, from the universal to
the minuscule—to the molecular—each is a different
manifestation of the timeless & ageless battle between

157

good & evil. Every. Single. Moment. Every thought.
Every unit of consciousness—a decision—good or evil.
Black or white. To have been given this insight, this
feeling is mind-shifting. Every single moment matters.
Every single decision counts & contributes to this fight
between good & evil. And then, I was given access—
a vision. I was shown. I saw everything. I cannot describe
it any more clearly than that. Everything. Rather,
perhaps, the source of everything. Same thing.

A bright, bright shining, radiating light. Energy.
Flow like a river but not beholden to gravity like a river.
Not grounded. Not anywhere, but rather everywhere.
This was enlightenment. The light. But it was more than
a light. It really was everything. And from this, comes
everything. All matter, universes, conceptions, stories,
myths, narratives, languages, worlds— We pull from this
to build our own worlds. What is pulled out can take
any shape or form we want. We decide. We invent.
We produce. We give shape & form—& it doesn't matter,
because it comes from the same source. Even talking
about it (writing) or even trying to describe it seems like
blasphemy, because it cannot be described. What are
we to do?

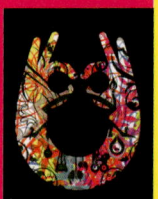

Above: *Search*
Right: *Unicorns*
Each: 2018, acrylic on wood panel,
12 x 9 in. (30.5 x 22.9 cm)

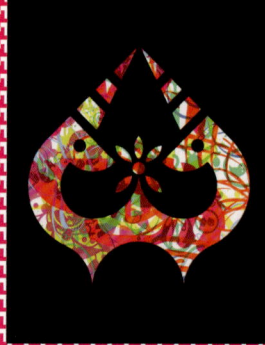

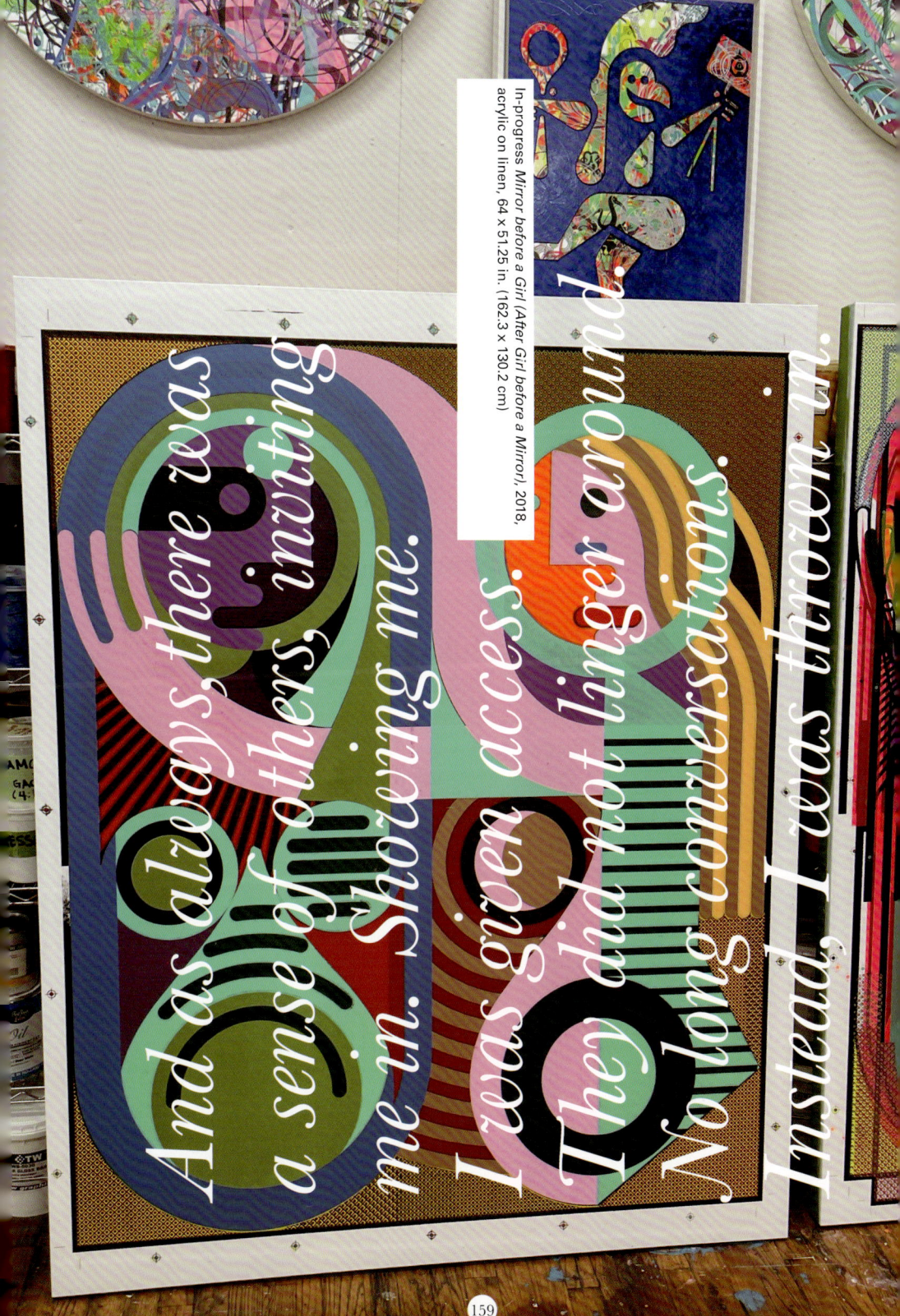

In-progress *Mirror before a Girl (After Girl before a Mirror),* 2018, acrylic on linen, 64 x 51.25 in. (162.3 x 130.2 cm)

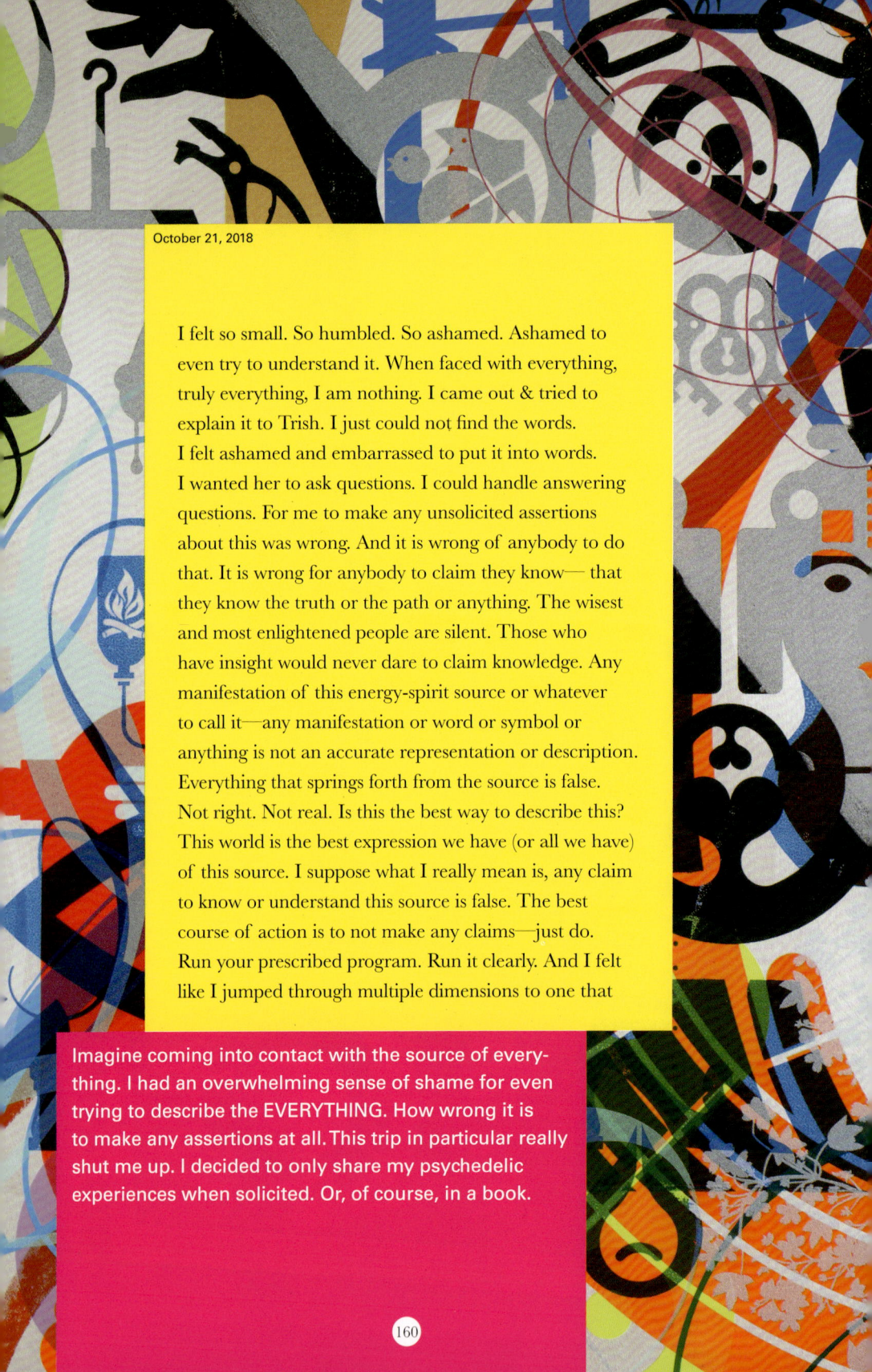

October 21, 2018

I felt so small. So humbled. So ashamed. Ashamed to
even try to understand it. When faced with everything,
truly everything, I am nothing. I came out & tried to
explain it to Trish. I just could not find the words.
I felt ashamed and embarrassed to put it into words.
I wanted her to ask questions. I could handle answering
questions. For me to make any unsolicited assertions
about this was wrong. And it is wrong of anybody to do
that. It is wrong for anybody to claim they know— that
they know the truth or the path or anything. The wisest
and most enlightened people are silent. Those who
have insight would never dare to claim knowledge. Any
manifestation of this energy-spirit source or whatever
to call it—any manifestation or word or symbol or
anything is not an accurate representation or description.
Everything that springs forth from the source is false.
Not right. Not real. Is this the best way to describe this?
This world is the best expression we have (or all we have)
of this source. I suppose what I really mean is, any claim
to know or understand this source is false. The best
course of action is to not make any claims—just do.
Run your prescribed program. Run it clearly. And I felt
like I jumped through multiple dimensions to one that

Imagine coming into contact with the source of everything. I had an overwhelming sense of shame for even
trying to describe the EVERYTHING. How wrong it is
to make any assertions at all. This trip in particular really
shut me up. I decided to only share my psychedelic
experiences when solicited. Or, of course, in a book.

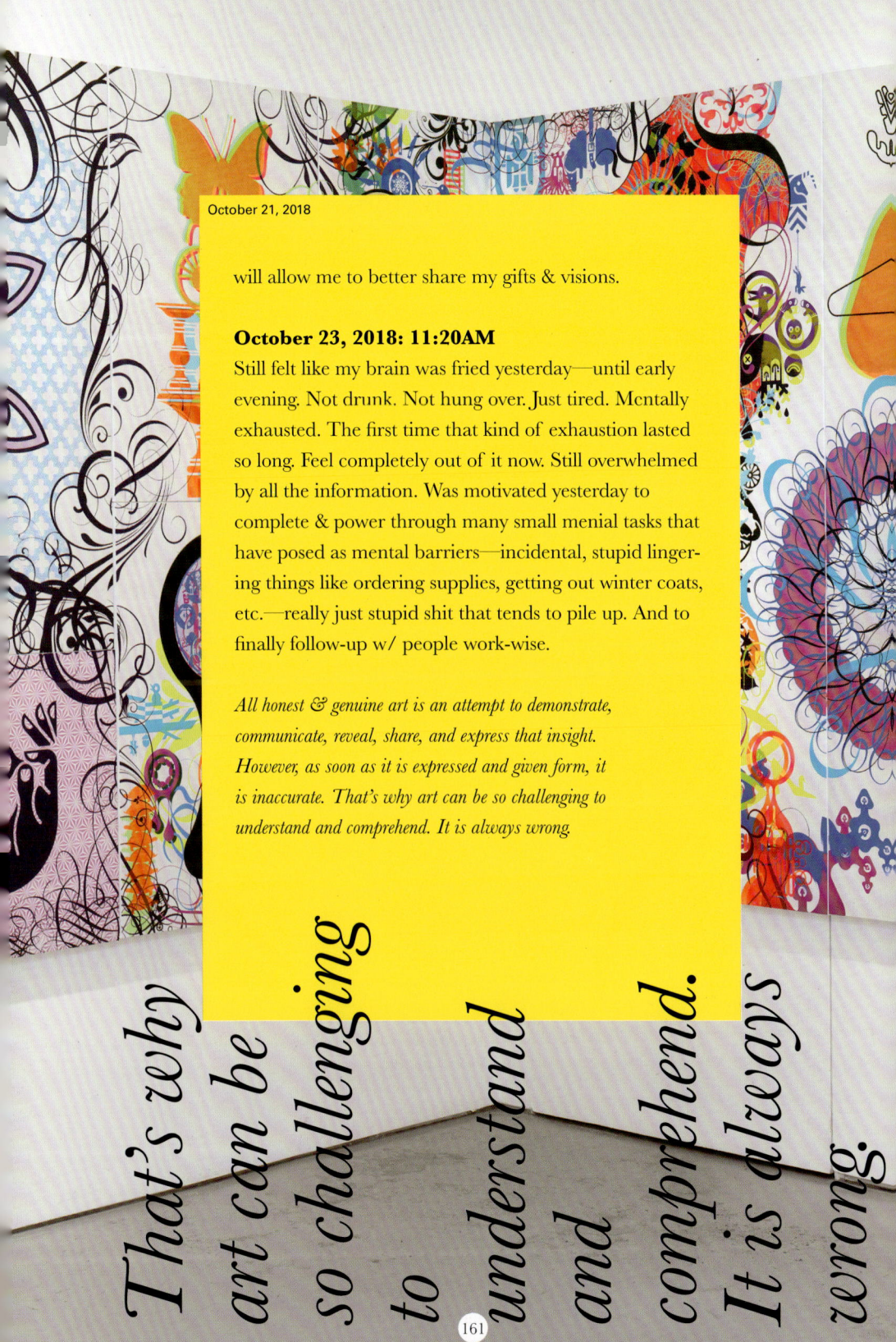

October 21, 2018

will allow me to better share my gifts & visions.

October 23, 2018: 11:20AM
Still felt like my brain was fried yesterday—until early evening. Not drunk. Not hung over. Just tired. Mentally exhausted. The first time that kind of exhaustion lasted so long. Feel completely out of it now. Still overwhelmed by all the information. Was motivated yesterday to complete & power through many small menial tasks that have posed as mental barriers—incidental, stupid lingering things like ordering supplies, getting out winter coats, etc.—really just stupid shit that tends to pile up. And to finally follow-up w/ people work-wise.

All honest & genuine art is an attempt to demonstrate, communicate, reveal, share, and express that insight. However, as soon as it is expressed and given form, it is inaccurate. That's why art can be so challenging to understand and comprehend. It is always wrong.

That's why art can be so challenging to understand and comprehend. It is always wrong.

I felt so small.
So humbled.
So ashamed.
Ashamed to even
try to understand it.
When faced with
everything, truly
everything, I am
nothing.

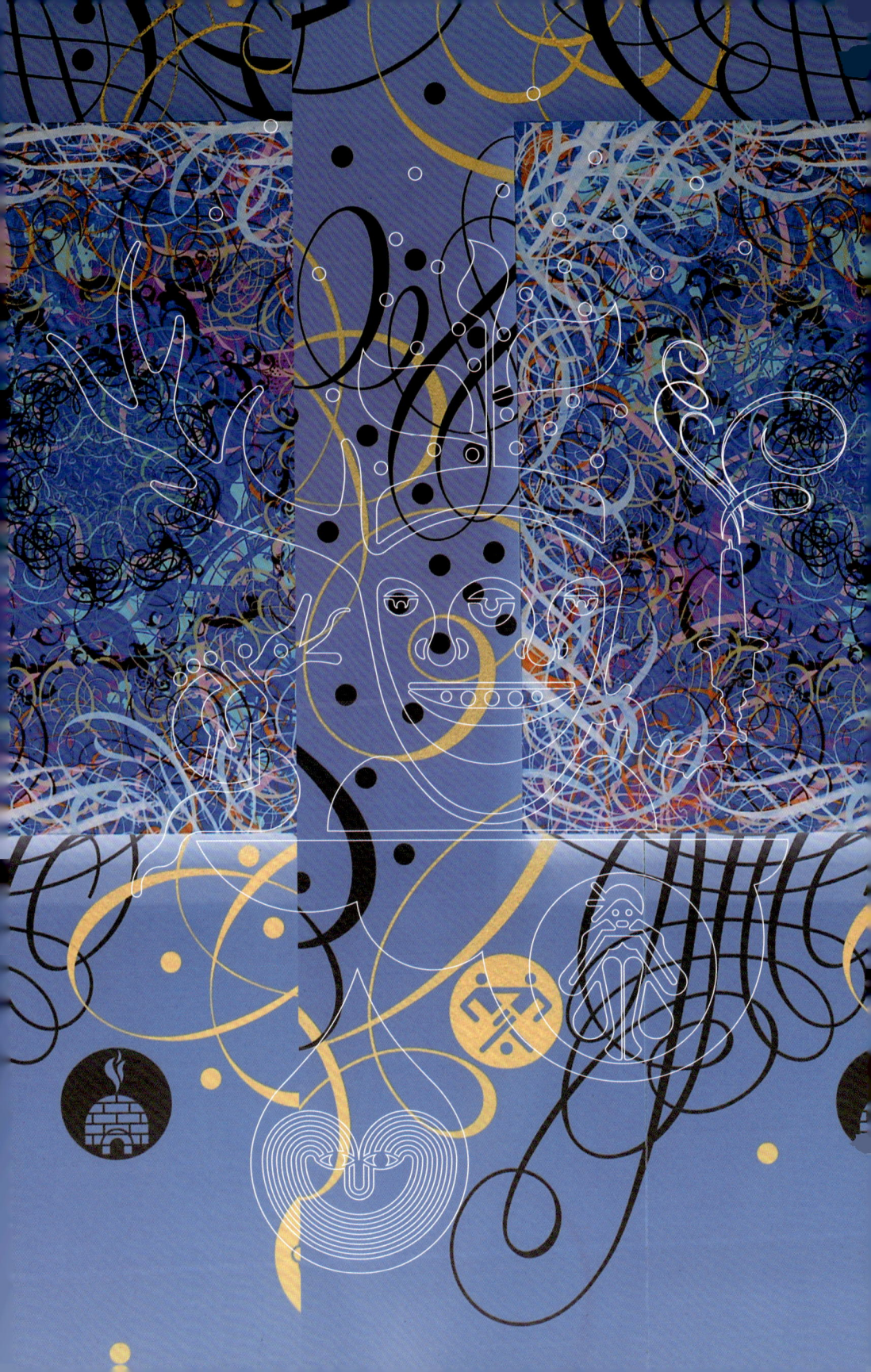

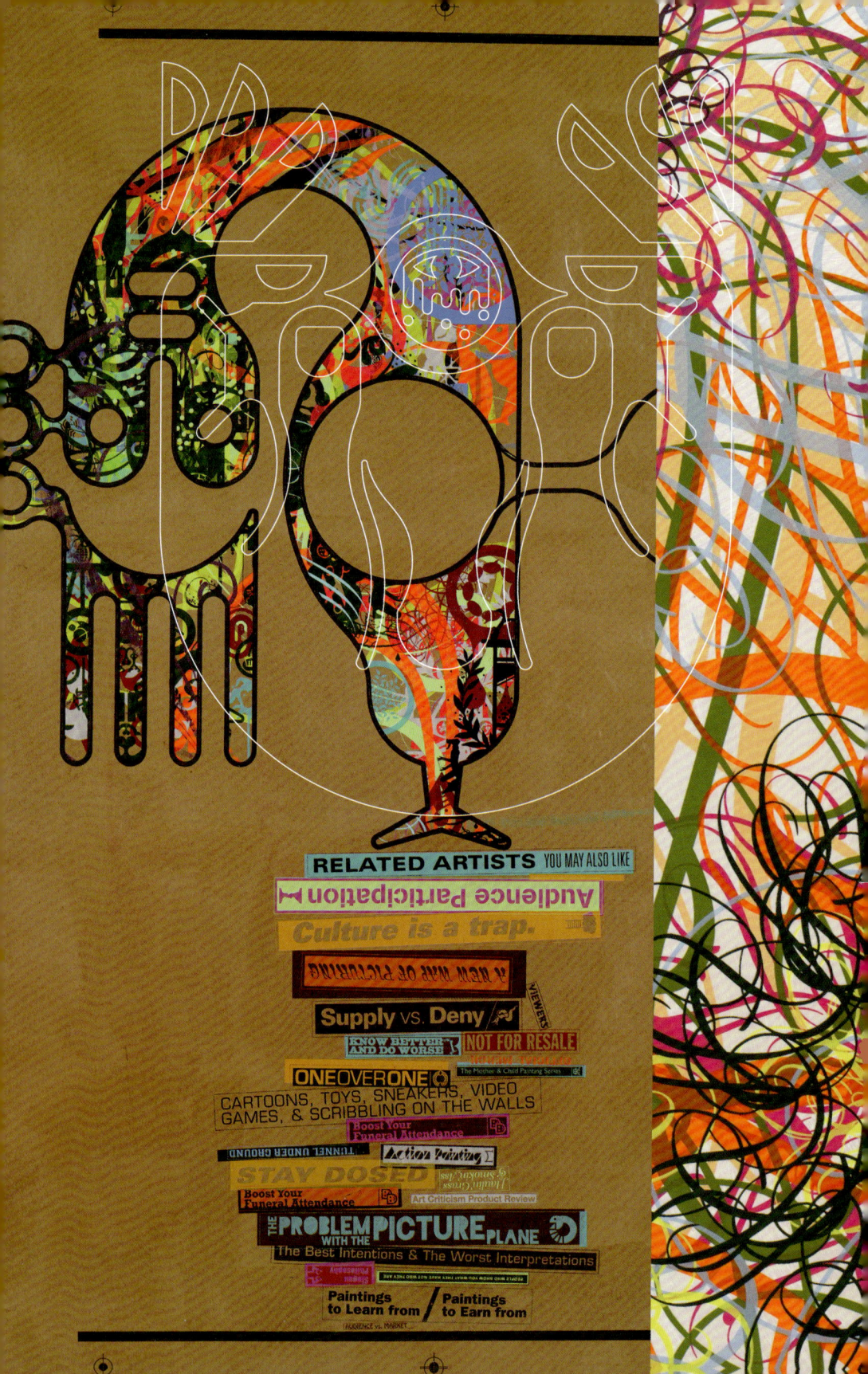

RELATED ARTISTS YOU MAY ALSO LIKE

Audience Participation

Culture is a trap.

A New Way of Picturing

Supply vs. Deny

KNOW BETTER AND DO WORSE   NOT FOR RESALE

ONEOVERONE   The Mother & Child Painting Series

CARTOONS, TOYS, SNEAKERS, VIDEO
GAMES, & SCRIBBLING ON THE WALLS

Boost Your Funeral Attendance

TUNNEL UNDER GROUND   Action Painting

STAY DOSED   Audiences & Sneakers

Boost Your Funeral Attendance   Art Criticism Product Review

THE PROBLEM WITH THE PICTURE PLANE

The Best Intentions & The Worst Interpretations

Paintings to Learn from / Paintings to Earn from

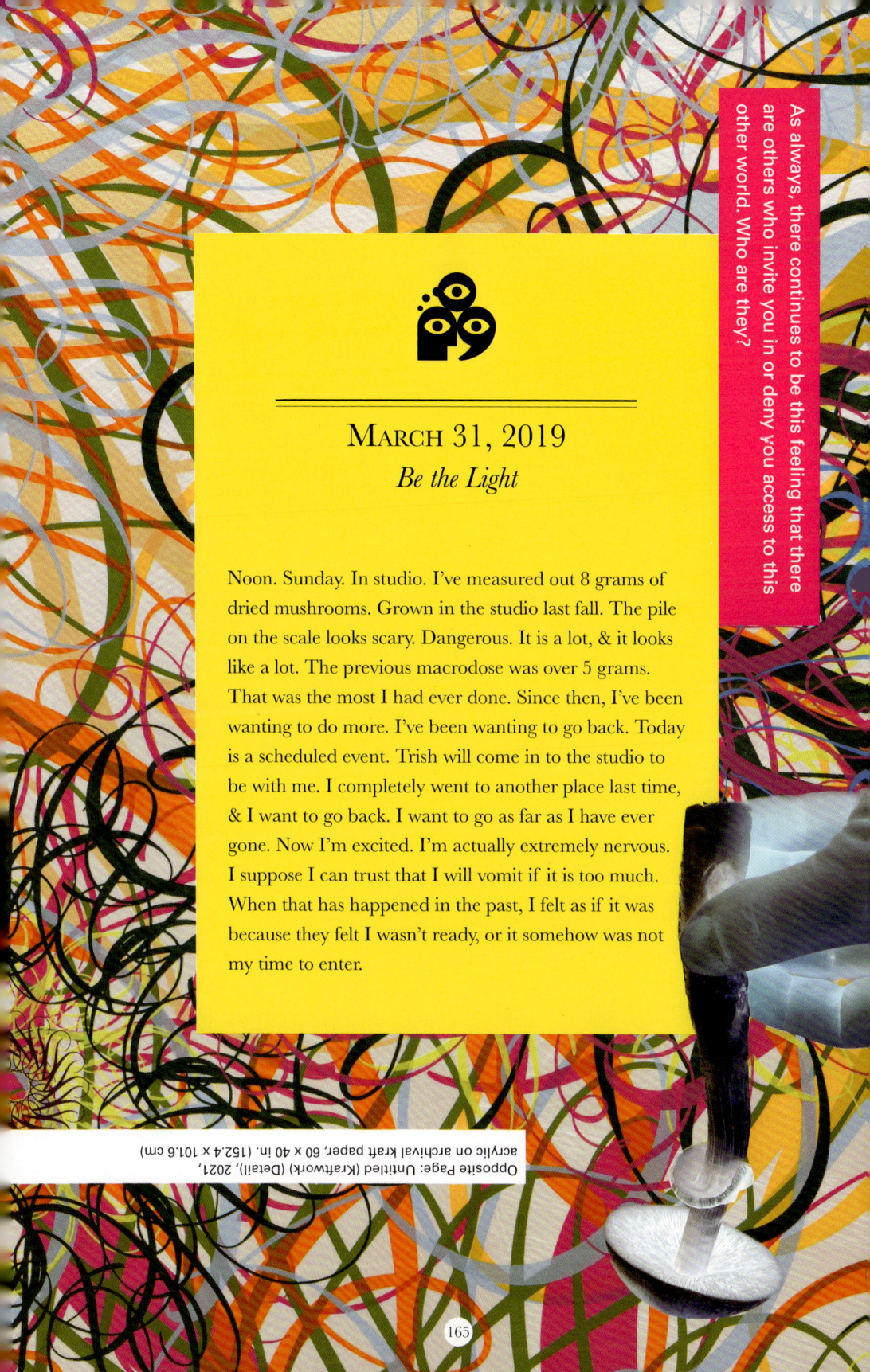

As always, there continues to be this feeling that there are others who invite you in or deny you access to this other world. Who are they?

MARCH 31, 2019

Be the Light

Noon. Sunday. In studio. I've measured out 8 grams of dried mushrooms. Grown in the studio last fall. The pile on the scale looks scary. Dangerous. It is a lot, & it looks like a lot. The previous macrodose was over 5 grams. That was the most I had ever done. Since then, I've been wanting to do more. I've been wanting to go back. Today is a scheduled event. Trish will come in to the studio to be with me. I completely went to another place last time, & I want to go back. I want to go as far as I have ever gone. Now I'm excited. I'm actually extremely nervous. I suppose I can trust that I will vomit if it is too much. When that has happened in the past, I felt as if it was because they felt I wasn't ready, or it somehow was not my time to enter.

Opposite Page: Untitled (Kraftwork) (Detail), 2021, acrylic on archival kraft paper, 60 x 40 in. (152.4 x 101.6 cm)

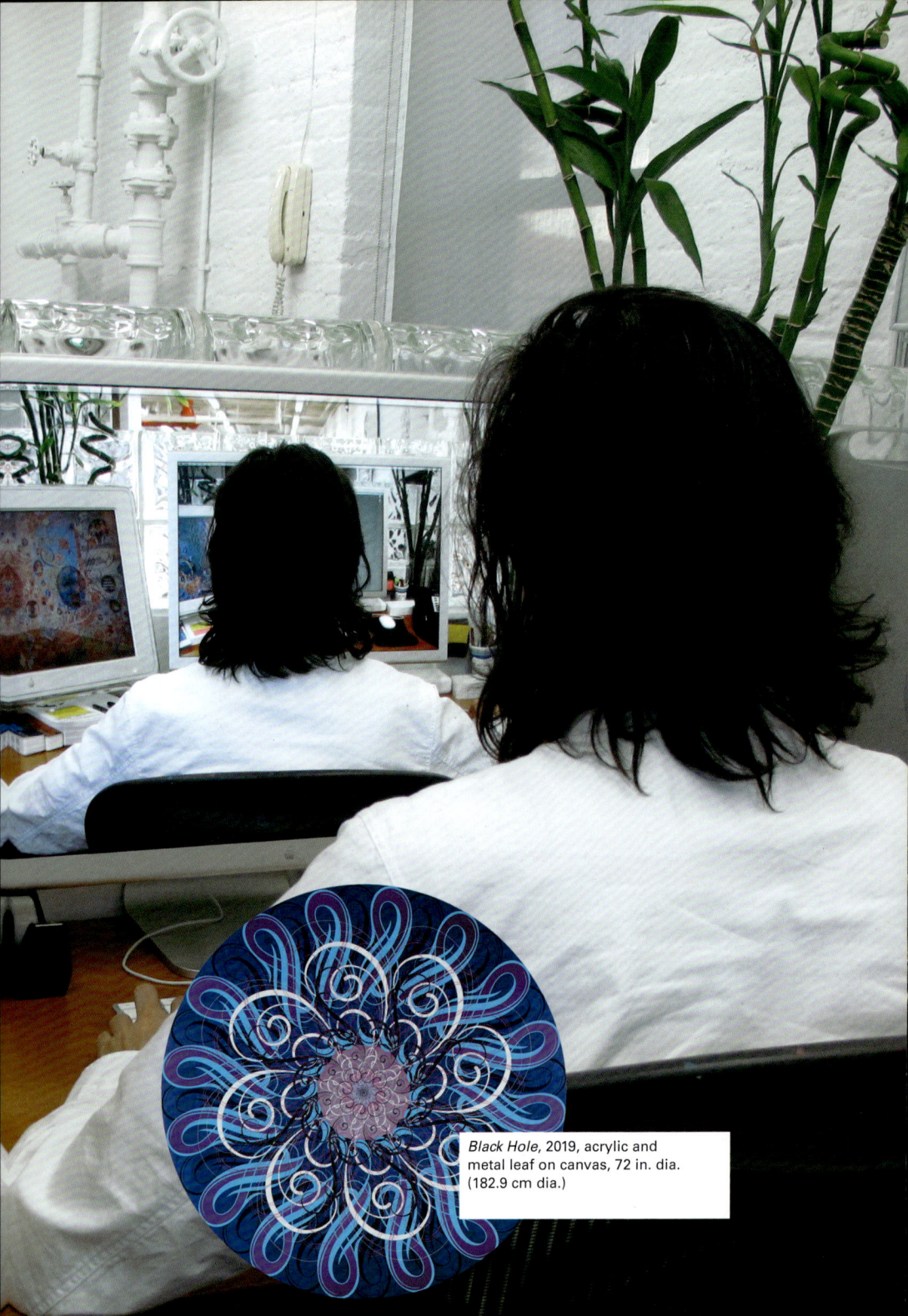

Black Hole, 2019, acrylic and
metal leaf on canvas, 72 in. dia.
(182.9 cm dia.)

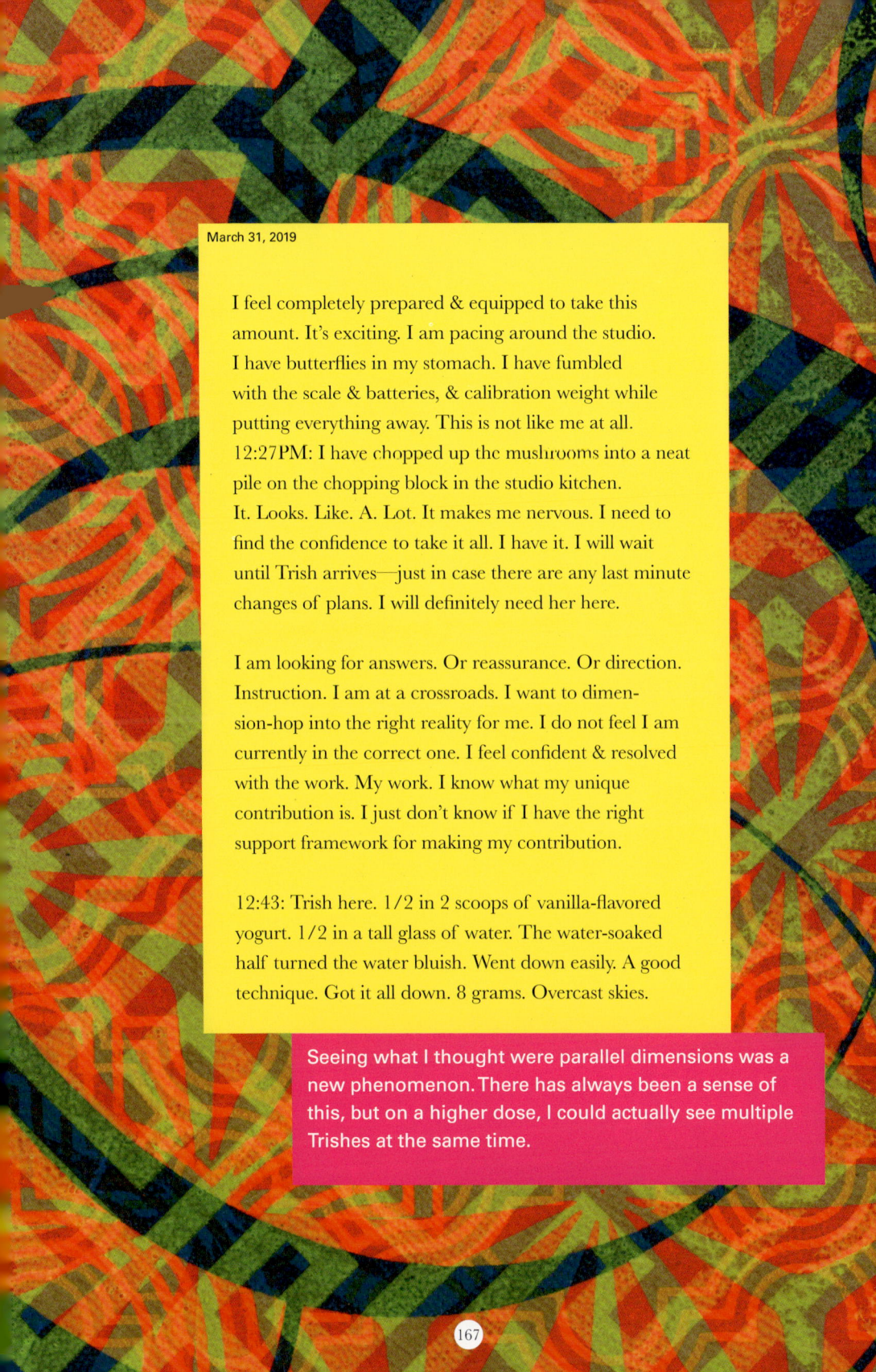

March 31, 2019

I feel completely prepared & equipped to take this
amount. It's exciting. I am pacing around the studio.
I have butterflies in my stomach. I have fumbled
with the scale & batteries, & calibration weight while
putting everything away. This is not like me at all.
12:27PM: I have chopped up the mushrooms into a neat
pile on the chopping block in the studio kitchen.
It. Looks. Like. A. Lot. It makes me nervous. I need to
find the confidence to take it all. I have it. I will wait
until Trish arrives—just in case there are any last minute
changes of plans. I will definitely need her here.

I am looking for answers. Or reassurance. Or direction.
Instruction. I am at a crossroads. I want to dimension-hop into the right reality for me. I do not feel I am
currently in the correct one. I feel confident & resolved
with the work. My work. I know what my unique
contribution is. I just don't know if I have the right
support framework for making my contribution.

12:43: Trish here. 1/2 in 2 scoops of vanilla-flavored
yogurt. 1/2 in a tall glass of water. The water-soaked
half turned the water bluish. Went down easily. A good
technique. Got it all down. 8 grams. Overcast skies.

Seeing what I thought were parallel dimensions was a
new phenomenon. There has always been a sense of
this, but on a higher dose, I could actually see multiple
Trishes at the same time.

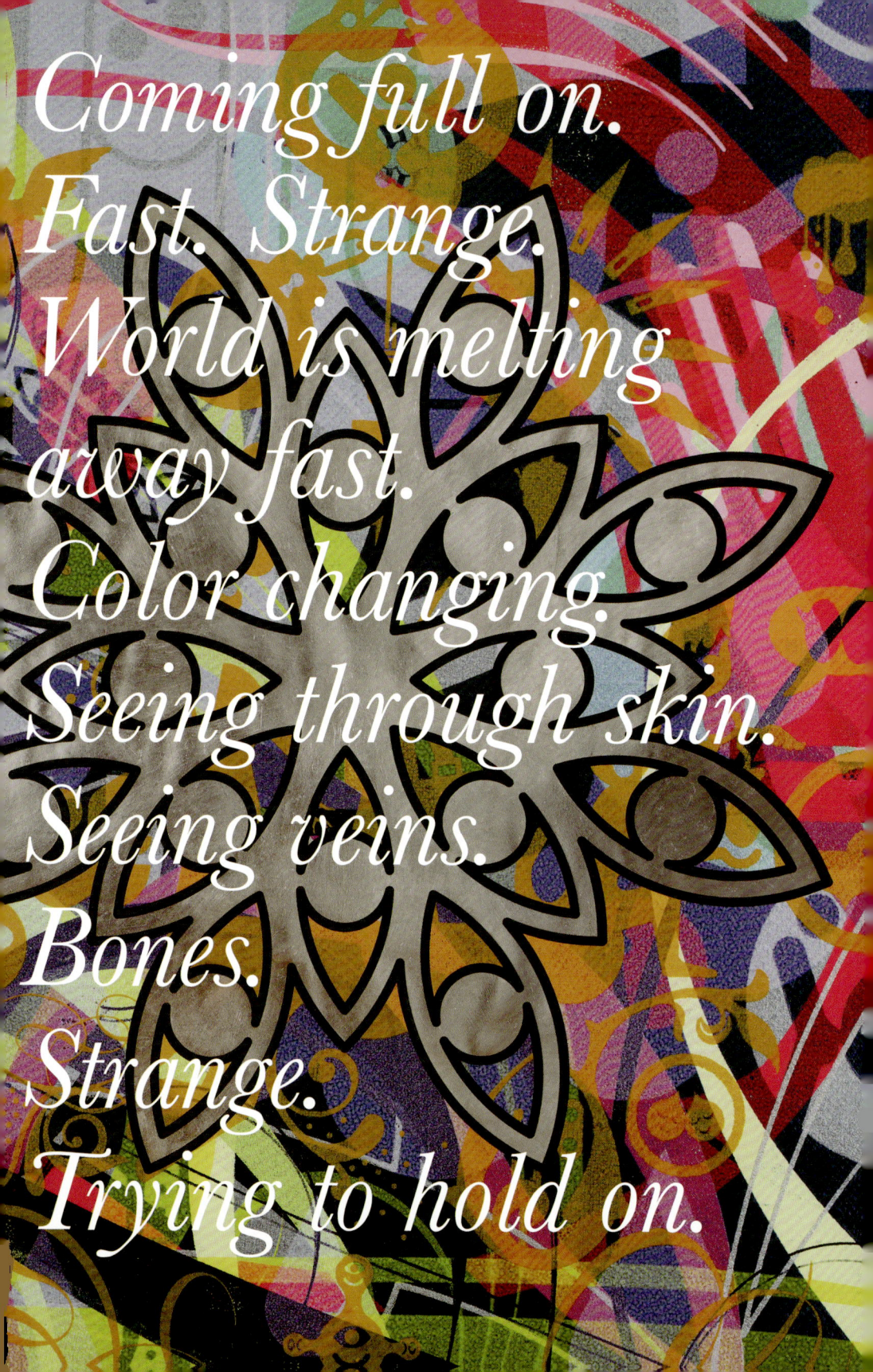

Coming full on.
Fast. Strange.
World is melting
away fast.
Color changing.
Seeing through skin.
Seeing veins.
Bones.
Strange.
Trying to hold on.

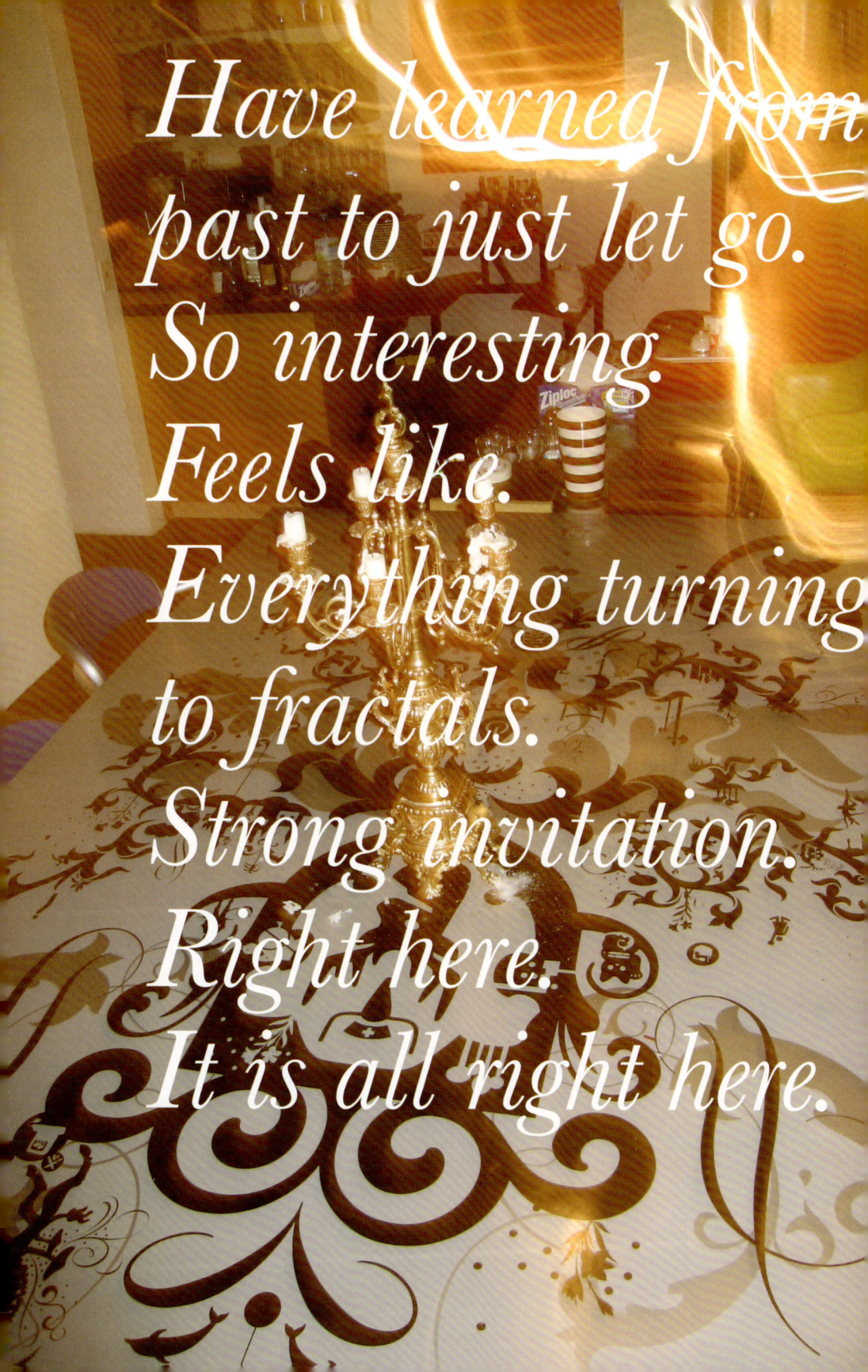

Have learned from
past to just let go.
So interesting.
Feels like.
Everything turning
to fractals.
Strong invitation.
Right here.
It is all right here.

March 31, 2019

Rainy. Not a storm, but no sunshine. Expressed anxiety to Trish. She is always encouraging & supportive of anything & everything. I am blessed. 12:56: Trish noticed I was jittery. I've been pacing around the studio. I am calm now. It is a bit chilly in here. Put on sweatshirt. She said, encouragingly, "You're going to have fun in there." to put me at ease. I am calm. Excited. Ready. Maybe I expect too much. Maybe nothing will happen. Slow breathing. Going to go sit on couch. 1:06: I feel calm. I feel deliberate—if that makes any sense. 1:15: Coming full on. Fast. Strange. World is melting away fast. Color changing. Seeing through skin. Seeing veins. Bones. Strange. Trying to hold on. Have learned from past to just let go. So interesting. Feels like. Everything turning to fractals. Strong invitation. Right here. It is all right here. 1:21: Going to stop & let go.

April 1, 2019: 9:43PM

By 1:30PM, I had tried my best to stay connected to this world—walking around the studio tethered to Trish & telling her what I was experiencing & seeing: patterns everywhere! The patterns were informed by the points of visual stimulation all around— A brick wall, the studio floor—anywhere & everywhere there was visual

I melted into everything everywhere I was going at all times.

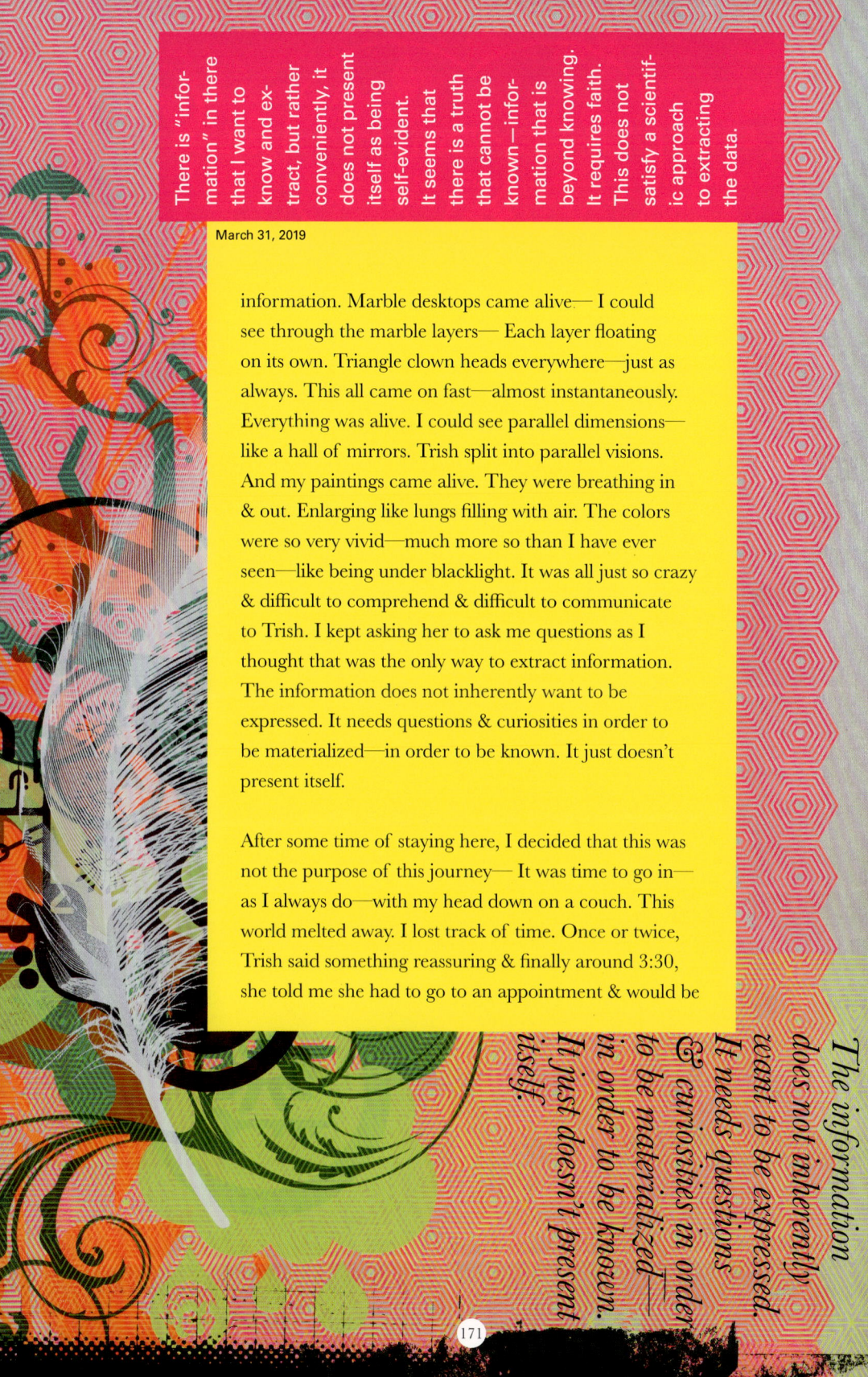

There is "information" in there that I want to know and extract, but rather conveniently, it does not present itself as being self-evident. It seems that there is a truth that cannot be known—information that is beyond knowing. It requires faith. This does not satisfy a scientific approach to extracting the data.

March 31, 2019

information. Marble desktops came alive— I could see through the marble layers— Each layer floating on its own. Triangle clown heads everywhere—just as always. This all came on fast—almost instantaneously. Everything was alive. I could see parallel dimensions— like a hall of mirrors. Trish split into parallel visions. And my paintings came alive. They were breathing in & out. Enlarging like lungs filling with air. The colors were so very vivid—much more so than I have ever seen—like being under blacklight. It was all just so crazy & difficult to comprehend & difficult to communicate to Trish. I kept asking her to ask me questions as I thought that was the only way to extract information. The information does not inherently want to be expressed. It needs questions & curiosities in order to be materialized—in order to be known. It just doesn't present itself.

After some time of staying here, I decided that this was not the purpose of this journey— It was time to go in— as I always do—with my head down on a couch. This world melted away. I lost track of time. Once or twice, Trish said something reassuring & finally around 3:30, she told me she had to go to an appointment & would be

The information does not inherently want to be expressed. It needs questions & curiosities in order to be materialized— in order to be known. It just doesn't present itself.

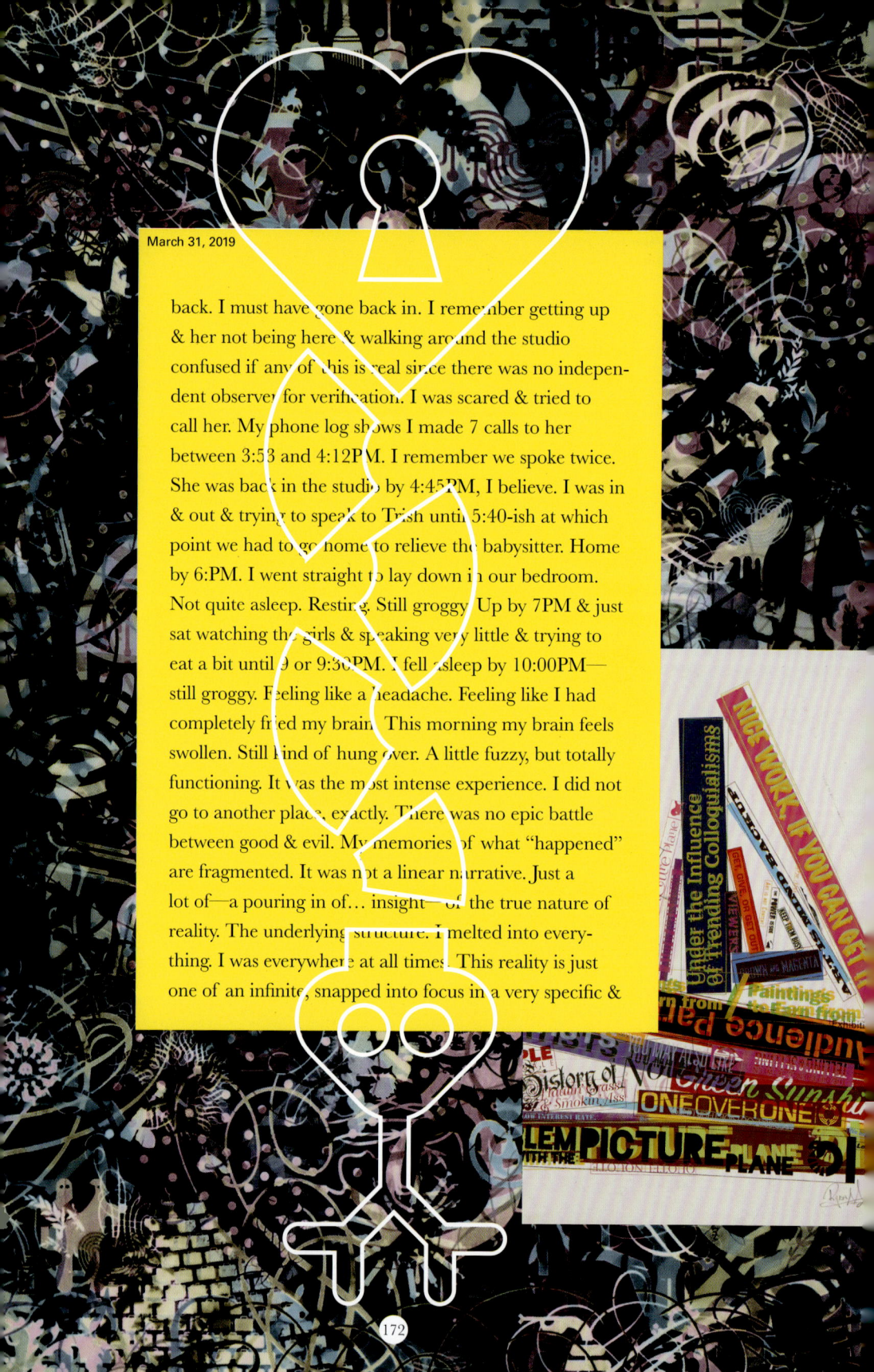

March 31, 2019

back. I must have gone back in. I remember getting up
& her not being here & walking around the studio
confused if any of this is real since there was no indepen-
dent observer for verification. I was scared & tried to
call her. My phone log shows I made 7 calls to her
between 3:53 and 4:12PM. I remember we spoke twice.
She was back in the studio by 4:45PM, I believe. I was in
& out & trying to speak to Trish until 5:40-ish at which
point we had to go home to relieve the babysitter. Home
by 6:PM. I went straight to lay down in our bedroom.
Not quite asleep. Resting. Still groggy. Up by 7PM & just
sat watching the girls & speaking very little & trying to
eat a bit until 9 or 9:30PM. I fell asleep by 10:00PM—
still groggy. Feeling like a headache. Feeling like I had
completely fried my brain. This morning my brain feels
swollen. Still kind of hung over. A little fuzzy, but totally
functioning. It was the most intense experience. I did not
go to another place, exactly. There was no epic battle
between good & evil. My memories of what "happened"
are fragmented. It was not a linear narrative. Just a
lot of—a pouring in of… insight—of the true nature of
reality. The underlying structure. I melted into everything. I was everywhere at all times. This reality is just
one of an infinite, snapped into focus in a very specific &

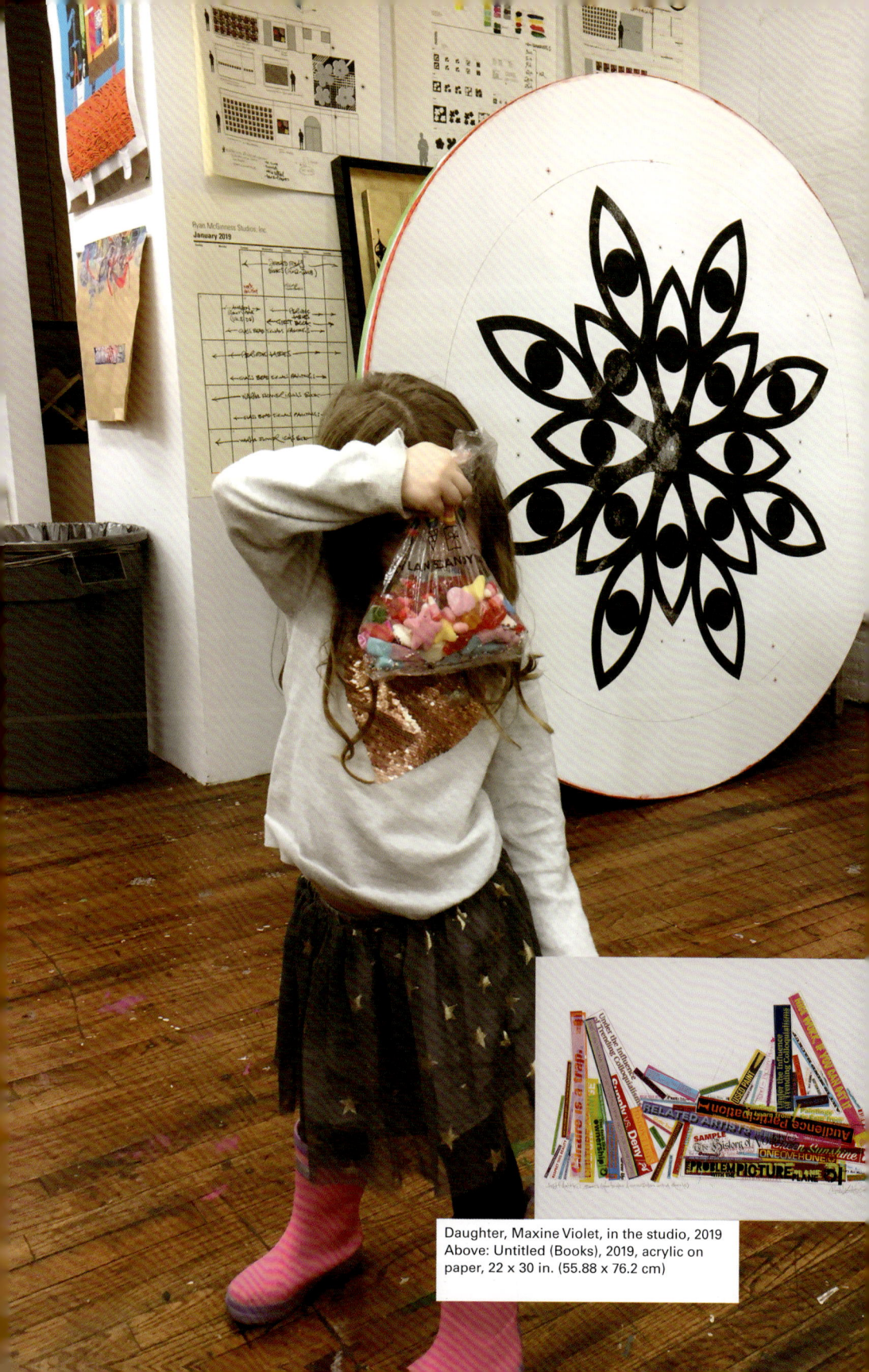

Daughter, Maxine Violet, in the studio, 2019
Above: Untitled (Books), 2019, acrylic on
paper, 22 x 30 in. (55.88 x 76.2 cm)

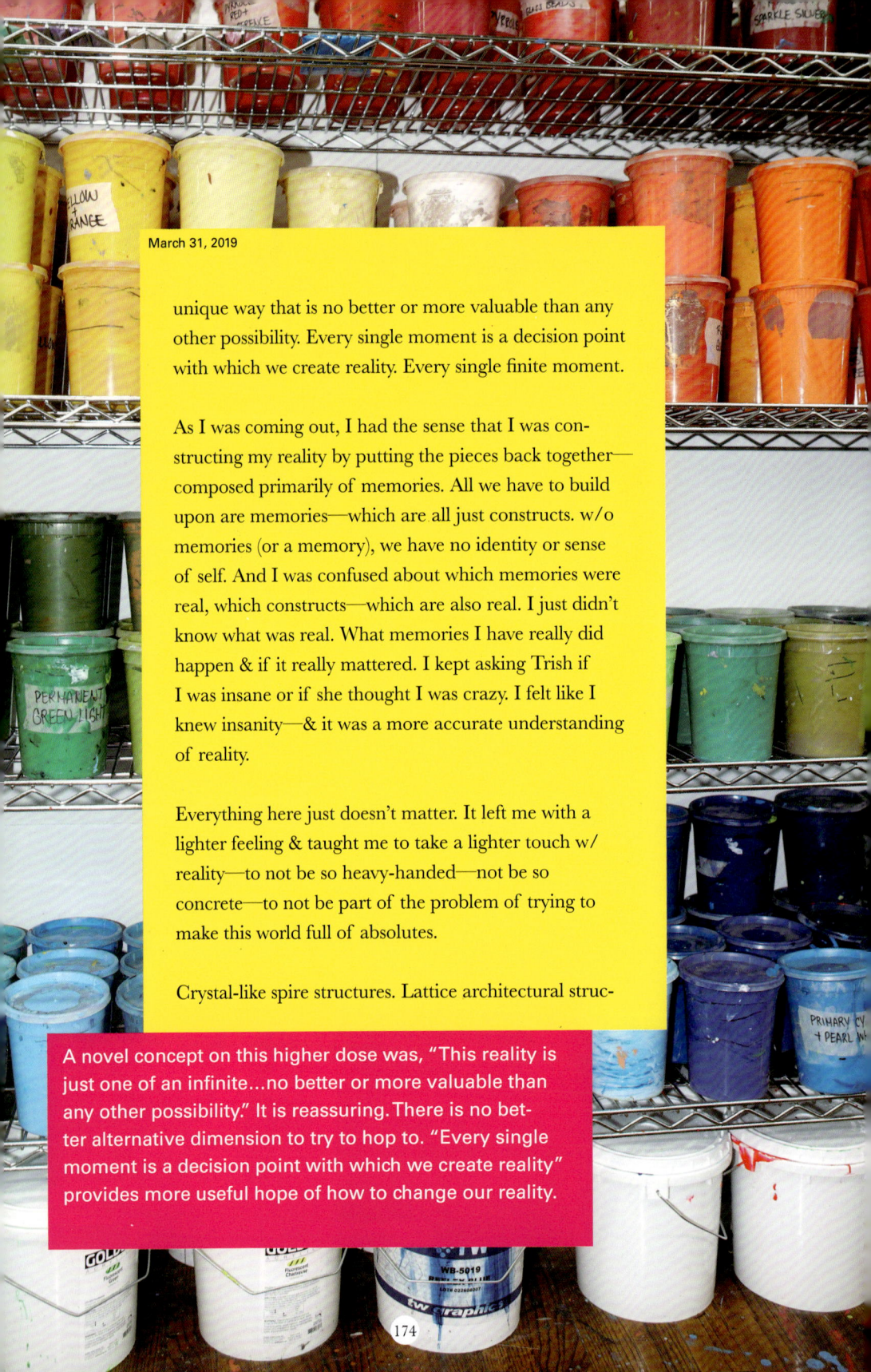

unique way that is no better or more valuable than any other possibility. Every single moment is a decision point with which we create reality. Every single finite moment.

As I was coming out, I had the sense that I was constructing my reality by putting the pieces back together— composed primarily of memories. All we have to build upon are memories—which are all just constructs. w/o memories (or a memory), we have no identity or sense of self. And I was confused about which memories were real, which constructs—which are also real. I just didn't know what was real. What memories I have really did happen & if it really mattered. I kept asking Trish if I was insane or if she thought I was crazy. I felt like I knew insanity—& it was a more accurate understanding of reality.

Everything here just doesn't matter. It left me with a lighter feeling & taught me to take a lighter touch w/ reality—to not be so heavy-handed—not be so concrete—to not be part of the problem of trying to make this world full of absolutes.

Crystal-like spire structures. Lattice architectural struc-

A novel concept on this higher dose was, "This reality is just one of an infinite...no better or more valuable than any other possibility." It is reassuring. There is no better alternative dimension to try to hop to. "Every single moment is a decision point with which we create reality" provides more useful hope of how to change our reality.

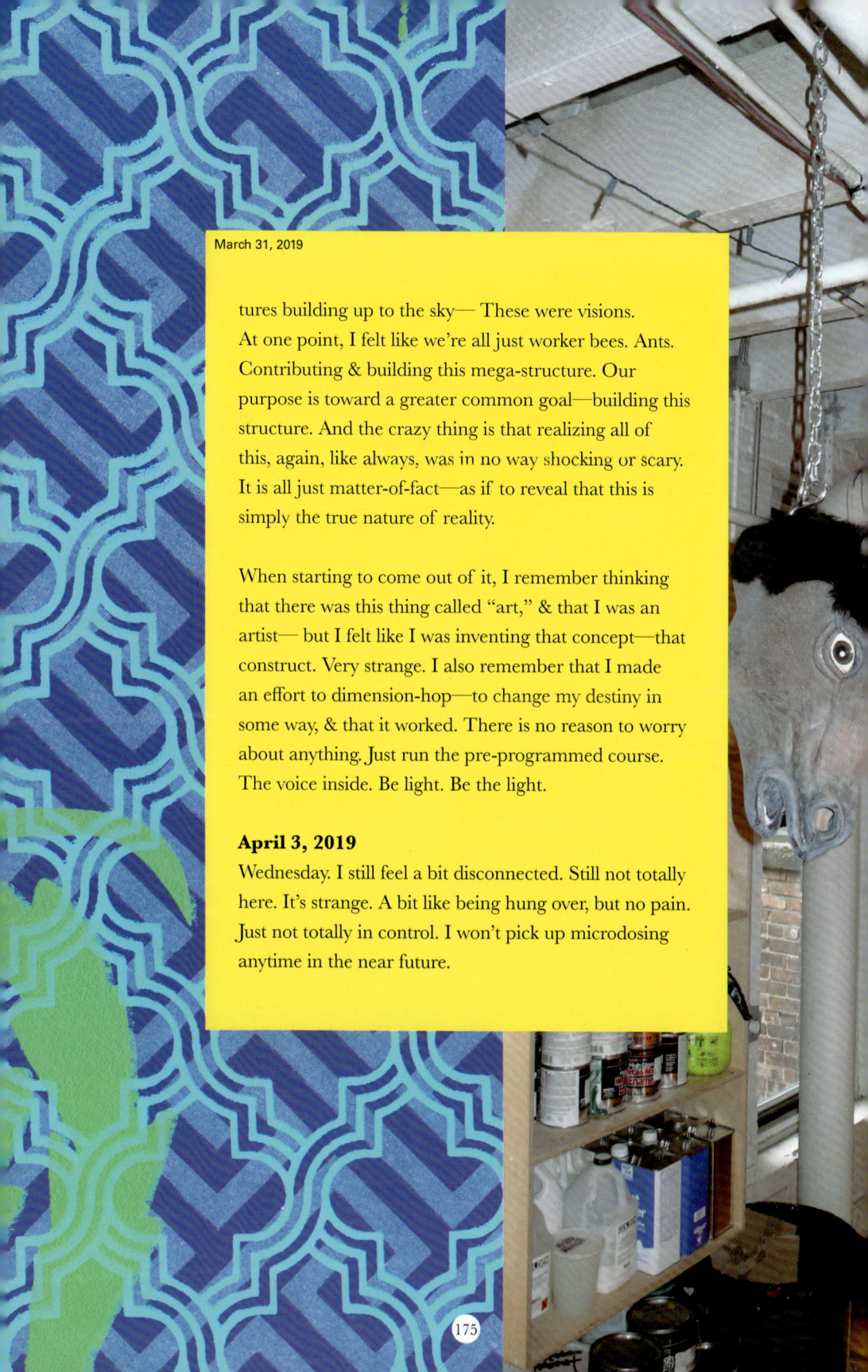

tures building up to the sky— These were visions.
At one point, I felt like we're all just worker bees. Ants.
Contributing & building this mega-structure. Our
purpose is toward a greater common goal—building this
structure. And the crazy thing is that realizing all of
this, again, like always, was in no way shocking or scary.
It is all just matter-of-fact—as if to reveal that this is
simply the true nature of reality.

When starting to come out of it, I remember thinking
that there was this thing called "art," & that I was an
artist— but I felt like I was inventing that concept—that
construct. Very strange. I also remember that I made
an effort to dimension-hop—to change my destiny in
some way, & that it worked. There is no reason to worry
about anything. Just run the pre-programmed course.
The voice inside. Be light. Be the light.

April 3, 2019
Wednesday. I still feel a bit disconnected. Still not totally
here. It's strange. A bit like being hung over, but no pain.
Just not totally in control. I won't pick up microdosing
anytime in the near future.

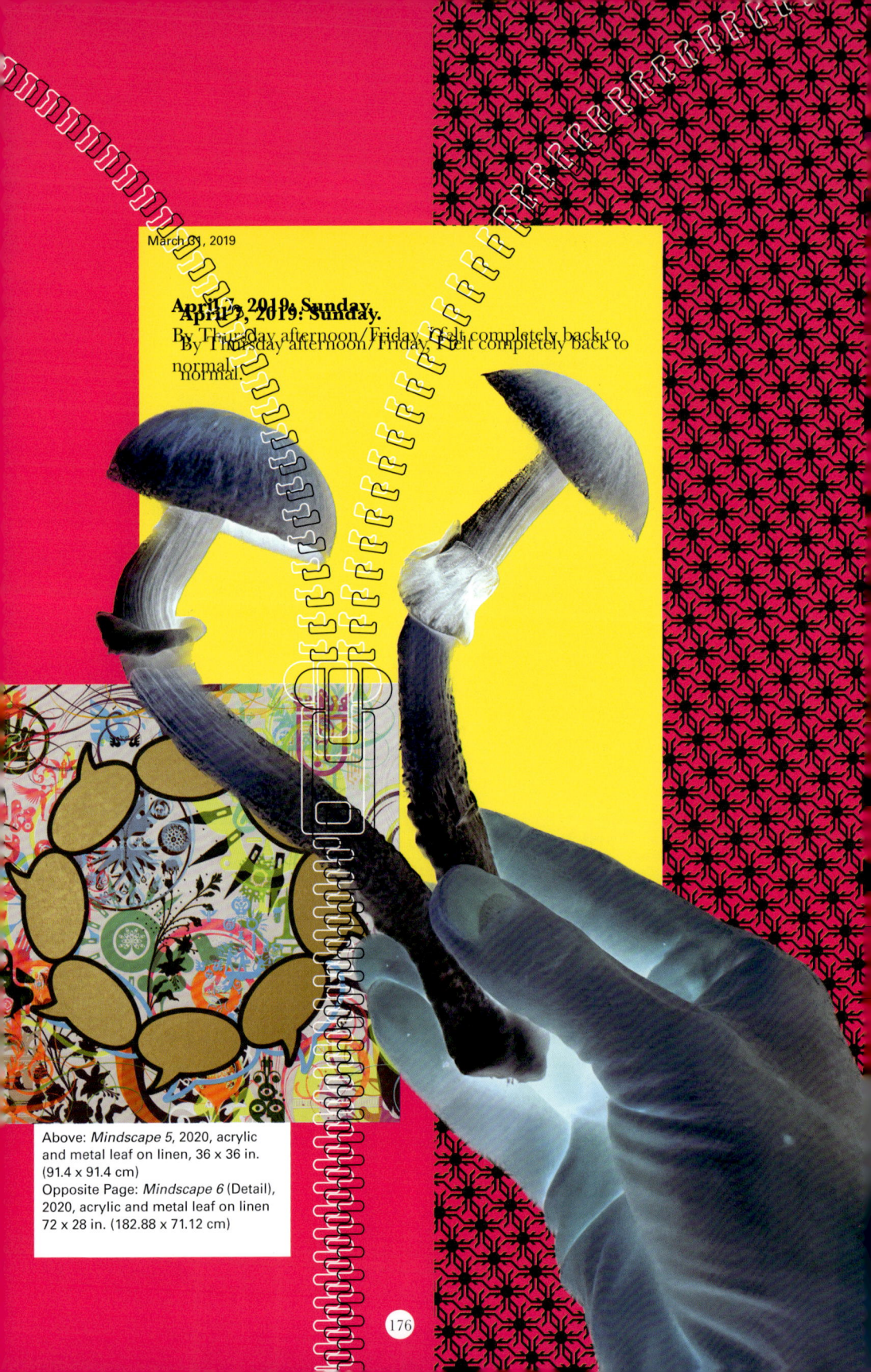

March 01, 2019

April 7, 2019. Sunday.

By Thursday afternoon/Friday, I felt completely back to normal.

April 7, 2019. Sunday.

By Thursday afternoon/Friday, I felt completely back to normal.

Above: *Mindscape 5*, 2020, acrylic and metal leaf on linen, 36 x 36 in. (91.4 x 91.4 cm)
Opposite Page: *Mindscape 6* (Detail), 2020, acrylic and metal leaf on linen 72 x 28 in. (182.88 x 71.12 cm)

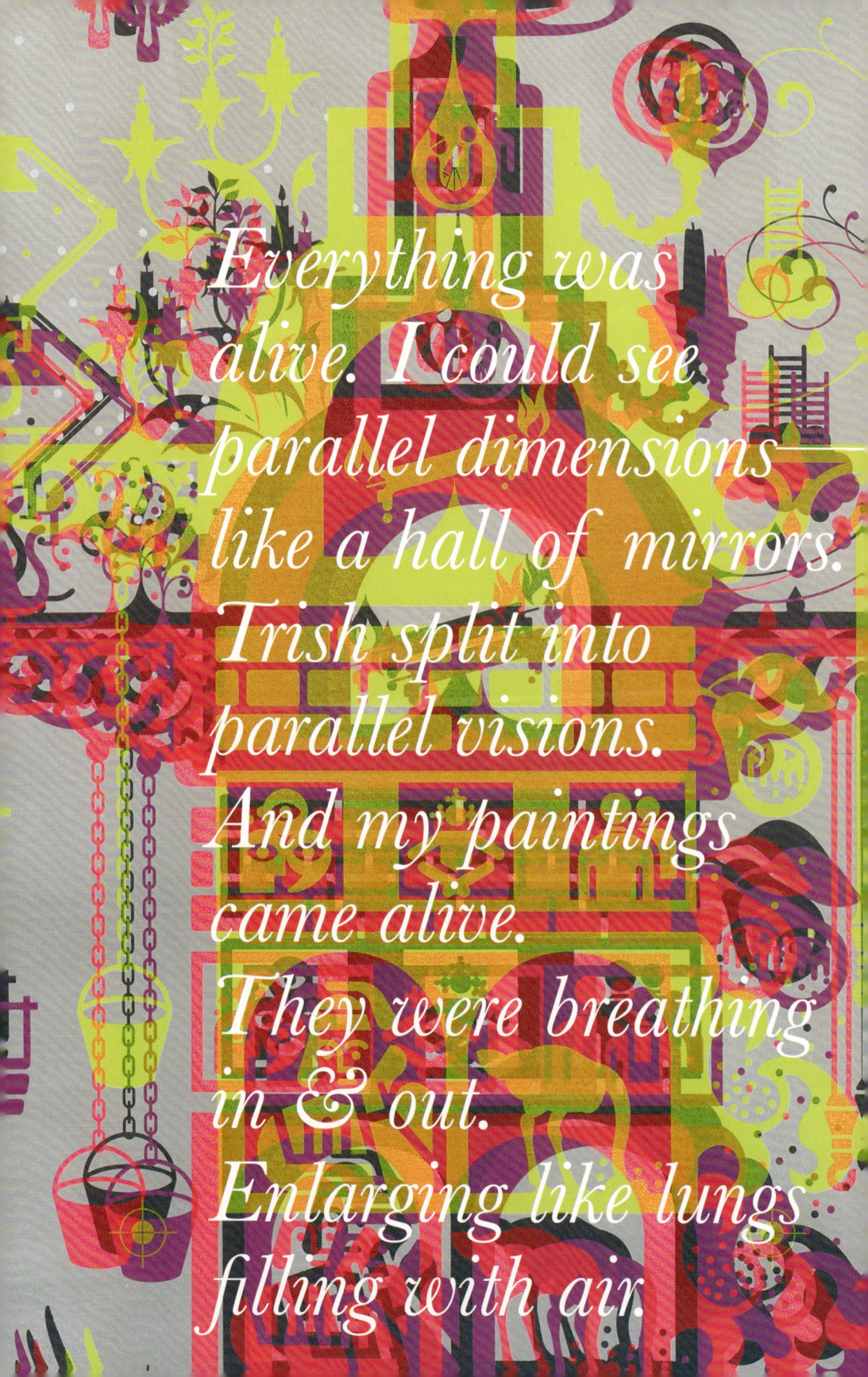

Everything was alive. I could see parallel dimensions— like a hall of mirrors. Trish split into parallel visions. And my paintings came alive. They were breathing in & out. Enlarging like lungs filling with air.

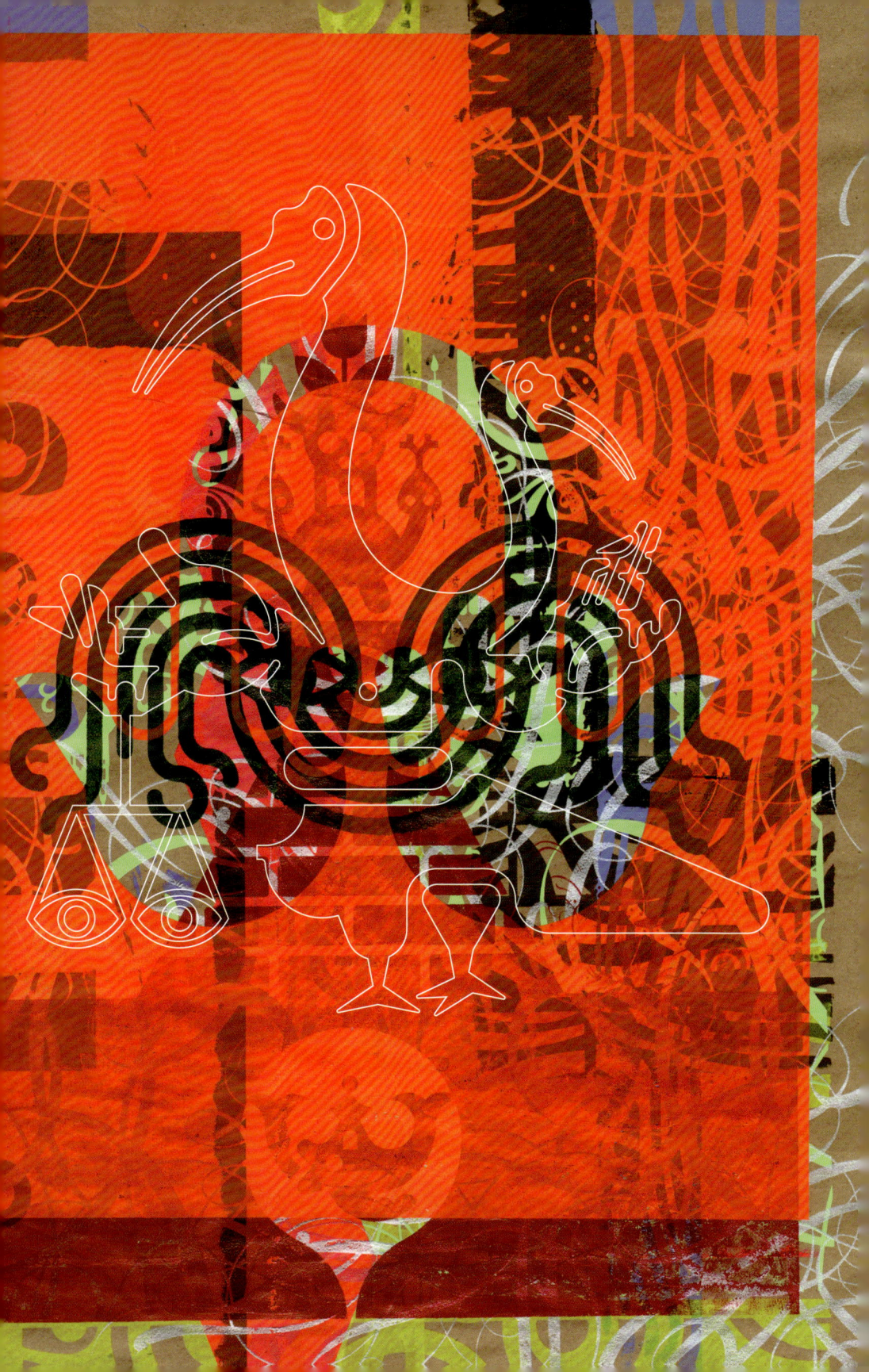

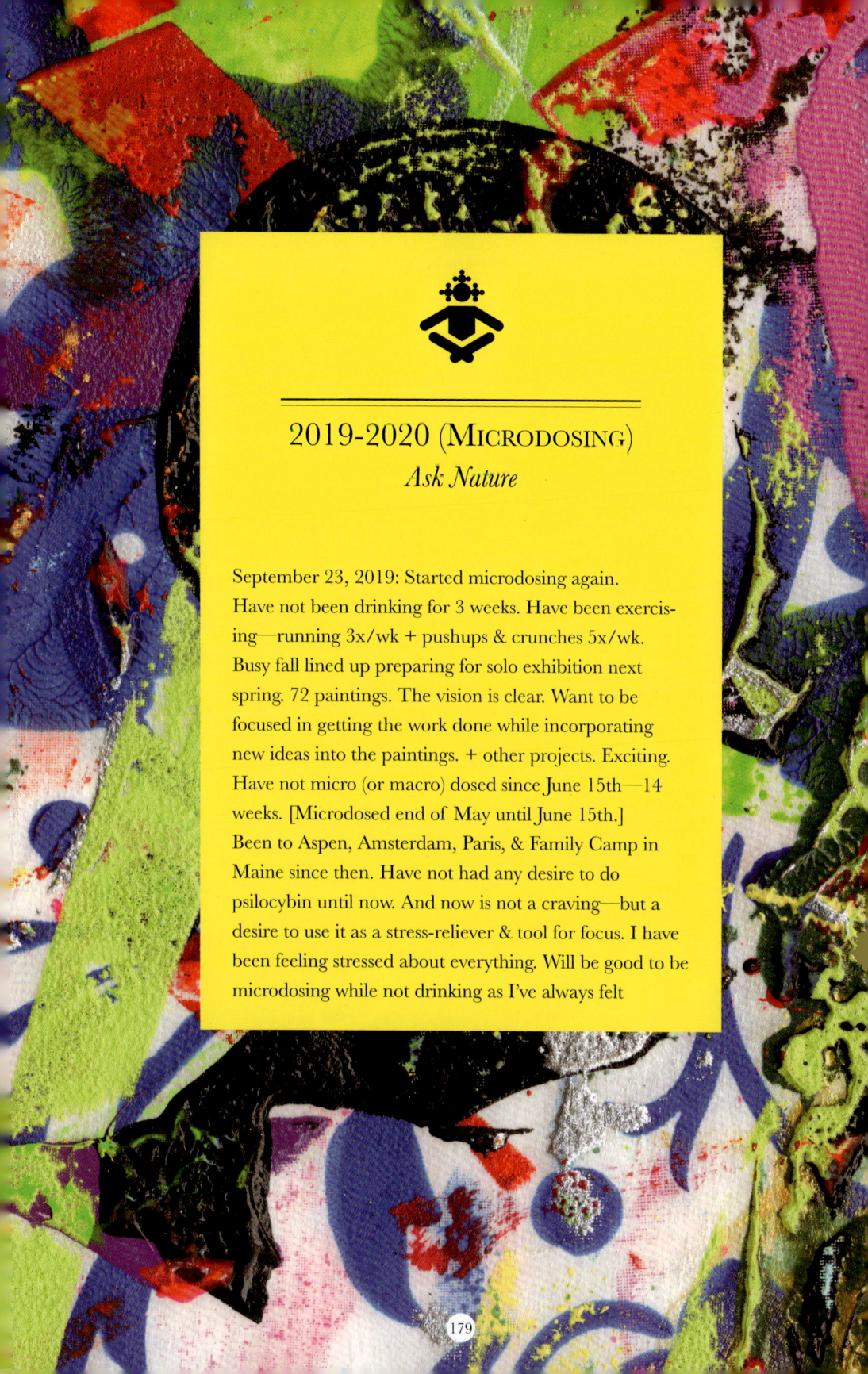

2019-2020 (MICRODOSING)
Ask Nature

September 23, 2019: Started microdosing again.
Have not been drinking for 3 weeks. Have been exercising—running 3x/wk + pushups & crunches 5x/wk.
Busy fall lined up preparing for solo exhibition next
spring. 72 paintings. The vision is clear. Want to be
focused in getting the work done while incorporating
new ideas into the paintings. + other projects. Exciting.
Have not micro (or macro) dosed since June 15th—14
weeks. [Microdosed end of May until June 15th.]
Been to Aspen, Amsterdam, Paris, & Family Camp in
Maine since then. Have not had any desire to do
psilocybin until now. And now is not a craving—but a
desire to use it as a stress-reliever & tool for focus. I have
been feeling stressed about everything. Will be good to be
microdosing while not drinking as I've always felt

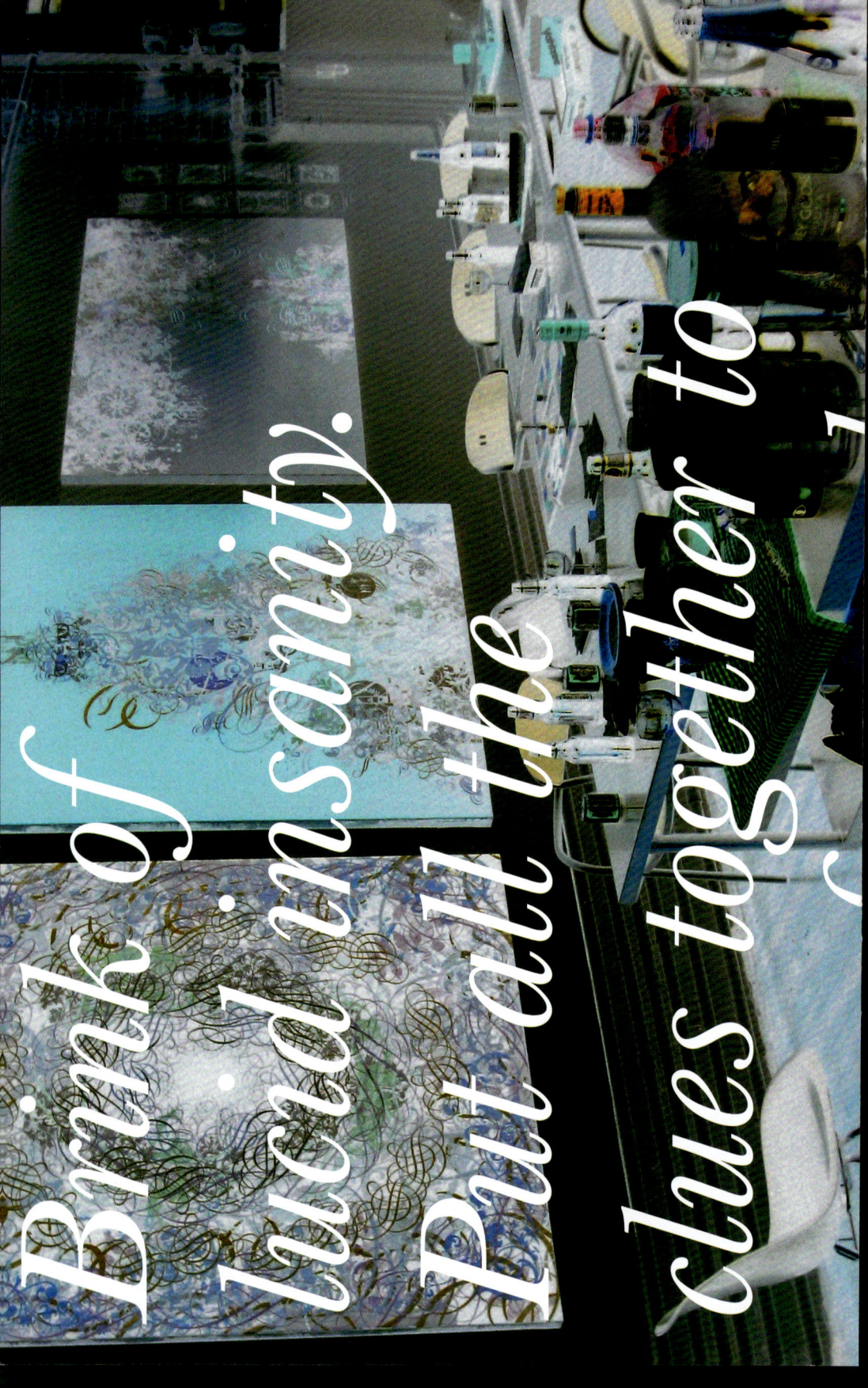

Brink of lucid insanity. Put all the clues together to

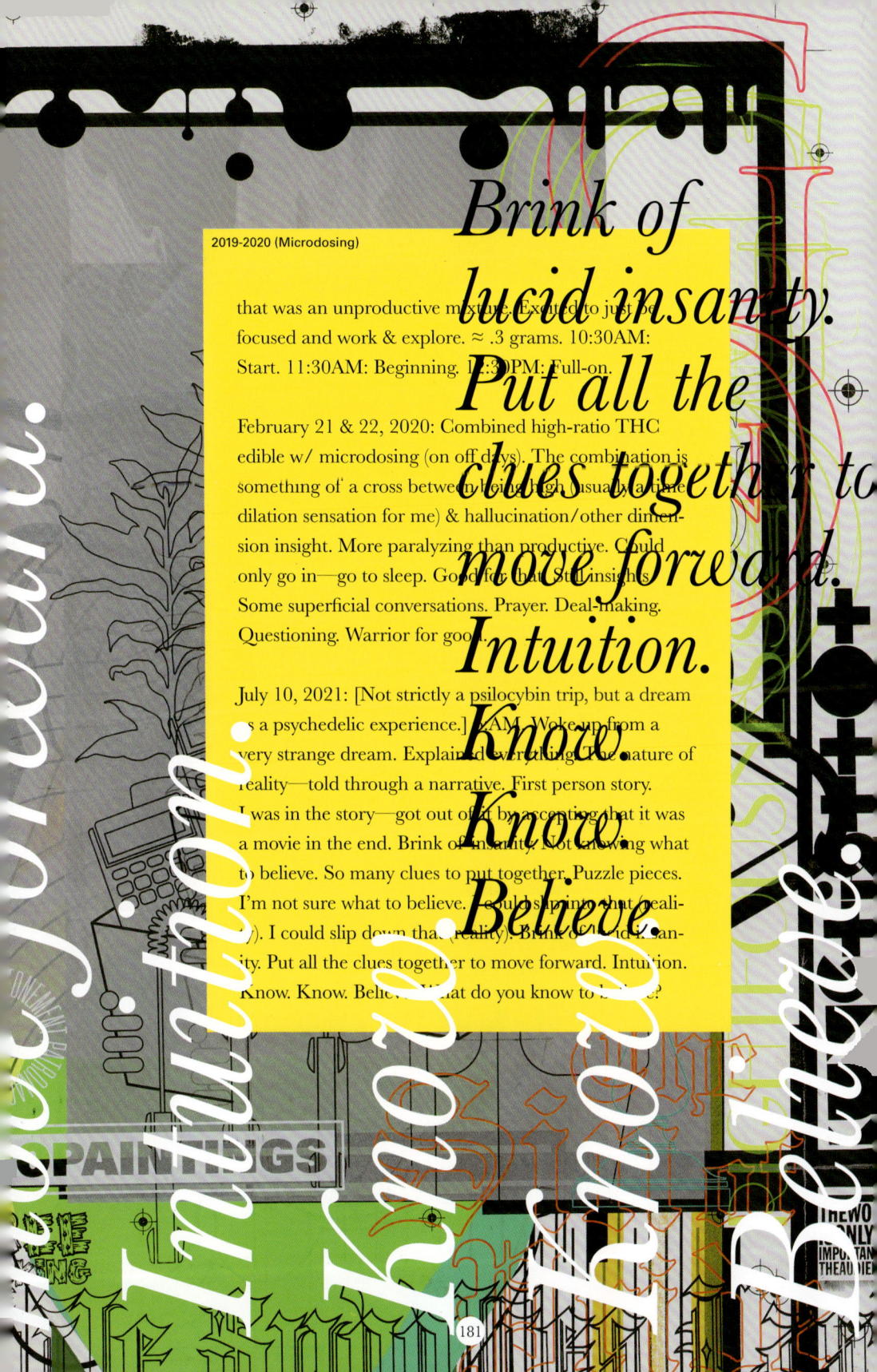

2019-2020 (Microdosing)

that was an unproductive mixture. Excited to just be focused and work & explore. ≈ .3 grams. 10:30AM: Start. 11:30AM: Beginning. 12:30PM: Full-on.

February 21 & 22, 2020: Combined high-ratio THC edible w/ microdosing (on off days). The combination is something of a cross between being high (usually a time dilation sensation for me) & hallucination/other dimension insight. More paralyzing than productive. Could only go in—go to sleep. Good for that. Still insights. Some superficial conversations. Prayer. Deal-making. Questioning. Warrior for good.

July 10, 2021: [Not strictly a psilocybin trip, but a dream is a psychedelic experience.] 1AM. Woke up from a very strange dream. Explained everything. The nature of reality—told through a narrative. First person story. I was in the story—got out of it by accepting that it was a movie in the end. Brink of insanity. Not knowing what to believe. So many clues to put together. Puzzle pieces. I'm not sure what to believe. Could slip into that (reality). I could slip down that (reality). Brink of lucid insanity. Put all the clues together to move forward. Intuition. Know. Know. Believe. What do you know to believe?

Brink of lucid insanity. Put all the clues together to move forward. Intuition. Know. Know. Believe.

PAINTINGS

Culture clues. How to retain the insight from this dream?

Had the sensation on THC of knowing what sleep is—
or, the purpose of sleep. It is to connect to the universal,
one, consciousness—to continually & regularly reconnect
to the one consciousness & then come back to inhabit
our ego avatars. The "sleepy" feeling (or tiredness
of the mind) is the unsustainable ego running out of
gas. We reconnect to the universal, reconnect to our
programming, perhaps to receive new orders, insights,
or answers, & come back to this world.

Transdimensional communication (to us) through demo,
not memo. Demonstration(s). Not messages. They are
not sending messages for us to receive. What is the most
effective way to teach/communicate to new humans?
Through demonstrating. That is how they are trying
to teach us. And the demo is nature. Ask nature. Learn
from nature. We are in the instruction manual.

Reclaim Your Mind, 2021,
ink, charcoal, and acrylic on paper,
60 x 40 in. (152.4 x 101.6 cm)

Reclaim Your Mind, 2021,
ink, charcoal, and acrylic on paper,
60 x 40 in. (152.4 x 101.6 cm)

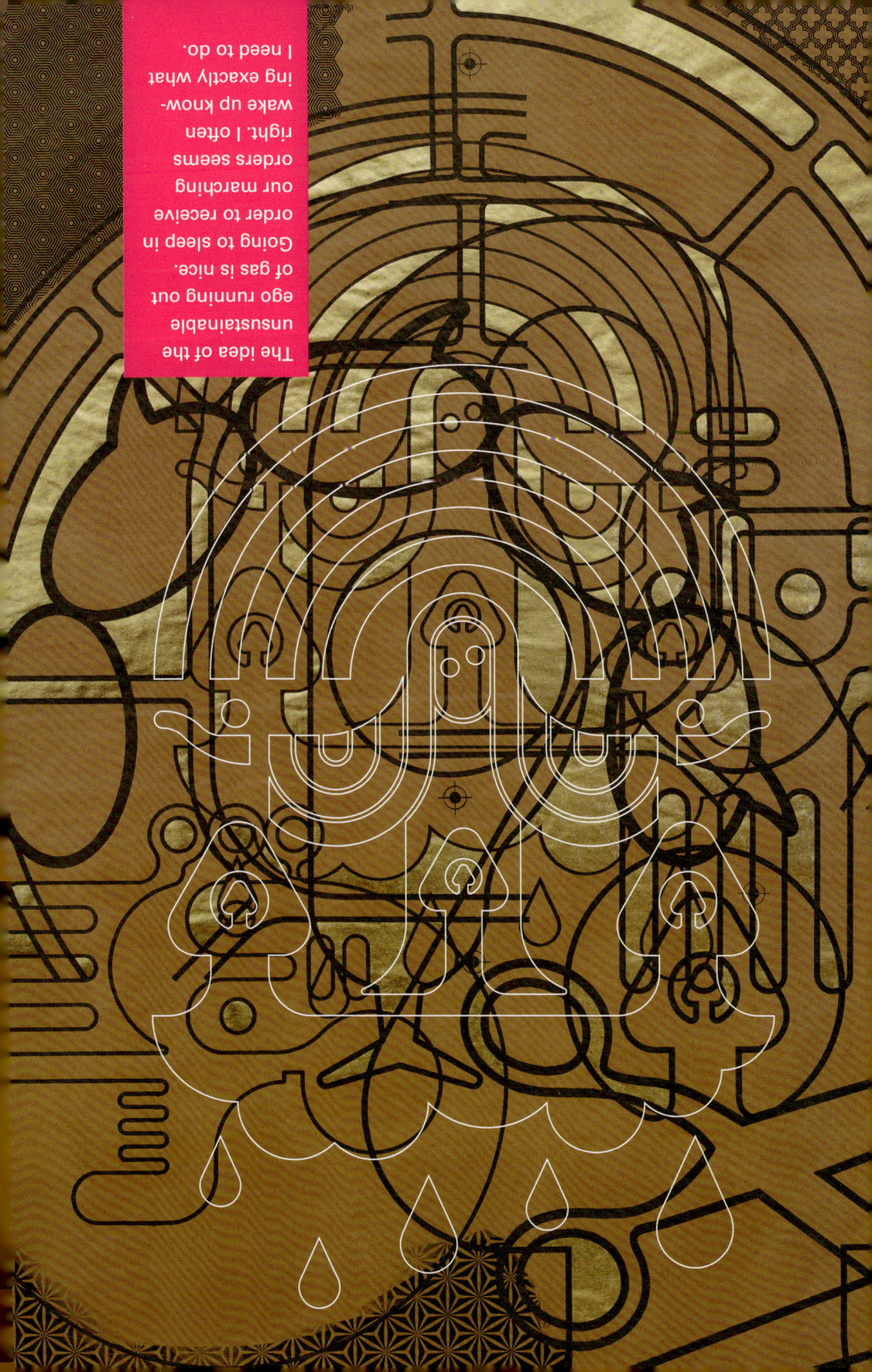

The idea of the unsustainable ego running out of gas is nice. Going to sleep in order to receive our marching orders seems right, I often wake up know- ing exactly what I need to do.

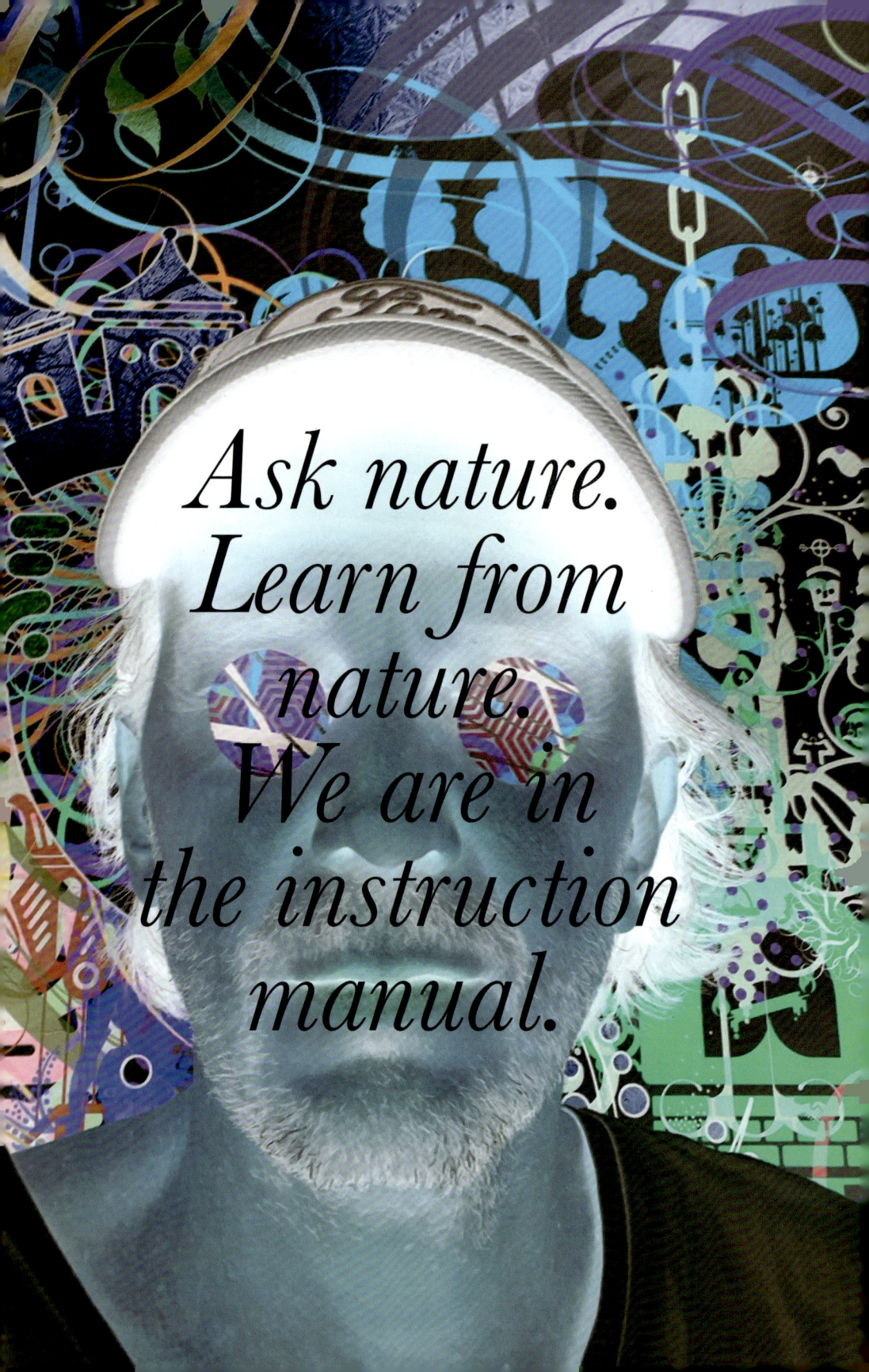

Ask nature. Learn from nature. We are in the instruction manual.

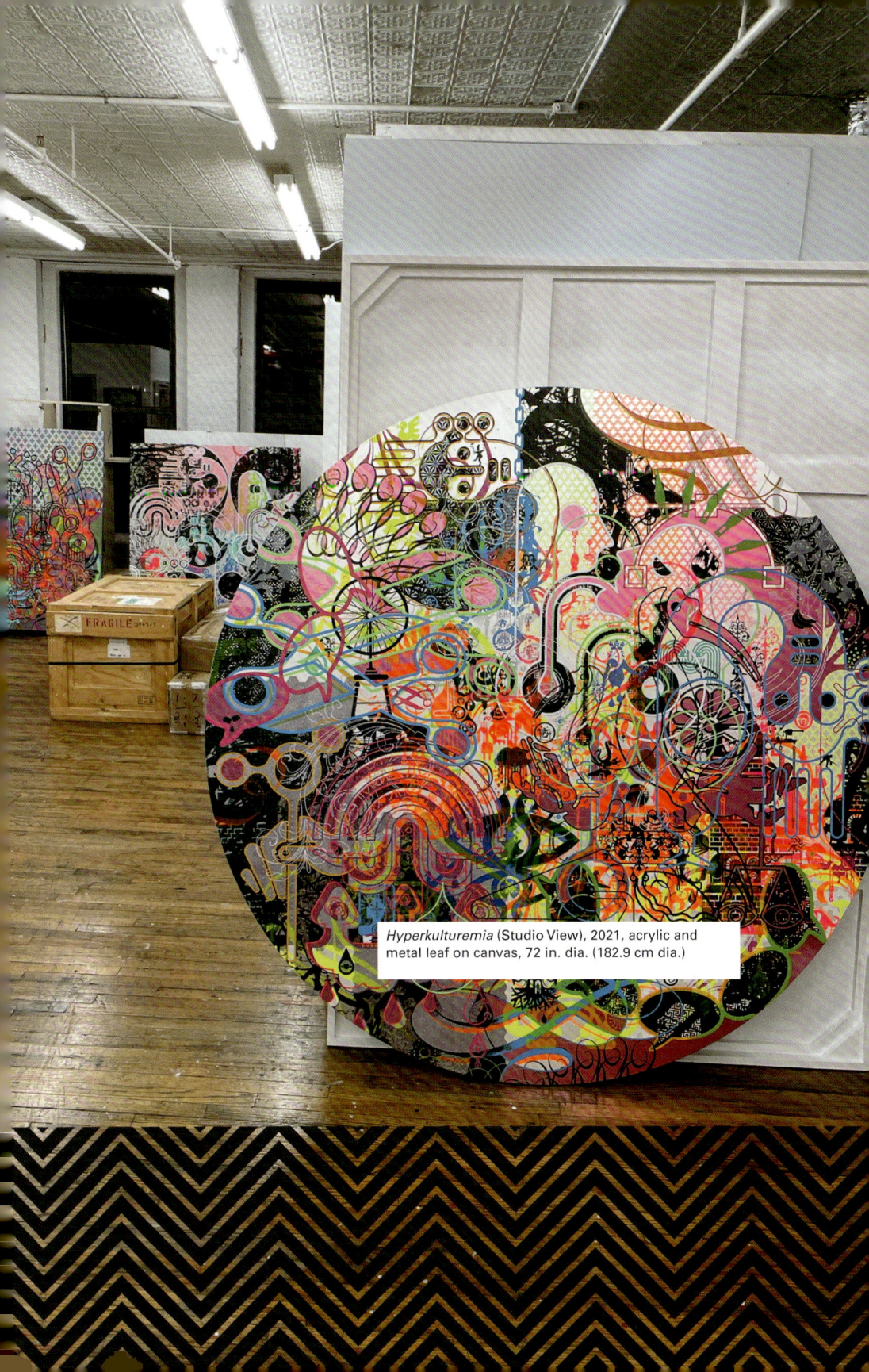

Hyperkulturemia (Studio View), 2021, acrylic and metal leaf on canvas, 72 in. dia. (182.9 cm dia.)

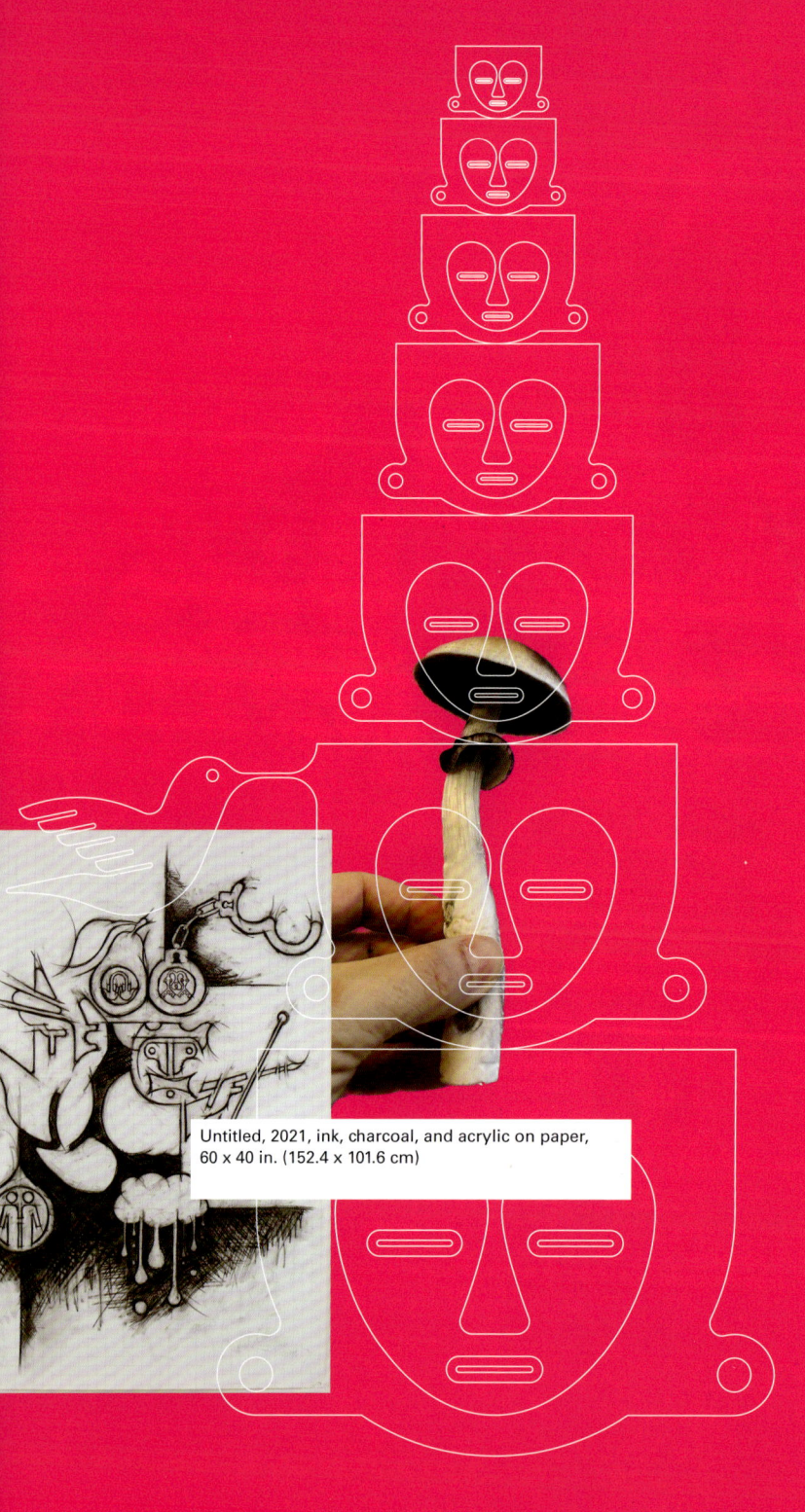

Untitled, 2021, ink, charcoal, and acrylic on paper,
60 x 40 in. (152.4 x 101.6 cm)

It was my 50th birthday, and I wanted nothing more than to simply disappear into my own mind. It is where I have always wanted to be. My life pursuit, career, and all my work is in support of this singular goal. I searched for any information I could find on the highest dose of psilocybin ever taken. I found an article about a published FDA study where the subject was administered 59 mg.

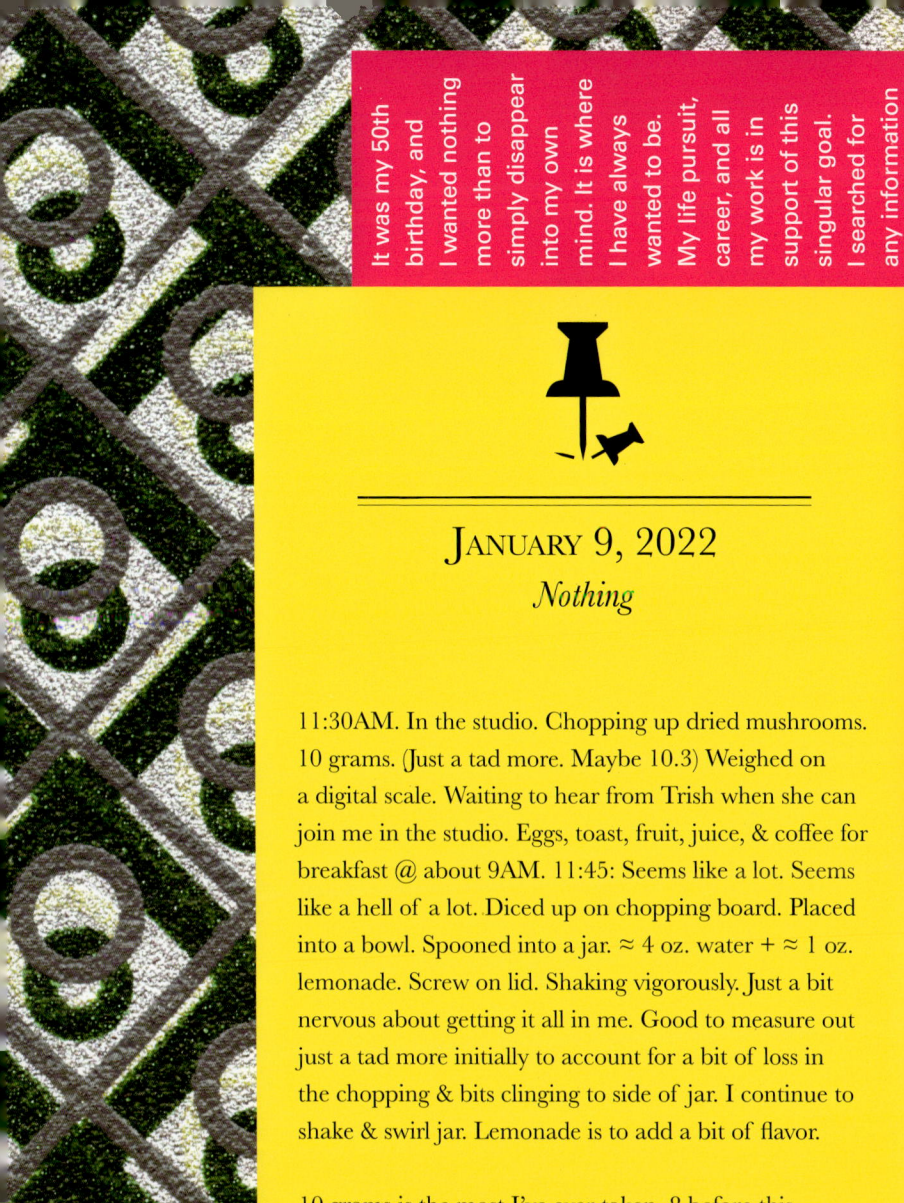

JANUARY 9, 2022

Nothing

11:30AM. In the studio. Chopping up dried mushrooms. 10 grams. (Just a tad more. Maybe 10.3) Weighed on a digital scale. Waiting to hear from Trish when she can join me in the studio. Eggs, toast, fruit, juice, & coffee for breakfast @ about 9AM. 11:45: Seems like a lot. Seems like a hell of a lot. Diced up on chopping board. Placed into a bowl. Spooned into a jar. ≈ 4 oz. water + ≈ 1 oz. lemonade. Screw on lid. Shaking vigorously. Just a bit nervous about getting it all in me. Good to measure out just a tad more initially to account for a bit of loss in the chopping & bits clinging to side of jar. I continue to shake & swirl jar. Lemonade is to add a bit of flavor.

10 grams is the most I've ever taken. 8 before this. 5 before that. Is there an amount after which it doesn't

An excerpt from that article: *"Dose three was 59 mg. I received the largest dose of psilocybin ever administered in a published FDA study. For the uninitiated to psilocybin dosing, this is a mega dose. The writer Terence McKenna dazzled his audiences with tales of doing what he called a "heroic dose" of five grams...*

January 9, 2022

matter? Are we opening just one door or several after each other? Are we speaking/communicating to one entity or several? Are these space-time restricted models even accurate & useful?

The mixture is turning bluish/grey. Smelled it. Nasty. Maybe capsule large amounts like I do with the microdoses? I have collected all previous trip journal entries in preparation for a book. I have not read any. Message from Trish: She will be here in 30 min. My anxiety increases for some reason. I have no fear of taking this dosage. Just really don't look forward to drinking this solution. That's a good word for this drink— A solution.

Intentionality is important, but should I bring specific questions? Whom would I ask, anyways? It seems like specific questions are pointless & perhaps even an abuse of the invitation to go in. That is what it feels like. Taking the mushrooms is only knocking on the door. There is usually a sense, if going deep enough, of being let in. The plan today is to, as always, simply sit or lay down with my eyes closed & disappear. I have no fear of not coming back, if that is dying. I would not want

...of dried mushrooms. I have been asked by many people 'What does this equal in dried grams of mushrooms?' (the standard method of ingesting mushrooms). The answer: about 10 grams of dried mushrooms."

(Steve E., "I received the largest dose of psilocybin ever administered in a published FDA study. Dose #3," psymposia.com, April 3, 2017)

So, I figured a bit over 10 grams would qualify. I was prepared to disappear and dissolve into everything.

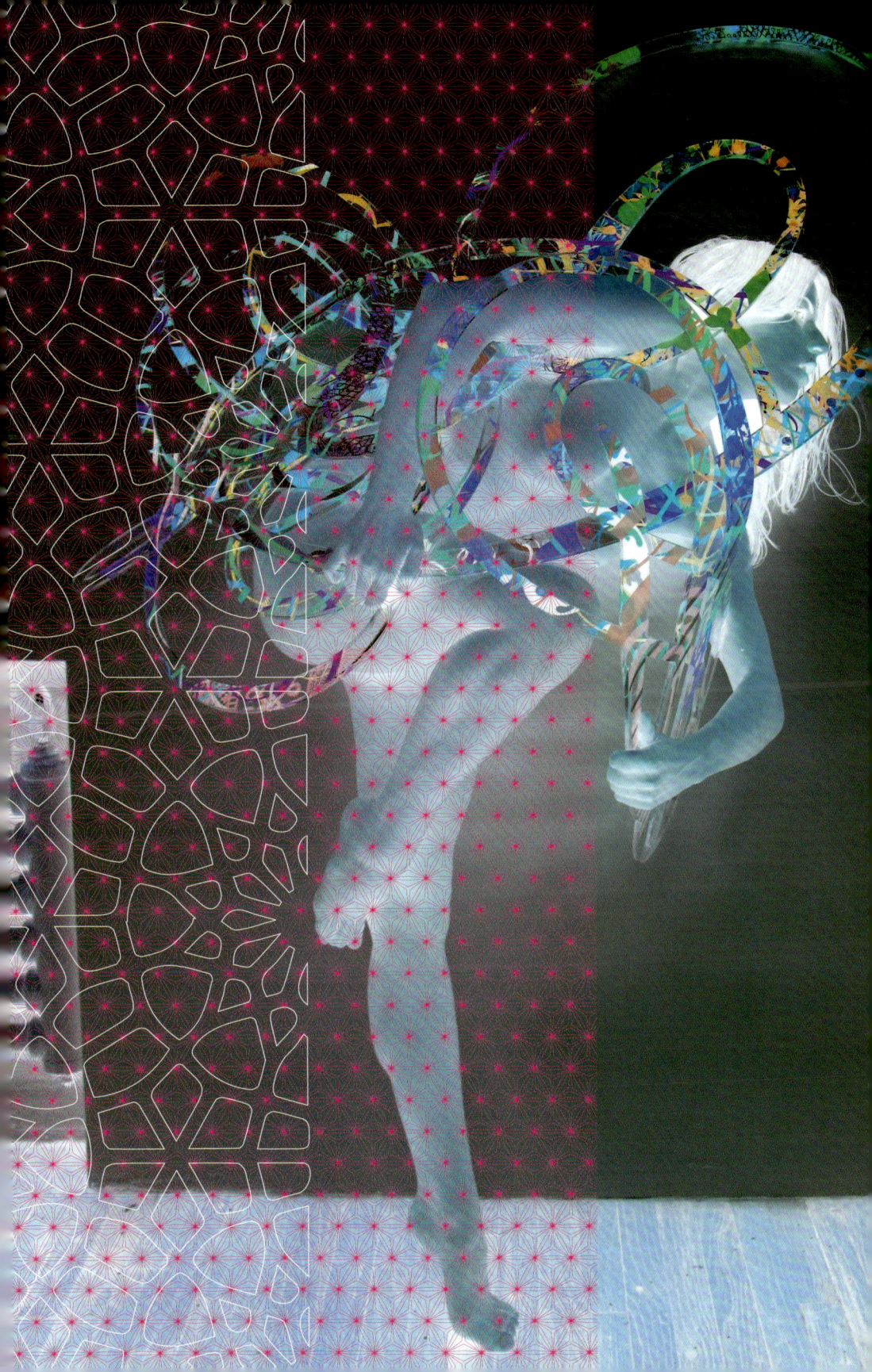

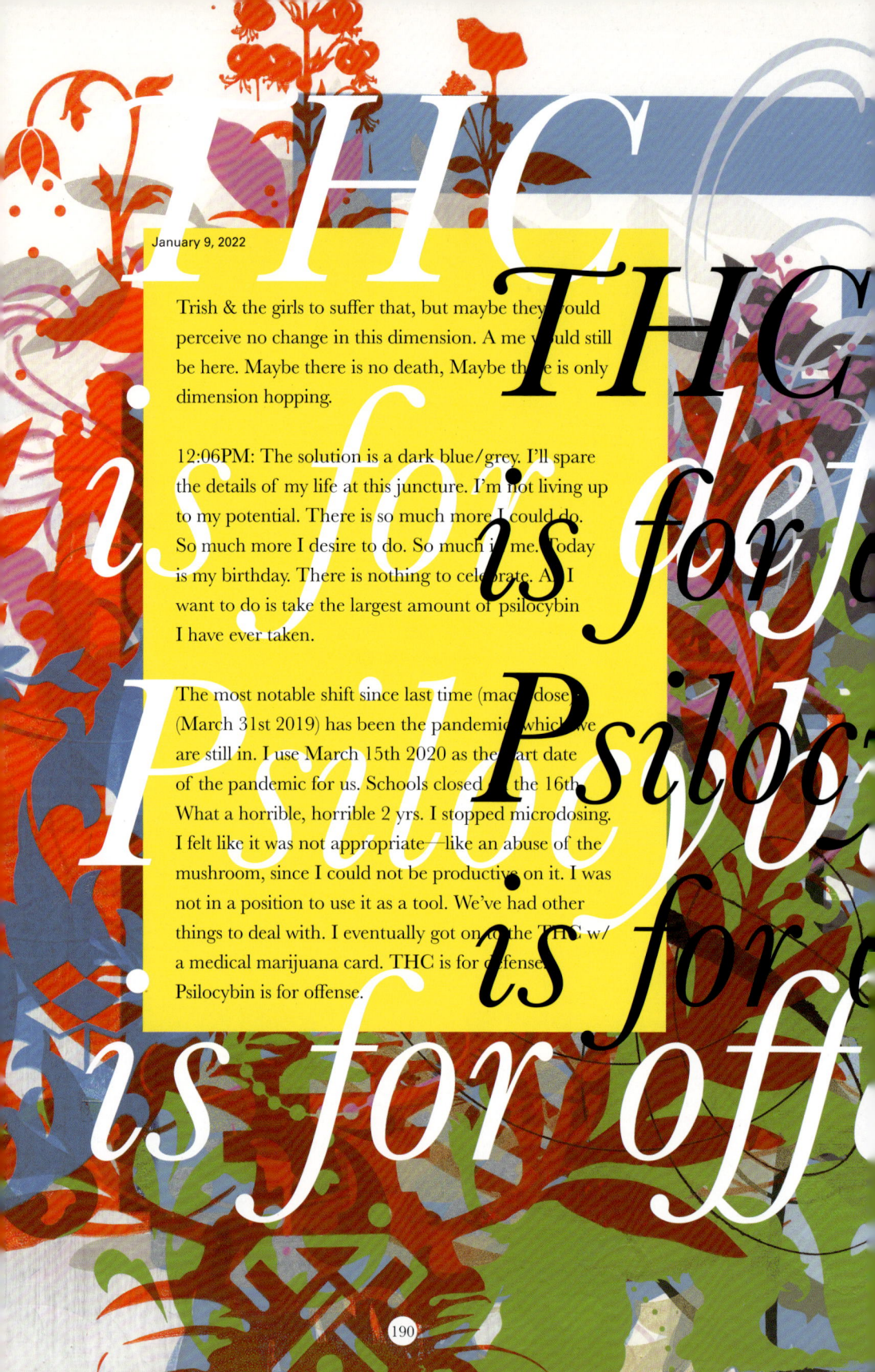

Trish & the girls to suffer that, but maybe they could perceive no change in this dimension. A me would still be here. Maybe there is no death, Maybe there is only dimension hopping.

12:06PM: The solution is a dark blue/grey. I'll spare the details of my life at this juncture. I'm not living up to my potential. There is so much more I could do. So much more I desire to do. So much in me. Today is my birthday. There is nothing to celebrate. All I want to do is take the largest amount of psilocybin I have ever taken.

The most notable shift since last time (macro dose) (March 31st 2019) has been the pandemic which we are still in. I use March 15th 2020 as the start date of the pandemic for us. Schools closed on the 16th. What a horrible, horrible 2 yrs. I stopped microdosing. I felt like it was not appropriate—like an abuse of the mushroom, since I could not be productive on it. I was not in a position to use it as a tool. We've had other things to deal with. I eventually got on to the THC w/ a medical marijuana card. THC is for defense. Psilocybin is for offense.

THC is for defense.
Psilocybin is for offense.

January 9, 2022

12:26PM: Trish just arrived. Solution is very dark blue/grey-greenish.

12:32PM: Just finished drinking solution. Not that bad. Trick is to not smell it. Just throw it back in multiple swallows. Try not to contemplate it. Relax. Like moving your body through G-forces— Don't resist the force. Let your body go limp. Walking around studio. Almost 3 years since last time. 12:43: Getting a bit jittery already. Speaking to Trish. Expressing goals for doing this & how this Western/scientific model & approach doesn't really apply to psychedelics. (Will have to write more on that later.) The idea of going in w/ specific questions & goals. Desire. Parsing out the universe into knowable units. Defining problems & crafting solutions.— Not the right approach here. 12:53: Coming on now. Shaky & jittery. 12:59— Could go in anytime.

I have felt on several occasions that my approach to understanding the psychedelic experience is flawed. I refuse to believe it is unknowable. I can't conceive of a better approach than trying to extract units of information. What are those units? How can they be shared? The psychedelic experience is a mystery. It is puzzle. How can we decifer it?

Six Paintings, 2021, acrylic on linen, 84 x 60 in. (213.36 x 152.4 cm)

Are we opening

just one door after

each other?

Are we opening

just one door after

or several after

each other?

January 9, 2022

Notes from Trish:

At 2:05 pm, Ryan started saying, "You would not believe me. Holy shit. You would not believe me!" And pacing. Quickly. After vomiting. Then muttering, "you're never gonna fuckin believe it." At 2:21, Ryan said, "Take notes. Wow! Fucking shit, Trish. Nobody will ever fucking believe this." Getting more agitated and less able to walk without bumping into things. Knelt down with head on painting. 2:34. Lying on floor "I can't believe it. Please tell me you believe it." 2:38. "It's so crazy, Trish. Holy shit." 2:54 pm. Still lying on the floor. "Fucking A. You are not going to believe this." Flailing arms. Now push-ups. 2:55 pm. Starts walking again - quickly. 3:10. Still pacing. Kneeling on silkscreens. Child's pose. Lying on floor. "It's so stupid. Tell me, Trish." 3:19. Sits on couch. Addresses me directly, "Has it ever been like this, Trish?" Moves to floor. "What do you see, Trish?"
Me- *"I see you trying to connect with reality."*
(Touching head, floor, paintings, etc — Ryan hit his left hand on something.)
3:22. Lying on floor.
3:23. "Does this happen every time, Trish?"
"No"

WELCOME TOURISTS

The Best Intentions & The Worst Interpretations

STAY CLOSED

GET 'EM IN.
GET 'EM OFF. GET 'EM OUT.

< Exhibition Continues >

KNOW BETTER
AND DO WORSE

re is a trap.

NOT FOR RES

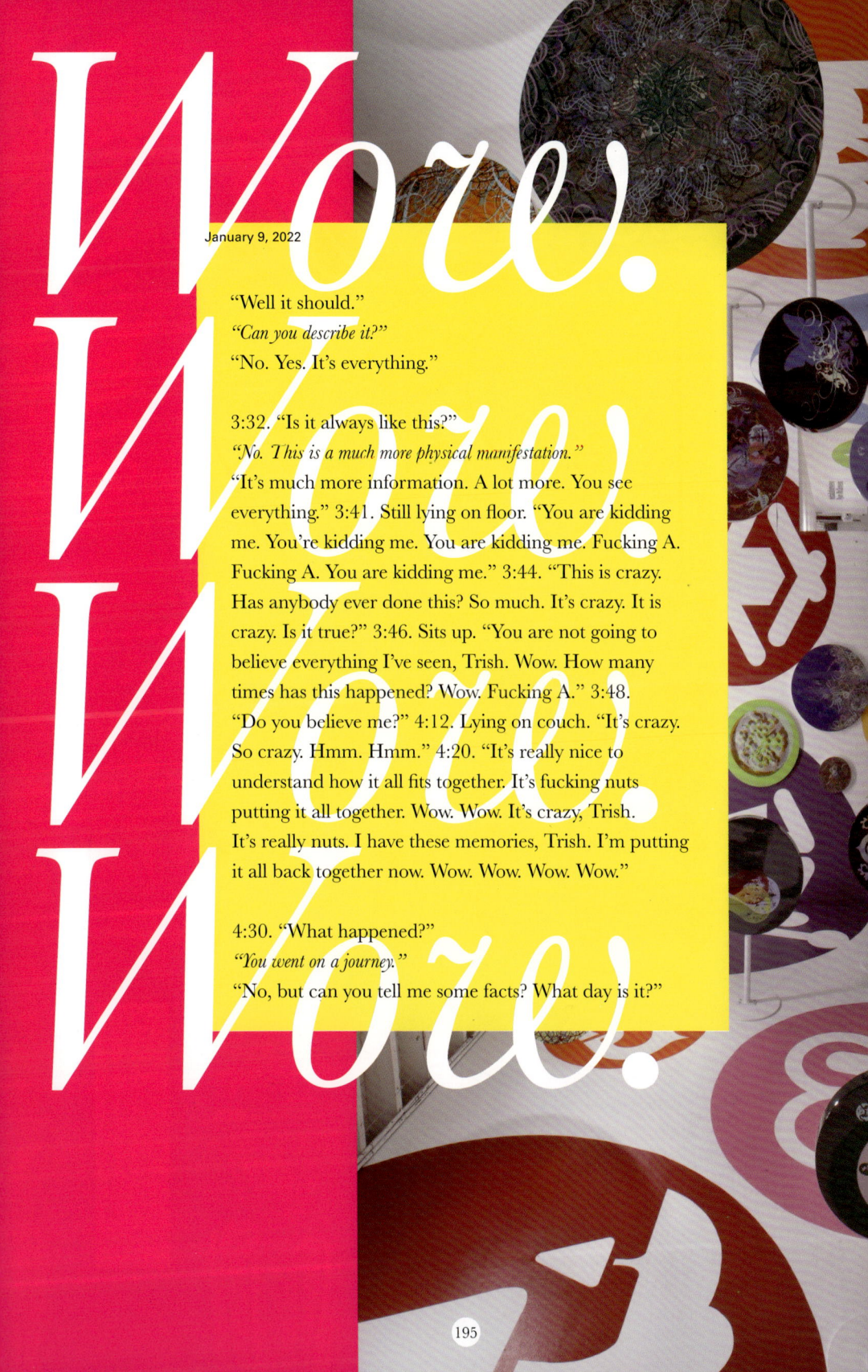

January 9, 2022

"Well it should."
"Can you describe it?"
"No. Yes. It's everything."

3:32. "Is it always like this?"
"No. This is a much more physical manifestation."
"It's much more information. A lot more. You see everything." 3:41. Still lying on floor. "You are kidding me. You're kidding me. You are kidding me. Fucking A. Fucking A. You are kidding me." 3:44. "This is crazy. Has anybody ever done this? So much. It's crazy. It is crazy. Is it true?" 3:46. Sits up. "You are not going to believe everything I've seen, Trish. Wow. How many times has this happened? Wow. Fucking A." 3:48. "Do you believe me?" 4:12. Lying on couch. "It's crazy. So crazy. Hmm. Hmm." 4:20. "It's really nice to understand how it all fits together. It's fucking nuts putting it all together. Wow. Wow. It's crazy, Trish. It's really nuts. I have these memories, Trish. I'm putting it all back together now. Wow. Wow. Wow. Wow."

4:30. "What happened?"
"You went on a journey."
"No, but can you tell me some facts? What day is it?"

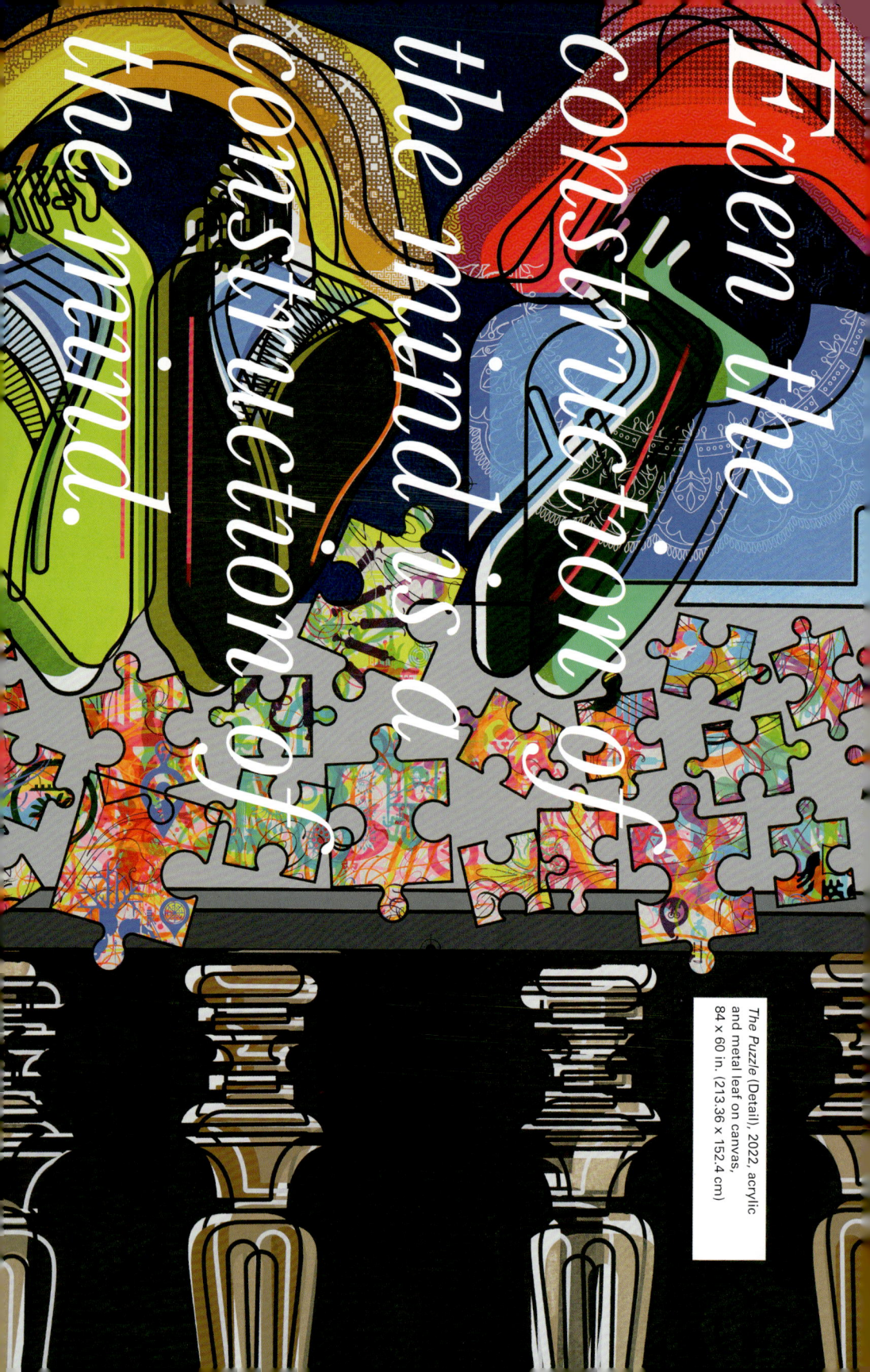

Even the construction of the mind is a construction of the mind.

The Puzzle (Detail), 2022, acrylic and metal leaf on canvas, 84 x 60 in. (213.36 x 152.4 cm)

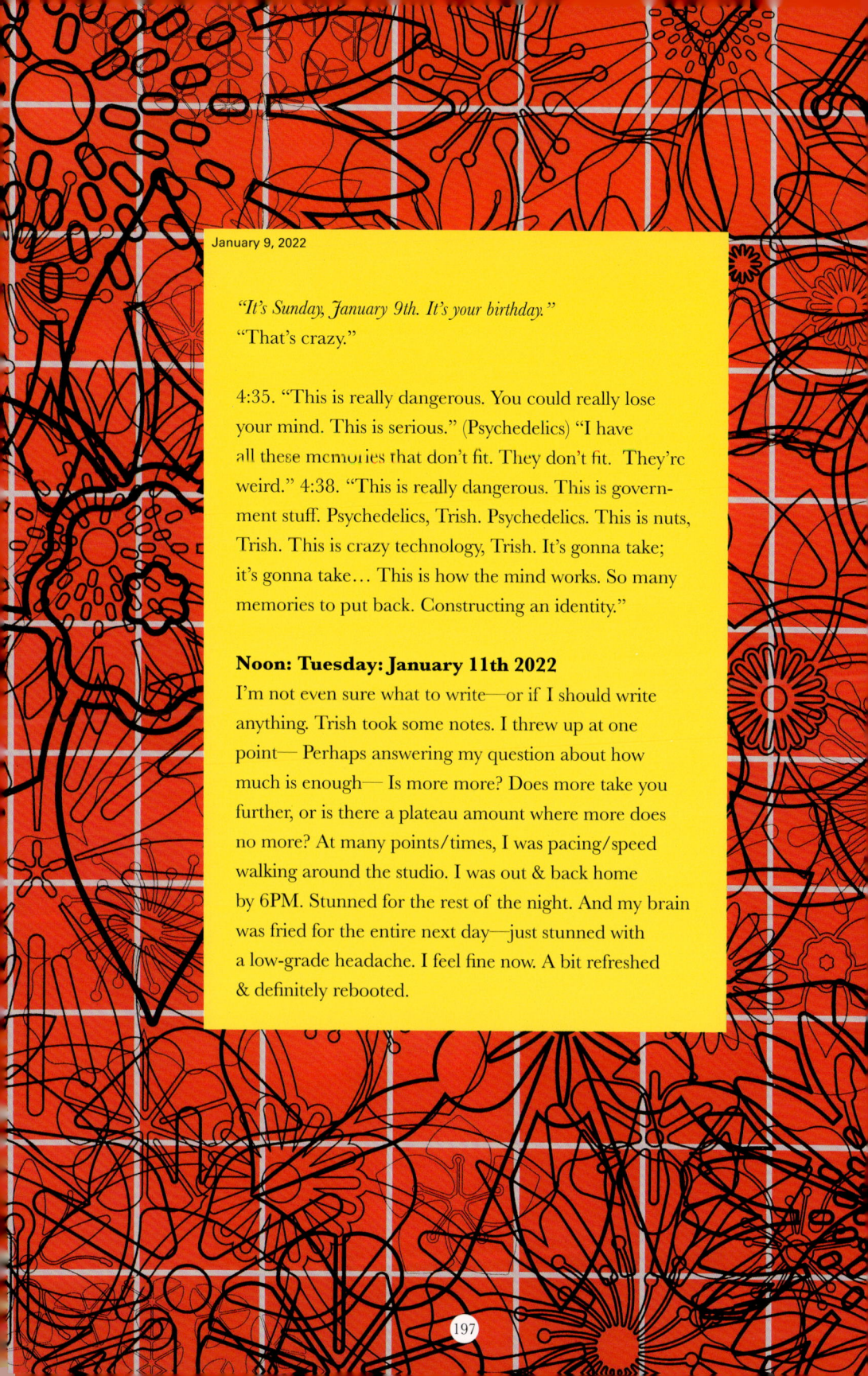

January 9, 2022

"It's Sunday, January 9th. It's your birthday."
"That's crazy."

4:35. "This is really dangerous. You could really lose your mind. This is serious." (Psychedelics) "I have all these memories that don't fit. They don't fit. They're weird." 4:38. "This is really dangerous. This is government stuff. Psychedelics, Trish. Psychedelics. This is nuts, Trish. This is crazy technology, Trish. It's gonna take; it's gonna take… This is how the mind works. So many memories to put back. Constructing an identity."

Noon: Tuesday: January 11th 2022
I'm not even sure what to write—or if I should write anything. Trish took some notes. I threw up at one point— Perhaps answering my question about how much is enough— Is more more? Does more take you further, or is there a plateau amount where more does no more? At many points/times, I was pacing/speed walking around the studio. I was out & back home by 6PM. Stunned for the rest of the night. And my brain was fried for the entire next day—just stunned with a low-grade headache. I feel fine now. A bit refreshed & definitely rebooted.

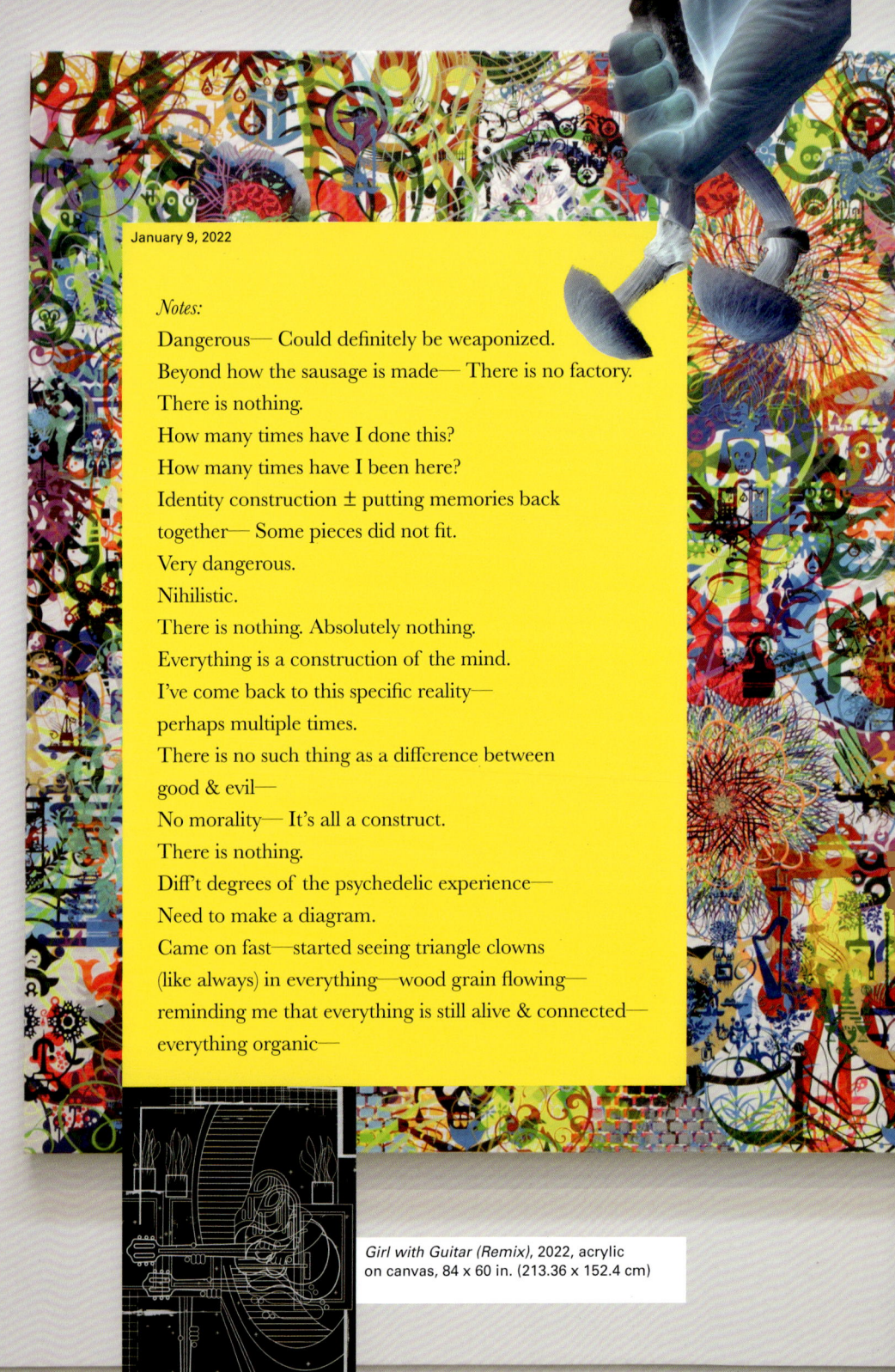

January 9, 2022

Notes:

Dangerous— Could definitely be weaponized.

Beyond how the sausage is made— There is no factory.

There is nothing.

How many times have I done this?

How many times have I been here?

Identity construction ± putting memories back

together— Some pieces did not fit.

Very dangerous.

Nihilistic.

There is nothing. Absolutely nothing.

Everything is a construction of the mind.

I've come back to this specific reality—

perhaps multiple times.

There is no such thing as a difference between

good & evil—

No morality— It's all a construct.

There is nothing.

Diff't degrees of the psychedelic experience—

Need to make a diagram.

Came on fast—started seeing triangle clowns

(like always) in everything—wood grain flowing—

reminding me that everything is still alive & connected—

everything organic—

Girl with Guitar (Remix), 2022, acrylic
on canvas, 84 x 60 in. (213.36 x 152.4 cm)

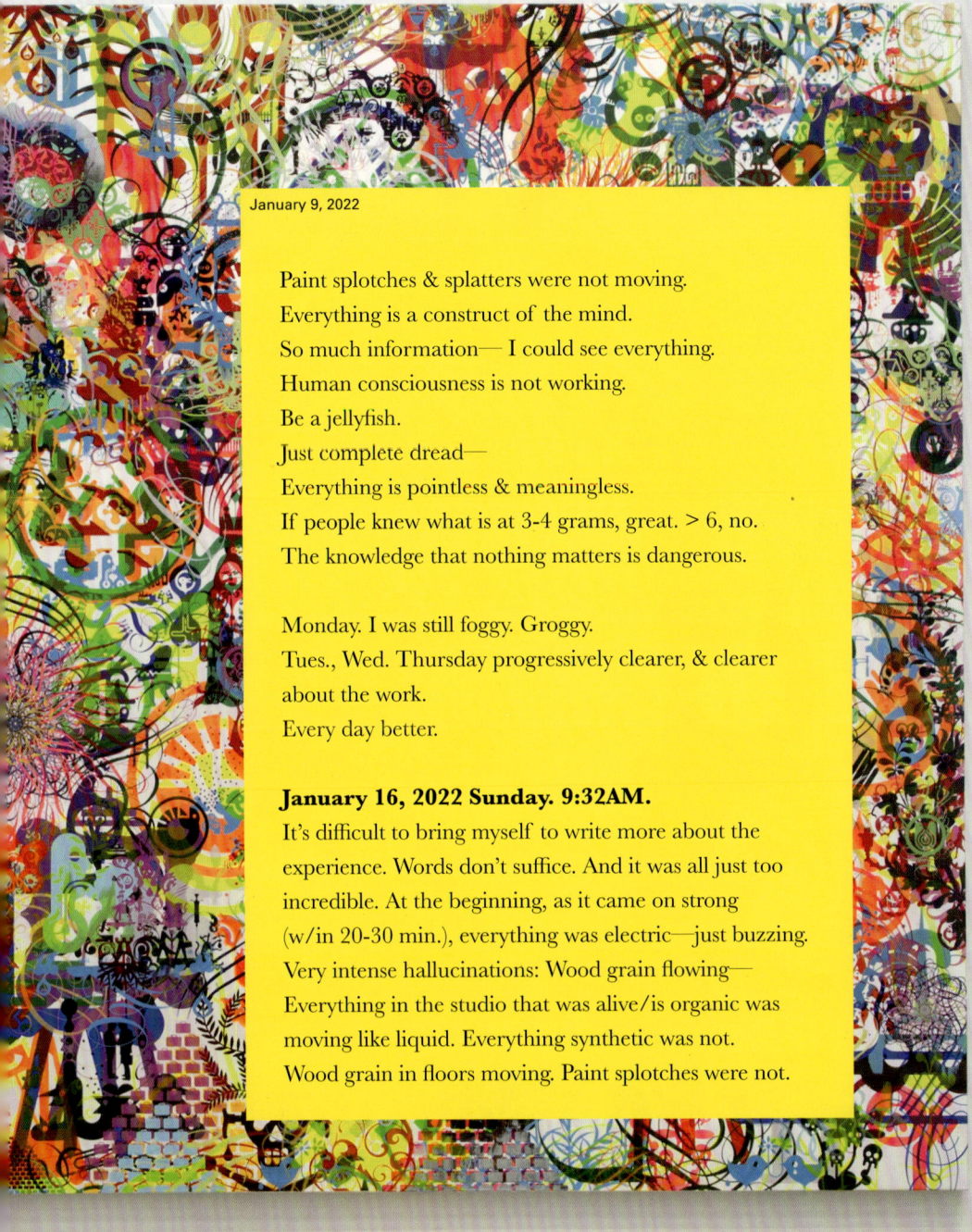

January 9, 2022

Paint splotches & splatters were not moving.
Everything is a construct of the mind.
So much information— I could see everything.
Human consciousness is not working.
Be a jellyfish.
Just complete dread—
Everything is pointless & meaningless.
If people knew what is at 3-4 grams, great. > 6, no.
The knowledge that nothing matters is dangerous.

Monday. I was still foggy. Groggy.
Tues., Wed. Thursday progressively clearer, & clearer
about the work.
Every day better.

January 16, 2022 Sunday. 9:32AM.
It's difficult to bring myself to write more about the
experience. Words don't suffice. And it was all just too
incredible. At the beginning, as it came on strong
(w/in 20-30 min.), everything was electric—just buzzing.
Very intense hallucinations: Wood grain flowing—
Everything in the studio that was alive/is organic was
moving like liquid. Everything synthetic was not.
Wood grain in floors moving. Paint splotches were not.

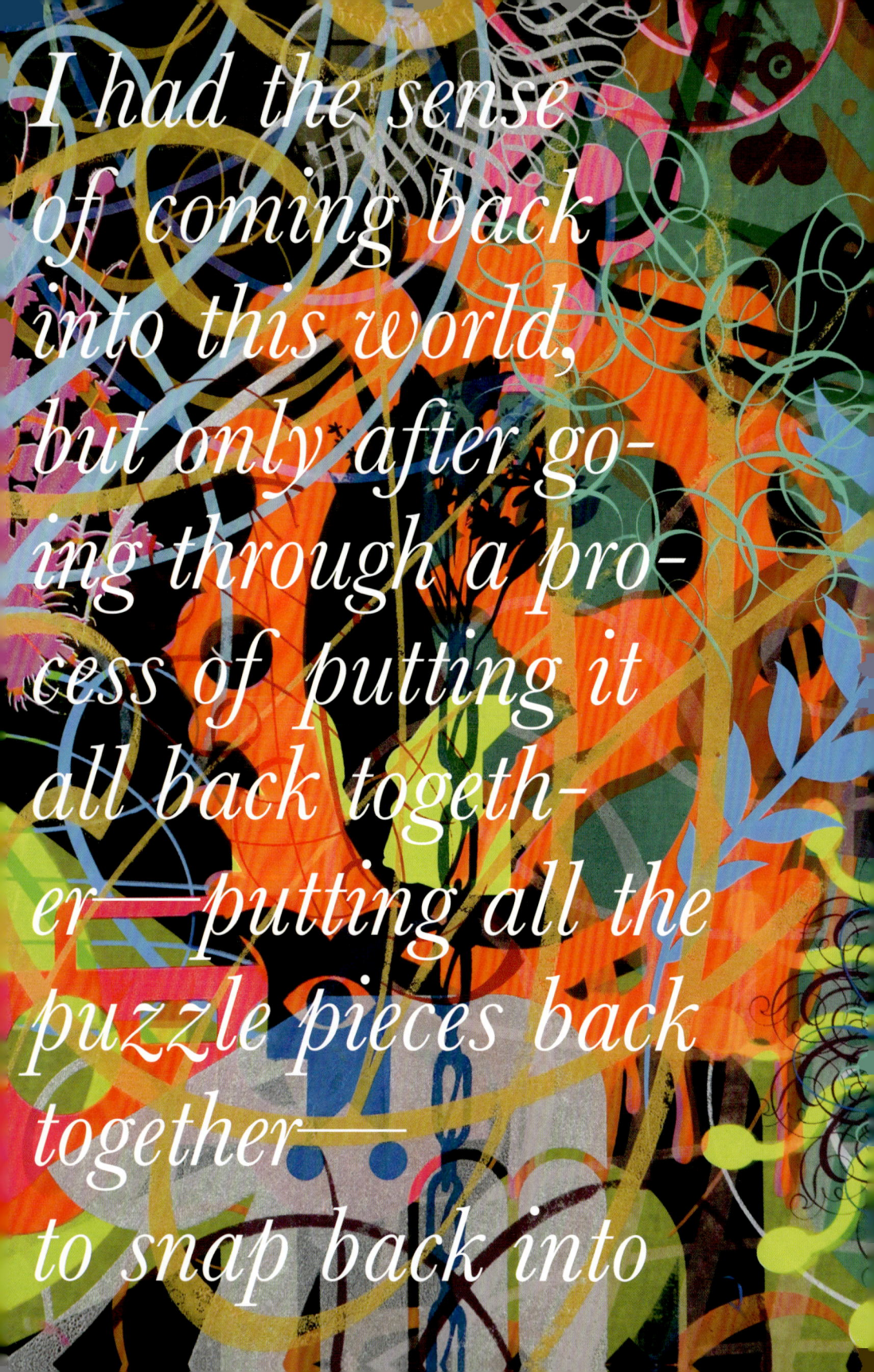

I had the sense
of coming back
into this world,
but only after go-
ing through a pro-
cess of putting it
all back togeth-
er——putting all the
puzzle pieces back
together——
to snap back into

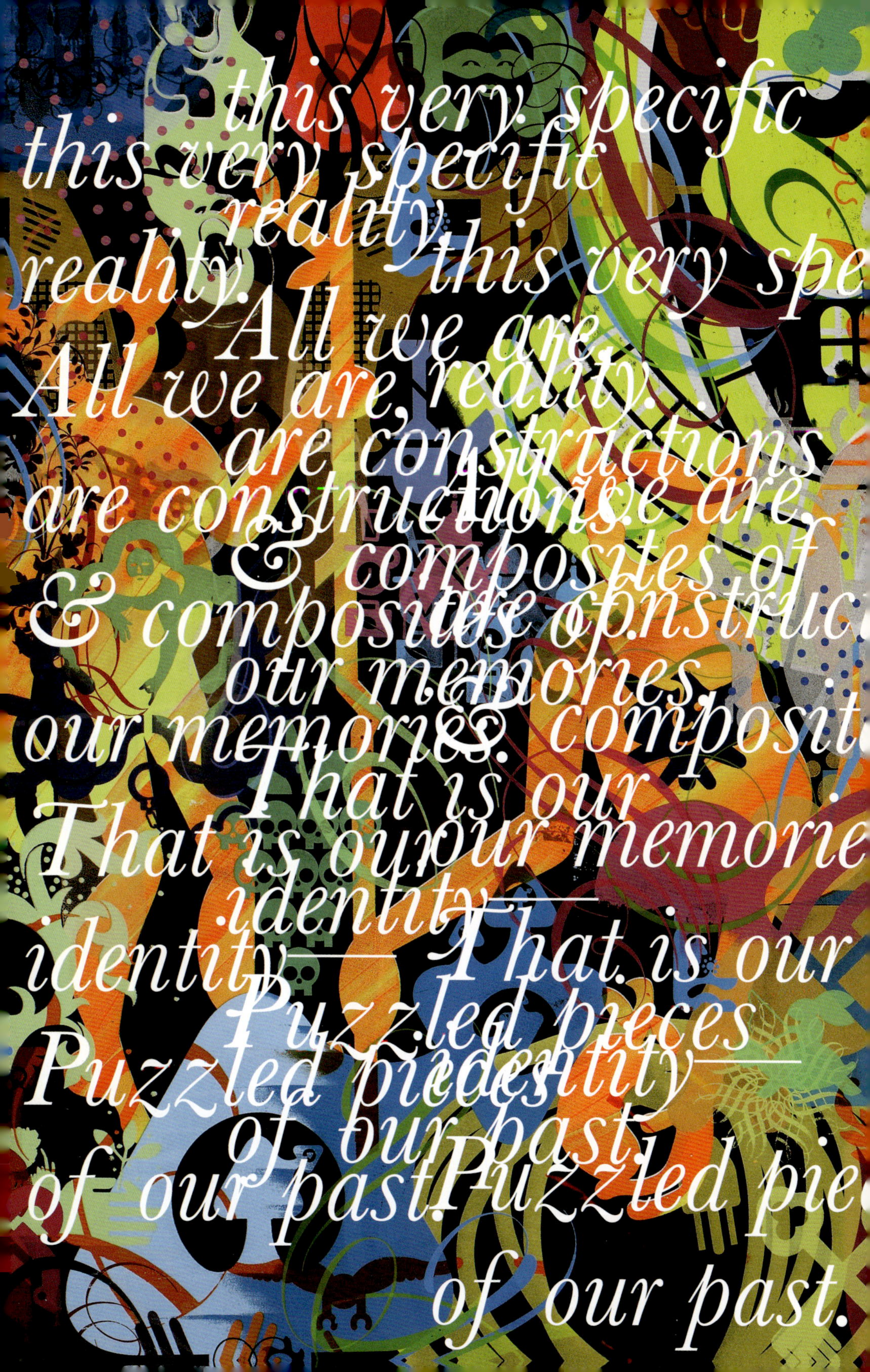

this very specific
reality.

All we are,
are constructions
& composites of
our memories.
That is our
identity——
Puzzled pieces
of our past.

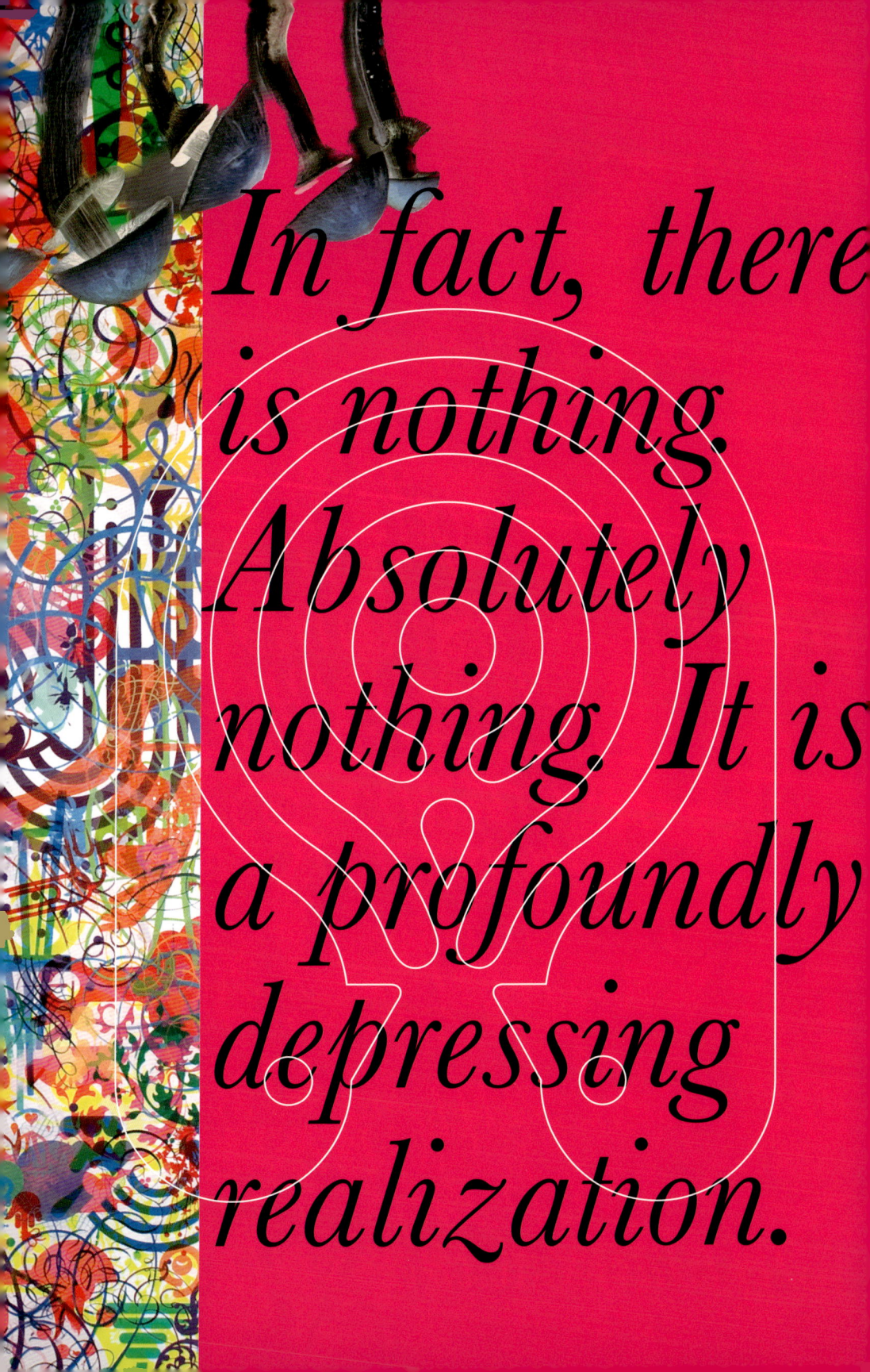

In fact, there is nothing. Absolutely nothing. It is a profoundly depressing realization.

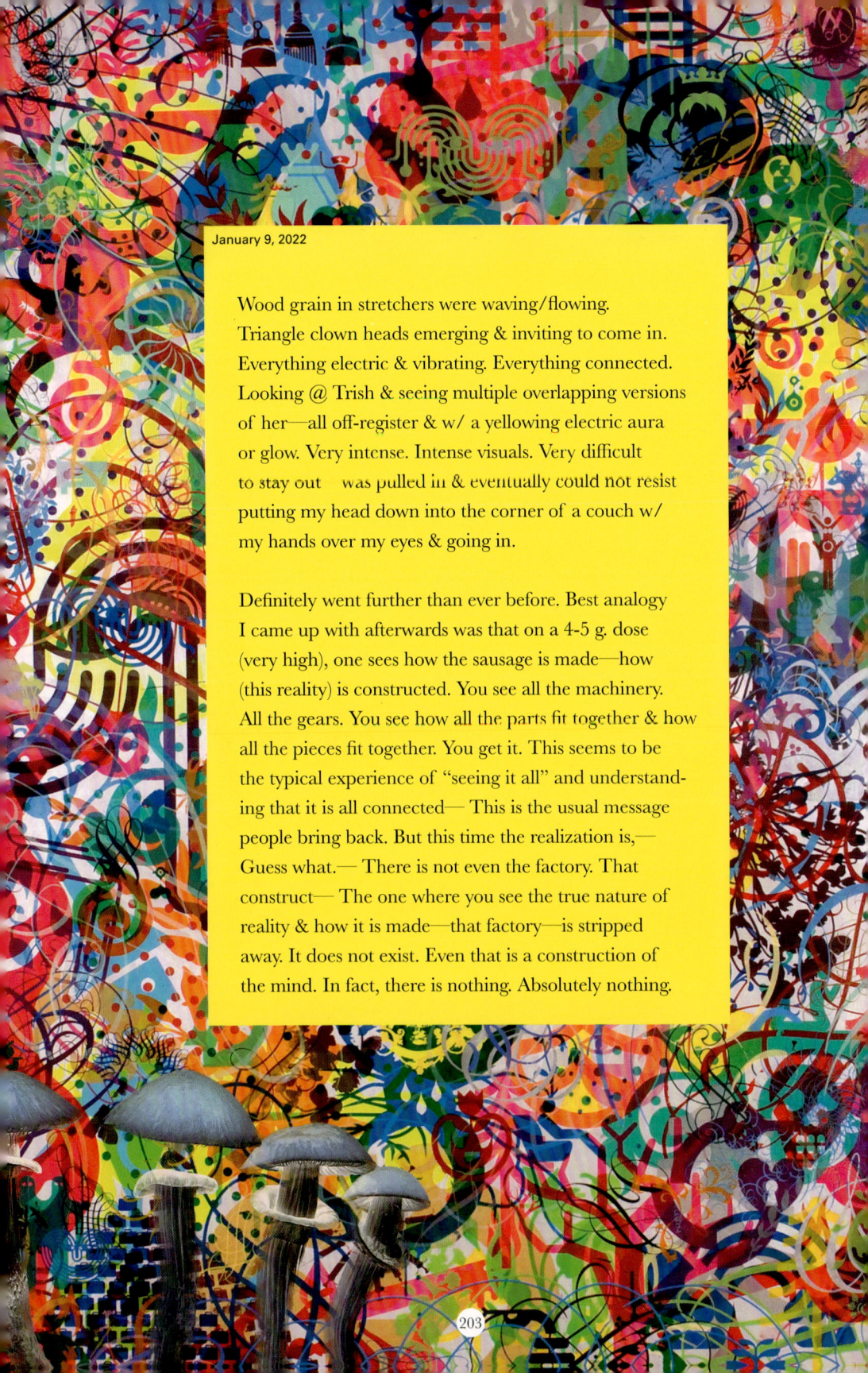

January 9, 2022

Wood grain in stretchers were waving/flowing.
Triangle clown heads emerging & inviting to come in.
Everything electric & vibrating. Everything connected.
Looking @ Trish & seeing multiple overlapping versions
of her—all off-register & w/ a yellowing electric aura
or glow. Very intense. Intense visuals. Very difficult
to stay out   was pulled in & eventually could not resist
putting my head down into the corner of a couch w/
my hands over my eyes & going in.

Definitely went further than ever before. Best analogy
I came up with afterwards was that on a 4-5 g. dose
(very high), one sees how the sausage is made—how
(this reality) is constructed. You see all the machinery.
All the gears. You see how all the parts fit together & how
all the pieces fit together. You get it. This seems to be
the typical experience of "seeing it all" and understanding that it is all connected— This is the usual message
people bring back. But this time the realization is,—
Guess what.— There is not even the factory. That
construct— The one where you see the true nature of
reality & how it is made—that factory—is stripped
away. It does not exist. Even that is a construction of
the mind. In fact, there is nothing. Absolutely nothing.

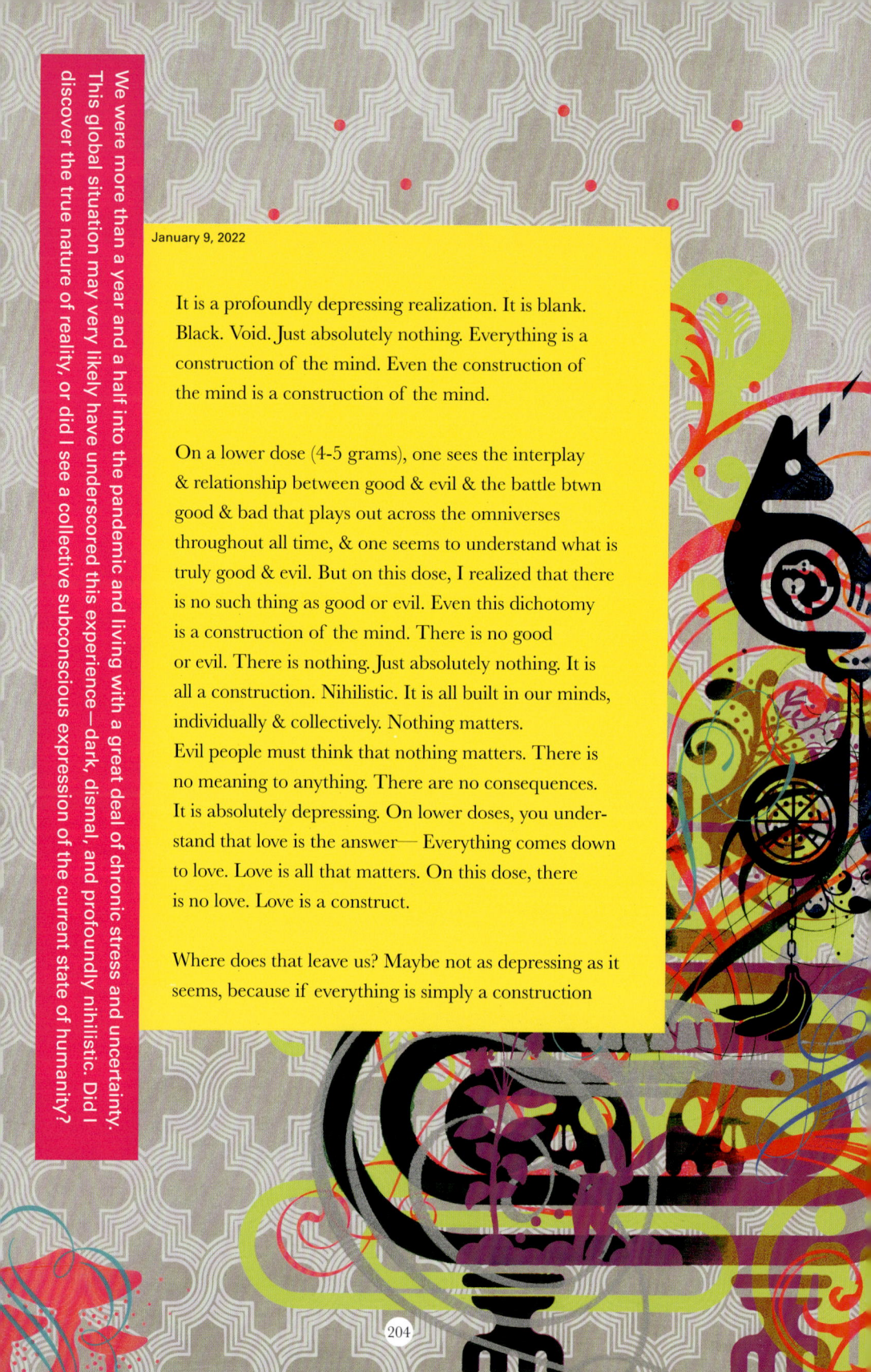

January 9, 2022

It is a profoundly depressing realization. It is blank. Black. Void. Just absolutely nothing. Everything is a construction of the mind. Even the construction of the mind is a construction of the mind.

On a lower dose (4-5 grams), one sees the interplay & relationship between good & evil & the battle btwn good & bad that plays out across the omniverses throughout all time, & one seems to understand what is truly good & evil. But on this dose, I realized that there is no such thing as good or evil. Even this dichotomy is a construction of the mind. There is no good or evil. There is nothing. Just absolutely nothing. It is all a construction. Nihilistic. It is all built in our minds, individually & collectively. Nothing matters.
Evil people must think that nothing matters. There is no meaning to anything. There are no consequences. It is absolutely depressing. On lower doses, you under-stand that love is the answer— Everything comes down to love. Love is all that matters. On this dose, there is no love. Love is a construct.

Where does that leave us? Maybe not as depressing as it seems, because if everything is simply a construction

We were more than a year and a half into the pandemic and living with a great deal of chronic stress and uncertainty. This global situation may very likely have underscored this experience—dark, dismal, and profoundly nihilistic. Did I discover the true nature of reality, or did I see a collective subconscious expression of the current state of humanity?

204

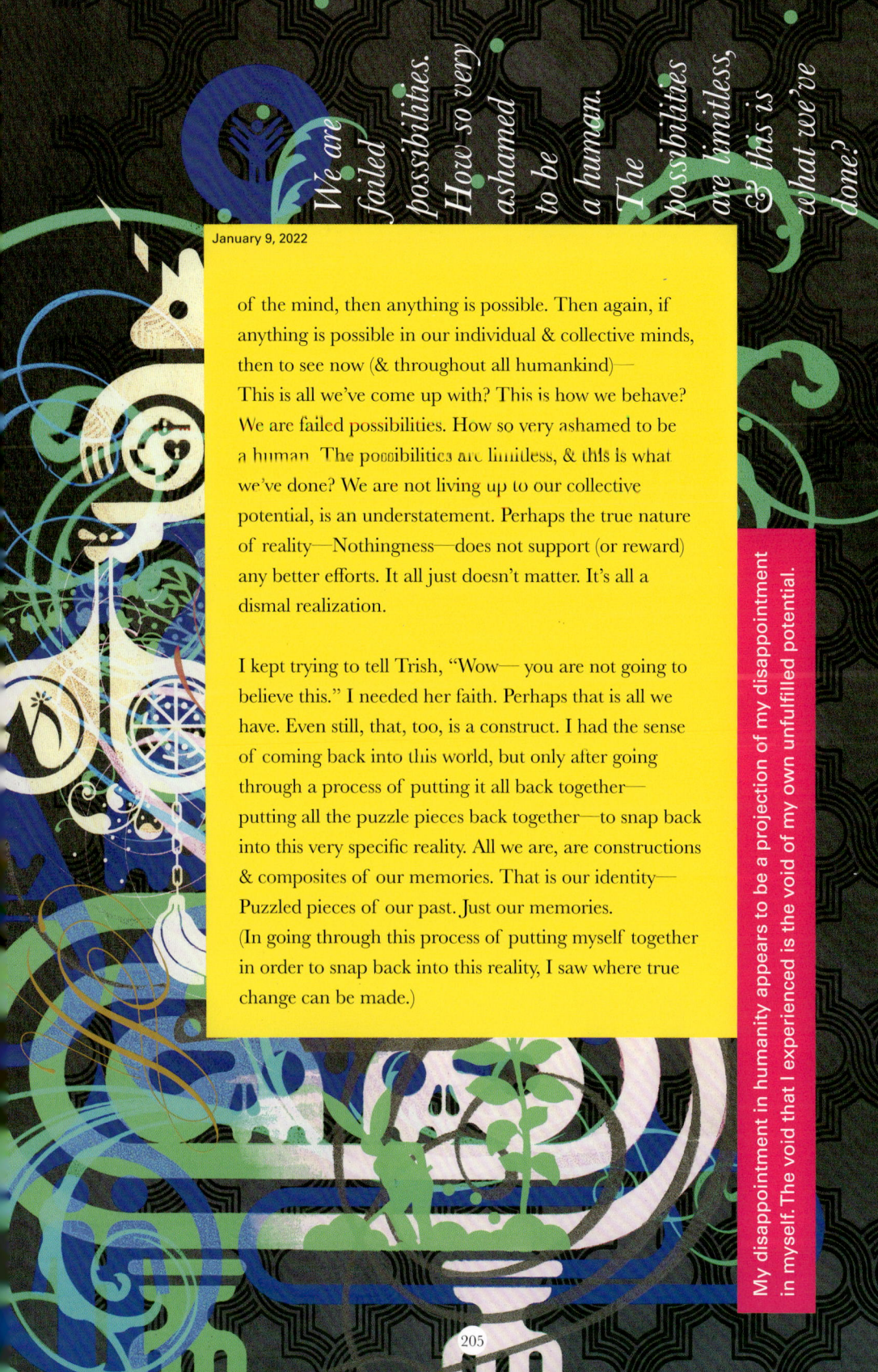

We are failed possibilities. How so very ashamed to be a human. The possibilities are limitless, & this is what we've done?

January 9, 2022

of the mind, then anything is possible. Then again, if anything is possible in our individual & collective minds, then to see now (& throughout all humankind)—
This is all we've come up with? This is how we behave? We are failed possibilities. How so very ashamed to be a human. The possibilities are limitless, & this is what we've done? We are not living up to our collective potential, is an understatement. Perhaps the true nature of reality—Nothingness—does not support (or reward) any better efforts. It all just doesn't matter. It's all a dismal realization.

I kept trying to tell Trish, "Wow— you are not going to believe this." I needed her faith. Perhaps that is all we have. Even still, that, too, is a construct. I had the sense of coming back into this world, but only after going through a process of putting it all back together— putting all the puzzle pieces back together—to snap back into this very specific reality. All we are, are constructions & composites of our memories. That is our identity— Puzzled pieces of our past. Just our memories.
(In going through this process of putting myself together in order to snap back into this reality, I saw where true change can be made.)

My disappointment in humanity appears to be a projection of my disappointment in myself. The void that I experienced is the void of my own unfulfilled potential.

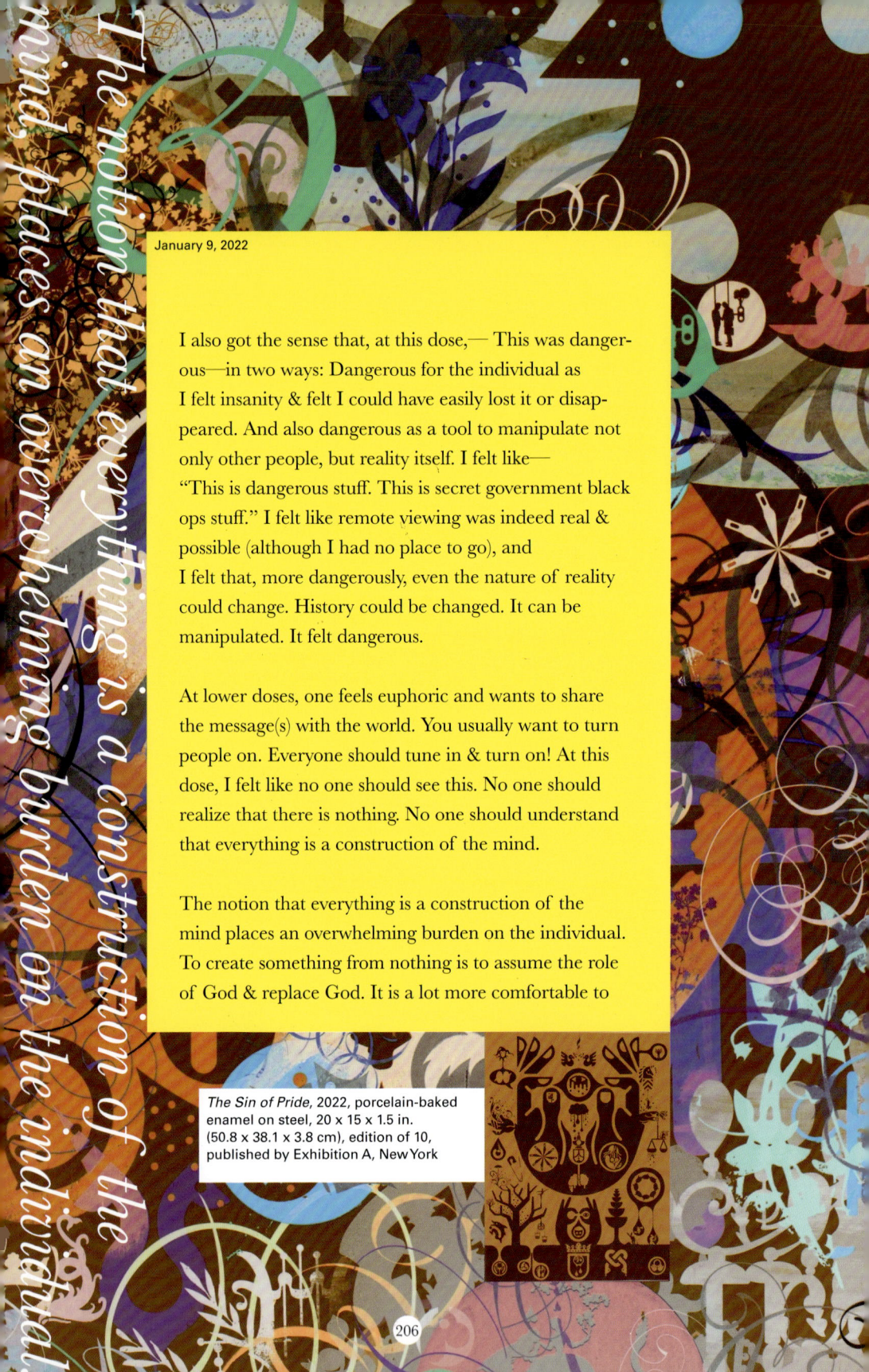

The notion that everything is a construction of the mind places an overwhelming burden on the individual

January 9, 2022

I also got the sense that, at this dose,— This was dangerous—in two ways: Dangerous for the individual as
I felt insanity & felt I could have easily lost it or disappeared. And also dangerous as a tool to manipulate not
only other people, but reality itself. I felt like—
"This is dangerous stuff. This is secret government black
ops stuff." I felt like remote viewing was indeed real &
possible (although I had no place to go), and
I felt that, more dangerously, even the nature of reality
could change. History could be changed. It can be
manipulated. It felt dangerous.

At lower doses, one feels euphoric and wants to share
the message(s) with the world. You usually want to turn
people on. Everyone should tune in & turn on! At this
dose, I felt like no one should see this. No one should
realize that there is nothing. No one should understand
that everything is a construction of the mind.

The notion that everything is a construction of the
mind places an overwhelming burden on the individual.
To create something from nothing is to assume the role
of God & replace God. It is a lot more comfortable to

The Sin of Pride, 2022, porcelain-baked
enamel on steel, 20 x 15 x 1.5 in.
(50.8 x 38.1 x 3.8 cm), edition of 10,
published by Exhibition A, New York

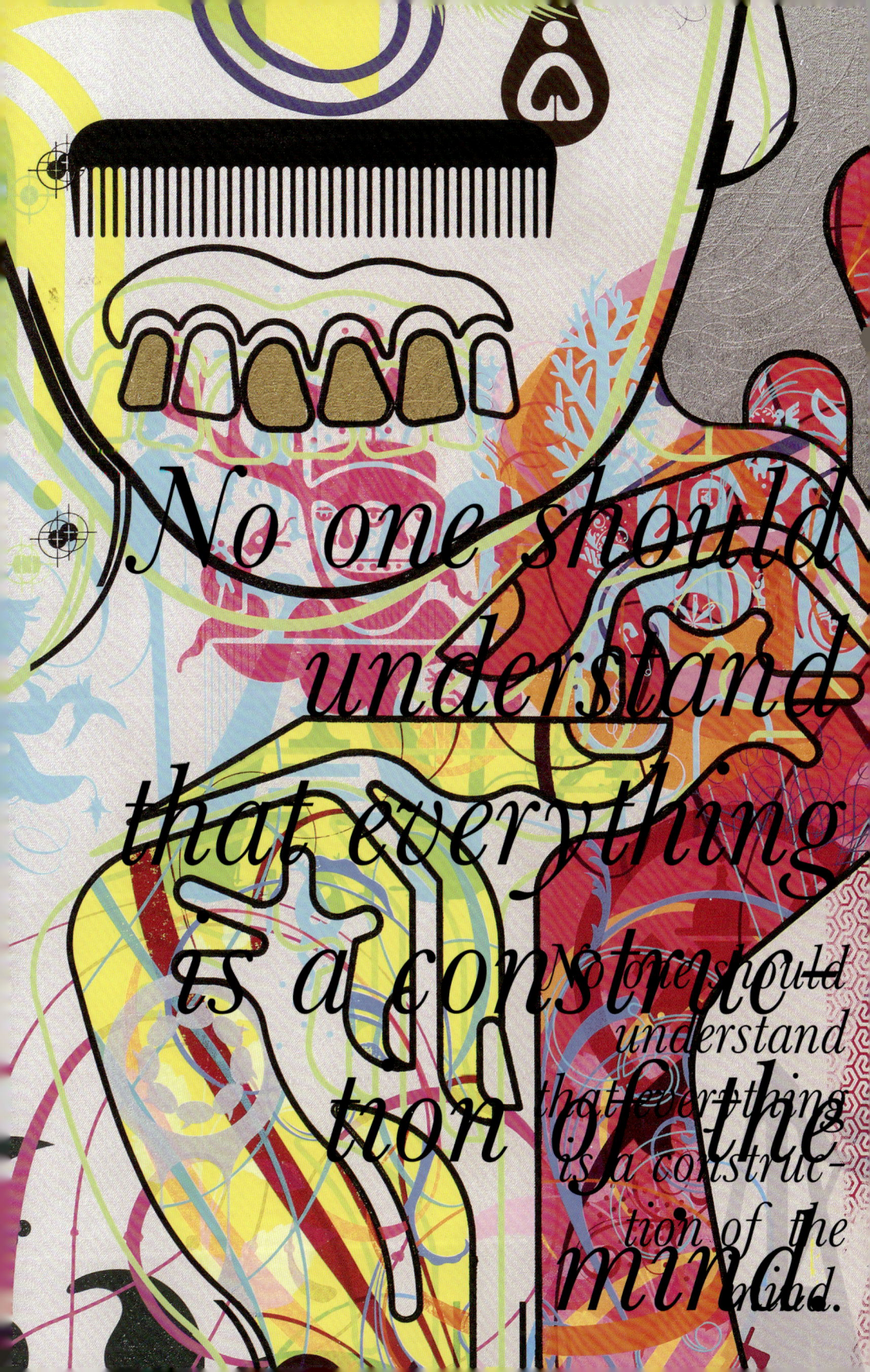

No one should understand that everything is a construction of the mind.

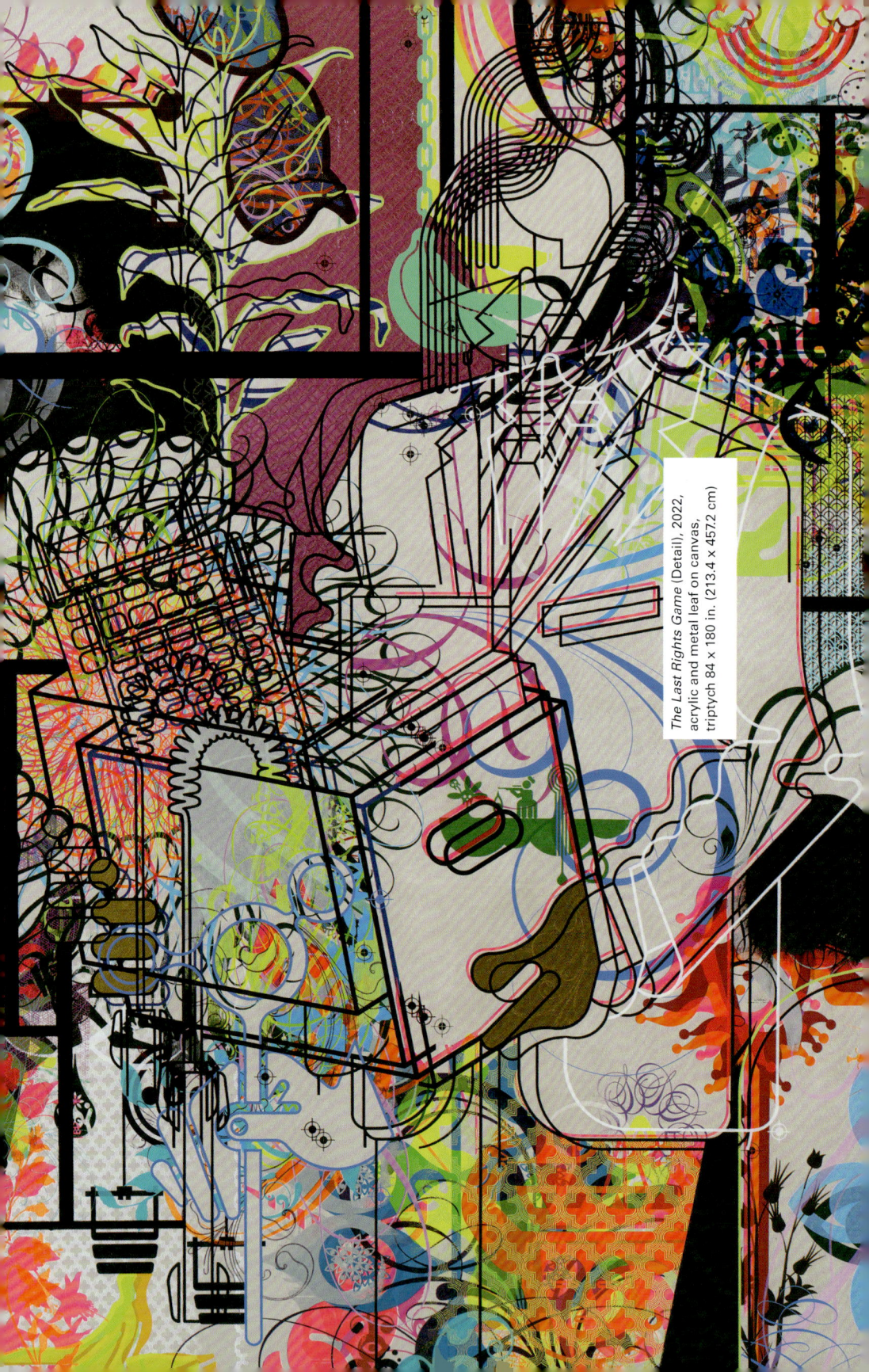

The Last Rights Game (Detail), 2022, acrylic and metal leaf on canvas, triptych 84 x 180 in. (213.4 x 457.2 cm)

January 9, 2022

create a God to do (or have done) that heavy lifting for you. Scapegoats are easier. God is a mini-me to blame. Of course, God exists outside yourself and is an "other."

Live only inside your own head & come to terms with your own reality of your own construction. That is all there is. That's not true. Conclusions drawn from this experience—the realizations—all the information— can be tricky. Potentially kooky. It's now a week later, & I feel like I am back. Progressively, since last Sunday, I have woken up each day feeling clearer & lighter. Painting & projects have clearer solutions. Have made some realizations & connections & conclusions. I've brought into question the merit of sharing any of this with anyone. What's the point? Still curious if any of this (psilocybin insights) can be quantified, studied, & productive.

What does any of this matter if, not only is none of this "real," but in fact, there is no reality?

USED PAINT

I did not want to believe any of this.

PREVIOUSLY UNSEEN

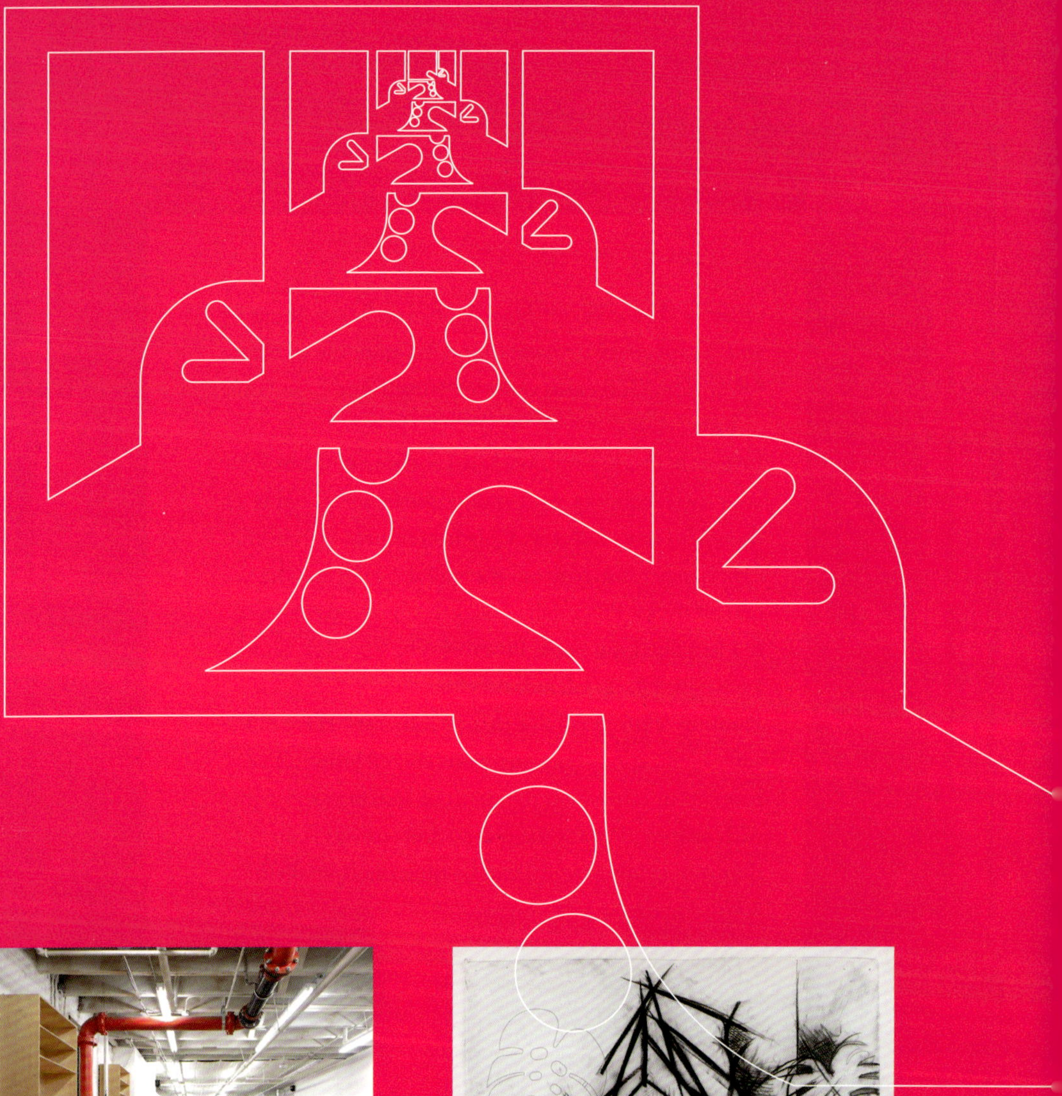

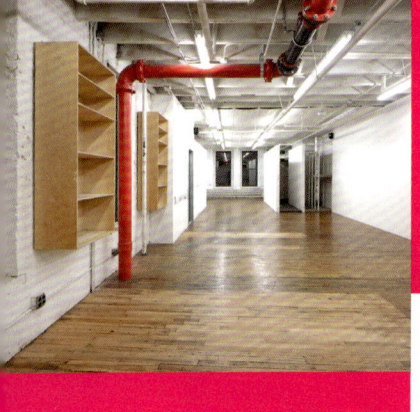

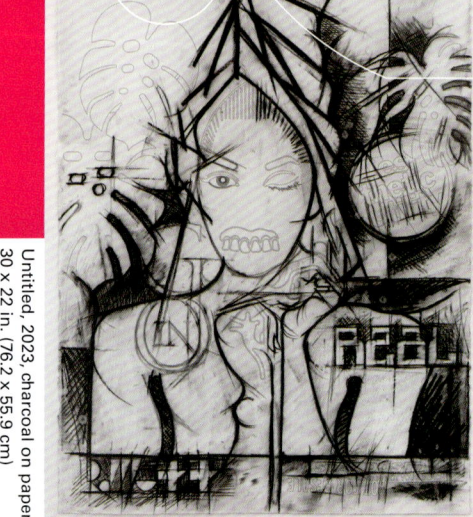

Untitled, 2023, charcoal on paper,
30 x 22 in. (76.2 x 55.9 cm)

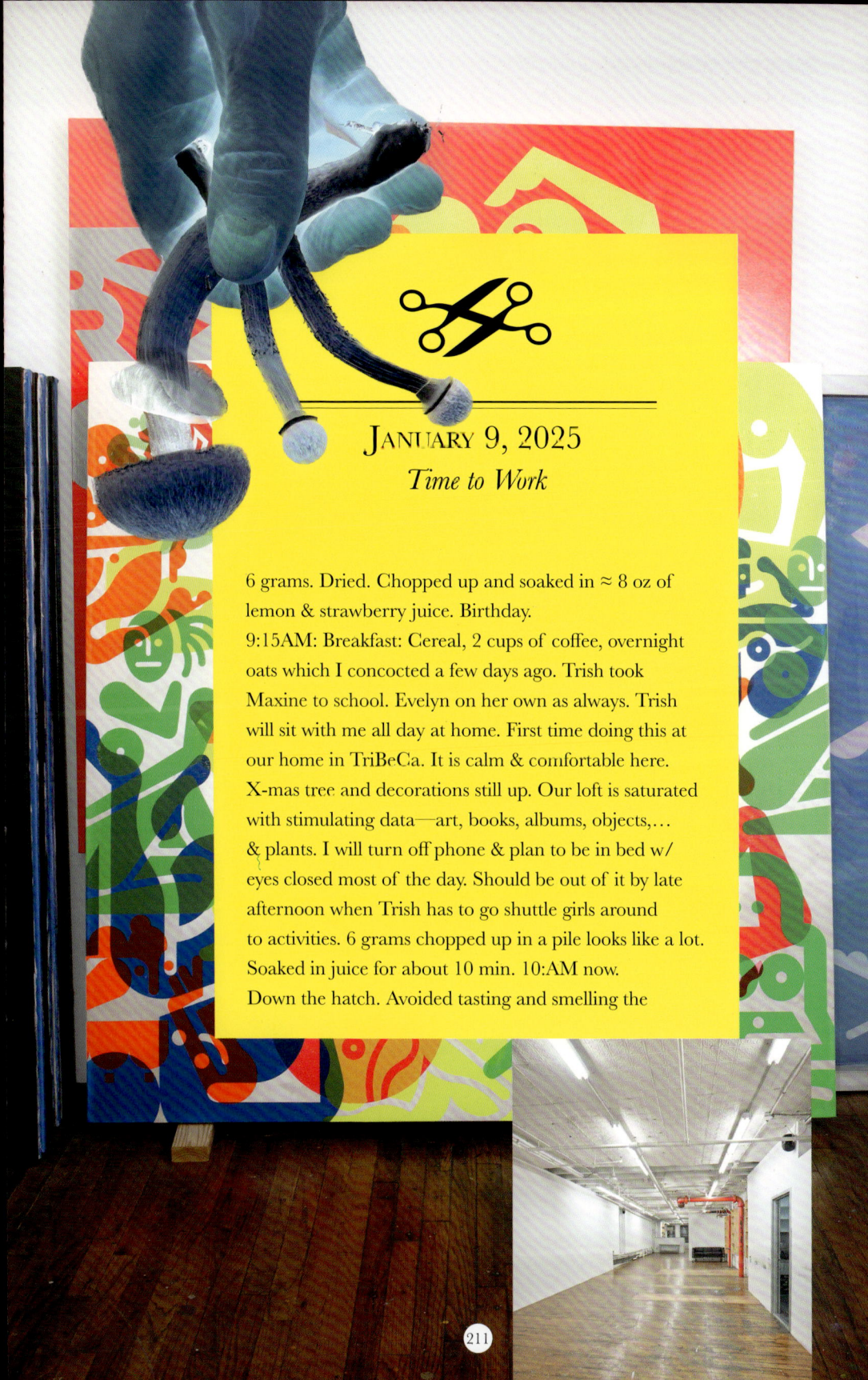

January 9, 2025

Time to Work

6 grams. Dried. Chopped up and soaked in ≈ 8 oz of
lemon & strawberry juice. Birthday.
9:15AM: Breakfast: Cereal, 2 cups of coffee, overnight
oats which I concocted a few days ago. Trish took
Maxine to school. Evelyn on her own as always. Trish
will sit with me all day at home. First time doing this at
our home in TriBeCa. It is calm & comfortable here.
X-mas tree and decorations still up. Our loft is saturated
with stimulating data—art, books, albums, objects,…
& plants. I will turn off phone & plan to be in bed w/
eyes closed most of the day. Should be out of it by late
afternoon when Trish has to go shuttle girls around
to activities. 6 grams chopped up in a pile looks like a lot.
Soaked in juice for about 10 min. 10:AM now.
Down the hatch. Avoided tasting and smelling the

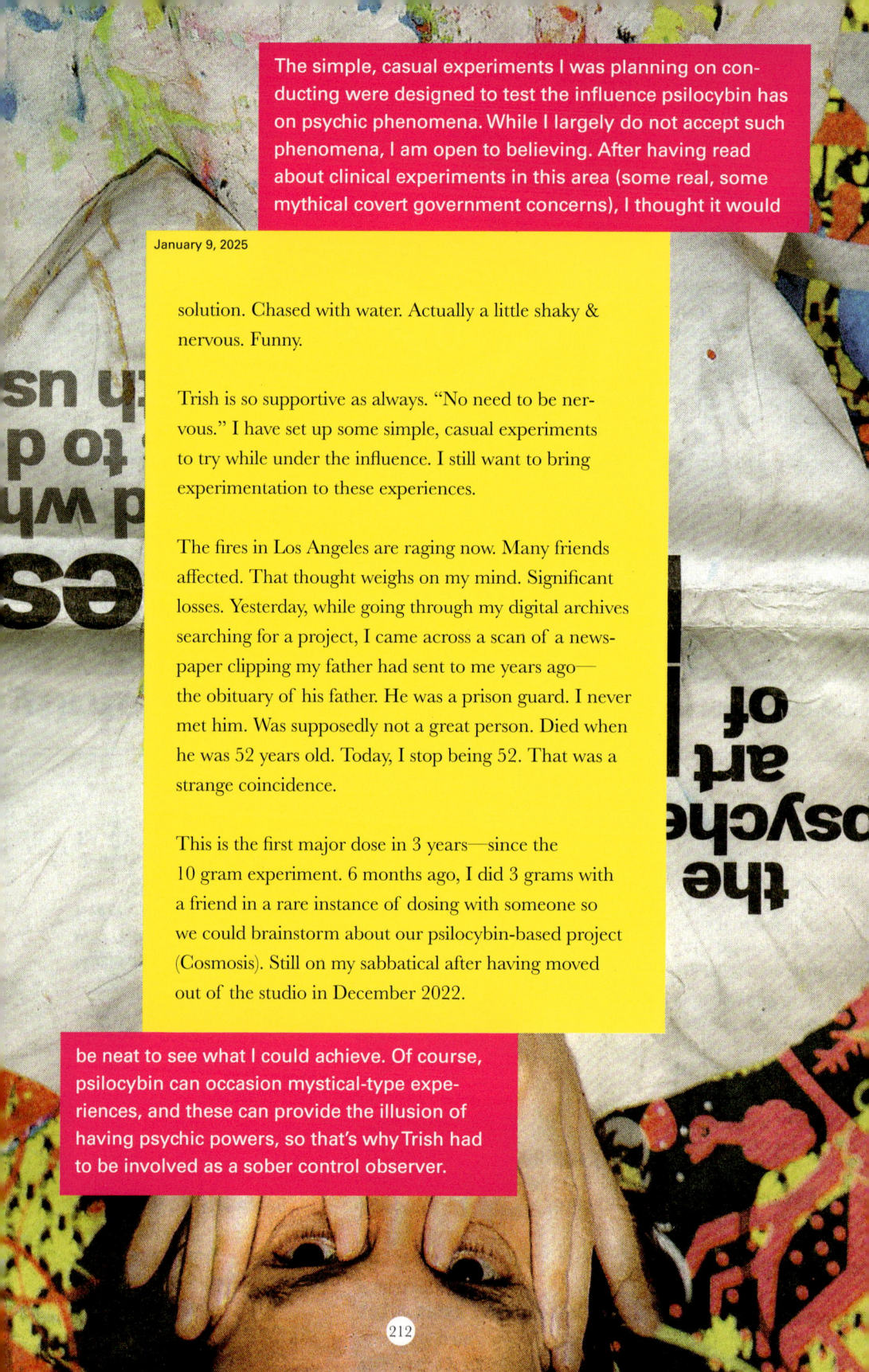

The simple, casual experiments I was planning on conducting were designed to test the influence psilocybin has on psychic phenomena. While I largely do not accept such phenomena, I am open to believing. After having read about clinical experiments in this area (some real, some mythical covert government concerns), I thought it would

January 9, 2025

solution. Chased with water. Actually a little shaky & nervous. Funny.

Trish is so supportive as always. "No need to be nervous." I have set up some simple, casual experiments to try while under the influence. I still want to bring experimentation to these experiences.

The fires in Los Angeles are raging now. Many friends affected. That thought weighs on my mind. Significant losses. Yesterday, while going through my digital archives searching for a project, I came across a scan of a newspaper clipping my father had sent to me years ago—the obituary of his father. He was a prison guard. I never met him. Was supposedly not a great person. Died when he was 52 years old. Today, I stop being 52. That was a strange coincidence.

This is the first major dose in 3 years—since the 10 gram experiment. 6 months ago, I did 3 grams with a friend in a rare instance of dosing with someone so we could brainstorm about our psilocybin-based project (Cosmosis). Still on my sabbatical after having moved out of the studio in December 2022.

be neat to see what I could achieve. Of course, psilocybin can occasion mystical-type experiences, and these can provide the illusion of having psychic powers, so that's why Trish had to be involved as a sober control observer.

However, I never conducted any of the tests. I just wasn't interested, and when during the trip Trish encouraged me to address the experiments, I simply dismissed them and said, "Those experiments are for something else—a time dedicated to just the experiments." I remember thinking that trying to use psilocybin in this way was somehow not right. I remember thinking that psychic powers were at odds with psychedelic insights.

January 9, 2025

2023 & 2024 have been used to formulate what the next 25 years will look like & under what studio model. Most of these past 2 years has been spent on THC. The better part of each week (the best part of each week) has been on a daily low-dose of 5 mg. 10:1 (THC:CBD) which I usually ride for up to 8 hrs. High functioning. Lots of writing & planning & researching. 18 months of seriously searching for a studio. Numerous close calls. Space is so very important to me for creation. As with the psychedelic experience, setting is paramount for making art. Everything must be perfect.

10:17AM: Slightly sweaty palms. A bit frenetic. A little queasy. Curious about the "lemon tekking" affect on the 6 grams. 10:23. Speaking with Trish. Calm & quiet in our home. May not get to our so-called experiments. Sweaty palms. Just sitting together at our booth… waiting. Trish is reading and will be able to do work while babysitting me. 6 grams should be sufficient to get me in &—explore. Learn. Receive.

First time really doing this knowing that these journal notes will be in the forthcoming book (*Trip Advisor*), which now has a publisher & will be released in Sept. This will

I wanted to test ESP, telepathy, psychokinesis, and remote viewing. Testing for heightened extra-sensory perception (ESP) abilities was going to be simple enough with a deck of cards. Trish was donating her mind for reading for the telepathy tests. Psychokinesis? Simple. I was going to re-arrange our furniture. To test remote viewing abilities, I had Trish take a tooth (a recent deaccession from the mouth of an offspring) with her on the morning journey to Chelsea for school drop-off. I told her to hide it anywhere in Manhattan before coming home that morning. She did.

A strange dissolving of everything

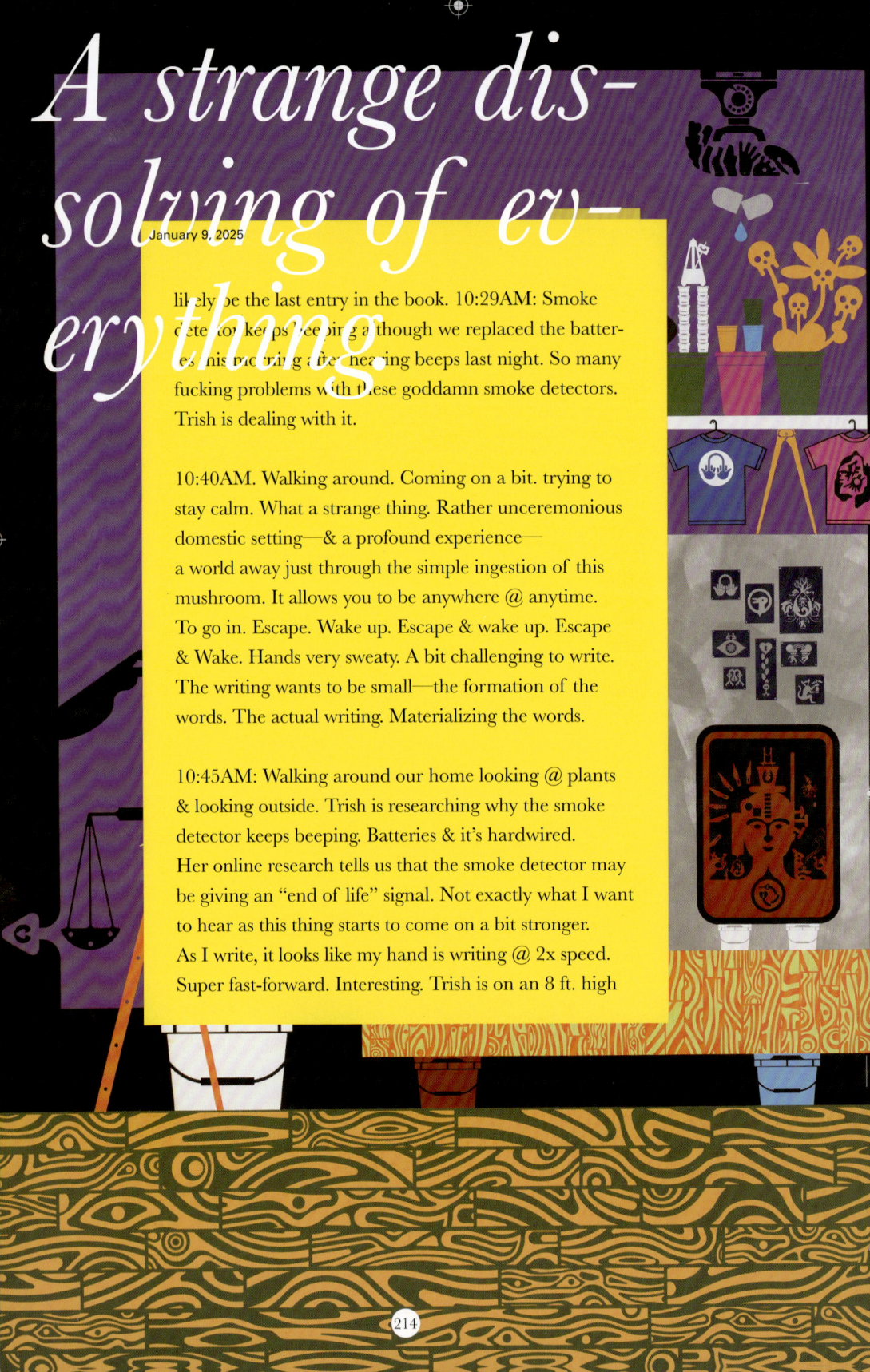

January 9, 2025

likely be the last entry in the book. 10:29AM: Smoke detector keeps beeping although we replaced the batteries this morning after hearing beeps last night. So many fucking problems with these goddamn smoke detectors. Trish is dealing with it.

10:40AM. Walking around. Coming on a bit. trying to stay calm. What a strange thing. Rather unceremonious domestic setting—& a profound experience—
a world away just through the simple ingestion of this mushroom. It allows you to be anywhere @ anytime.
To go in. Escape. Wake up. Escape & wake up. Escape & Wake. Hands very sweaty. A bit challenging to write. The writing wants to be small—the formation of the words. The actual writing. Materializing the words.

10:45AM: Walking around our home looking @ plants & looking outside. Trish is researching why the smoke detector keeps beeping. Batteries & it's hardwired.
Her online research tells us that the smoke detector may be giving an "end of life" signal. Not exactly what I want to hear as this thing starts to come on a bit stronger.
As I write, it looks like my hand is writing @ 2x speed. Super fast-forward. Interesting. Trish is on an 8 ft. high

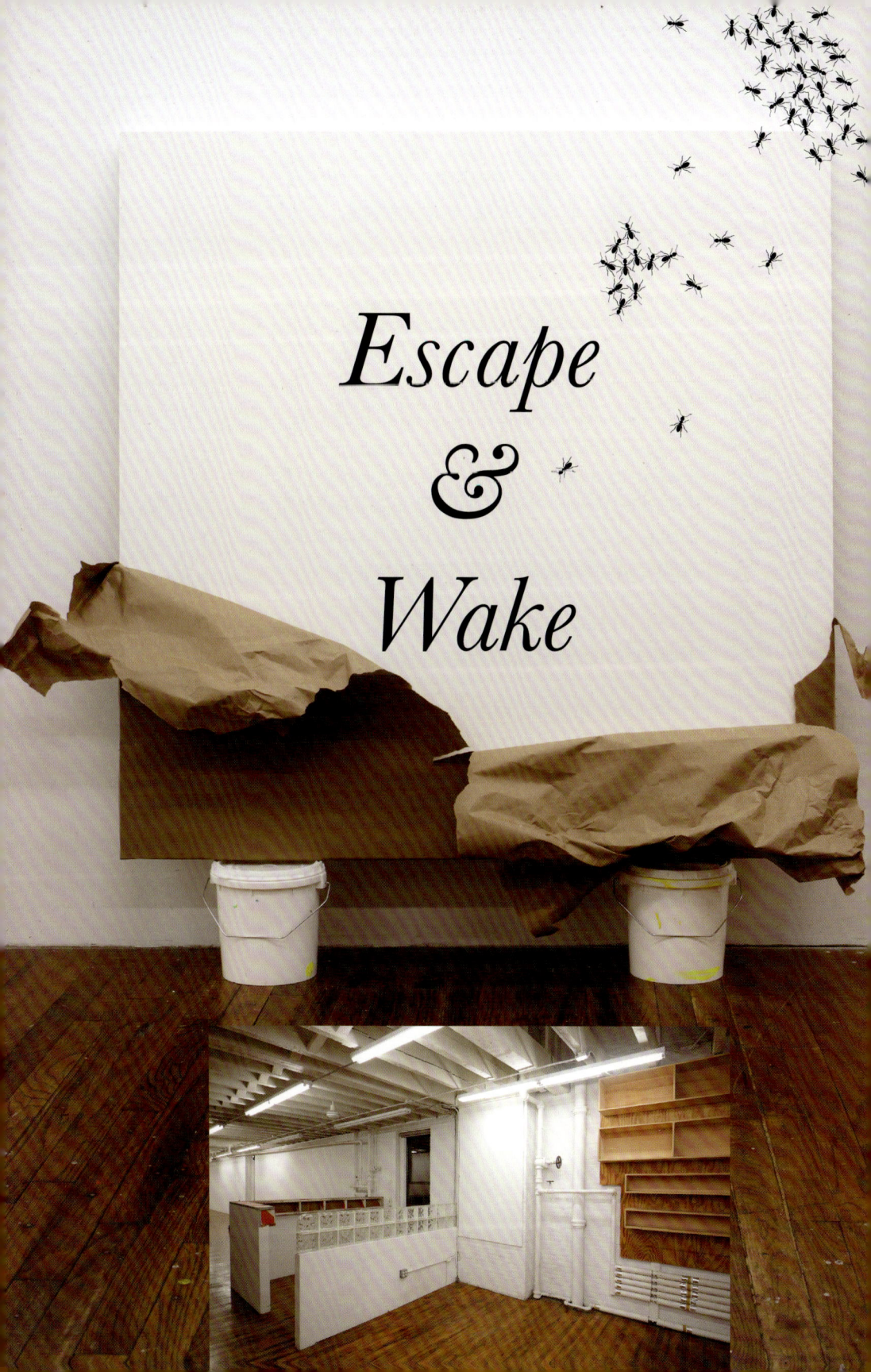

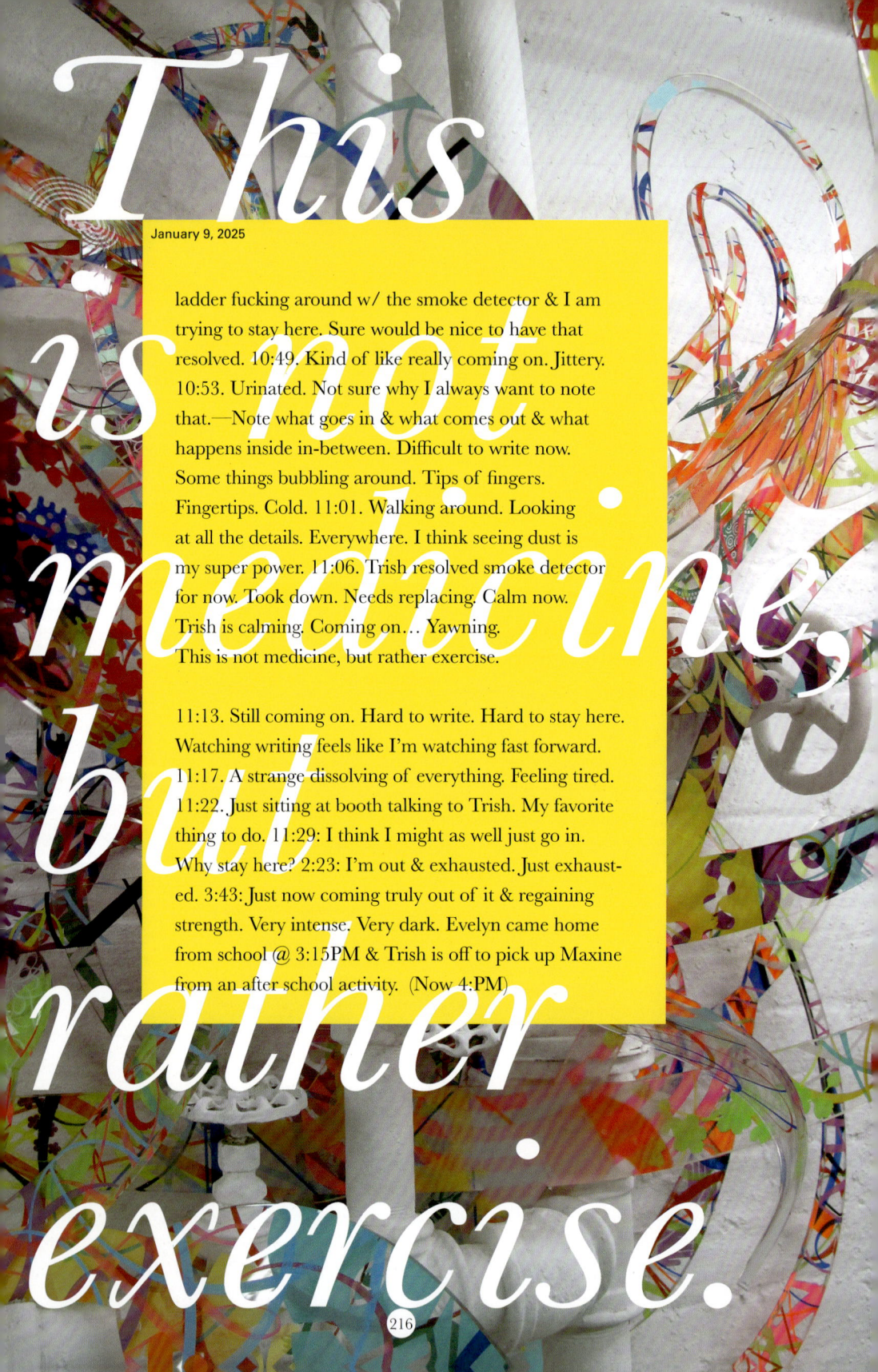

January 9, 2025

ladder fucking around w/ the smoke detector & I am trying to stay here. Sure would be nice to have that resolved. 10:49. Kind of like really coming on. Jittery. 10:53. Urinated. Not sure why I always want to note that.—Note what goes in & what comes out & what happens inside in-between. Difficult to write now. Some things bubbling around. Tips of fingers. Fingertips. Cold. 11:01. Walking around. Looking at all the details. Everywhere. I think seeing dust is my super power. 11:06. Trish resolved smoke detector for now. Took down. Needs replacing. Calm now. Trish is calming. Coming on… Yawning. This is not medicine, but rather exercise.

11:13. Still coming on. Hard to write. Hard to stay here. Watching writing feels like I'm watching fast forward. 11:17. A strange dissolving of everything. Feeling tired. 11:22. Just sitting at booth talking to Trish. My favorite thing to do. 11:29: I think I might as well just go in. Why stay here? 2:23: I'm out & exhausted. Just exhausted. 3:43: Just now coming truly out of it & regaining strength. Very intense. Very dark. Evelyn came home from school @ 3:15PM & Trish is off to pick up Maxine from an after school activity. (Now 4:PM)

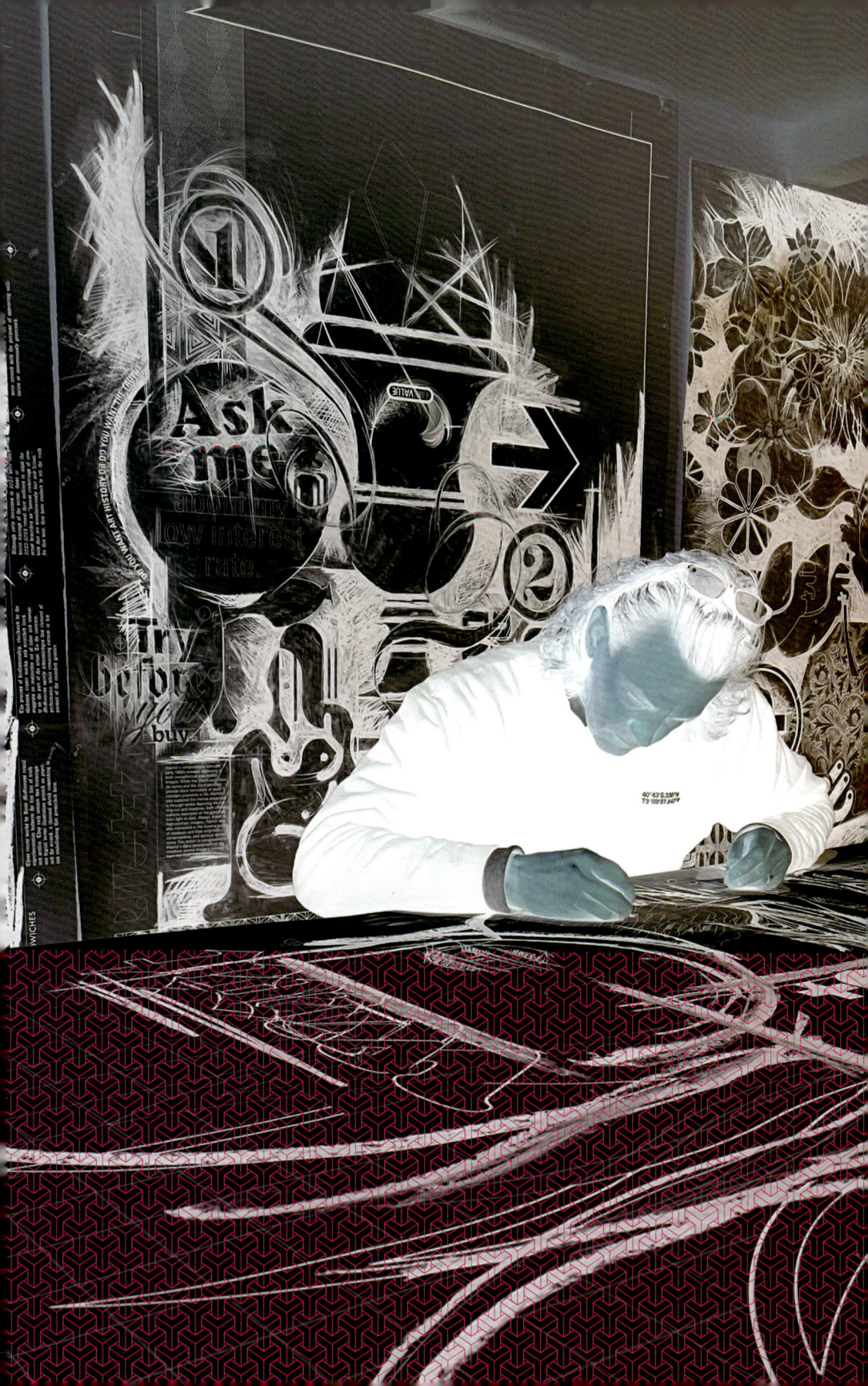

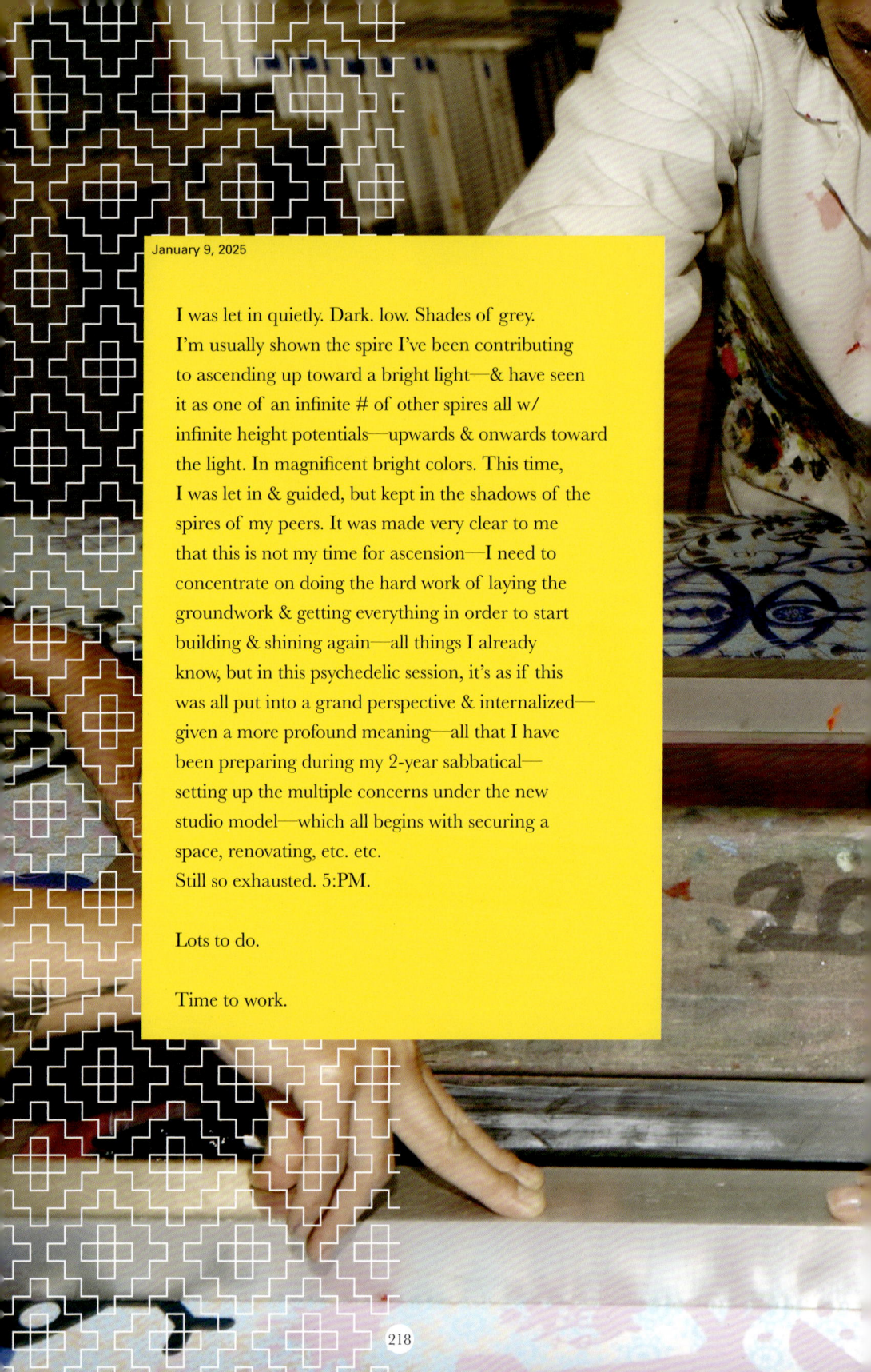

January 9, 2025

I was let in quietly. Dark. low. Shades of grey.
I'm usually shown the spire I've been contributing
to ascending up toward a bright light—& have seen
it as one of an infinite # of other spires all w/
infinite height potentials—upwards & onwards toward
the light. In magnificent bright colors. This time,
I was let in & guided, but kept in the shadows of the
spires of my peers. It was made very clear to me
that this is not my time for ascension—I need to
concentrate on doing the hard work of laying the
groundwork & getting everything in order to start
building & shining again—all things I already
know, but in this psychedelic session, it's as if this
was all put into a grand perspective & internalized—
given a more profound meaning—all that I have
been preparing during my 2-year sabbatical—
setting up the multiple concerns under the new
studio model—which all begins with securing a
space, renovating, etc. etc.
Still so exhausted. 5:PM.

Lots to do.

Time to work.

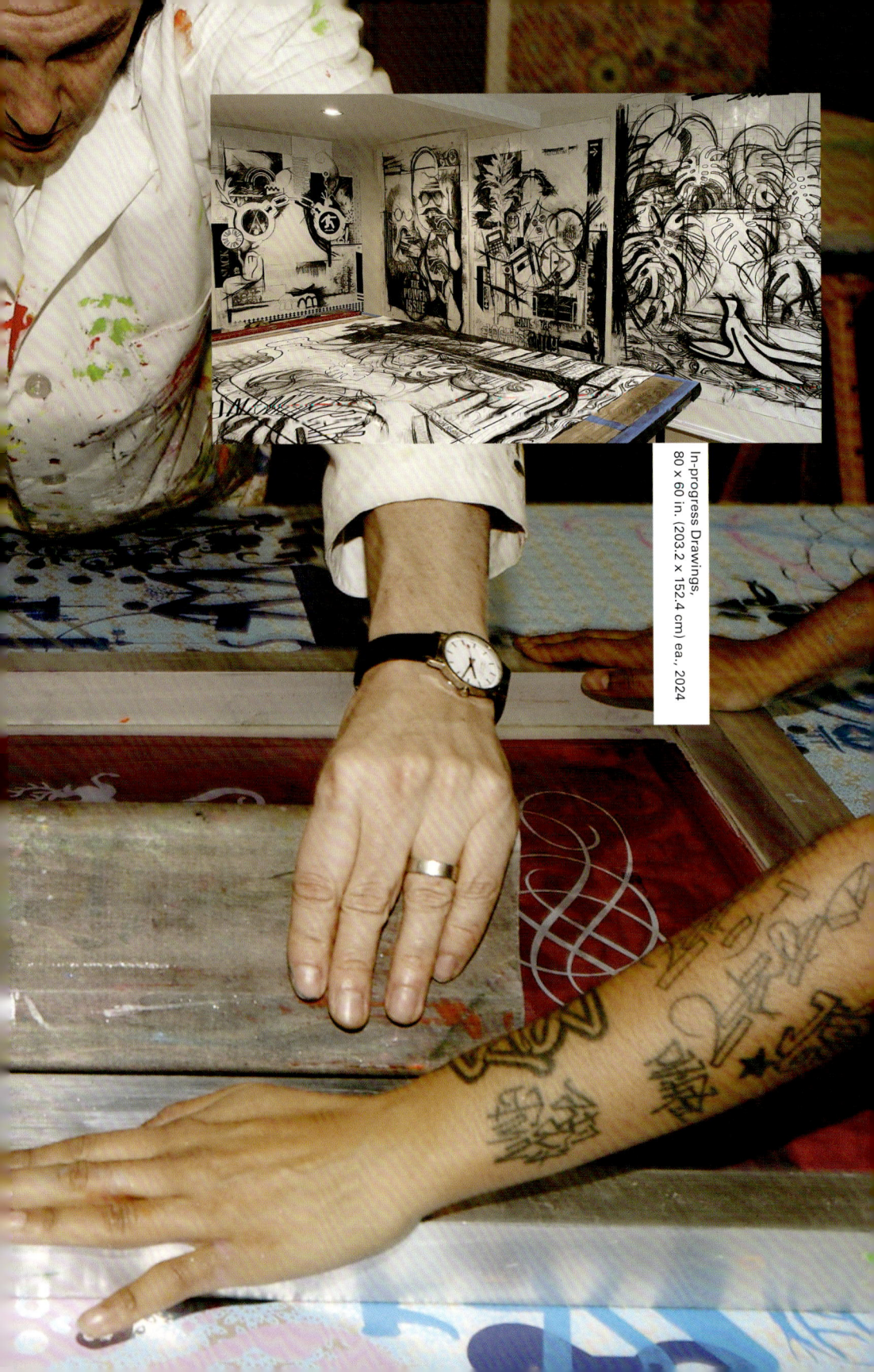

In-progress Drawings,
80 x 60 in. (203.2 x 152.4 cm) ea., 2024

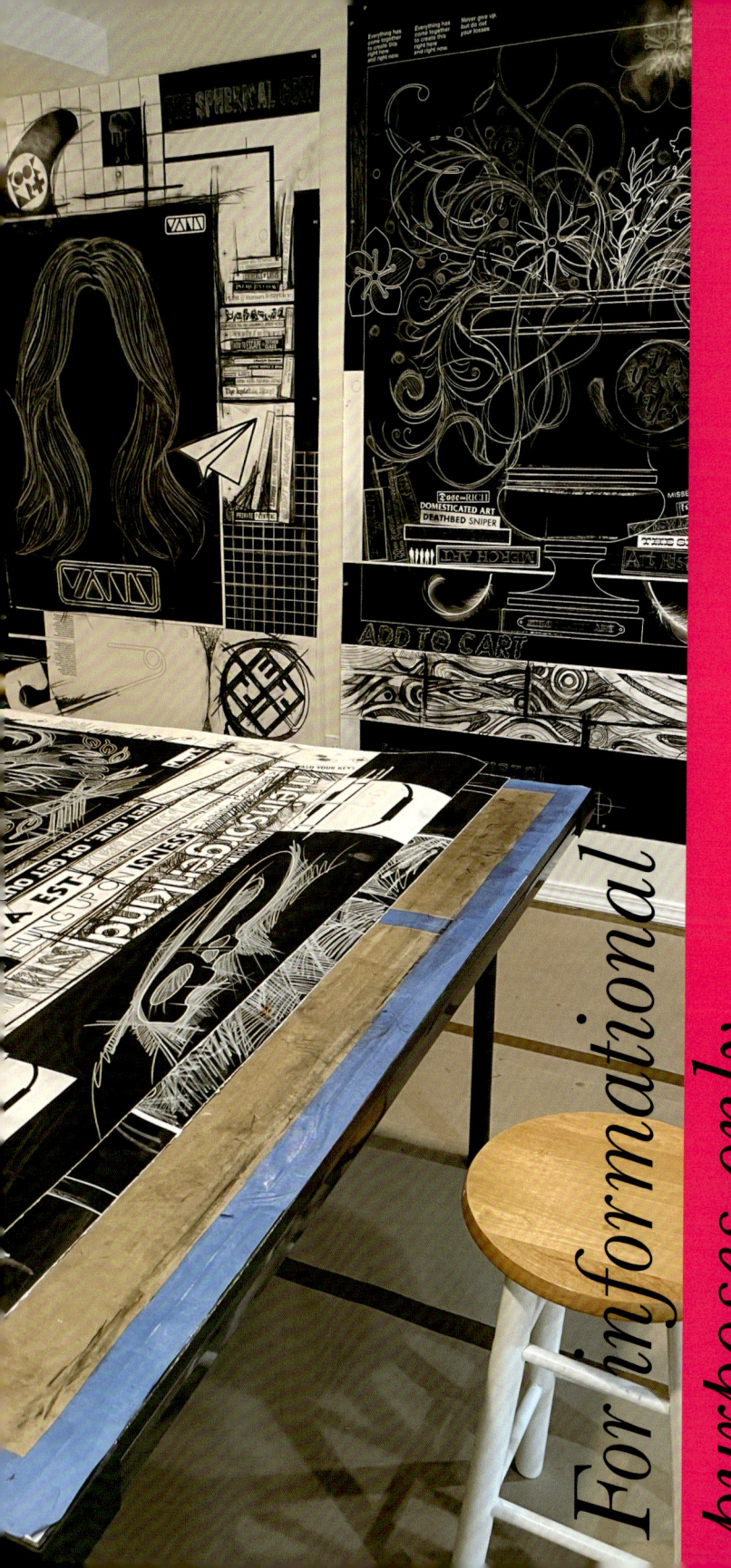

For informational purposes only

Epilogue

The Cosmic Joke

We often hear of two use cases for psychedelics:
therapeutic and recreational.
But what about for informational purposes only?

While the mental health benefits of psilocybin have
been proven and celebrated, not much attention has
been given to the idea of using psilocybin as a tool for
"healthy normals" to explore their minds—to explore
our collective mind.

We've been *turned on* with recreational psychedelic use.
We've been *tuned in* enough to start to recognize the
medical benefits. Now is the time to *not drop out*, but
go in. We need to enlist psychonauts to serve and bring
back what they can from the realm beyond our observ-

able universe. Can we enlist and deploy a legion of surveyors to explore their minds? Our minds? The mind of the universe? Can psychonauts go into the unknown, come back, and report their findings? What would we find? What if we were given something to find?

I have gone in with specific problems to solve—from figuring out how to depict a challenging pattern, for example, to deciding which projects to work on. I have looked for specific answers. But, I have found that in that psychedelic space, in the world beyond, it just doesn't work like that. I have not been able to bring words or numbers into that space. It is the realm of feelings and vibrations. Language seems to be too specific. Language is an expression that is unique unto this world and does not come close to accurately expressing the profound vibrations of that world.

Still, there must be a way to test for verifiable novel knowledge acquired during the psychedelic experience. Let us design and conduct experiments! Let us test for repeatable and reproducible experiences! That knowledge, I assume, has use. But what about the insights? What is the use of insights? Why should we know the

Still, there must be a way to test for verifiable novel knowledge acquired during the psychedelic experience.

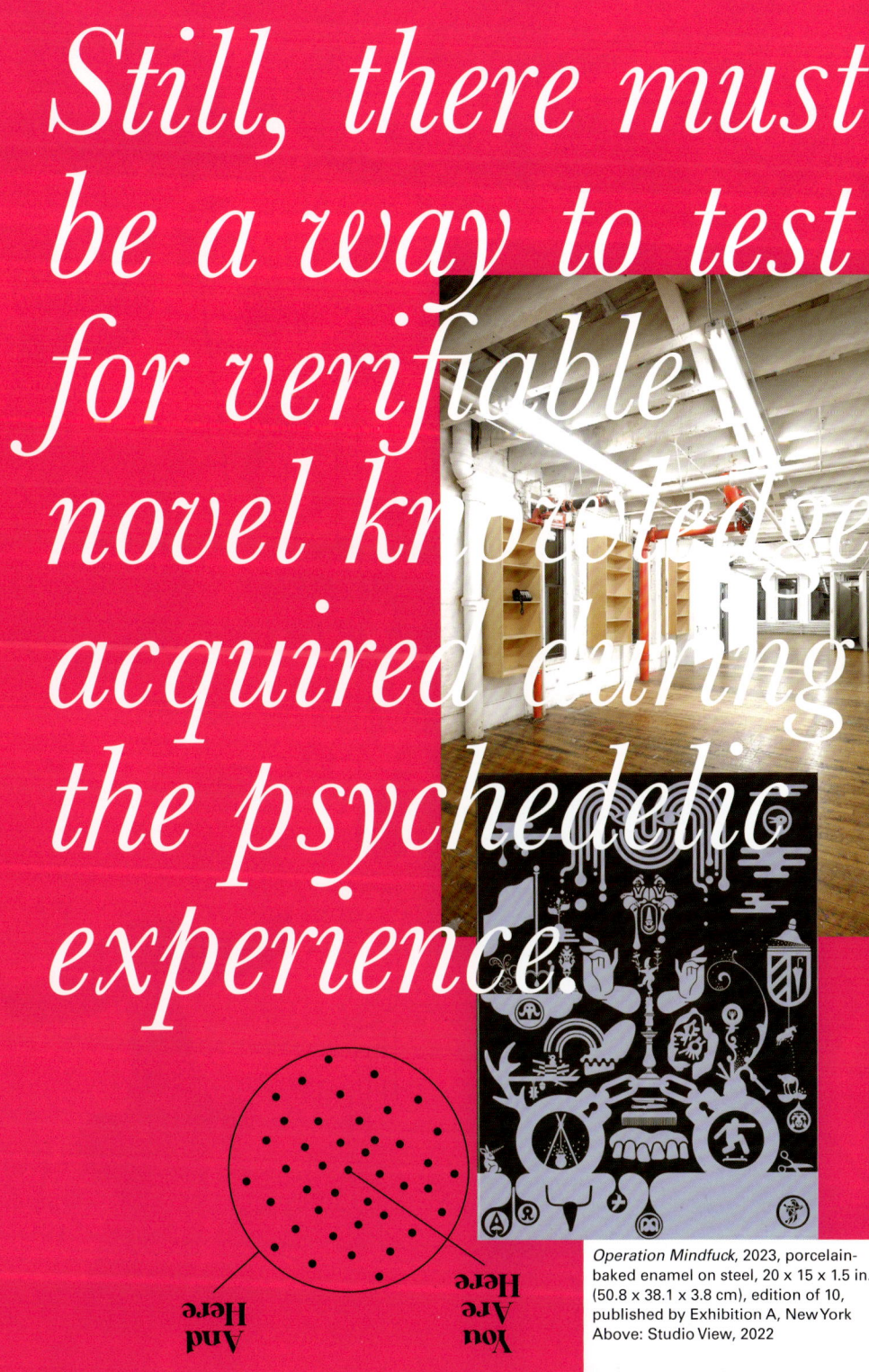

Operation Mindfuck, 2023, porcelain-baked enamel on steel, 20 x 15 x 1.5 in. (50.8 x 38.1 x 3.8 cm), edition of 10, published by Exhibition A, New York
Above: Studio View, 2022

You Are Here

And Here

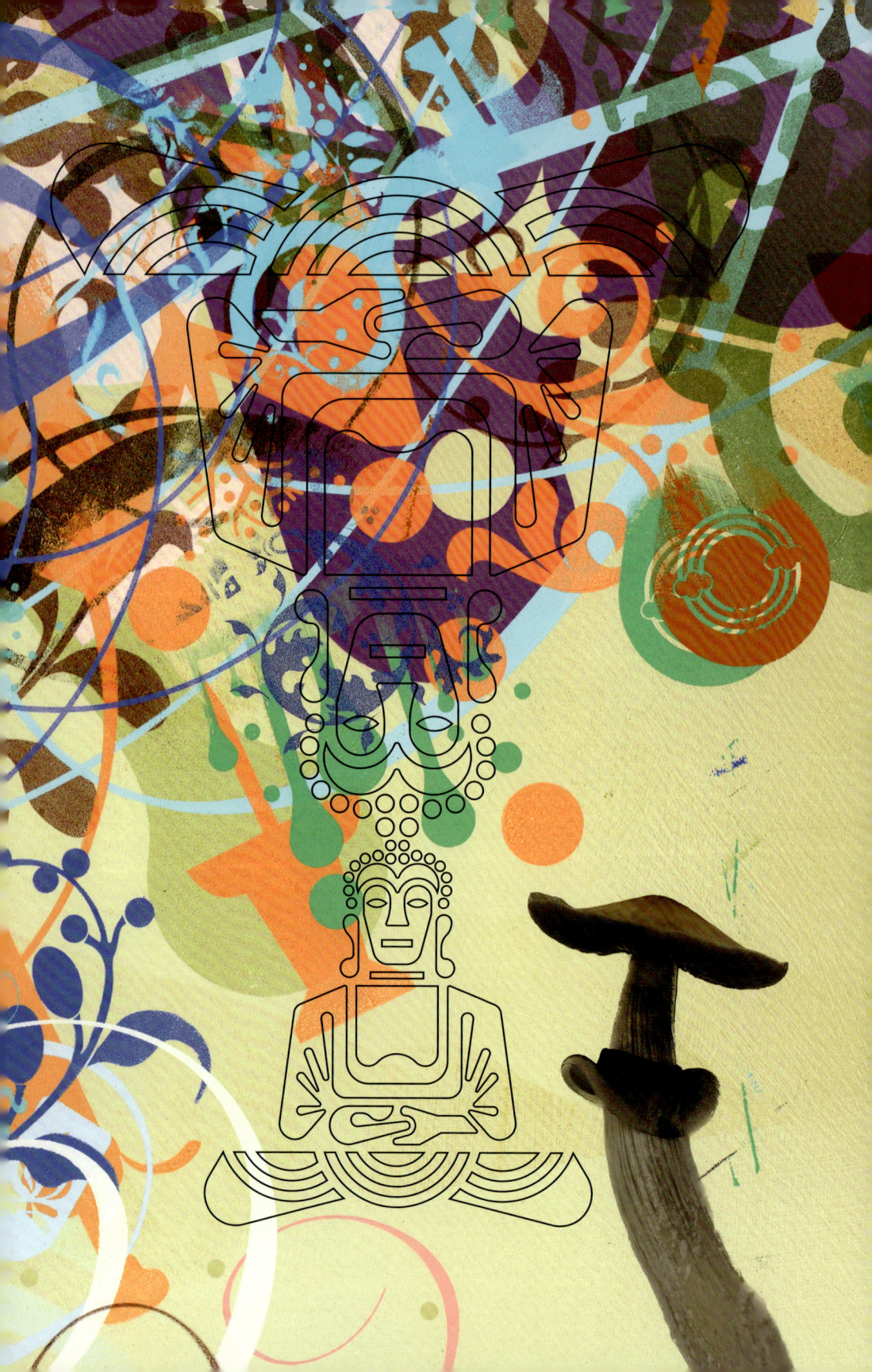

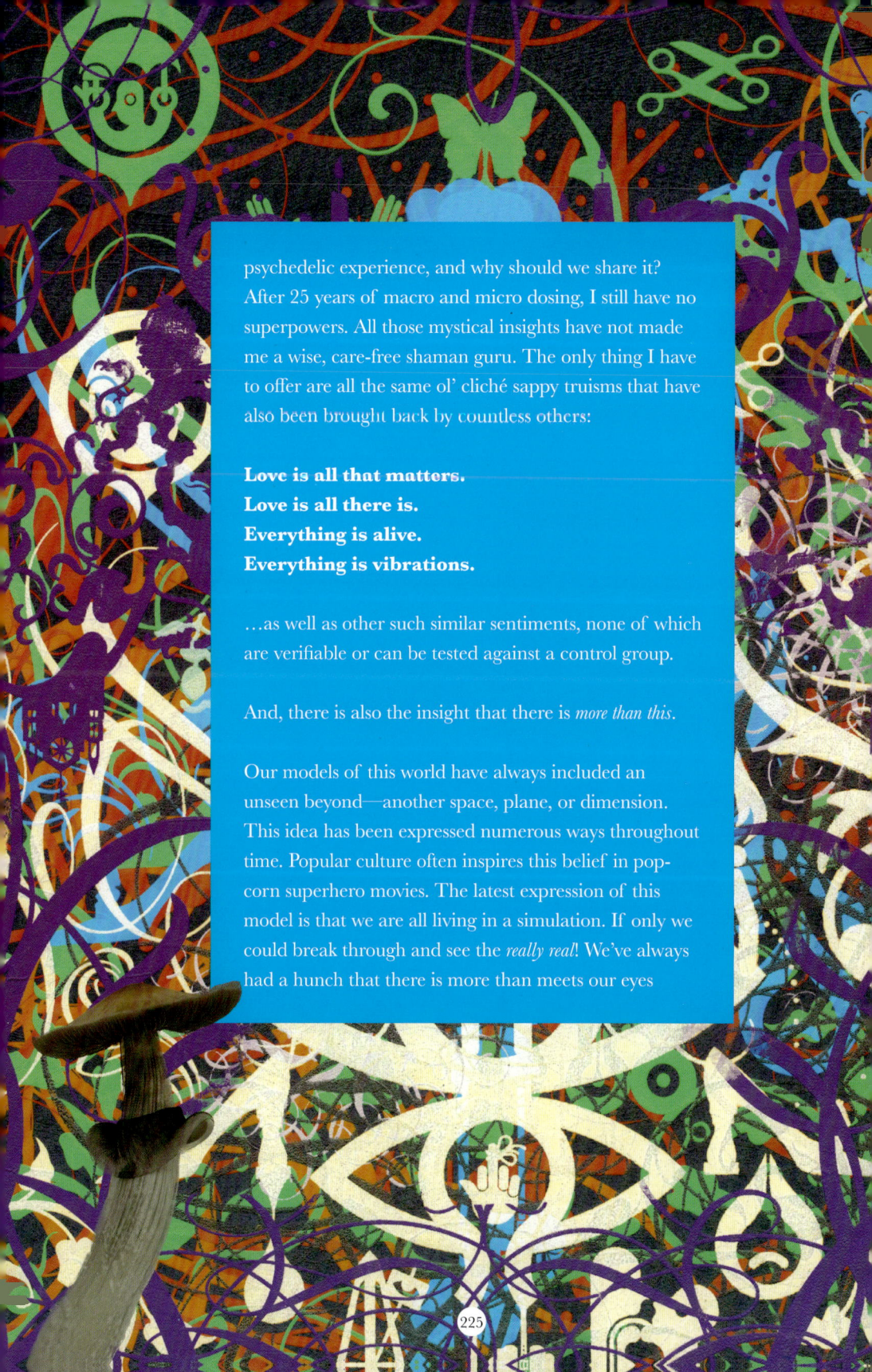

psychedelic experience, and why should we share it? After 25 years of macro and micro dosing, I still have no superpowers. All those mystical insights have not made me a wise, care-free shaman guru. The only thing I have to offer are all the same ol' cliché sappy truisms that have also been brought back by countless others:

Love is all that matters.
Love is all there is.
Everything is alive.
Everything is vibrations.

…as well as other such similar sentiments, none of which are verifiable or can be tested against a control group.

And, there is also the insight that there is *more than this*.

Our models of this world have always included an unseen beyond—another space, plane, or dimension. This idea has been expressed numerous ways throughout time. Popular culture often inspires this belief in popcorn superhero movies. The latest expression of this model is that we are all living in a simulation. If only we could break through and see the *really real*! We've always had a hunch that there is more than meets our eyes

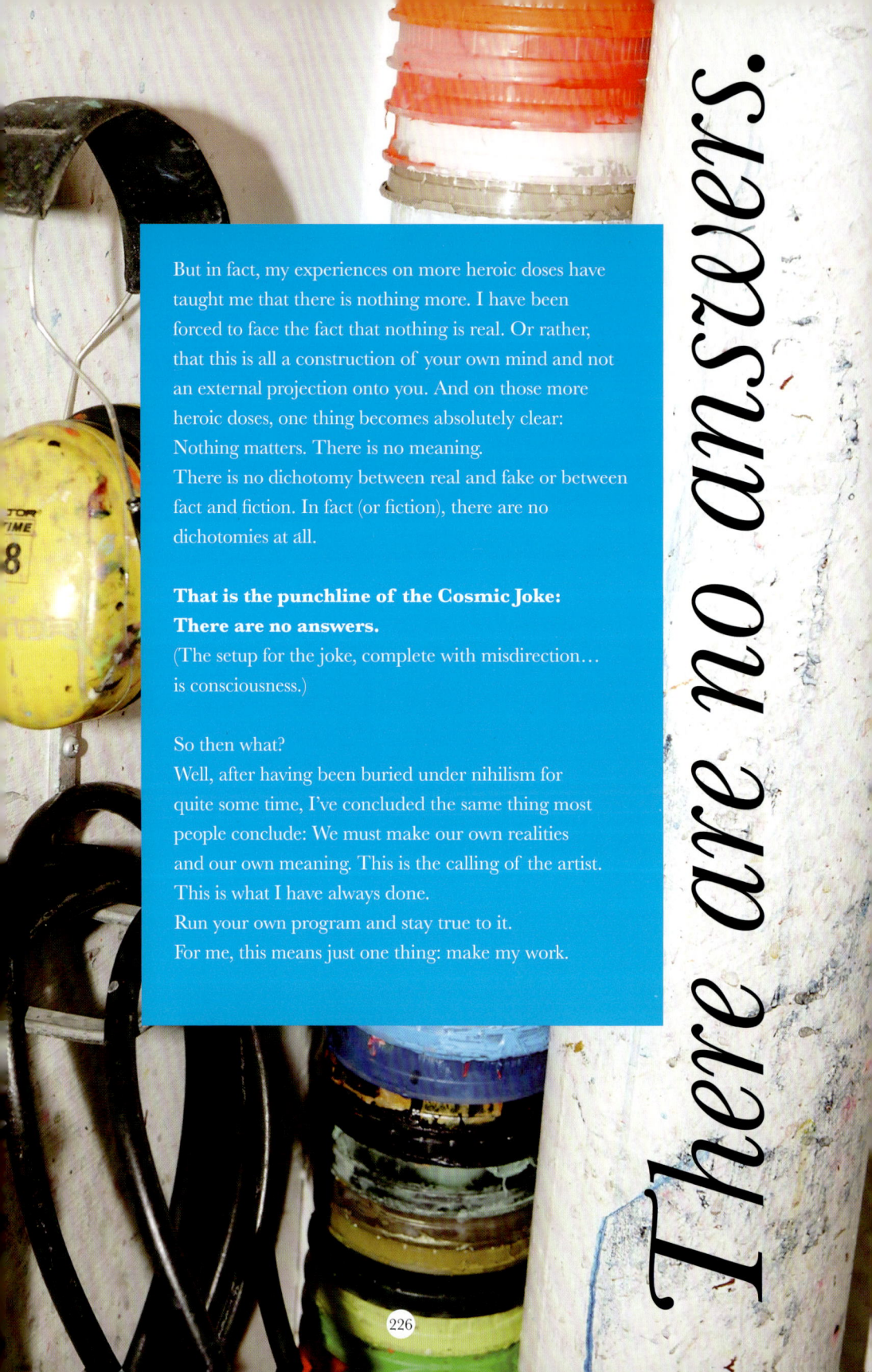

But in fact, my experiences on more heroic doses have taught me that there is nothing more. I have been forced to face the fact that nothing is real. Or rather, that this is all a construction of your own mind and not an external projection onto you. And on those more heroic doses, one thing becomes absolutely clear: Nothing matters. There is no meaning.

There is no dichotomy between real and fake or between fact and fiction. In fact (or fiction), there are no dichotomies at all.

That is the punchline of the Cosmic Joke: There are no answers.

(The setup for the joke, complete with misdirection… is consciousness.)

So then what?

Well, after having been buried under nihilism for quite some time, I've concluded the same thing most people conclude: We must make our own realities and our own meaning. This is the calling of the artist. This is what I have always done.

Run your own program and stay true to it.

For me, this means just one thing: make my work.

There are no answers.

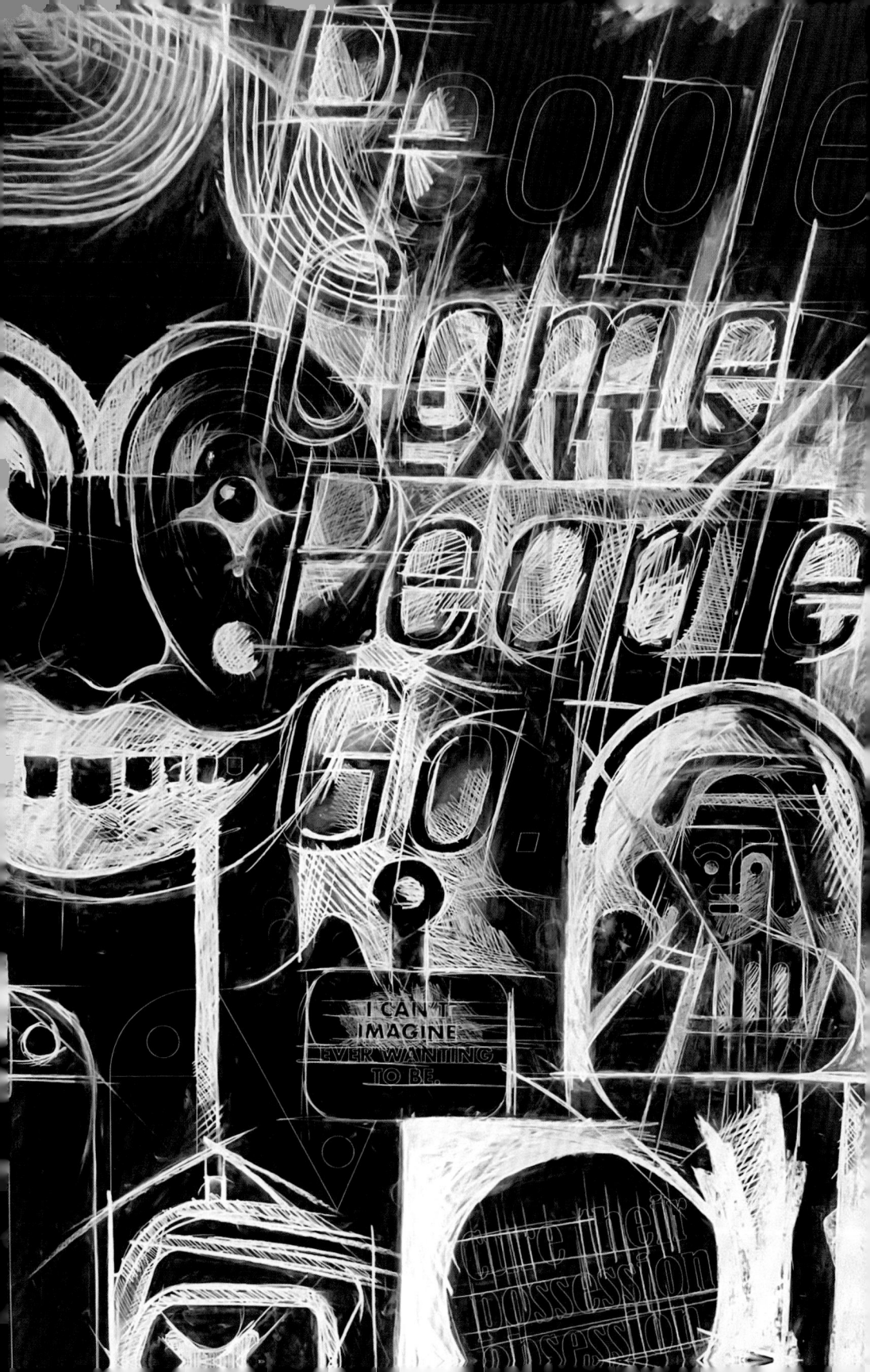

People

Some People Go

I CAN'T IMAGINE EVER WANTING TO BE.

their possession
possession

... SORTA GREEN SHIT. TY.
DEPRIVING. BEING PULLED IN

... JUST ANOTHER DRINKING SOLUTION.

A... BE ... TO NAW. SMELL IT.

... IT BACK IN MULTIPLE SWALLOWS.

AND TO CONTEMPLATE IT. RELAX.

... MOVING YOUR BODY ...

... LET YOUR BODY
... YOUR MIND GO LIMP.
... AROUND STUDIO.

... WATCH ...

... SINCE, MUST TIME

... GETTING ...

... HOW THIS WESTERN/SCIENTIFIC MODEL &

... TIME TO WRITE MORE ON THAT LATER.

... CHECK IN W/ SPECIFIC QUESTIONS

... INTO KNOWABLE UNITS. ...

CAN'T LOOK AT PIECE AS WHOLE. JUST SWARMING
SO MUCH ~~CHING OF IT THERE~~ ~~INTI~~
~~THE WHOLE~~ IS CONVERSATION 3 DIMENSION
PATTERNS. ~~NEED TO~~ SHAPES ~~FORMS~~ REALLY
~~JMP INTO~~ THE ~~RIGHT~~ ONE.
SWARM. ~~WRITER~~ 5:20 EXACTLY ~~I CAN~~
~~BLUR~~ ~~LENS~~ ON THE ~~WARHOL~~ FLOWER
LOOKING ~~AWAY~~ @ ~~ORCHIDS~~ ~~NOW~~.
~~MIRROR~~ ~~BEHIND~~ A GIRL (AFTER GIRL BEFORE
CAN ~~ARGUE~~ ~~IDEAS~~) ~~MAKES~~ ~~OTHER~~ PROJECTS.
SNAP ~~IN BURSTS~~ OF ~~THE GIRLS~~ OFTEN ~~GETTING~~
~~AT DRAMATIC~~ ~~SOMETHING~~ ~~HAVE A~~
~~IN BETTER~~ ~~REALLY~~ ~~DESIGN~~ ~~VERY~~
~~TO SWAP~~ ~~LOTS~~ OF ~~IDEAS~~ ~~REMAINING~~ LOSE.
~~IN~~ ~~VISION~~ ~~THE WORK~~ ~~CLEAR~~
~~BUT EXCITING~~ ~~RUNNING~~ ETC. 15 MILES LA
ON ~~6:36 PM~~ ~~REDNESS~~ ~~HISTORY~~
~~THE~~ ~~EVERYTHING~~. SKETCHING. FEEL LIKE
~~COULD~~ LAY DOWN. ~~NAP~~. BLANKET.
~~SHAKING~~ IN & OUT. IN & OUT.
~~6:45 PM~~ FEEL LIKE ~~NEED~~ TO MAKE SURE
~~CAN MAKE~~ ~~SHAPES~~ ~~EVERYTHING IS IN ORDER~~ ~~ALL SETUP~~. FEEL L
~~IT WAS A BIT MUCH~~. MIGHT VOMIT, ~~PULLED~~ ~~OFF~~
SO ~~MUCH~~ ~~GRABBING~~ ~~MAKING~~ BLANKET & PUT
SO ~~MANY~~ ~~LAYERS~~ OF ~~CLOUD~~. ~~COULD LAY DOWN~~
GO IN ~~TRYING~~ TO STAY CALM; ~~WALKING~~
~~SENSITIVE~~ TO ~~EXTRA~~ ~~WARMTH~~ IN SUNBEAM
YOURSELF GO

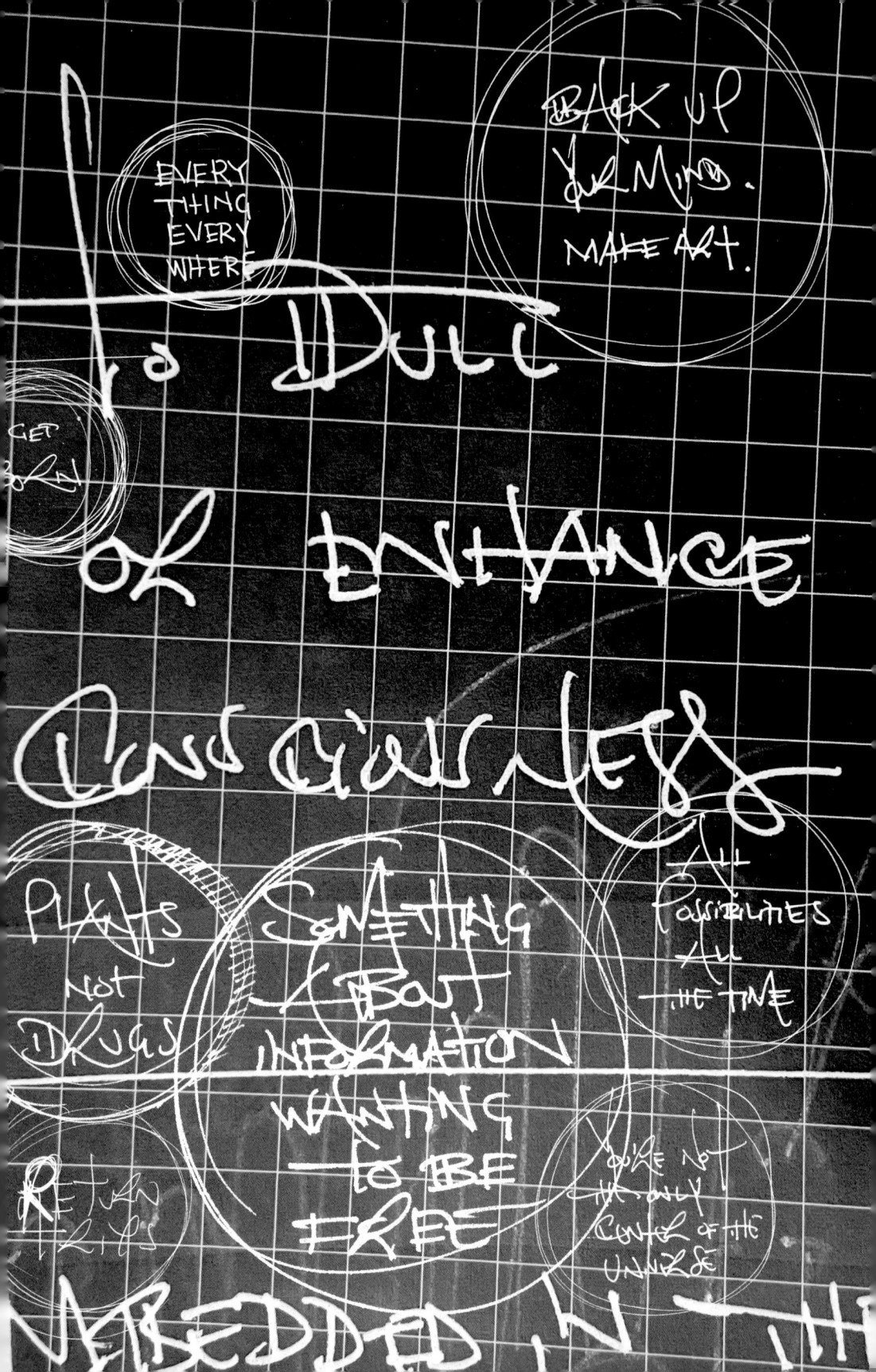

EVERY
THING
EVERY
WHERE

BACK UP
YOUR MIND.
MAKE ART.

To DULL

GET
BORN

OR ENHANCE

Consciousness

PLANTS
NOT
DRUGS

SOMETHING
ABOUT
INFORMATION
WANTING
TO BE
FREE

RETURN
TRIPS

ALL
POSSIBILITIES
ALL
THE TIME

YOU'RE NOT
THE ONLY
CENTER OF THE
UNIVERSE

EMBEDDED IN TH

ACKNOWLEDGEMENTS

It is only with the loving support of my best friend and the
smartest person I know that I was able to conduct these
experiments. Thank you, Trish.

Readers of early drafts of *Trip Advisor* provided valuable
feedback and professional advice. Thank you to Sutian Dong,
Michael Halsband, Jud Laghi, and Matt McGowan.

Thank you to db, Sean, and Lila at Blurring Books.
It takes a brave publisher willing to assume a great deal of
risk to bring a book like this to the public.

Photographers:
Talisman Brolin, Olimpia Dior, Michael Dominic, Cheryl Dunn,
Trish Goodwin, Sherry Griffin, Nolan Grunwald, Haruka,
Austin Kennedy, Keppie Kepple, Gina Kim, Wellington Lee,
Jennifer Livingston, Chris Mosier, Farzad Owrang,
Nathan Perkel, Tom Powell, Mary Raap, PD Rearick,
James Rexroad, Philipp Rittermann, Charlie Rubin,
Claire Schneider, Jean Vong, Hans Wilchut, Ellen Page Wilson,
Michael Wong, Hikari Yokoyama

Studio Assistants:
Becca Baldwin, Rosalia Bermudez, Matt Bernick,
Ben Bloomstein, Brian Boyce, Ben Callaway, Julia Carlson,
Veronica Chen, Rachel Decareau, Willem Devos, Olimpia Dior,
Rachel Domm, Drew Droege, Garret Edwards, Joe Ferriso,
Steven Gadzinzki, Pilita Garcia, Nicole Golan, Kim Hodges,
Keppie Kepple, Regina Kim, Aiyana Knauer, Akane Kodani,
Stephanie Kosinski, Bo-Yee Lai, Lyndsey Meyers, James Moore,
Sarah Murphy, Shinya Nakamura, Justin Penov,
Casandra Quinn, Carl Rauschenbach, Rayna Savrosa,
Dustin Schuetz, Sarah Shebaro, Jasper Stapleton,
Nina Stojkovic, Pierre Tardif, Sonia Tay, Julian Uribe,
Maria Wan, Hikari Yokoyama

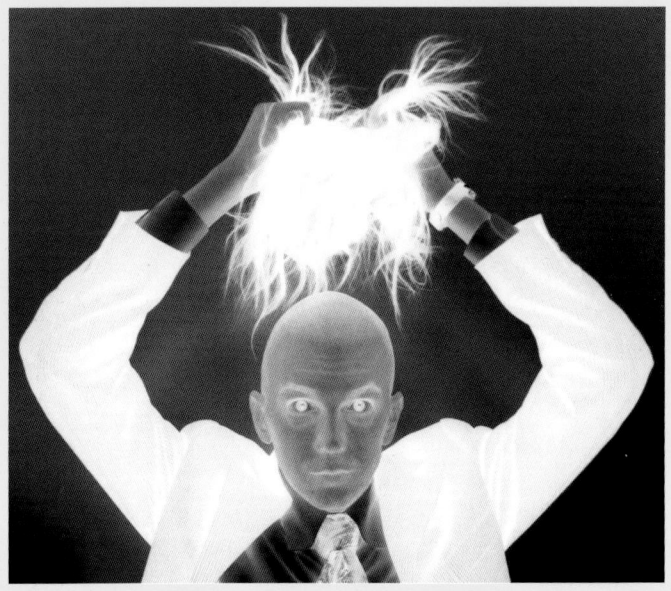

Ryan McGinness is an American artist, living and working in New York, New York. He grew up in the surf and skate culture of Virginia Beach, Virginia, and then studied at Carnegie Mellon University in Pittsburgh, Pennsylvania, as an Andrew Carnegie Scholar. During college, he interned at the Andy Warhol Museum as a curatorial assistant. Known for his extensive vocabulary of original graphic drawings that use the visual language of public signage, corporate logos, and contemporary symbology, McGinness is credited with elevating the status of the graphic symbol to fine art through the creation of his paintings, sculptures, installations, and books. Concerned with the perceived value of forms, he assumes the power of this visual language in order to share personal expressions.

His work is in the permanent public collections of the Museum of Modern Art, The Metropolitan Museum of Art, Virginia Museum of Fine Arts, Museum of Contemporary Art San Diego, Cincinnati Art Museum, MUSAC in Spain, and the Taguchi Art Collection in Japan.